HARD ROCK EPIC

HARD ROCK EPIC

Western Miners and the Industrial Revolution, 1860–1910

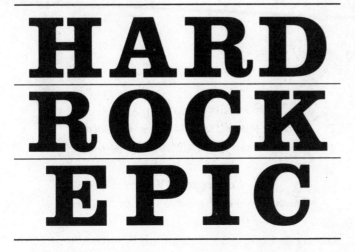

MARK WYMAN

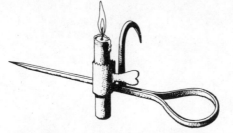

University of California Press

Berkeley · Los Angeles · London

University of California Press
Berkeley and Los Angeles, California
University of California Press, Ltd.
London, England
Copyright © 1979 by
The Regents of the University of California

Library of Congress Catalog Card Number: 78-54805
Printed in the United States of America

First Paperback Printing 1989
ISBN 0-520-06803-3

1   2   3   4   5   6   7   8   9

This book is for my family

CONTENTS

PREFACE

This book is an attempt to examine the impact of the Industrial Revolution upon the men who mined gold, silver, and other metals underground in the West in the 1860–1910 period. Believing that some previous studies have emphasized the spectacular and violent at the expense of historical understanding, I have sought to approach the topic from many angles while avoiding favoritism to, or condemnation of, any specific group.

At every step of my research and writing there were persons who—like those who grubstaked prospectors in the mountains a century ago—provided encouragement and assistance. Chief among these was Professor Vernon Carstensen of the University of Washington, whose ideas and suggestions regarding Western workers as part of larger economic processes have been absolutely crucial in the genesis and development of this book. Robert Romig and Merle Wells of the Idaho Historical Society have repeatedly shared their extensive knowledge of mining with me, including in Romig's case a trip to his Boise Basin mine. Professor Rodman Paul of the California Institute of Technology offered numerous suggestions from his broad background in mining history, and took the time to read the finished manuscript. Encouragement and suggestions also came from Professor Melvyn Dubofsky of the State University of New York at Binghamton, and Professor Vernon Jensen of Cornell University.

Earlier there were others who helped stimulate my concern for workmen caught amid fast-changing technology. During my stint as labor reporter for the Minneapolis *Tribune*, my interest in this was especially developed by two men: Clarence

Meter, then regional director of the National Labor Relations Board, and Professor John Flagler of the Department of Industrial Relations of the University of Minnesota.

Many institutions provided assistance, chief among them being Illinois State University. My colleagues in the university's Department of History have willingly offered criticisms of my writing, just as Milner Library staff members have always been helpful despite my unending demands on them. The university has provided assistance through financial aid, released time for writing, and typing.

I am also indebted to the following: the state historical societies of Colorado, Idaho, Montana, Nevada, and Wisconsin; Colorado State Archives; University of Washington libraries and Northwest Collections; University of Illinois libraries; University of Nevada Library Special Collections and Mackay School of Mines Library; Western Historical Collections of the University of Colorado (special thanks to curator John Brennan); Colorado School of Mines Library; Bancroft Library of the University of California; Beinecke Library of Yale University; Western History Collections of the Denver Public Library; Boise Public Library; Helena Public Library; Seattle Public Library; and the Washoe County Library in Reno. Officials of St. Peter's Hospital (Helena, Montana) and St. Vincent's Hospital (Leadville, Colorado) permitted me to scrutinize their records of the 1880–1910 years. Teller County, Colorado, records were made available through the courtesy of Mrs. Grace Sterrett. Thanks are also extended to the *Western Historical Quarterly* for permission to use material that originally appeared in my article, "Industrial Revolution in the West: Hard-Rock Miners and the New Technology," in Vol. V, No. 1 (January, 1974), 39–57, of that journal.

Finally, many near and distant relatives have encouraged and helped me over the years; this includes Emil and Edith Goldschmidt, my parents-in-law, who have aided me in many ways. My debt is especially great to my parents, Walker D. and Helen B. Wyman, and to my brother Bryant and his wife Barbara. During the writing of this book the main burden, of course, has fallen on my wife Eva and our children Daniel, Ruth, and Miriam. This book is for all of them.

M. W.

Illinois State University, Normal

PART ONE
IMPACT

CHAPTER I

Machinery on the Route to the Mines

First the huge machines were transported up the rivers, forcing steamboats to struggle against the currents of the Sacramento, the Missouri, and the Columbia. When the fall line was reached, or when the water's course diverged from the route to the mines, the mechanical devices were landed and transferred to sturdy wagons. Then they were carried up into the mountains.

These mammoth pieces of mining and milling equipment, moved in steamboats and wagons, were among the mechanical wonders of an age that prided itself on technological innovations. Both this fact and their sheer immensity attracted attention along the way. From San Francisco in 1864 came a steam engine and shaft bound for the Gould & Curry enterprise on the Comstock Lode in Nevada; the 300-horsepower engine was "said to be the largest high-pressure" engine ever made in California, and the shaft was described as being "as large around as an ordinary man's body." When the ship *Yosemite* landed the shaft at the Sacramento docks, the reporter for the *Bee* called it simply "an immense affair," but he was left little time to scrutinize it, because "it was at once passed along toward the mountains," bound for the Comstock across the Sierras.[1]

Other routes provided entry for the gigantic and intricate machinery which Western metal mining required from the 1860s onward. It took from thirty to fifty wagons to transport

3

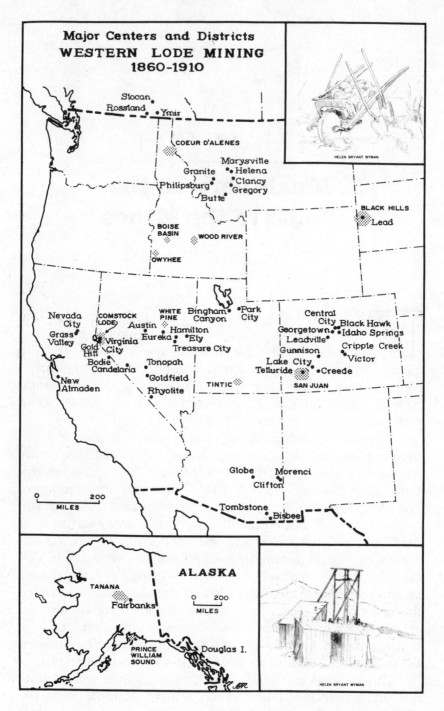

Major Centers and Districts
WESTERN LODE MINING
1860-1910

Slocan
Rossland
Ymir

COEUR D'ALENES

Marysville
Granite • Helena
Philipsburg • Clancy
Butte • Gregory

BLACK HILLS
• Lead

BOISE BASIN
WOOD RIVER

OWYHEE

Nevada City
Grass Valley
Gold Hill
Bodie
Candelaria
New Almaden

COMSTOCK LODE
Austin
Virginia City

WHITE PINE
Eureka
Hamilton
Ely
Treasure City

Bingham Canyon
• Park City

Central City
Georgetown • Black Hawk
Leadville • Idaho Springs
Gunnison
Lake City • Cripple Creek
Telluride • Victor
• Creede
SAN JUAN

Tonopah
Goldfield
Rhyolite

TINTIC

Globe • Morenci
Clifton
Tombstone
• Bisbee

0   200
MILES

HELEN BRYANT WYMAN

ALASKA

TANANA
Fairbanks

0   200
MILES

PRINCE WILLIAM SOUND
Douglas I.

HELEN BRYANT WYMAN

a quartz mill across the plains to the Montana mines, or from Fort Benton on the Missouri after a steamboat trip from St. Louis. The *Idaho World* eagerly announced in 1865 that "the forty stamp power crusher belonging to the Pittsburg & Idaho Gold & Silver Mining Company is within a few days journey of us." Eighteen wagons were used in this haul, which was marred by the engineer's death from "complications following a gunshot wound." When a new eleven-ton roaster made its way into the Grass Valley district of California in 1869, it was transported in specially constructed wagons brought from San Francisco, over bridges that had been strengthened in anticipation, and pulled by ten yoke of oxen which were aided in turning corners by blocks and tackles. This slow-moving spectacle "resembled a circus coming to town" in Grass Valley, where "an immense crowd" watched the roaster make its way to the Rivot Company works on Canada Hill.[2]

Such were the devices that traveled, and occasionally clogged, the routes to the Western mines. They were the advance agents of the Industrial Revolution, helping conquer the mountain fastness of a primitive frontier. While it is true that the basic changes involved in industrialization occurred over decades or even centuries, when industrialization entered this Western frontier the clash of old and new was dramatic. Spaniards who had moved into the West in the colonial era were not accompanied by the massive paraphernalia of industrialism; nor were the early groups of other Europeans and Americans who came later. Explorers, priests, *hacendados*, soldiers, fur traders, placer miners—the noise they knew was the roar of a gun, the bellow of an injured animal, the shouts of drunken revelry. Their basic mechanical equipment was limited to firearms, wagons, and traps.[3]

More than machines went into the creation of that historical transformation known as the Industrial Revolution. Attitudes of businessmen, governmental leaders, inventors, and workmen were also crucial in the shift from animal to machine power, as was the availability of natural resources, labor, and paying customers.

The workman was located at a key point in this transformation. Usually drawn into industrial enterprises from a nonindustrial tradition, the new worker was beset by changing demands in job skills and work discipline which frequently led to severe tensions. These new industrial workers carried with them habits and values "not associated with industrial necessities and the industrial ethos," in Herbert Gutman's words.[4]

Such tensions were not limited to workers in the throbbing industrial centers of the East. They were present as well as the industrialization of underground metal mining proceeded on the Western frontier from the early 1860s through 1910. By the latter date the basic transformation was completed in technology, work organization, union formation, and protective legislation. The changes in lode mining over this fifty-year span were especially dramatic because of the juxtaposition of the world's most modern, complex technology alongside conditions matching the most primitive anywhere.* By 1880, Nevada had thirty-seven mines sunk beyond 1,000 feet in depth and five below 3,000 feet; outside the West, no American mine went as deep as 1,000 feet. That same year, Colorado's growing mine kingdom used 118 steam engines, and Nevada's used 90. These were outposts of modernity. Short distances away, however, were unconquered peaks, wild game, and Indians whose childhood memories included no white men or steam engines.[5]

The broad impact of this transformation for the Western

---

*Lode mining refers to underground mining below bedrock, the term being derived from the *lode* that occurs where several veins of gold, silver, or other metals run closely together; these and the ground between them contain metal-bearing rock, or *ore*. This differs from *placer* mining, which is the recovery of flakes, nuggets, and other particles of gold or silver that were freed when a vein was exposed to the elements and eroded. A *lead* (pronounced *leed*) is synonymous with a lode, although the term is also used to refer to an unexplored vein.

Other key mining terms include the following: In a lode mine, a *shaft* is a vertical opening from the surface. Occasionally a shaft follows a vein and is off the vertical; this is called an *inclined shaft*. *Tunnels* are horizontal passageways; *adits* are tunnels from the surface. *Drifts* are tunnels that follow a vein or ore body; *crosscuts* are tunnels that cross the trend of the ore or rock structure. Passageways that connect on the same general horizontal plane constitute a *level*. Ore is generally extracted in a *stope*, which is any enlargement of a drift or crosscut penetrating an ore body. *Raises* are passageways driven upward from one level to the next; *winzes* are passageways driven downward, usually to explore continuation of the ore.

Protection from cave-ins is provided by *timbering*, which consists of placing *posts*, *caps*, and *lagging* in excavated areas. *Stulls* are timber props or timbers wedged between the walls of a stope; planks laid across the stulls provide a platform for miners working higher up the sides of the stope.

1. *In the beginning: shallow mines, a hand windlass, and miners who provided much of their own financing. This small operation was in the Breckenridge district of Colorado, circa 1900.*

Colorado School of Mines photo

2. *The contrast: changing the shift in a Comstock Lode silver mine, where dozens of miners lined up to be checked in before the long ride into the bowels of the earth. This involved fast-moving machinery, large crews, an elaborate division of labor—and all these industrial phenomena had been little known earlier to the men who became hard-rock miners in the frontier era.*

Lithograph from Frank Leslie's Illustrated Newspaper *in 1877.*

Nevada State Historical Society photo

mine worker may perhaps be grasped by first focusing briefly upon a miner who was present at the turning point—at that "elbow in history" when an old way of life watches the birth of the new. Such a person was Albert Byron Sanford, who worked in Colorado in the summer of 1881 when lode mining in the Gunnison area was still on or near the surface, and who recorded his activities in a diary. Sanford described his job in the shallow mine, which mainly involved cutting and lowering trees for use as timbers. It was difficult labor, but in contrast with what came later—and was then already the case in many Western mines—Sanford's summer seems almost bucolic. He picked berries, went fishing, and enjoyed incidents such as these:

> Just above where we are working, there is a long rock juts out. A big wood chuck comes out and sits there every morning and watches us work.
> Tonight we all got together and serenaded Mac. Our instruments consisted of drills pans cans &c. It was highly appreciated.
> We have nice times of evenings when the boys from the other camps come around and relate stories of war, hunting Indian scouts and so on. Tonight Oscar gave us an account of the great fight of Sand Creek where so many Indians were killed.[6]

But it could not last, this life of independence and berry-picking. Every foot of rock blasted out of their shaft brought Sanford and his fellow workers closer to that day when their simple, inexpensive mine operation would have to give way to costly processes of hoisting, timbering, and milling. And with these changes would come the need for work discipline and a sharp differentiation between labor time and leisure time.

Sanford noted—perhaps unwittingly—an incident which pointed to the imminent changes. In the shallow-lode mining operation that Sanford was engaged in, as in placer mining, there was seldom a problem in stopping work for any reason. Sanford was largely his own employer. But at a nearby mine, he reported, a "row" occurred "and one of them left and threw up the contract because his pardner would not let him go fishing while he worked." Such problems were largely unknown in placer or shallow-lode mines. This change never confronted Albert Sanford, however, for in September his father showed up and the two of them journeyed together back home to the "farm," apparently located on the plains or in the Midwest. There, presumably, Albert Sanford might continue for some time to live without taking orders from an employer, and to retain the right of fishing or not fishing as his whims—not his boss—dictated.

As revealed in his diary, Sanford still retained much control over his own actions on the job. But such control would be drastically reduced for workers as industrialism spread. The contrast between Sanford's mining day and the start of a new shift at the mammoth Gould & Curry enterprise on the Comstock dramatically reveals one aspect of the transformation:

> The operatives . . . were collected in a large room connected with the engine-room, waiting for the roll-call, which took place at 5 o'clock, each man answering to his name as the same was called by the time-keeper, and immediately after starting to his place—and as the last name was called, those that had been at work passed out, each one giving his name as he passed, which was checked by the time-keeper. By this means no mistake is made, and punctuality is secured which otherwise could not be done.[7]

The change in economic organization from Albert Sanford's shallow mine to the Gould & Curry did not occur everywhere across the region, did not follow any schedule, and did not result in identical approaches to enforcing work discipline. The varied rhythm of industrialism meant instead that placer mining continued down to 1910, repeatedly attracting lode miners and then releasing them back to wage labor. It also meant that the West was pockmarked by small lode mines which provided far different experiences for workmen than did

---

3a and b. New methods of timbering made deep mining possible on the Comstock, creating an underground labyrinth that became a daily home to thousands of men from the 1860s on. Such operations were far beyond the capabilities of individuals, and they ushered in the era of the corporation in Western mining.

a. Lithograph from Frank Leslie's Illustrated Newspaper, March 16, 1878.

Nevada State Historical Society photo

b. Lithograph from Views of the Works of the Gould & Curry Silver Mining Company (San Francisco, n.d.).

Nevada State Historical Society photo

large enterprises. Many of these shallow mines, often employing less than a dozen workmen, existed side by side with mammoth lode operations of several hundred workers. Such contrasting conditions would complicate lawmaking, union organization, and especially attempts by later historians to generalize on the life of hard-rock miners.[8]

Although some placer operations became large enterprises as hydraulicking developed in the late 'fifties, it is still basically true that the industrialization of Western metal mining stood in sharp contrast to what had been known earlier. This was especially true of its large machinery, speed of operation, and numbers of workmen. Observers saw at once that lode mining *was* different from California gulch mining—vastly different from any occupation followed before by large numbers of men. Neither contemporary placer operations nor underground mining during previous centuries knew the fast-moving steel "cage" (a sort of elevator) which took the hard-rock miner hundreds and thousands of feet below the surface to a dark world of creaking timbers, dripping water, and unpleasant or dangerous gases. Nor did earlier periods know blasting: in former times, miners working underground had picked down the rock, or sometimes built fires to crack it loose. Western hard-rock miners, however, drilled holes in a pattern in the rock, so that blasting powder could be inserted. A longtime hard-rock miner, Frank Crampton, recalled his work:

> Single jacking was one-armed swinging of the short-handled four-pound, iron hammer, while turning a drill steel with the left hand a fraction of an inch after each stroke. Two-armed swings with the long-handled, eight-pound hammer, while a partner turned the steel after each stroke, was double jacking. Either required fifty or more strokes a minute to be effective, from every position, excepting standing on one's head, and in all directions—up, down, at an angle, or to one side.

(That this speed could be maintained over long periods is doubtful. An 1872 account stated that a miner working "at ordinary speed" struck "20 blows per minute.") After years of experimentation, shots were fired by using different lengths of fuse so the rock would break toward space opened by the preceding shot. This also made it possible for men to listen (from a safe distance) to ascertain which ones "missed." Explosions

12

in the carefully planned row of holes shattered the rock on the floor, where it was loaded into mine cars by *muckers* and removed by *trammers* to the dump outside, to the mill or the smelter, or sometimes to other underground areas where it was used for support.[9]

As will be discussed in Chapter 4, some mines were hot and full of unhealthful gases, a problem which worsened as they were pushed deeper into the earth. Water was a continuing problem, requiring the wearing of "gum" boots, and occasionally "gum" hats and jackets as well. The widow of a former Colorado miner recalled lovingly the ritual of her husband's return each evening from the mine: "He came with muddy boots," she said, stretching her arms to indicate their great length, "and I hung them up to dry behind the stove." Until carbide lamps began to appear early in this century, hard-rock miners worked by the flickering light of candles, usually issued three to a man per shift. These were held on the sides of the drift or stope by "a splatch of wet clay" in some early mines, but generally were positioned in candleholders of bent wires or iron rods. The latter became identified with hard-rock mining, and were supplied with a hook for hanging the miner's jacket and a sharp point to be poked into the rock or timber. They could have other uses as well: Comstock newspapers reported after-hours brawls in which miners set upon each other, inflicting deep wounds with these devices. "The steel prong of a miner's candlestick," the *Territorial Enterprise* noted, "is about as long and as sharp, and produces the same kind of wound, as an Italian stiletto."[10]

As it expanded in the Gilded Age, lode mining came to involve more than the men who drilled and blasted or mucked and trammed. It included such varied types as carpenters and timbermen, pumpmen, engineers who ran the hoists and steam engines, powder men who stored and sometimes distributed the blasting materials, cagers who moved the mine cars on and off the cage, and pick boys who retrieved dull drills and picks, carried them to the blacksmith for sharpening, and hauled water to the men. In shallow mines all of these operations were often carried out by the same men. Larger mines had specialization and also had various echelons of shift bosses and foremen; by the 'nineties, there were large numbers

13

of workmen as well in mills and smelters—often located adjacent to mines—who worked for the same employers as the miners.[11]

The term *miner* changed as well, undergoing refinement with this growing specialization underground. During the placer era's dominance, anyone employed in any way in the search for gold and silver merited the label; now it was increasingly restricted to those actually excavating rock. The additional label of *hard-rock miner* came to distinguish Western metal miners from placer or coal miners. This new, narrower definition explains why the percentage of men identified as miners could decline in a district despite an expansion of mine operations. In Grass Valley, for example, the growth of quartz (lode) mining in the 1860s required many more largely unskilled employees for such duties on top as breaking rock prior to delivering it to the mill; many new skilled artisans were needed as well for mill work, running and maintaining machines, and construction. Under the new definition, however, none of these groups were classified as miners. In Grass Valley this meant that the proportion of men called miners decreased while the percentage of men employed in mining increased.[12]

Soon, large numbers labored for single companies: in 1866, one mine on the Comstock and two in Grass Valley each employed more than 150 men, but by 1890 the major Butte mines had 300, 350, 400, 500, and 900 employees, topped by Anaconda's total of 3,000 in mining and smelting.[13]

While this led to a chronic labor shortage in the West, because of a variety of factors an employment agency's paradise did not materialize. When ore piled up faster than the mill could handle it, or when a hoist broke down, or when supplies ran short due to bad roads or other causes, hundreds or thousands of men could be suddenly left jobless in an isolated frontier economy which frequently held little prospect for alternate employment. Although Butte was known for its job opportunities, in 1885 the oversupply of job-seekers was so great that "as many as 20 and 30 can be counted at one time round every hoisting work supplicating for work which they cannot get," forced to remain because they chose not to "count railroad ties on an empty stomach. . . ." Employment was also affected by the railroad and telegraph links which soon reached the

14

West's mining camps and smelters, for they drew the hard-rock miner closely into a world economy beset by sharp fluctuations. Now, a drop in the copper price in Paris could immediately cause layoffs in Butte. This was especially noticeable after the silver panic of 1893 hit the West: when the news arrived in Granite, Montana, it immediately caused the town's silver mine to close and set off a stampede of the more than 3,000 residents, who fled within twenty-four hours. All the while the mine whistle wailed on, finally becoming inaudible as the steam pressure subsided amid the tumult of a community sent reeling by events thousands of miles away. The Western miner was isolated no more.[14]

The hard-rock miner's community life was usually boisterous, following the tradition established by the California placer mining camps in the days of the forty-niners. But new noises echoed through the Western canyons now: on the Comstock the quartz-crushing mills "are kept thumping, crushing, screetching with their steam whistles almost continually . . . ," and visitors noticed "the steady puff! puff! puff!" of the steam engine, "the shrill sound of the steam whistle calling off the night hands," or the quartz mill "whose roar of many stamps made the echo resound through the surrounding mountains." (When the Homestake operation in the South Dakota Black Hills suddenly shut down its machinery in 1909 after thirty-two years of operation, the town's inhabitants felt themselves in a strange world. "You could even hear the dogs bark," one resident recalled.)[15]

In addition, life was more dangerous in a crowded, noisy lode-mining community than it had been in a placer camp. Streets were clogged with quartz wagons, while miners blasting too near the surface caused sagging homes and roads, and their dynamite frequently carried missiles beyond company property. A correspondent in Nevada's White Pine district reported that he saw "a sockdolager" of twenty-five or thirty pounds come sailing through the air from the Aladdin's Lamp mine "and gently pass through the roof of the Company's house." It made a hole "about the size of a flour barrel" in the roof, dropping at the feet of the camp cook. "It seemed to annoy him," the correspondent added. Aerial tramways stretched across mountain valleys would later have a similar impact on other camps, spilling ore on homes, humans, and lesser animals below as the cables moved another load to the mill.[16]

Citizens of the modern era who are sensitive to noise, air, and other pollution will perhaps greet with disbelief the fact that the din of a mining camp generally did not stir the wrath of the citizenry. Far from it: the noise, the bustle, and the rocks in midair were considered symbols of the new industrial prosperity and a necessary accompaniment to progress. And there was no argument on the necessity for progress. The noise of quartz mills in Centreville, Montana, in 1864, was therefore described in lilting phrases: "The music of the engines and the ceaseless clatter of the stamps are agreeable to the ear, give encouraging promise of the future, and raise the village to a fixed and important place in the territory." Similarly, at Silver City in southwestern Idaho, the cacophony of engines and dynamiting was called "music to her people." An observer in Butte's early period noted the starting up of the Lexington mill and commented that ever since "we have enjoyed our favorite melody, the 'music of the stamps.' Long may the merry tune continue." When the district later became known as well for the billowing clouds of smoke which spewed from the copper smelters, killing vegetation, a local newspaper could still see the bright side: "The thicker the fumes the greater our financial vitality, and Butteites feel best when the fumes are thickest."[17]

The noise of mills and blasting and the fumes from the smelters combined with the jerry-built nature of mining camps to produce communities noted for dissipation and transience rather than lasting monuments of brick and stone. Especially in a camp's early years, life was centered in the unsavory demimonde of saloons, gambling dens, hurdy-gurdy dance halls, and "the line," where prostitutes waited to break the monotony of a miner's life while relieving him of his pay. One estimate puts one hundred saloons in Virginia City by 1880—every second building downtown—and violence was so common there that a Comstock newspaper once exclaimed with surprise: "There was no one shot in Virginia [City] yesterday!" Responding to a report of a Nevada murder—in which two desperadoes shot an enemy while he slept in a railroad station, then fired randomly at nearby houses and a passing train—the *Alta California* lamented, "This is life on the mining frontier." The popularity of Shakespeare's works among miners, which

16

startled both contemporaries and later historians, was notable primarily because it was such an unexpected growth in such surroundings.[18]

But as welcome as Shakespeare was in Leadville, Virginia City, or Butte, one other visitor from afar was longed for with greater expectations. This was the railroad, at once providing other routes to the mines, permitting more rapid shipment of the latest technological devices, and opening up hundreds of low-grade properties with its cheaper rates for bulk shipment. Comstock mine owners predicted that the coming of the railroad would cut the district's costs in half. In Butte, the Iron Horse arrived precisely at that moment when large-scale copper discoveries called for an alternative to ox teams for hauling ore. Small wonder, then, that railroad men had such little trouble drumming up support in the mining districts: voters of Gilpin County, Colorado, for example, supported by 1,139 to 58 a plan for the county to purchase $300,000 worth of railroad bonds. The U.S. Geological Survey agreed with the spirit behind these moves. The opening of the Western mines, it stated in its 1884 report, "may be regarded as the direct result of the rapid extension of the railroads in the Rocky mountains, cheapening the cost of suitable fuel and the shipment of product. . . ."[19]

Soon there were extensive intricate equipment, great depth of operations, and a growing division of labor in the vast labyrinths below bedrock—all having a major impact on the Western hard-rock miner. And these were tied to another development which would also profoundly affect his life: the rise of large-scale capital investment, the unavoidable prerequisite for any lode mining that went more than a short distance below bedrock. As early as 1856, the Sacramento *Union* saw few places in Western mining where individuals or companies could make three dollars a day without "considerable" capital investment. A Comstock newspaper stated the situation bluntly eight years later: the miner was beginning to discover, it noted, that "a pick and shovel and sack of flour, though backed up by brave heart and willing hands, are hardly adequate to the work of driving tunnels and sinking shafts, to say nothing of the mills and reduction works necessary to silver mining."[20]

It would be difficult to overemphasize either the enormity

of lode mining expenses or the restrictions they imposed upon hard-rock miners dreaming of opening their own mines. Construction of the Gould & Curry mill on the Comstock cost the firm nearly $900,000 by the close of 1863, during a period when the company was also forced to excavate the equivalent of two and one-half miles through poor rock in order to run an efficient operation. (The expenses brought dividends in this case: from 1862 to 1865, the Gould & Curry produced $14.5 million in silver and gold.)[21]

The rebellious ores being encountered on the Comstock and elsewhere soon required a variety of milling and smelting devices and methods, such as the "Washoe Process," the "Reese River reverberatory," or by 1908 the electrical dredge, chlorination, and cyanidation. All this brought additional expenses beyond the never-ending daily overhead and operation costs—explosives, candles, timbering, deadwork, and water removal. (The latter could be extremely costly, as the owners of an Aspen mine learned when they had to provide pumps to handle a daily water flow of four million gallons. A mine in Idaho Springs, Colorado, was only slightly better off when it had to pump out forty tons of water for each ton of ore removed.) Litigation was the inseparable companion of high technology and high finance in the West, overloading the court dockets and crowding courtrooms with elaborate models of mineral veins and tons of specimens, thus swelling mining expenses further.[22]

By 1863, Colorado's mines could no longer be adequately supplied by local capital, one study has estimated. This condition occurred early in other districts as well, for mining preceded settlement in virtually all Western states and territories. The miners of Desert City, Nevada, sent out a plea that "the mines of the district, to pay, must needs be developed as other districts, by means of tunnels, shafts and—capital." The thought was widely repeated. San Francisco became the early center of Western mining finance, and by 1869 it was estimated that three-fourths of the mines of White Pine were financed from there; a similar dependence was registered in many other districts.[23]

But soon San Francisco was inadequate to supply the voracious appetite of the West's growing metal-mining industry, and help was sought in the East. When mine owners in Philipsburg, Montana, realized their need for expensive smelting procedures, "it was not long," one writer wryly observed, "until the residents of the little camp ceased looking to the hills as a source of wealth: they looked toward Philadelphia." From the Western mining districts, travelers set out with ore samples and literature; an Idaho mine agent transported fully a ton of rock to New York, and in 1865 a quartz mining agency for Idaho territory was set up there. Easterners came to investigate on their own as well: "There were 33 Bostonians came in last night on a special train," a youthful resident of Lake City, Colorado, recorded in his diary one day during the summer of 1901. "They came in at 6:30 p.m. and went right up to the Contention Mine. Quite a crowd gathered at the Depot to see them come in." Four days later the Bostonians left— "the whole push"—presumably having a clearer view of what their funds would go for.[24]

Eventually, even Eastern financial centers proved inadequate, and this left one major alternative: Europe. Thus, when the Colorado Legislature passed a law in 1887 "Preventing Non-Resident Aliens from Acquiring Real Estate in Colorado," the solons carefully specified that this prohibition would *not* apply to "foreign corporations, syndicates, or individuals acquiring, owning, holding or working mines. . . ." Foreigners were not welcome if their aim was to buy up farm and ranch acreage needed by settlers; the welcome mat was out only if they came to invest in the mines.[25]

European money came eagerly, aided by completion of the transatlantic cable in 1867 and by continued railroad and steamship improvements which reduced the trip from London to the Comstock to a total of twenty days by 1868. The gradual pacification of Indian tribes encouraged travel by European investors also. One of the early European companies operating in Colorado was Mining Company Nederland, a Dutch firm organized in 1873 to take over a productive mine at Caribou. Most active across the region were the British, registering at least 518 joint stock companies for Western mining from 1860 to 1901. In Montana, the Lexington mines were purchased by French capitalists in 1881. Troubles beset many of these companies, however: Mining Company Nederland was ruined by

1876 due to a series of problems, and the leading historian of British investment in Western mines has concluded that only one British company in nine paid any dividends, and "many of these were but token payments of slight significance."[26]

This transfer of mine ownership away from mining districts to a point beyond the mountains or seas proved another crucial change in labor-management relations in the mining West. Partly this stemmed from the continued competition for this capital, for the use of puffery or outright fraud became widespread in mine finance. Many leaders of the industry were angered by this financial chicanery. The famous mine expert T. A. Rickard concluded that the Comstock, for all its wealth and advanced engineering techniques, "did more harm than good to legitimate mining." This was because of the encouragement it gave to finding sudden riches without systematic work, and because of "forming share-mongering companies on mere expectations, with a view to market jugglery." A Colorado businessman warned a Scottish investor that "the keenest Yorkshire horse dealer is a mere innocent babe in comparison to a dealer in mines . . . ," and another critic complained that whole communities were "demoralized by the spirit of gambling" because citizens were "over-anxious to capture the capitalist, so impatiently waited for in every mining camp." Eben Smith, a leading Colorado mine owner, would have agreed: he wrote to an out-of-state investor that "this country is full of more petty propositions in the way of mining stocks than Hell is full of imps. . . . They [are] sent over the country broadcast to catch suckers. . . ."[27]

To many persons the situation did not call for laughter, but former Comstock journalist Mark Twain could not resist. After the Eastern press had reported straightforwardly that springs with gold-bearing water were for sale in California, Twain could hold back no longer. The humorist explained that he did not doubt the authenticity of the news, for he had once owned the same springs and got "a dollar a dipperful," letting them go because of "the badness of the roads and the difficulty of getting the gold to market." But Twain found this no more remarkable than "the gold-bearing air of Catgut Cañon, up there toward the head of the auriferous range." The wind blew through six hundred miles of rich quartz croppings for seventy-five minutes "every day except Sundays" and picked up minute particles of gold, which could best be precipitated by contact with "human flesh heated by passion." Lovers had special problems in such a wind, and two men arguing over a dog "had to stop and make a dividend" every three or four minutes or their jaws could clog up. Twain said Catgut Cañon locations would be stocked for the New York market; "They will sell, too." Coming during a period of extravagant claims for mine stocks, many readers must have nodded in agreement with his prediction. The sentiment was likely shared by a Montana judge who ruled in a case where—typically—the price of a mine's stock had no relation whatever to the mine's value. This custom, the judge stated, "has made the very word 'mine' in financial centers of the world almost synonymous with conspiracy to defraud."[28]

The popular image of absentee control has generally been made up of pictures showing arbitrary dictation by distant owners, in ignorance of or in opposition to employees' needs. A recent generalization states that "giant corporations" in the West "did not allow local managers to make ultimate labor policy. . . ." However, evidence from a variety of sources, to be presented in this book, prohibits such a broad conclusion. Some firms were run with an iron hand from corporate headquarters; others allowed local managers considerable leeway.[29]

British-owned companies, for example, usually gave one man charge of operations at the mine, frequently authorizing him to accumulate debts and hire and fire his own assistants as well as miners. When the question of a wage raise went before Pittsburgh officials of the Trade Dollar mine in Owyhee County in southwestern Idaho, they referred it to the company's board of directors, who voted to return it to the mine superintendent on the scene in Idaho and let him do as he pleased. Ernest Le Neve Foster, a well-known Colorado mine manager, struck back after he was bombarded with suggestions and criticisms from New York headquarters:

> I should like to know what authority I have here, if I cannot work the property, for if I have to submit every contract or agreement to pay money for the Co. to the trustees for their action, then I am a mere clerk, and that I don't intend to be. If I am manager of your property, I intend to have all the authority a manager needs. . . .

A pretty pass things have come to if the board of Directors
in N.Y. must know every time their manager required a new
mine car, a pick or a drill. . . .[30]

Not everyone got away with such independence, of course.
Another Colorado agent was dressed down by a New York official after he disobeyed orders regarding the dispersing of company funds. If the company's hopes were ever to be achieved,
the official warned, it would only be done through New York
fund-raising—"You cannot do it at the Colorado end, never."
Similar tales dot mining company records.[31]

What remained, obviously, was considerable variety in the
type of control exercised from afar. Wages, for example, remained fabulously high in the Western metal mines compared
to workmen's wages in Eastern cities, where the officials of
most mining companies resided. But even if these distant owners had all exercised total control over minute details of their
Western enterprises, this would not have resulted in disaster
or a life of serfdom for all hard-rock miners. The record of
Western mining does not support an accusation that mine
owners were all ogres; many, in fact, are shown to have had
real sympathies for their workmen, but their policies were
carried out by foremen who understood ore removal better
than labor relations. Others won their workmen's support
through fair practices. The hard-rock mining story is replete
with incidents of miners going to battle against crews in other
mines to help their employer control a valuable stretch of
ground, as took place when armed employees of the Ophir
mine blasted into the Burning Moscow property on the Comstock in 1863 and "a general row occurred." Cases of workmen
presenting gifts to retiring mine officials also dot mine camp
records.[32]

The evidence showing that hard-rock miners frequently
got along well with their employers, won labor disputes
against them, or simply held their own brought further complexity to the dilemma which the need for large-scale financing
forced upon the frontier. Briefly stated, this dilemma was
whether capital was so indispensable to the success of lode
mining as to render intolerable anything that would discourage
it. If capital was sacrosanct, then many of the normal com-

ments and activities of free individuals and a free-swinging press—traditions sacred long before settlement crossed the Great Plains—would have to be abandoned in the mining West. On the other hand, if the rights of criticism and free association were to be maintained in full vigor, some frightened investors might elect to place their capital elsewhere, and if so, Western mines would remain undeveloped. One side of the argument was stated baldly by the *Owyhee Avalanche* as southwestern Idaho's lode mining industry developed in the mid-1860s:

> The prosperity of Owyhee depends solely upon quartz mines; such mines are of no general value until opened up and the ore crushed; and to effect this, much capital is a pre-requisite. Therefore, anything that tends to discourage capitalists in making investments is detrimental to the public welfare.[33]

Others, however, feared the consequences of relying on wealthy outsiders. The dilemma was debated as early as the 1863 Nevada Constitutional Convention; as the Comstock's boom developed. Some delegates sought to provide individual stockholders with legal protection from liability for debts of the entire corporation; this was regarded as crucial in attracting investments. Warning of disaster if investors were frightened, one delegate claimed that "some of the heavy capitalists" in New York had refused to incorporate to work Nevada mines "solely on account of this personal liability clause." But another argued against obedience to outsiders: "Unless we hold these foreign capitalists individually responsible, they will not only own you, but will sell you." The convention voted to protect the individual stockholders, a decision that foreshadowed the ease with which mining firms would operate under Nevada laws.[34]

Financiers and investors soon emerged in the minds of some critics as opponents of the common people—as creators of "soulless corporations"—while at the same time other Westerners attempted to lure them and complained that not enough money was forthcoming. An Owyhee miner who angrily criticized companies which had left without paying their debts added that "some will say we should not publish such things of the mines; it will deter capitalists from investing. . . ." Not so, he added: "The country would be blessed if there never had

a. Lithograph from Frank Leslie's Illustrated Newspaper, *March 30, 1878.*
Nevada State Historical Society photo

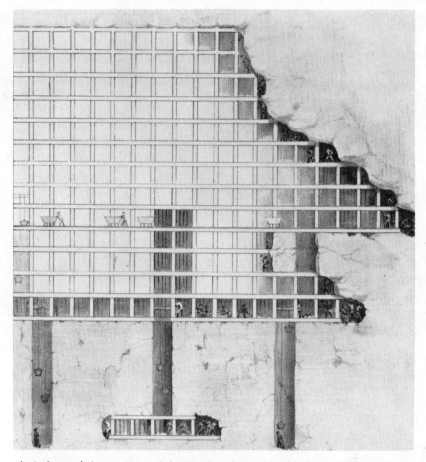

b. Lithograph from Views of the Works of the Gould & Curry Silver Mining Company *(San Francisco, n.d.).*

Nevada State Historical Society photo

4a. and b. Elaborate timbering, ore chutes, tracks for mine cars, and extensive haulage systems characterized larger mines across the West. But these worked to reduce the laborer to the position of a cog in a large machine, dependent for his income, security, and safety upon the actions of others distant from him. The one-dimensional cross section of the Gould & Curry Mine provides a hint of the elaborate organization needed and the relative weakness of the position of the individual miner.

5. The Cornish Pump—shown here in an 1879 version installed in the Union Shaft on the Comstock—made deeper mining possible by rapidly removing enormous amounts of water. Only through such employment of the latest developments in mine technology was lode mining able to expand in the decades after 1860.

Nevada State Historical Society photo

been a dollar of San Francisco capital invested in it by such thieves. . . ." By the end of the century, this was developed into an anticapitalist philosophy by several leaders of the Western Federation of Miners, whose president held that "there can be no harmony between organized capitalists and organized labor," nor between employer and employee, or millionaire and working man.[35]

The persistence of this dilemma over capital tore many Westerners who saw merit and error on both sides. It was especially hard on mining camp editors, since believers of one argument (miners and their allies) purchased most of the copies of the newspaper, while the other side (mine owners) kept the community from becoming a ghost town—there were always nearby examples of camps which had gone *that* way. The editor of the Clancy *Miner*, in a small camp near Helena in the 1890s, had particular trouble with the dilemma when the miners sought to end compulsory patronage of a company boardinghouse. The editor supported the miners but also ventured that when a capitalist is "putting every cent he can rake and scrape" into a mine, "giving employment in the meantime to all the men he can work at the going rate of wages, he should be helped and encouraged in every way possible. . . ." Caught between the two sides, the editor added: "While we have always held that if there is a class of men on the face of the earth who earn their wages it is the American gold and silver miner, we would still regret to see them take such action as would close down any of the mines of Lump gulch and throw everybody out of work."[36]

Various efforts were made to avoid the necessity for outside capital, although local interest rates of 30 to 40 percent reduced the alternatives. Homemade equipment attempted to provide new technology without the exactness possible in a large-scale foundry or factory; other would-be entrepreneurs sought to pool their savings as well as their labor. Such an effort brought confusion to an underfinanced Comstock mine,

6. *The end product: industrial enterprise in the wilderness. Gold Hill on the Comstock Lode at the height of the district's boom years represented all the modernity, ugliness, bustle, and optimism of America in the Gilded Age. Less visible to the photographer were the myriad evils that industrialization posed for workmen.*
University of Nevada Special Collections photo

where each shareholder was required to work several days for the group's enterprise. Since each was a part-owner, each played the role of director underground: after one drove a tunnel, "another would come in and obstinately start off upon the opposite tack—he would show those who preceded him that they had wasted their time and strength in a wild goose chase after the ledge, that it was the other way—he knew it, and he would convince them of it by showing them the ledge before he had worked his shift out." The result: a twisting, mixed-up passageway that caused an exasperated visitor to observe, "We have heard of dips, spurs, and angles of ledges, but we never knew that those terms could properly apply to a tunnel until we undertook to perambulate this one."[37]

Others sought to avoid capital's grasp by going back to prospecting—seeking to either find and sell, or find and operate, their own claims. Many descriptions of the hard-rock miners' mobility reveal these goals. When men left the Comstock in a massive exodus to the Boise Basin in 1864, the Gold Hill *News* observed that many of them had formerly been placer miners in California; the news of a gold discovery in Idaho was sufficient to induce such veterans "to leave this place, where the mines are worked only by companies, for a country where every man can work for himself." And when miners flocked out of Utah camps to join the rush for the Salmon River district, the Salt Lake *Tribune* understood that dull times had not driven them away, "but the great majority of the miners had been working for wages and concluded to try their luck in the new and rich mines of Idaho." At least into the 'nineties, the Gold Hill Miners' Union—made up of men who labored for wages —maintained a supply of prospecting tools for the use of members.[38]

This spirit did not die among hard-rock miners. As the Coeur d'Alenes of northern Idaho began to develop into a major lode-mining center in 1886, most of the 2,500 men working there were reported to be "independent miners" operating in pairs or squads. And by 1902, when the district was closely identified with such mammoth enterprises as the Bunker Hill & Sullivan, at least five hundred of the Coeur d'Alenes' three thousand miners were working in small lode mines or placer claims.[39]

The point is that the arrival of the absentee owner in Western metal mining did not completely close out other options, any more than signing on as wage laborers could totally erase dreams of wealth from the minds of hard-rock miners. These dreams would remain, though not pursued, even when apparently blocked by high costs, rebellious ore, or family obligations. Through it all, the miners' desire to win a piece of the Western *El Dorado* for themselves would continue to color labor relations in hard-rock mining.

For many other miners, however, a solution to the dilemma over the need for capital led in a different direction. These men responded to their loss of power under industrialism by developing a host of self-protection devices and associations to challenge company control. These will be examined in the following chapters, but at the outset it should be noted that the formation of labor unions aimed at overturning employer policies came very early in the Western hard-rock mining experience. By 1870, at the close of the first decade of large-scale lode mining in the West, miners' unions had been formed in the major camps and had successfully rebuffed several attempts by capitalists to dictate conditions that the workers found offensive. In Grass Valley in 1869, the miners even blocked efforts to switch to dynamite (instead of black powder) for blasting, forcing the abandonment as well of plans to substitute Chinese workmen for whites. These early union successes meant that the acquiescence of hard-rock miners would be a factor in the spread of lode mining during ensuing decades.[40]

With the hindsight offered by the twentieth century, such developments show that various traditions were being challenged by the industrial system then aborning—especially traditions of self-government and individualism. Part of the drama of this clash in the West stemmed from the fact that the immediate forerunners of the hard-rock miners were the California placer miners, whose dedication to self-government in each gulch and canyon was widely hailed. It seemed natural to continue this system. When a rush to the new Nevada lode-mining camp at White Pine in the late 'sixties brought the rapid creation of a miners' government, an admiring editorial writer observed that whatever the circumstances when miners come together, "they are never at a loss in forming the rules necessary for the promotion of the common weal." He considered White Pine and other miners' meetings to be outstanding examples of American democracy: "No grander spectacle, no higher evidence of man's capacity for self-government have ever been presented." Events in that raw mining district, the editorial concluded, "speak volumes for the progress of the nineteenth century."[41]

But with the spread of the Industrial Revolution, the century was giving birth to other institutions that would increasingly challenge these traditions of American democracy. Some were inherent in the rise of the corporation, in the investment requirements that transferred the economic control of a community to some distant point. Brazen displays of this new control were fairly rare; more often, the simple fact that most workmen were employed by absentee-owned companies was enough to erode some aspects of self-government.

But occasionally the realization of this change came suddenly. It occurred when orders arrived from Europe to close a mine, or when miners waited powerless while a superintendent left for the East to discuss wage changes. The Comstock had this issue presented bluntly in the summer of 1867, after some citizens chafed over the requirement that miners labor on Sundays. They formed a committee to stop the "public desecration of the Sabbath day," but did not take their plea to the city council. Instead, they turned to the Comstock's mine owners, who lived in San Francisco, arguing in a fiery petition that "such violation of divine and moral law would not be tolerated in San Francisco; you yourselves would be the first to suppress it, why should you uphold or permit it here?" The committee had accurately pinpointed the seat of power over the Comstock's basic activities.[42]

Such developments stand as historical monuments along the uneven path of industrialism across the mining West. They aid later travelers seeking to understand the drama that was played out there from 1860 to 1910. The machinery on the route to the mines was an early symbol of these changes, but few then could envision what this economic transformation would mean for social, cultural, political, and other aspects of life. Because such machinery became both a godsend and a curse, issues began to arise concerning the recruitment of workmen, the maintenance of high wages, the health and safety of work-

30

ers, and the power of citizens to control their own destinies. For the route to the mines was traveled by men, too—men who would provide the labor for this expanding industry. Their own search for protection would affect the future course of life in this vast region. That they came as free men, carrying traditions and expectations of independence and self-government, gave their acts special significance in the epic that unfolded as industrialism came to the Western frontier.

CHAPTER II

Who Will Work?

The "great Dago question" confronted hard-rock miners in Colorado's Gilpin County in early 1888. Faced with rising unemployment as the winter snows deepened, the predominantly Cornish and Irish crews in the district's gold and silver mines held boisterous mass meetings to protest the continued arrivals of Italians, "a horde of men who belong to the lowest class of the civilized world."

The Dago question was not, of course, limited to the mining West. Gilpin County's 1888 controversy was parallel in some ways to campaigns against immigrants in Eastern industrial centers. This was particularly true regarding the workmen's concern over an increase of cheap labor during a time of unemployment for many. In Gilpin County, resident miners charged that newcomers from Italy were taking their jobs by accepting wages below the district's scale of $2.25 to $3 per day, and that they were being imported from New York through the connivance of a local mining company with a steamship firm. Anti-Italian poetry, jokes, and editorials filled the local press, while rallies passed resolutions that "the Dago, who does not speak our language, does not respect our laws, does not understand our institutions," and is clannish and "treacherous," was not "a desirable acquisition to our population." [1]

Gilpin County was scarcely unique. Similar complaints were heard in many areas outside the West that also experienced an influx of immigrants. Not only wage laborers voiced such opinions; they appeared in various levels of American society. It is obvious that many citizens who watched unhappily as the immigrant hordes arrived on American shores shared the opinion of two eminent economists, John R. Commons and John B. Andrews. The two scholars concluded that "it cannot be denied that the newer immigrants were as a rule willing to work for less wages, to endure harder conditions, and to lower the general plane of living of unskilled laborers." Because of these developments, organized labor became the moving force nationally behind legislation banning the importation of aliens as contract labor, as well as a variety of other efforts to limit immigration.[2]

But in the final analysis there were limits to parallels between the mining West and Eastern industrial centers. Nowhere was this demonstrated better than in Gilpin County, where the campaign against Italians collapsed within weeks of its initiation. Support for forceful action against the new arrivals faded rapidly when the investigating committee—appointed by the Cornish and the Irish—found no truth in the charges that Italians had been imported into the district, or that they were working as cheap labor. "They no doubt drifted into the mountains from the various railroad camps of the state where they were employed last summer and fall," one observer commented, helping squelch the importation argument. These developments hit an anti-Italian rally like a "cold shower bath," the local newspaper reported. Succeeding weeks saw the anti-Italian movement weakened further; the immigrants were just not fitting into the stereotypes laid out for them by the community's Dago-baiters. Soon the Italians were taking out citizenship papers, further destroying the charge that they were only temporarily in America. By 1899, a report noted that large numbers of Italians were working as hard-rock miners in Colorado, and added: "They are all union men and get the union scale of $3 per day."[3]

Behind the rallies, investigations, and charges lay one of the major issues in the mining West in the late nineteenth century: the need for a supply of labor. And both the posing and the answering of "the great Dago question" involved issues that were important in this larger problem as it kept reappearing from the Comstock Lode onward. One facet centered on attracting, hiring, and retaining workers. Here the "pull" of the West mingled with the "push" factor in the homeland, and helped create a labor mobility surpassed by few other occupational groups. Another issue involved relations between immigrants and native Americans, and the question of why most European immigrants were accepted in the mining West while others (principally the Chinese) were not. Closely related to this, why did some groups that were scorned in Eastern industrial centers find a high degree of acceptance in the mining West? Clearly the issue of the uniqueness of the West is raised here. The native-born American was also present in the growth of the Western mining labor force, but his contribution was complicated by the fact that he was often a minority in mining camps and was frequently brought in as a strikebreaker—against union militants who were overwhelmingly European. And finally, the characteristics of this Western mining labor force can perhaps be better understood by examining the makeup of this diverse population.

All of these issues—most of them evident to some degree in the "Dago" dispute in Gilpin County—were part of the crucial question for the mining West: who will work? This chapter will explore the West's answers to this question; union dealings with immigrants will receive further discussion in Chapter 6.

Basic to any consideration of luring men westward after 1849 was the existence of precious metals, a persistent attraction that affected Christopher Columbus and most colonial-era explorers as well as the men who later crossed the plains. This lure was not suddenly extinguished when the sporadic gold rushes collapsed and placer mining gave way to lode mining. Although the corporation became dominant in many mining areas by the 1890s, the mountains continued to bear the tracks of prospectors; and individuals and small groups of miners still poked down to bedrock for evidence of a lead which they might work themselves or peddle to capitalists. Even company employees—a classification which covered most Western metal miners by then—often scoured the nearby hills in their spare time, seeking to discover and develop their own claims.[4]

The unquenchable nature of this dream, so nurtured by the gold rush, can be seen in a letter that a Colorado miner wrote to his Ohio cousin in 1885, from a small lode-mining operation near Leadville. As the snow piled higher and higher outside, Horace Mathews explained his reasons for working on amid difficult conditions:

> Yes, Bessie, there are other countries which I prefer to this, but, my dear girl, a poor man can not always do as he wishes—not that I have to stay here, for I could go east if I was so minded. Mining is certainly a dangerous and uncertain business, but there is something about it which draws a man on, ever hoping to become rich suddenly.[5]

This desire to "become rich suddenly" remained a compelling attraction for thousands. It became part of the composite picture of the region which developed in America after 1849, but it took other forms than finding nuggets. A Canadian who quit his Eastern lumberjack job and headed West to work on the Comstock Lode said it was "the lure of the West and high wages" that drew him. High wages, then, eventually merged with the dream of finding precious metals to produce an image of hard-rock mining that was irresistible to many Europeans and Americans.

The importance of high wages in building a labor force can be best understood by comparing Western metal-mining wages with what most working men were receiving anywhere else in the country or the world. Starting at $6 and $7 a day as lode mining began in the early 1860s, hard-rock miners were soon receiving a standard $4 on the Comstock Lode and other areas; and while this dropped slightly across the region in ensuing decades, it was usually no lower than $2.50 to $3, and frequently higher.[6]

These wages contrasted dramatically with the national daily average for nonfarm labor of $1.04 to $1.57 in the 1870–1899 period; for carpenters, $2.23 to $3; wool manufacture, $1.42 to $1.47; shoe manufacture, $1.67 to $1.80; and iron manufacture, $1.99 to $2.03. Coal miners—who had job skills making them more open to the idea of Western mining employment—had daily earnings of from $1.61 to $2.37 in Illinois in the 1880s and 1890s, and from $1 to $2 in Pennsylvania, according to an 1897 study. But even these daily figures do not provide an accurate view of workers' incomes. Building-trades workmen were then, as now, forced into lengthy layoffs for weather and

7. *Labor needs increased sharply once deep mining began. Single-jack men, working at the side of the stope, muckers (such as the one shown here), and a legion of carpenters, timbermen, dynamite experts, hoist operators, and others were required. They worked under the watchful eye of the "super," pictured inspecting underground operations in the Primos Chemical Company Mine in San Miguel County, Colorado. Undated.*
Denver Public Library, Western History Collection photo

business reasons, and short workweeks drastically reduced the earnings of many coal miners. Western miners' wages, therefore, were considerably above the pay in Eastern industrial and mining centers.[7]

The contrast with European wages was often greater and provided even more of an impetus to emigration. The president of the British Miners' National Union, Alexander Mac-Donald, toured the West in 1877 and later told his members that high wages for miners and cheap land were major reasons for moving to the region. In the Tyrol at the turn of the century, "You worked in a field, for maybe 40 cents a day," recalled Mrs. Ermira Visintin, widow of an Italian who emigrated to Colorado then. Her husband did considerably better, therefore, when he signed on at the Liberty Bell Mine near Telluride at $3 a day for a seven-day week. Later studies by economists have given statistical backing to such observations and recollections.[8]

Wages were high in Western mining for several reasons. From the bonanzas of the gold rush era a tradition of high earnings—and costs—was carried over into lode mining. In addition, the rapid extension of underground operations called for large numbers of workmen, and the demand kept wages high. A leading figure in the industry termed the "great want of the region" in the post-Civil War decades "a full supply of labor." San Francisco and the East could supply most of the capital and technology required, but workmen were not shifted so easily across the intervening miles of mountains and plains into thinly-populated states and territories. High wages, however, could stimulate men to bear the hardships of Western travel.[9]

The need was met rapidly. By the mid-1860s, many mines on the Comstock already had crews of forty to fifty men, while the Yellow Jacket employed 125 and the Savage, 150. Two large lode mines in the Owyhee district of Idaho called for "one hundred more men" in 1873, while a newspaper correspondent wrote from Rocky Bar that "the greatest drawback to this camp is the scarcity of laborers." Amid such shortages of workmen, high wages emerged to complement—and increasingly to supplant—the lure of gold nuggets. They drew to the West men whose closest previous contact with mining consisted of scooping coal into a stove. Their lack of skill proved of little long-range importance, however; as one mining engineer put it, superintendents soon discovered that "ordinary 'laboring men' under experienced supervision can be trained to become efficient miners in a short time."[10]

One solution to the need for labor appeared early. It seemed logical and fortuitous to many: hire the Chinese, who were pouring into California after having been driven from their homeland by poor economic conditions. A Comstock Lode editor in 1868 reported that cheap labor—meaning the Chinese—was considered "a great desideratum" by those who had investigated Nevada's political economy. As long as such labor was available so easily, he added, "it will no doubt be a sore temptation" to other employers besides railroad foremen to hire such workers. A year later, the same editor surveyed the number of mines in his district that were lying quiet because of inability to meet operating costs, and asserted: "Let us have 'cheap labor.'" Across the Sierras in California, another editor predicted that the use of Chinese labor in the lode mines of California and Nevada would boost production more than 100 percent. The Colorado Legislature took up the cry, calling on its citizens in 1870 to assist Chinese immigration because it was "eminently calculated to hasten the development and early prosperity of the territory by supplying the demands for cheap labor."[11]

The Chinese spread rapidly from their entry point in California, and by 1870 over half of the 6,600 miners in Idaho Territory were Chinese. They usually worked as placer miners along Western streams, but were also employed as ditchdiggers, cooks, laundrymen, domestics, or as hands laying track for railroads.

While some Westerners looked eagerly at the influx of Chinese, others considered the newcomers a strange phenomenon —first a curiosity, increasingly a menace. The Chinese came into southern Idaho in 1866, passing over ditches and woodpiles, "forcibly reminding one of a huge drove of crickets on their march." Later that year, Chinese were "getting thick as blackberries" in the new Montana gold camp of Virginia City. Since they often bought used-up placer claims from white miners, the Chinese were allowed into many districts despite grumbling from the residents. But an underlying fear remained, surfacing only occasionally, as when an Idaho mining town's Star Spangled Banner was replaced on the community flagpole by a triangular Chinese flag—"sufficient proof in itself of decay and degeneracy," a newspaper correspondent complained.[12]

The rise of lode mining, however, rapidly diminished tolerance for Chinese in the mining districts. As placer miners, the Chinese were potential buyers of used-up claims; as lode miners, they were only cheap competition for jobs. A Nevada editor put his finger on the importance of their *potential* damage when he argued that "the problem was not so much what the Chinese were doing then but what they would do in the future over the labor market. . . ." As a result, in district after district the Chinese were either driven out, banned by legislation, or made to understand that they would not be tolerated as underground miners.

White miners rioted against Chinese on the Comstock Lode in 1869, causing a local business leader to report to an associate: "The miners drove off the Chinamen yesterday, for which I am quite sorry, they gain nothing by it all." He was wrong, for the miners did gain: they won a promise that Chinese railroad construction men working toward the district would not be hired for mine labor when the railway was completed. Uprisings against Chinese occurred as well in other lode-mining districts—Idaho's Owyhee district in 1873; Caribou and Leadville, Colorado, in the 1870s; Rico, Colorado, in 1882; Tombstone in 1887; the Coeur d'Alenes in 1891; Butte in 1897; and in many other centers of underground mining. Community support for (or at least acquiescence in) the miners' actions was evident in most of these incidents, but was shown most dramatically when Nevada citizens balloted in 1880 on a question of whether or not to allow further Chinese immigration. The results showed 17,259 against the Chinese, 183 for.[13]

As a result, Chinese—and all other Orientals—were completely barred from most camps and were only barely tolerated as cooks and laundrymen in others. One study found that while the Japanese who came at the turn of the century sometimes obtained jobs as coal miners in Colorado, "the metalliferous mines were closed to them." The passing of time did not weaken the white miners' opposition, and in 1902 the Victor Miners' Union in Colorado voted to request that Congress "exclude not only the Chinese, but the Mongolian race, from the United States, not only for a limited time, but for all time."[14]

Complaints against the Chinese were based on incidents, rumors, and a host of beliefs that had wide currency throughout the West. The Chinese, it was said, came not as independent workmen but in gangs, as contract labor under a headman. The Colorado Bureau of Labor Statistics repeated this charge, alleging that the Chinese "pay $6 each per year to some of the Chinese companies in San Francisco. It is also claimed that they are under the control of the Emperor of China and are compelled to send all of their surplus earnings back

39

8. The Chinese were excluded from Western hard-rock mining. They were kept out by laws, by threats, and sometimes by mob violence, such as the rioting that killed C. Lung in Tonopah, Nevada in 1903.

Nevada State Historical Society photo

to the Flowery Kingdom. . . ." Others argued that the Chinese were temporary sojourners only, saving money for their return to China. As Montana Governor James M. Ashley stated in 1869: "The coolie laborer has no family to support or educate, . . . he has no interest in our society or government, and does not expect to become a citizen, and until he does he cannot be forced to enter our army." A third complaint was that the Chinese—with their queues, opium dens, and strange smells—were culturally too different to assimilate into American communities.[15]

But the major opposition to the Chinese stemmed from the fact that they were cheap labor in the West, receiving as little as half the wages paid to whites. Because of this wage differential, Chinese were hired and white workmen fired in several widely publicized instances. The Chinese were used extensively in railroad work and coal mines, and gained wide notoriety among white workingmen throughout the country when they took the places of striking whites in a Massachusetts shoe factory. They also replaced whites in Western lode mines on several occasions—at least often enough to remain a credible threat to the livelihood of the hard-rock miner.[16]

These incidents and fears formed an important part of the background when members of the Western Federation of Miners were warned at their convention in 1901: "What will it avail us to enact eight-hour laws and employers' liability acts if corporations are permitted to import cheap yellow men to supplant the Caucasians?" Using their political strength in the West, miners spearheaded a variety of anti-Chinese legislative acts. These ranged from Idaho's 1866 law taxing all Chinese miners $5 a month (while specifying that "all Mongolians, whether male or female, and of whatever occupation," had to pay the tax), to Nevada's prohibition in 1879 on the importation of contract Chinese labor into the state, to British Columbia's 1884 ban on the immigration of "any Chinese" into the province, followed by the province's outright ban in 1897 on the employment of Chinese or Japanese in any underground mine.[17]

In these ways—ranging from violence to more subtle forms of pressure—the Chinese were kept from supplying the labor needs of the growing Western metal-mining industry. The question, who will work?, was still open.

Immigration from another direction served to minimize the labor shortage that the Chinese had once been expected to fill. Europeans, lured by the aura of precious metals and by news of high wages, and often pushed by conditions in their homelands, moved into Western hard-rock mining in vast numbers. Publicity about the West increased dramatically in Europe; one study notes 129 books published about the West in England from 1865 to 1900. Nevada, which had the first extensively developed lode-mining district, became the nation's immigrant capital, percentagewise, by 1870—44.2 percent, mostly European, falling slightly to 41.2 percent by 1880. The state's major city, Virginia City, the Comstock's largest community, boasted a foreign-born percentage of 63.5 for the 1870 census. The diversity of the mining regions was borne out in the birthplace records that year for Storey County, which encompassed the Comstock. Major sources were:

Native-born Americans (5,557)	Foreign-born (5,802)	
1,244 Nevada	484	British America (Canada)
742 New York	981	England and Wales
909 California		(includes Cornwall)
363 Ohio	2,155	Ireland
332 Pennsylvania	172	Scotland
170 Illinois	613	Germany
	113	France
	60	Sweden and Norway

Westward over the mountains, the 1870 census of the major California lode-mining center of Grass Valley showed that 75 percent of the population was foreign-born. Although percentages of native-born had increased by the 1880 census, mining districts still recorded heavy proportions of Europeans. Colorado's native-born dominated the state's census by almost a four-to-one ratio that year; but in the major mining district of Gilpin County, the census showed 3,772 native-born and 2,717 foreign-born.[18]

As miners moved from job to job, nationality group proportions shifted sharply in specific districts. A mine engineer recalled his first employment, in Leadville in 1885, when "over three-quarters of the miners in the Small Hopes were Cornish, with mining in their blood for generations." Soon, however, the proportion of Cornishmen began to decrease as more Americans and Irish came, followed by Austrians and Scandinavians. The Butte cycle was described as Yankees, Cornishmen, Irishmen, Missourians, South Dakotans, and—by 1910—Balkan immigrants. These waves of workers made Western mining a conglomeration of nationalities, as demonstrated by the 1894 crew list in the Bunker Hill & Sullivan mine of northern Idaho: it had 84 native-born Americans, 76 Irish, 27 Germans, 24 Italians, 23 Swedes, 19 English, 14 Scots, 14 Welsh, 12 Finns, 11 Austrians, 8 Norwegians, 7 French, 5 Danes, 2 Swiss, and one each from Spain, Portugal, and Iceland.[19]

Rivalry and friction between European groups was common. Much of this took place in saloons, but occasionally the public was made aware of these divisions. The Cornish-Irish competition frequently boiled over in communities where both groups were numerous, such as Grass Valley and Butte. In the former, a letter writer complained in 1868 that he had been told "that unless a man came from the same town, village, or neighborhood as the boss, that there was a poor show for him to get work"—an obvious reference to immigrants' mutual support. Even the Montana Legislature faced the question, during its 1889 debate over a proposal to bar the foreign-born from serving as mine inspectors. The bill's sponsor asked "if the miners employed at Anaconda were not almost exclusively Irishmen, and those at Granite almost exclusively Cornish. Would a man appointed to the office from either of these nationalities be likely to prove as impartial in the exercise of his duties as one who was not influenced by prejudices that these facts showed to exist?" Another legislator agreed that "the laborers at Anaconda were almost exclusively Irish, and of two men equally competent to fill a position the Irishman invariably got it."[20]

Some Europeans were assisted in their immigration. English mine owners in the West frequently preferred skilled Cornishmen and brought them over under contract. A Denver syndicate sent agents to Italy to hire workmen for mining and other Colorado enterprises. Hard times in Britain caused the miners' unions of Manchester and North Wales to offer funds to their members wishing to emigrate.[21]

The actual instances of assisted immigration to the West appear to have been few, however—especially when compared to the number of allegations and rumors. Most Europeans came West independently, usually after stopovers in the East. Finns who poured into Butte at the end of the century, for example, came mainly from jobs in the copper mines of the Upper Peninsula of Michigan. Similarly, many Cornishmen showed up in Western mining districts after first working in the Wisconsin or Upper Michigan diggings. It was the Cornish who developed one of the best systems for spreading the word on Western job opportunities, the "Cornish grapevine," which by letters and word of mouth brought thousands of miners to America from Cornwall's declining tin-mining industry. The usual nickname for Cornish miners, "Cousin Jacks," arose from their custom of urging mine superintendents to hold a job for a cousin back in Cornwall or in some other state.[22]

The "grapevine" was used extensively by other nationality

43

groups as well. Three Italian widows residing today in Telluride, Colorado, recall that their late husbands all entered Western hard-rock mining not through company recruitment in their native Tyrol, but through emigrating on their own to other parts of the United States and then hearing of good jobs in Colorado. Mrs. Albina Clementi's report was typical: her father-in-law had gone to Northern Michigan to work in the mines, then returned to the Tyrol, and soon went back to Michigan with his son, in 1897. The son (eventually Mrs. Clementi's husband) soon heard from a friend of a better mining job in Ouray, Colorado, and traveled West to obtain employment there.[23]

But the mere fact that Europeans were so numerous could bring on bad feelings, even though they were not cheap labor and had no contact with company agents prior to appearing outside the shaft house asking for work. A Colorado miner's complaint about the Finns was repeated elsewhere concerning other nationalities: "The people are ignorant of the language and ways of working in this country, and will take from the bosses any insult they may offer, and are willing to accept any usage in the company's boardinghouse." When Cornish miners were fired at a Montana mine in 1890, a newspaper alleged that they were replaced "by Italians and others who are more amenable to the wishes of their employers" and would vote Democratic as directed at the coming election. Colorado's deputy labor commissioner called Italians "clannish" and said they did not follow American customs; they were "not a desirable class of citizens." The arrivals of large numbers of immigrants from Austria-Hungary, Italy, and Russia stimulated harsh editorial attacks in Butte, with its heavy British Isles and North European population.[24]

Occasionally the anti-immigrant feelings went beyond words. Grass Valley in 1851 was torn by a riot between Americans and foreigners, on the eve of the expansion of lode mining there. The following year, Americans petitioned the California legislature to bar the foreign-born from the town. In 1855, the Know-Nothings in Grass Valley used an anti-Irish platform to help them win the county election. By the 1880s and 1890s, epithets once used against the Irish, Cornish, and North Europeans were being turned against the New Immigration—but still physical abuse was rare. Rebuffing a group of job-seeking Italians, a Colorado mine superintendent warned that "No S-- of a B---- who wears rings in his ears can work for me." The Eureka, California, Miners' Union found sixteen non-union Italians working on a mine lease in 1884, and forced them to join. Company spies in Leadville regularly reported on intra-union conflicts between the Irish and Cornish and between Americans and immigrants. Five men mistakenly identified as Italians—they were Austrians, probably from the Tyrol—were kept from entering the Victor district during Colorado's mine wars of 1903, under what was claimed to be "the unwritten law of many Western mining camps that no Italian should be allowed to live" there. Similarly, a union campaign to organize in Bingham, Utah, was frustrated when the Italians dropped out after being insulted by English-speaking members. Butte exploded briefly with an anti-"Bohunk" (Balkan) campaign in 1910, when the Butte *Evening News* ran a front-page feature with photos depicting the grimy living conditions of the latest arrivals, and reporting that these workers were forced to rent such hovels from mine foremen or lose their jobs. The newspaper exposé quickly ended the system of forced rentals to workers, but it also drove some of the immigrants (and foremen) from the area.[25]

But such concerted actions against Europeans were, on the whole, rare and short-lived in the mining West. This pattern contrasts sharply with what occurred in many Eastern industrial areas—where Europeans dominated the industrial labor force—and with what might have been expected given the similarities between the rapid industrial development in the two regions.

Something was different in the West. Three possibilities are suggested by available evidence.

First, Europeans came into the new Western states and territories in such large numbers that an anti-European campaign would have been aimed at a very large minority or even a majority of the local population in most areas. This was evident on the Comstock, the West's first extensive lode-mining district, where the Gold Hill Miners' Union had to decline an invitation to march as a unit in the 1867 St. Patrick's Day parade because most of its members were already scheduled to march with the Swaney Guards and other Irish organizations: "Our numbers would be so diminished on that day that we could not make so good an appearance as the Union Merits —thus the Union would be injured." While it is true that the Chinese also constituted majorities or large minorities in some placer districts, these European groups were sharply different from the Orientals in their understanding of the language (Irish, Cornish, Welsh, and English spoke the same tongue as Americans) and of the political system.[26]

In addition, Europeans who entered Western metal mining usually did not come as cheap labor, or at least did not remain as such for long and escaped such permanent identification.

There are few cases on record of European immigrants working for less than standard wages. They were apparently encouraged in this regard by the reputation of Chinese throughout the region. Chinese were "the indispensable enemy," regarded as tools of employers, and white miners could unite against them by refusing to adopt any characteristics of the Orientals.[27]

Thirdly, the lack of established unions in the West meant a lack of traditions—traditions which might have closed membership to certain groups. Present when unions were being formed, immigrants were often founding fathers or joined as charter members, or at least during the movement's infancy in a new district. Miners' unions from the beginning were inclusivist organizations, seeking to take in all miners and, eventually, all employees of the company. Immigrants therefore were not forced to remain non-union.

Western history provides much evidence of the Europeans' active support for the miners' union movement. Irish names were prominent in the growth of union locals from the Comstock Lode of the 1860s through the end of the century. Mooney, Fitzsimmons, Duffy, Burke, Breen, Boyce—a variety of Irish surnames can be found in leadership positions in hard-rock miners' unions. Whether belonging to first- or second-generation Irishmen, they fostered the identification of the Irish with unionism across the West. Irishmen were the majority in the Park City district in Utah, and one-third of the miners in Cripple Creek at the time of the 1894 strike were Irish, maintaining close identification with the union. (Cripple Creek's major union organizer was not, however, an Irishman, but a Scot: John Calderwood, who came West after first working in the Pennsylvania coal fields.)[28]

The Cornish were also active in forming hard-rock miners' unions, starting with the first union at Grass Valley in 1869. Like other European groups, they resisted pressures to become cheap labor. When a company made plans to cut costs by importing Cornishmen into Nevada's White Pine district in 1870, paying them below the area's minimum, local newspapers reminded their readers that when this was tried earlier in California and another Nevada district it had backfired: the imported "Cousin Jacks" refused to continue as cheap labor. The plan was quickly abandoned in White Pine as well. Building on this reputation, Cornish miners in the Central City district of Colorado struck in 1873 after their employers cut wages fifty cents below the standard three dollars a day. Later a miners' union was formed there with Cornishmen as a nucleus.[29]

While some Europeans did serve as strikebreakers during various labor-management disputes, such attempts often failed because of opposition from the immigrants themselves. This occurred with Slavic and Italian workers imported from the United States to British Columbia during hard-rock miners' strikes there in 1899. And in Cripple Creek's turmoil in 1903, fifty-one strikebreakers—mainly Finns and Norwegians, only two of whom could speak English—were transported into the city. But after learning that a strike was in progress, eighteen quit the first night. The rest dropped out over the next three days until all "had left the city at the expense of unions, be it ever recorded to the foreigners' credit," according to the strike's chronicler.[30]

Refusing to play the role of cheap labor or strikebreakers, Europeans became union members in large numbers, although leadership positions were generally taken by native-born Americans. Of the 528 union men held by authorities after violence in the 1899 Coeur d'Alenes strike, only 132 were native-born Americans; most of the remaining 396 were Swedes, Italians, Finns, and Irish. Imposing testimony to the Europeans' union militancy can be seen today at Telluride, Colorado, in the San Juan region. The cemetery's dominant monument—its white marble columns rising majestically over other gravestones marking victims of mine accidents, snowslides, and more typical deaths—proclaims:

Erected by
16 to 1 Miners Union
In memory of
JOHN BARTHELL
Born in Kovjoki Wora, Finland
Died at Smuggler, Col.
July 3, 1901
aged 27 years.
In the world's broad field of battle
In the bivouac of life
Be not like dumb driven cattle
Be a hero in the strife.

This Finnish native, a member of the Western Federation of Miners, was one of three persons (and the only union member) killed during a union attack on strikebreakers. Some 2,000 miners marched to the unveiling ceremonies at the monument one year after his death.[31] (See Plate 9.)

Union militancy by European immigrants did not change when the New Immigration began to constitute a large proportion of the non-American miners. Italians became vigorous participants in miners' unions, especially by the 1890s, when they were still largely a low-wage, anti-union force in many areas of the East.[32]

The Italians' enthusiasm for the hard-rock miners' unions was shown repeatedly. The heavily Italian crews of two gold mines in Hinsdale County, Colorado, went on strike in 1896 when employers fell two months behind in paying wages. A Colorado report in 1899 noted that Italian metal miners in the state were "all union men" working at union wages. In Lake City, Colorado, that year, two mining companies ordered all single employees to board only at company boardinghouses. This angered the large group of Italian miners, who refused to obey the edict and tried unsuccessfully to get the native-born American miners to join them. The Italians armed themselves by raiding the local National Guard Armory, and then closed the mine to the American workmen, who were largely non-union. State troops crushed the strike quickly. With the Italian consul on hand for negotiations, the companies with-

9. *The immigrant played a key role as union militant, leading some of the most violent actions in Western mining history. One of them was John Barthell, a Finn who fought strikebreakers in the Smuggler Mine in 1901. This monument erected in his honor by the miners' union still stands in the Telluride Cemetery.*

photo by the author

drew their boardinghouse requirement but nevertheless forced all the Italian strikers to leave the district; only Americans were to be employed thereafter.[33]

Militancy by Italians appeared again during the WFM's bitter conflicts in the Coeur d'Alenes and Colorado in the late 1890s and early 1900s. An Idaho mine manager testified that Italians—who made up half his labor force prior to the 1899 Coeur d'Alenes strike—had been joining the union promptly upon arrival in the region. Strikebreakers who came into Wallace, Idaho, in 1901, wrote home that they were met by "a lot of Italians" who demanded that they turn back. Italians were so active in the WFM's Colorado strikes in 1903–1904 that Governor Peabody obtained the assistance of the Italian secret service and the Italian consul in Denver regarding the removal of undesirable aliens from the district. An attempt to dynamite a company transformer plant during a miners' strike in Idaho Springs, Colorado, in 1903, resulted in accidental death for the dynamiter, Filippo Fuoco, an Italian. Noting the Italians' support for the union, the members of the Citizens Protective League of Idaho Springs proclaimed that they had "more sympathy for the Italians touching the fuse that destroyed the transformer house and resulted in the death of one of them than we have for the agitators who inspired them to do it." Italians had immigrated with little understanding of "the full meaning of republican liberty," the League added, "and when Americans tell them that their employers are robbers and tyrants it is little wonder that it makes anarchists of them."[34]

The somewhat nonplused anger of the Citizens Protective League revealed the enormous distance that Italians had put between themselves and their reputation outside the West of being non-union. Further evidence of this came in Telluride, where the manager of the Smuggler Union Mine remarked that the "scab list" given to him by the union "was interesting because the names upon it could be pronounced!—that is, they belonged to men of American and English descent, against the bulk of miners in the district who are Austrians, Italians, Slavs, etc." Italian names, conversely, were prominent in the lists of union men forcefully transported from the district in 1904 by vigilantes. One outbound train, for example, carried WFM members Tony Marchinado, Tony Sartoris, Leuis Sartoris, Matt Lingol, and Battiste Monchiando.[35]

The New Immigration eventually sided with the WFM in many camps in Utah and Nevada, also. Some two hundred striking Italians were attacked by militia in Scofield, Utah, in late 1903, and the WFM's state organizer—an Italian—was arrested. The reopening of copper mines in the White Pine district of Nevada initially attracted hundreds of low-wage Greeks, Hungarians, Slavs, and Japanese in the early 1900s. By 1908 and 1909, however, these foreigners were chafing at their required "tribute" payments to employers, and many began joining the union. In July, 1909, some three hundred copper miners—mostly Greeks and Serbians—launched a strike there for a flat $3.50 per day for all underground work, and held out for two years before giving up. Like the Irish, Cornish, and other European groups who preceded them into Western hard-rock mining, the New Immigration cast its lot with the miners' unions, and a top WFM official was on safe ground when he told the federation's 1909 convention that "fully one-half of the entire membership of the WFM" was made up of the foreign-born. As will be discussed in Chapter 6, much of the WFM's popularity among the New Immigration stemmed from the leadership's attempts to include everyone employed by the mining companies within the union movement.[36]

The changing labor scene that the West knew during the Gilded Age brought frequent needs for strikebreakers. The unions' thoroughness in gaining support from working men drove some employers to great lengths—both in miles and in effort—to obtain men who would work for lower pay and/or refrain from joining the union.

Early hopes to use immigrants for these purposes were usually frustrated. As has been noted, the Chinese became unavailable for strikebreaking because of the effectiveness of the anti-Chinese movement. Europeans as a whole supported the miners' union movement, and even as non-union employees they usually showed little enthusiasm for working for lower wages or serving as union-busters. The general unavailability of these two large immigrant groups forced employers to scour the countryside for vast numbers of non-union men, preferably with mining experience, who could be transported rapidly to strike areas in the West.

They found two major sources: the Upper Peninsula of

Michigan, an iron and copper area; and the Joplin district of Missouri, a lead and zinc mining center that included adjacent counties of Kansas and Oklahoma. Both had lower wages and less union development than the mountain West. Not all Western hard-rock miners originating in these districts were strikebreakers, for many had first learned mining skills in Michigan or Missouri before moving on to the Rockies. But during several major labor disputes in the 1890s and 1900s, Western mine superintendents found hundreds—possibly several thousands—of new workmen there who were recruited as strikebreakers. Available evidence further indicates that most of these were native-born Americans.

Their recruitment relied heavily upon the promise of high miners' wages, although deception also came into play. The latter was noted by a Michigan man who jumped from a westbound train as it crossed Montana in 1892. Interviewed by a newspaper reporter in Missoula, John Handersohn described the exit which he and fifteen others made as "very much in the nature of an escape from the custody of the guards who accompanied the train." He said the group was induced to sign on "through misrepresentations." In his case, the lure was high wages and the assurance "that anyone could do the kind of mining work required." A newspaper in Ironwood, Michigan, reported during that spring of 1892 that "a couple of gentlemen" were in the city seeking miners for jobs "in the mines of Montana"—an apparent ruse to obtain strikebreakers for the Coeur d'Alenes. Advertisements carried by Upper Peninsula newspapers did not mention the existence of a strike:

More Miners Wanted.

First train for Idaho arrived safely. Men all at work and well pleased with situation. Work guaranteed to miners at $3.50 per day; trammers, $3.00 per day. Shipments will be made from Duluth, Saturdays and Wednesdays. Apply to Capt. John Carbis or to Thos. G. White & Co., opposite Union depot, Duluth.[37]

After a group of fifty men from the Upper Peninsula went to work as miners in Wallace, Idaho, one of them sent a telegram to a newspaper in Iron Mountain, Michigan, proclaiming that "the company has not misrepresented anything." But a Danish immigrant transported to Colorado as a strikebreaker reported after quitting that when he was recruited in Duluth, "they had a newspaper in the office, saying: 'No strike in gold camp; all men go to work.'"[38]

Such sporadic, small-scale efforts typified the recruitment of strikebreakers for Western metal mines in the early 1890s. This pattern changed dramatically, however, with the Leadville strike of 1896.

The Leadville dispute became a bitter confrontation as summer gave way to autumn without a settlement, and each side feared it would be reduced to a powerless position if it lost. Eben Smith, a leading mine owner, admitted to a London investor that "we cannot afford to give up unless we expect to move out of the country." By October, the options had narrowed so much in the employers' eyes that operating without union workers appeared to be the only alternative to turning over management entirely to them. "There is only one thing we can do but which would be attended with more or less trouble," Smith advised, "and that is to bring in miners from the outside, from Missouri and Wisconsin." One group was "already shipped in," he wrote, and another group of 150 men was to be transported soon.[39]

This effort to stave off disaster launched the importation of Missouri strikebreakers into the Western mines. A Missouri native serving as a Leadville mine superintendent may have been responsible for the proposal. In reminiscences published fifty-four years later, Joseph Gazzam, the former superintendent, claimed credit for initiating the importation. The Joplin men, he wrote, "were native-born Americans and could not be intimidated by the gunmen. . . . The Missourians fully justified my faith in them."[40]

Joplin quickly superseded the Upper Peninsula as the major source of Western strikebreakers, possibly because of the Missourians' more fervent opposition to unionism. "There is no organization among the miners of that [Joplin] district," complained the Missouri Commissioner of Labor Statistics in 1903. The ease of railroad communications between southwestern Missouri and Colorado may have encouraged recruitment as well.[41]

Not all of the Missourians remained as strikebreakers as harsh winter weather and violence visited Leadville frequently in the fall of 1896 and the following winter. Some of the Joplin men quit mining and joined the militia guarding company property. Others used their employment as an opportunity to travel West cheaply, and continued on their journeys after a brief stay in the district. One recruit returned to Missouri blaming the Colorado climate for his rapid departure, although a friend claimed that "Jim and another miner stuck their heads outside the stockade and . . . the 'other fellow' got shot and Jim very prudently took the next train home." A group of seventeen Joplin miners told reporters as they made their exit that they were leaving Leadville forever. They said they were "not in the least concerned for their personal safety," but found the climate "too dangerous" and the wages inadequate to cover high costs of board and clothing. But most stayed; three hundred of the companies' four hundred new employees were Missourians by the time the strike ended.[42]

The employers' successful use of Missourians in breaking the Leadville strike led to further recruitment in the Joplin area during subsequent labor-management disputes in the Western mines. A new source of labor for the mines had been found —antipathetic to unions, eager for the higher pay of hard-rock mining, and quite possibly less friendly to the unionized European workers than persons originating in areas with numerous immigrants. Within the Missouri-Kansas lead region, heading westward to work as strikebreakers in the mines soon became an accepted thing to do, and a local critic of this recruitment admitted that he and his friends "are in the minority" in their opposition but held out hope that someday Joplin men would "not be looked upon as scabs wherever they go."[43]

The eight-hour strike in British Columbia and the nearby Coeur d'Alenes strike, both in 1899, provided the next occasion for large-scale recruitment in the Joplin area. Missourians arrived in Rossland, B.C., and the related smelter at Northport, Washington, in groups of 62, 75, 100, and 120 in the late summer and early autumn of 1899. A Coeur d'Alenes mine official testified that after workers dynamited an ore concentrator, "we therefore concluded to import men to operate our mines, and sent agents to California, Colorado, Lake Superior, and Missouri, and we have secured several hundred men, who are at work here." Other evidence indicates that most were Missourians. Since their wages went from $2 per day in the Joplin district to $3.50 in Idaho, "they are naturally rather pleased with their situation here," the official added. Some 150 Joplin miners were imported to northern Idaho in early July, 1899, along with a group of men from the California Copper Company's works at Keswick, California. One agent of the Coeur d'Alenes companies reportedly brought in 1,100 Joplin miners as strikebreakers during the dispute, then returned to recruit more in 1901.[44]

There was ample precedent to recruit in Missouri, therefore, when warfare resumed in Colorado between mine and smelter owners and the Western Federation of Miners in 1903. While some newly-hired men from Joplin quit after learning of the strike, many more stayed on, deepening the chasm between the employers and union miners. The decision to recruit again in Joplin would "undoubtedly . . . be the signal for immediate trouble" unless adequate troops were present, warned the *Mining and Scientific Press*. But it admitted that Missouri miners had by then "demonstrated their ability to take care of themselves, pretty well." The following year, more Joplin area miners were sought through advertisements which proclaimed: "No trouble in Telluride or Cripple Creek; union wages, $3.50 and $4, for eight hours' work." Similar appeals were made— plus an offer of free transportation—during the Bisbee strike of 1907; and again in 1910, most strikebreakers employed in the Homestake Mine in the Black Hills came from the Joplin district.[45]

This new source of hard-rock miners ultimately changed the makeup of Western metal-mining labor. Some districts which had previously been heavily European now shifted to a preponderance of Missourians and other native-born Americans. The trend was most noticeable in the Coeur d'Alenes, where by the end of July, 1899, the mammoth Bunker Hill & Sullivan Company reported that three-fourths of its miners were native-born Americans. The remaining 25 percent were mainly British and Canadians, with only "2 or 3 Italians"—and this in a mine which in 1894 had only 84 American-born employees in a crew of 329! At the nearby Helena-Frisco Mine, the percentage of native-born Americans jumped, from 10 to 12 percent before the strike, to 80 percent after the strike. Italians, who constituted half of the crew before the 1899 dispute, were now sharply reduced in number.[46]

The transformation was evident in statistics released in

1901 by an employment agency run by nine of the Coeur d'A-
lenes' ten major mines. The agency reported that 1,065 of the
1,677 miners hired through the agency were native-born Americans. Three years later, three-fourths of the miners hired
through the agency were native-born; in the Wallace mines
26 percent were Missourians. This trend was encouraged by
an 1897 Idaho law which in context appears to have focused
on the immigrants' increasing militancy: the act limited both
public and private employment in the state to native-born or
naturalized United States citizens, or to those who had declared
their intentions to become citizens. A similar rule in Cripple
Creek raised the number of native-born in one major mine to
346 out of 469—almost 75 percent. The motive behind the Mine
Owners' Association policy in the Colorado camp was described as a desire "to maintain a supply of non-union laborers
who are not easily influenced by labor agitators."[47]

The Missourians' popularity with employers was not shared
by their fellow hard-rock miners. One Joplin native admitted
in a letter sent home from Leadville in 1896 that "Missourians
are in bad repute here, and about the worst epithet you can
apply to a fellow is 'flat-footed Missourian.'" Colorado's deputy labor commissioner basically agreed. He condemned the Missourians imported into Leadville as "the worst lot of all-around
thugs that ever came in a body to the State of Colorado." Their
presence increased criminality in the district and kept the police
court busy, he added.[48]

The Western Federation of Miners bitterly denounced Joplin's role. The WFM's *Miners' Magazine* labeled the district "the
recruiting station for scabs," and claimed in 1901 that Cripple
Creek, Leadville, the San Juans, and the Coeur d'Alenes "were
overrun with so-called miners from this abominable region.
. . ." These strikebreakers were not high-quality; wherever
they went "they acted the part of the bully and thug . . . and
proved themselves to be hirelings competent to carry out the
wishes of the corporations that employed them." Noting reports that Missourians were writing home urging their friends
to come West as strikebreakers, the magazine complained: "It
is strange how degraded some men can become, when, for a
miserable job in a cold, damp mine, they will sell their honor
and manhood and try to deceive others so they may follow
in their footsteps."[49]

Typical of the "odium that has smirched the character" of Joplin's miners was a poem appearing in the WFM *Miners' Magazine*. Four verses follow:

Strike Breaker's Lament

A miner from Missouri lay dying in the hills—
He was sick with mountain fever and various other ills—
He called his partner to him and murmured soft and low:
"I wish I was in Joplin, in Joplin down in Mo.

"They shipped me here to Mullan and gave me a permit,
The men who worked before me got orders then to quit;
They all were first-class miners, but then they had to go,
Their jobs were filled with greenhorns who came from Joplin, Mo.

. . . .

"Please write and tell the old folks I'm sorry that I left
And came to work in Mullan, for I've lost my heft—"
Just then his voice it faltered, he ceased to murmur low,
His soul it went a-scooting to Joplin, Joplin, Mo.

His partner wept above him, and sadly fell his tears,
Then tried to drown his sorrow by drinking many beers,
He boxed the stiff and shipped him, as fast as he could go,
To the land of scabbing miners in Joplin, Joplin, Mo.

—Anonymous[50]

Although repeated attempts were made to organize the Kansas-Missouri lead region to block the shipment of strikebreakers westward, by 1910 the WFM appeared disheartened and President Moyer admitted that "the unorganized of Missouri are always with us."[51]

The growing anger at the Missourians' presence further reduced the likelihood of anti-European campaigns among hard-rock miners. On one side stood the miners' unions—a diverse group which included large numbers of Europeans. On the other: the mine owners, mainly American, aided by importations of other native-born Americans from Missouri and elsewhere. "What a splendid sight it is," the *Miners' Magazine* commented bitterly as shipments of Missouri strikebreakers arrived in British Columbia, "to see those 'free born' American citizens . . . crossing the Canadian line, armed with a six shooter and bowie knife, in the employ of London capitalists to reduce the wages of the men employed in the mines at Rossland." Such a combination of circumstances went far to weaken latent nativism among the hard-rock miners at the very time when the New Immigration was arriving in large numbers.[52]

From such developments a generalization emerges concerning Western hard-rock mining: more strikebreakers were drawn from the ranks of native-born Americans than from any other nationality group—a statement inapplicable in Eastern industrial centers of the period.

The reluctance of many of the native-born to support miners' unions began early. In the Grass Valley dispute in the spring of 1869, the Empire Mine reopened with forty unskilled and often cumbersome miners, "most Americans," while the Cornish and Irish were on strike. Later that year in White Pine, a parade of 110 strikers drew the comment that only "two were said to be of American birth." By 1907, reports to the WFM convention showed that the Americans' reluctance was unchanged: in organizing the 3,000 employees of mines in Cle Elum and Roslyn, Washington, it was reported that "a very small percentage of the English-speaking miners are taking any active part in the organization," the WFM there being composed mainly of Italians.[53]

The answer to the basic question—who will work?—was therefore a conglomeration: a heterogeneous labor force drawn from all parts of Europe and North America, a mass of men who developed toleration for national differences while forging solidarity in confronting employers. Divisions were present, especially in housing districts in the larger camps. But the divisions were gradually broken down, mainly through the mobility that became characteristic of the hard-rock miners. It was "almost instinctive" for miners to keep moving, an Idaho editor observed, for they were "the Arabs of the American wilderness, content with nothing but constant change and exploration." They moved on for a variety of reasons—or for no apparent reason—but dissatisfaction with a particular mine or foreman, and the hope of a better situation elsewhere, apparently accounted for many of the changes in locale. It was the Western version of the much-documented mobility among Eastern factory workers who rebelled against industrial discipline, but it was conducted in an extreme form on the closing frontier. Alexander MacDonald of the British Miners' National Union concluded that "migratory habits seem almost to become part and parcel of the miners' existence in the West," for he encountered men who had left $5-a-day jobs to search for something better —and were eventually forced to settle for as little as $2.50.[54]

The existence of "ten-day miners" and "journeyman miners" (so-called because they were always journeying) meant that nationalities became thoroughly mixed. However, this characteristic also created problems of instability in both mine crews and labor unions. Within the span of a single year, the miners' union of Gold Hill, Nevada, lost four of its officers. "Leaving the Country" was the reason given for each. Another union, at Victor, Colorado, issued sixty-seven transfer cards over a nine-year period to members moving to join twenty-six other Western miners' union locals. This was in addition to issuing large numbers of "Traveling" and "Withdrawal" cards during the period.[55]

A perplexed mine manager in Central City, Colorado, complained in 1880 that "our work at the mine has not advanced as rapidly as I could wish to have it, on account of the uneasiness and shifting of the men. It is out of town and they do not stick to their work up there, and we are all the time short." The situation was unchanged twenty-five years later, when another Colorado mine manager reported to the company's English owners that operations were delayed by "a scarcity of miners, due to various causes, prominent among which are the exodus to the new goldfields of Nevada" and "attractions of leasing [mines] in Cripple Creek. . . ."[56]

Western miners therefore developed first-hand knowledge of the region's geography. When 32-year-old John Quinn ran for sheriff of Butte in 1902, he had already worked in mines in Arizona, Park City (Utah), and the Coeur d'Alenes, as well as Butte. Charles MacKinnon, a miners' union leader in Goldfield, Nevada, also knew the West well. He testified in a court case in 1908 that since coming West from Pennsylvania twenty-one years earlier, he had mined in British Columbia, in Lake City and Victor, Colorado, in Tonopah, Rhyolite, and several small mines in Nevada, as well as having held various other jobs in Mexico, Texas, the Indian Territory, and Arkansas. He was therefore close to the truth when he admitted, ". . . I was rambling a good deal during them years."[57]

With such mobility, the Western frontier was quickly overrun with men of diverse national and occupational backgrounds. Moving continuously, they spread ideas of high wages and unionism throughout the region. Nativist ideas occasionally spread too, and corollaries of "the great Dago question" reappeared from time to time. But the forces drawing miners together proved stronger than those dividing them. The mining West became a conglomeration of nationalities, a conglomeration somehow united despite the occasional arguments heard from a boisterous saloon crowd. This overriding unity in the face of diversity of origins remains one of the major results of the era of the industrialization of Western hard-rock mining.

CHAPTER III

Payday–Perhaps

I t was an unusual winter scene for a tiny Montana mining camp. There were the 225 miners marching down the main street, escorting four company representatives. Parades had been held in the town of Gregory before, but usually in summer—and never in January, when the Rocky Mountain winter drove men indoors to their cabins or the saloons.

On that morning—January 27, 1887—Gregory's unusual happenings began at 7 o'clock, when the recently arrived company officials called a meeting to announce that the mine would shut down. It was the old story of the Western frontier—transportation costs excessive, output low, development work too costly. This news was not unexpected by the miners, but they waited in vain for word on the $75,000 still due them in back wages.

That word did not come. Their announcements made, the four Gregory Consolidated officials began rummaging through the mine and mill buildings, collecting papers, locking doors, and boarding up windows. The miners, meanwhile, talked among themselves. By 8 o'clock, they had decided to act, realizing that the company men would soon return to the safety of New York.

Suddenly the miners surrounded the four, paraded with them down Gregory's main street to a noisy meeting where "speeches were made on both sides," then told the New Yorkers they would be held prisoners until the $75,000 in back pay arrived. Miners' committees closed the saloons, inspected incoming and outgoing mail and telegrams, and guarded company property. They also watched over the company men, allowing them only the freedom to saunter about the town and send out approved messages.

By 2 P.M., information was received through nearby Helena that payment was being arranged, and the miners freed all but A. J. Seligman, son of Jesse Seligman, a noted New York banker. Young Seligman then sent his father a telegram pleading with him to arrange payment or the son would not answer for the consequences. Although the Seligman banking firm owned only a portion of the Gregory Consolidated stock, the company immediately arranged for the full $75,000 to be sent from its coffers.

Late that night, a lone horseman galloped through the mountains from Helena to Gregory, bearing the news that the Seligman money was being sent from New York, with the territorial governor serving as intermediary for the transfer. The next day, the Gregory miners got their wages for the previous two months' work, and it was reported that "all hands are happy." Newspaper accounts stressed that the miners had been sober and well-behaved and had treated the prisoners with respect and courtesy.[1]

Desperation shines through these events of a winter's day in Gregory—desperation based on the miners' realization that wages due would not be paid unless forceful action was taken immediately. Possible illegality was of less concern than economic survival. This sort of desperation was not uncommon on the Western frontier, where law was frequently inoperative, where distances upset communications and even good intentions, and where regulations and traditions of another time and place were often applied with difficulty. And when wages had to compete with costly but essential mine and mill equipment in the ledger books, the temptation was great to let wages slide another week, another month. Although this situation was most notorious after absentee owners became numerous, it also existed in some shallow, primitive enterprises where owners were striving to acquire more costly equipment.[2]

This was the less attractive side of the hard-rock miner's

high wages. A mine could promise $3, or $4, or even $4.50 a day, but if miners had to wait months to collect this they were often driven into poverty or forced to live at the mercy of storekeepers who advanced credit. The *Mining and Scientific Press*—which frequently groused at the high wages paid in mining camps—admitted that "hardly a week passes in which there is not reported a case where laborers have been left without their pay and with no means of securing it from the property itself." The issue became a center of controversy early in the Western lode-mining experience. It figured in the Nevada Constitutional Convention of 1863, when a critic charged that he had seen cases "a hundred times" where miners had sought to obtain back pay from "exploded corporations." Not once, he alleged, had enough been obtained by the miners to pay the costs of filing the complaint. A Cornish miner wrote home in 1876 that an Idaho mine was paying its miners off at five cents on the dollar; he lamented that this was a frequent occurrence, for "there is hardly a camp on the coast where working men have not been wronged out of their earnings in a similar way."[3]

An Idaho judge facing a similar case flatly condemned the system. "To say that the laborer is worthy of his hire is to tell him what he already knows," Judge Ailshie observed. But what the miner wants to know, he emphasized, is whether "he will get his pay, and that the property upon or about which he worked shall be liable for such pay." The famous high wages were made less glamorous in other ways, also—required patronage of company stores, payment in scrip or "truck," or the use of overvalued gold dust.[4]

To protect themselves, miners turned to a variety of approaches. They tried the law; they launched strikes; they leased mines or set up cooperative endeavors to better control their own income. And some turned to stealing high-grade ore where they worked, or they resorted to violence. This chapter will examine the individual miner's plight under problems of unpaid wages, and his attempts to obtain the money he felt was rightfully his.

At the root of the problem were absentee owners, called variously simply foreign capitalists or "thieving gambling corporations." The superintendent of a mining company in southern Idaho called absentee ownership "the great evil," mainly because the distant owners refused to answer requests for funds, and this led to loss of local confidence in the firm's agents, delays in operations, and the growth of distrust. Significantly, the superintendent added that if mines were allowed to keep a sufficient amount of funds on hand to meet payrolls, "labor could be procured for at least twenty percent less for ready cash than the present uncertainty of their ever getting their pay."[5]

Delayed paydays had a variety of causes. Chief among them was simply the geographical distance from the Western mine to the mine's owners. Distance facilitated efforts by stockholders to switch company money to other projects, lose it through bank failure or their own ineptness, and otherwise delay wages in order to meet other obligations. Mismanagement frequently worsened this situation, a fact noted by an Idaho editor who complained that when superintendents were required to order "unnecessary dead work" as part of the directors' attempts at "bearing the stocks," not enough ore could be produced to pay the miners. Stockholders had to be kept happy, as when the principal owner of a Leadville mine instructed the superintendent in 1894 to "put off payday until, say, the 10th or 15th" so a dividend could be paid. The miners could wait.[6]

Sometimes the large distance between owner and miner worked the other way: it permitted local mine managers to hoodwink absentee employers. Two Cornishmen wrote home that Idaho mines were going broke because the "reckless 'supers'" became rich by reporting to the faraway owners that rock worth $100 a ton was only valued at $20—"the choice grain is the supers' portion while the gleanings fall to the companies, and the worthless chaff may be divided among the workmen." Similar results for the miners came from the practice in some areas of paying workmen in other forms than coin—such as greenbacks, bank scrip, or gold dust. Local managers would then report to the home office that they had paid, for example, $10,000 in wages for a month, when in reality they had paid the men greenbacks worth only three-fourths of that.[7]

The frequency of such incidents provoked an angry reaction against "thieving corporations," a reaction which deepened in intensity as industrialism continued to transform Western mining. It appeared with special bitterness after the failure of the Bank of California in 1875 nearly wiped out several Idaho companies and left miners months behind in wages ($80,000 at the Empire Mine alone). Meanwhile, it was charged, the owners "riot in luxury in San Francisco," and a Boise editor lashed out at the "soulless corporations, located in a foreign State," who treated workers like machines: "They pay when they are obliged to, the same as they oil the engine when it will not run any longer without." One "Quartz Miner" contended that "the country would be blessed if there never had been a dollar of San Francisco capital invested in it by such thieves. . . ." Another reported that he had waited eight months for his wages, "but starvation is now at my door and I cannot wait longer." Many were leaving, he added, but several families were "really in need" and could not get out.[8]

Corporations had other ways of reducing the burden forced on them by the West's high wage scales. One of the principal methods was to require miners to reside in company boardinghouses and to patronize company stores. The problem defied simple solution, however, and those who study the problem from another time and place must be wary of blanket condemnation of company practices. This is because the isolation of many mining districts usually forced new enterprises to provide sleeping and eating facilities if they expected to employ large numbers of workers. For example, the Coeur d'Alenes was a rugged, lightly inhabited region in the 1880s when a mining boom began which eventually created the Bunker Hill & Sullivan properties. Because alternative facilities were lacking, the company built a boardinghouse in 1887, and six years later a local editor argued that if the Bunker Hill and other new companies had not followed such a course, "employees at many of the mines would have been greatly inconvenienced." Similarly, a union member confessed in 1907 that the company store and boardinghouse "will have to be tolerated" along Prince William Sound on the rugged coast of southern Alaska. Camps there were small and scattered, he said, and far from distributing centers.[9]

The issue was further complicated by the fact that boardinghouses were usually more healthful and commodious than

10. *The company store and boardinghouse were often prerequisites for mining in isolated regions. In the rush into Tonopah in early 1901, Nay and Stimler's boardinghouse provided the sole eating facilities for miners, many of whom are posed here. But as camps grew into towns and additional eating facilities appeared, miners chafed at continued requirements that they patronize company facilities.*

Nevada State Historical Society photo

alternative housing, especially the cabins in which three or four miners would "batch," or the rooms in fleabag hotels. This was glaringly evident when the manager of a Colorado mine called on some of his employees and found that "the cabin is a regular hog-pen & two of the men are 'crummy.' I don't like to write such stuff, but it is true. . . ." Such quarters contrasted sharply with what the Idaho Inspector of Mines encountered in the Coeur d'Alenes:

> Some of the big company boardinghouses are complete hotels, steam-heated, and include a large dining hall, sitting room, commodious lavatories and bath rooms, provided with plenty of hot and cold water, and separate numbered lockers to hang clothes in. They are generally divided into small sleeping rooms in the second story with two single beds, and while they are

not noted for plush finish and frescoes, they are usually kept scrupulously clean by regular attendants, and afford comfortable quarters.

Charges for board and lodging at these places are from $32.50 to $35 per month, or $30 per month for board without lodging.[10]

Not all company facilities were this elaborate or clean, of course. A union report described company boardinghouses as roughly constructed and poorly lit, letting in the cold winter air. Wet working clothes hung on a nail by the heater, while the floor was covered with candle grease and tobacco juice. This mess was cleaned up only when a miner became disgusted with his surroundings, but such a break with tradition was "seldom undertaken." Except for some isolated lumber camps, the union account concluded, "it is difficult to find a more undesirable place for a man to live than the average mine bunkhouse. . . ."[11]

It was the compulsory feature of company boardinghouses and stores that rankled, and this erupted into major political and labor-management disputes by the 'nineties. These attempts to change required patronage will be examined in Chapter 8.

But incidents involving the "pluck-me" (or company) stores, boardinghouses, and long-overdue paydays were not generally included in the tales that were spread throughout the country and around the world of the fabulous opportunities for riches in the Western mines. How could a complaint about the company boardinghouse, for example, nullify the enthusiastic reports being told afar of wages at $6 and $7 *per day* in early mining ventures in Idaho and Montana, which equaled the pay for *two weeks* of the tin miners back in Cornwall? Or the $4 that became the Comstock Lode's basic daily wage for decades? Or the $3.50 in Butte? In fact, very few Western hard-rock miners got below $2.50 for an eight- to ten-hour day, six or seven days a week.[12]

Government statistics fortified the reputation of high wages. Gold and silver miners were "better paid and more productive . . . than any of the other industries of the country," a report concluded from the 1890 census. Their yearly earnings averaged $729, compared to $431 for workers in granite quarrying, or $474 in coal mining west of the Mississippi.[13]

This meant that some miners could do well in the West

—particularly if they had the good fortune to be single, un-encumbered by medical bills, free of the need to support relatives, and regularly employed by a company that did not miss paydays. But such a combination did not occur often. These factors came together for Richard Thomas, a Cornish immigrant working in the Coeur d'Alenes, who wrote home that he was averaging twenty-nine shifts a month, at $3.50 per day. From this monthly income of over $100, he paid $36 for board and room, insurance, and a hospital fee; some money was also withdrawn in certain months for taxes. Still, he told his family, "I must say it's one of the best places going to save money. Last month I deposited $30 of my wages with the Company and also bought a new hat and a pair of shoes and a few little things to stock my trunk." [14]

There were few Richard Thomases, however. Seldom did the factors exist in fortuitous combination for a miner for long periods—wages were delayed, or a mine accident occurred, or bad weather closed the roads and the mine shut down for lack of supplies. And even when such conditions were absent, the apparent affluence of hard-rock miners was reduced by the high cost of living that pervaded the Western frontier. Caused by isolation, poor transportation, and resulting scarcities, this legacy of the gold-rush period remained for years. A Cornish miner in Nevada County, California, warned his fellow countrymen in 1864 against coming West "to seek for riches," and he noted the costs: wages were $3 a day, but employment was irregular; board was at least $1 per day, boots $20 a year, poll tax $6 and road tax $4 a year, a foreign miner's license $4 per year, and clothing was expensive. Improved transportation in ensuing years cut living costs somewhat in many districts, but "the almost universal system of credit" in mining camps sent prices "out of proportion to the cost of the goods sold." In addition, many miners had unusual working expenses, such as the men laboring underground in the Coeur d'Alenes who needed $8 to $10 worth of new rubber clothing each month to survive in the district's wet stopes. [15]

Protecting themselves from economic uncertainties brought a host of responses from Western miners, culminating in the rise of the union movement and the turn to legislation which will be discussed in Chapters 6 through 9. As individuals or in small groups, they also tried the lease system of mining, filed liens against the property of nonpaying employers, and through peaceful and violent takeovers of mines sought to obtain payment for what they had legally earned. Or occasionally they were lucky and a good income was obtainable through highgrading.

The tremendous popularity of mine leasing, also known as "tributing," provided a continuing example of the insufficiency of the much-heralded high wages in meeting the expectations and/or needs of hard-rock miners. Originating in Cornwall, the system was carried by Cornishmen into Eureka and Austin, Nevada, in the early years, and spread rapidly across the West. By 1886, a third of the mining in the Leadville district was under leases, and the system was widespread in Colorado in the 1890s.

Leasing was risky. It was generally limited to mines which were previously opened but had been shut down for various reasons, usually linked to declining production. Lessees were given either a specific part of the mine to work, or a limited time period, or both. Six months or a year were common limits. The mine owner received a predetermined royalty from the output, a percentage that varied according to the known value of the ore remaining underground. Occasionally, fairly large companies took out leases, but most were small groups of miners and often men of the same nationality, especially the Cornish.

Several factors lay behind the spread of leasing. Chief among these were the miners' frustrations in company employment (such as delayed wages, pay in greenbacks, and obnoxious foremen), the desire for independence, and the hope of making more than going wages. Whether most lessees did better than $3 or $4 a day cannot be ascertained from the conflicting evidence, although the system's continued popularity through the end of the century indicates that adequate earnings were probably obtainable.[16]

Some miners tried to obtain overdue wages through legal action. In such cases, bankruptcy became a special barrier to their efforts, especially if caused by "a squabble among certain stockholders" located in distant cities. Distance and the layers of lawsuits and appeals thus insulated the employer from the hard-rock miners' legal actions. Even a court-appointed receiver for a bankrupt firm could not always do well by the men, as a Colorado miner explained to the U.S. Industrial Commission in 1899. The miners' worst objection concerning wages, said John C. Sullivan of Victor, "is that they do not receive their pay at all." He went on to show a time check for $96, issued by the receiver for a Cripple Creek mine three years earlier. The mine was paying dividends again, Sullivan noted, but not back wages. When pressed as to whether he had brought legal action against the stockholders, he said: "It seems as if that failed in the cases that the other employees gave to the lawyers. . . ."[17]

A company's reputation was sometimes worth guarding in back-pay disputes, especially if it wished to buy locally on credit and obtain high production from its crew. Colorado mine owner Eben Smith noted that unpaid wages at one mine created an "inability to get the men to do a good day's work until they are satisfied that they will be paid. . . ." To satisfy inquiring workmen, some employers sent out elaborate details to explain just why funds were not available. On one occasion when some back pay was sent to "*hardship* or *suffering*" cases, the money was ordered given "quietly" to avoid creating further troubles for the company among the unpaid. The embarrassments for a large firm over this issue were noted by a Colorado entrepreneur associated with Horace Tabor:

> Very nice it was for me, when for instance a Mr. Rouse was discharged to have to tell him that he had to wait for his wages. —(I had given him $20—out of my own pocket—afterwards refunded) he refused to go.—he was legally entitled to do so until paid & stopped on that way for about ten days—telling everybody—every workman, every visitor how that big $5,000,000 Company—could not pay his wages. . . . The dunning letters show all the lovely variations from an Andante moderato to an Allegro.[18]

The mechanic's lien was the traditional legal weapon for use by unpaid American working men. But its application in the mining West was often weakened through several factors, chief among them being company control by diverse and usually distant stockholders.

The mechanic's lien developed historically from the practice of giving unpaid contractors and builders a claim on buildings that they had constructed as well as on the land upon which these were built. This had gradually broadened over the years to cover other workmen. Usually the structure would be sold and the funds used to pay off employees. Western territories and states passed mechanic's lien laws early in their development, carrying over the language and experience of Eastern states but increasingly making the laws more protective of miners.[19]

When a lien worked, it was of enormous assistance. When a group of miners won a suit for $21,891.57 in 1866 against an Owyhee County mine, it was believed to be "the first case of day laborers in a mine getting judgment for wages under the Lien Law. . . ." A group of lien cases settled in the same county in 1877 brought individual awards to persons suing mining companies of $3,484 and $3,769.60, and also lesser amounts.[20]

But the lien did not always work. Any system encountered difficulties when the employer's assets were "nothing," as in an early Grass Valley case when fifty unpaid miners brought suit. Legal complexities could block employees' demands as well, as a group of miners from Clancy, Montana, discovered in a back-pay suit in 1897. Their lien action against the Baby Helen Mine—involving some $700—initially resulted in a verdict for the miners, but this was set aside when a question arose as to one of the absentee defendants' connections with the mine. A local editor conceded that "the case just now has a dubious look. . . ." Liens for $21,000 against another Clancy district mine, the Golden Scepter, were unsatisfied for months while the receiver scurried about the East trying to raise money —and then "adverse reports" arrived, "destroying the confidence of the money lenders" and putting off settlement again. Eventually the company paid three-fourths of the claims in cash, promising the rest when the mine could be sold.[21]

But some lien problems had little to do with the location of the mine owner. Leaseholding proved a major culprit in this category. The basic problem was that in a leased mine, the miner's employer—the lessee—was not the owner and had no legal control over the property, hence nothing to attach a lien to. A miner running for office as a Populist in Montana's 1892 campaign reported that he was still owed money by a lessee, but saw no prospects for ever obtaining it under existing laws. Miners in Colorado, which had the largest amount of leasing, suffered extensive losses under these circumstances.

A state law kept the mechanic's lien from applying to property worked under a lease, and a series of court decisions buttressed the owner's protection against his lessee's unpaid workmen. California courts took an identical stand.[22]

One bright spot appeared in the lien picture, however. Western legislatures began to frown on stockholders who had not paid the full value of their stocks, but were holding them for manipulation or other purposes. Obviously, since these persons had not paid the full value of their stocks, the companies did not have these funds available to pay workers when production declined. Montana's 1872 act sought to correct this difficulty. It held stockholders liable for company debts "to the amount of unpaid stock held by them," until all capital stock was paid. Colorado's 1877 law was similar. Obtaining these funds from a stockholder located in a distant state or country could be difficult, however.[23]

Frustrated by the courts, miners quickly turned to a variety of more forceful steps—illegal or extralegal—to get around the judicial and economic barriers that kept them from obtaining their wages.

The mine where they had worked was still there, even if their employer was far away. It was usually poorly guarded or unguarded, and so miners could return to the stopes to extract what they thought was due. As early as 1866, when Western lode mining was in its infancy, miners who were due $20,000 from the Morning Star & Oro Fino Mine in Owyhee County proposed that they be allowed to continue working under two foremen in order to obtain their back wages. The owner had failed due to "becoming involved in other enterprises," and eager creditors agreed to the miners' plan because it offered them a share of the proceeds as well. The miners even agreed to permit compulsory arbitration to settle disagreements between the two foremen, and to prevent "gutting" the mine. Such worries proved baseless—finding the workings in poor condition, the miners labored with perseverance and eventually paid off the debt. Then they opened the mine deeper "and found a great increase in its richness," getting as high as $160 per ton from an 80-ton yield.[24]

Such incidents were fairly common. Throughout the period down to 1910, many Western metal mines were briefly operated by unpaid workmen who sought to recoup back wages. Sometimes they did better than that—as when miners at the Gambrinus Mine in Whiskytown, Shasta County, California, were given a month's control and "quickly struck a good pay streak," averaging $10 each per day and sometimes clearing $16. Since miners knew where the "pay streak" ran, they could ignore lower-quality ore.[25]

Miners' control fitted in with the growing cooperative movement, under which working men being hurt or threatened by the spread of industrialism banded together to produce or purchase cooperatively. Farmers were enthusiastic about the system in many areas.

In the West, the cooperative movement won many adherents among the Western Federation of Miners, which viewed mining cooperatives as devices to get around the less savory aspects of corporate control. Others urged cooperatives as a means of survival for unemployed miners during hard times. A notable example of this was lessee D. B. Huntley's attempt to run the Morning Mine as a cooperative in the Coeur d'A-lenes during the Depression of 1894. Huntley advertised that 25 percent of the production would go to the company for taxes and other expenses, while the remainder would be ear-marked for mine development, operating expenses, and the workers' share. The project was launched amid widespread interest but some doubts as to its success. Twenty men signed up to work initially, but within a month 105 were working, and the figure rose to 150 in two months. The expectations were that each miner's daily share would come to between $2.50 and $3.00, somewhat below the prevailing union rate of $3.50. When only $2.68 was paid for each day's work after the October settlement, the Miners' Union protested and eventually blocked Huntley's project from continuing.[26]

In view of the West's reputation for violence, it may seem contradictory to report that most back-pay cases appear to have been resolved through peaceful means or left unresolved. Pleas were made to the mine owners, liens were levied, men carried IOU's in their pockets for years—and little violence occurred. Men due $30,000 in Custer County, Colorado, in 1885, were reported to be "orderly and very patient under their misfortunes" as they waited three months for wages. In 1897, a company president was allowed by Montana miners to return to

Delaware to attempt to secure the $21,000 due them; within two months he had placed three-fourths of the money in their hands and a due bill for the remainder. The pages of such publications as the *Mining and Scientific Press* and the *Engineering and Mining Journal*, as well as mining camp newspapers, contain frequent cases of the patient suffering of unpaid miners and their occasional rewards.[27]

This is not to claim that all miners could remain passive in the face of long overdue wages. Sometimes only threats were made, as when the superintendent of an Owyhee County mine with extensive wages in arrears received a note threatening arson at company properties. But more forceful action occurred as well.[28]

The strike proved highly popular as a means of forcing employers to meet their obligations to workers. It usually came as a last resort, however. "Men seldom strike unless driven to it," a Colorado miner explained in describing employees' efforts to collect three months' pay. Frustration led to desperation and violence fairly often, beginning with the early years of Western lode mining. When a new stamp mill erected at Red Warrior in the South Boise district of Idaho in 1865 ate up company funds and caused wages to be passed over, the employees wasted no time. While the teamsters seized the superintendent, the miners and other employees barricaded the mill and refused passage to anyone until they were paid.[29]

A similar incident occurred again in Idaho as lode mining expanded rapidly in the Owyhee district in 1875. Continued problems in collecting their overdue wages drove miners to abandon strikes and petitions. "It is useless to talk to men who are starving for bread," an editor concluded as frustration reached the danger point. He added that there was "only one chance out [of] ten thousand for these men to disperse without revenge of some sort, unless they are paid off." His prediction was accurate. What one mine owner initially described as "a speck of trouble" soon mushroomed into disorder when the men observed company officials closing a mine and removing equipment. Some one hundred miners—due two months' wages—seized the superintendent of the Golden Chariot Mine at midnight on June 30, 1876, and vowed to hold him until company officers in San Francisco came up with their pay. Three weeks later, they permitted him to leave to secure promised funds in San Francisco. He kept his word, returning in late August with the overdue wages.[30]

The Dutch-owned Mining Company Nederland encountered similar problems with its employees in Colorado in 1876 when they seized the mine after liens and other attempts had failed to supply their unpaid wages. The company's new owners came up with the required funds then, but in 1882 they were able to provide only seventy-five cents on the dollar to men unpaid for three months. Similar cases are numerous in Western records, including an 1889 case at Castle, Montana, where the miners rioted and the manager "escaped a lynching . . . by the possession of a fast horse." Other managers were driven off or kidnapped while the miners tried to remove ore to cover their overdue wages.[31]

One other salvation remained for the unpaid or underpaid miner: highgrading. It fell somewhere between legality and illegality for most miners, although in the eyes of employers and the law it was unquestionably a crime. Highgrading lacked the desperation and organization that characterized kidnaping mine officials; neither did it require filing lengthy lien documents, interpreting statutory jargon, or waiting months for action. In certain districts it was the individual miner's opportunity to get even with a "thieving corporation" by appropriating ore for himself. Highgrading worked only in rich mines (in high-grade ore—hence the term), where miners could remove enough ore from the property to bring satisfactory returns from local illegal assayers. In such mines, the closing whistle signaled the start of a strange-looking procession of men leaving work with bulging clothes. They walked lumpily homeward under the weight of ore secreted in double-crowned hats, belt pouches, shirts sewed together and pants lined with interior-stitched pockets, enormous boots, spacious lunch pails, and specially made harnesses worn inside their clothing. In Grass Valley, a miner was noticed with a rag tied around his boot because it had a hole; in the dry room, he took off the rag and threw it out the window. Before he could retrieve it, however, a company man investigated and found it contained a specimen worth $60. Other Grass Valley miners swallowed rich specimens to hide them from inspectors, and one miner needed a surgical operation because of his intimate approach

11. *High-grade ore was too valuable to be transported by usual means; often it was immediately sacked before it could be appropriated by "dinner pail shipments" and other maneuvers that miners used to augment their wages. These men are sacking ore worth $1 per pound, in the Mizpah Stope of the January Lease, Tonopah, Nevada, 1904.*

Nevada State Historical Society photo

to removing rich ore from the premises. T. A. Rickard recalled seeing Goldfield miners stumbling clumsily as they shuffled off toward home, including one who was so loaded with hidden rock that he sprawled in front of the superintendent when leaving the hoist. This was removing ore through "dinner pail shipments."[32]

Highgrading began as soon as mining went underground, but thrived on a grand scale only in bonanza camps such as Cripple Creek and Goldfield. It was noted as early as 1866 in one of the early lode mines in Owyhee County; it figured in the buildup to the Grass Valley strike of 1869; companies in Utah's Tintic district fought the practice in the 1870s; and highgraders robbed the Elkton Company of an entire dividend

—$75,000—in Cripple Creek in 1900. A miner arrested in Baker City, Oregon, in 1903 had 150 pounds of ore which he was selling for $10 a pound; the company estimated it had lost $10,000 in this way. A trunkful of highgrade ore recaptured in 1905 in Cripple Creek was worth $4,000.[33]

Highgrading required a local assayer who could receive the illegal ore, and it often entailed a home grinder; frequently a small "tube mill" was used in the mine to pulverize the rock. This grinding facilitated removal from the mine as well as confounding lawmen who might seek to determine the ore's source. Jim Sterrett, an old-time miner in Cripple Creek today, recalls that his community had fifteen "highgrade shops," and nearby Victor had seven or eight, in the early years of this century. Once the high-grade ore reached these assayers, tracing it to a specific mine was well-nigh impossible.[34]

But the zenith of highgrading on the North American continent occurred in Goldfield, the Nevada camp where "extraordinary freedom" to appropriate ore advanced the practice to a highly developed art. Companies claimed that they lost $1,250,000 to highgrading in 1906, while recovering only $250,000. Such developments were predictable in Goldfield because—as Rickard noted—"the ore was rich indeed." An eight-inch vein in the Mohawk ran $250,000 per ton, and the several leases there yielded at least $50,000 a day for 106 consecutive days.[35]

One of the few generalizations that may be advanced with complete confidence regarding Western mining is that "rich ore invites theft." When Goldfield miners were breaking ore worth from $10 to $40 per *pound*, that invitation was particularly difficult to decline. Men refused to work in non-high-grade mines as the extent of the bonanza became known. Teamwork made even larger removals possible, as Frank P. Tondel learned when he went to Goldfield in 1906 from his job as a Pinkerton agent in Los Angeles. One miner luckily had a friend who was employed by the company to examine workers as they left the shaft: consequently, the miner was passed without question when he arrived with his high walking boots filled to the brim with specimen rocks. The plot was uncovered through a drunk's loose tongue, and $14,000 in ore was found hidden in the miner's cabin. Due to such large-scale highgrading, it was estimated that of the fifty-four assayers operating in Goldfield in

1907, only three dealt with legitimate ores. It was truly a high-grader's paradise. This was the only explanation for the reports of miners who received $5 per day from their employers but spent $100 or more by night patronizing the saloons, monte tables, and red-light houses.[36]

Leases were the catalyst that brought the highgraders and the rich ore together. In Goldfield's heyday, mining in the bonanza claims—the Mohawk, Red Top, Combination, and Florence mines—was carried on under leases. The owners were generally inexperienced capitalists who granted leases to more seasoned operators. The leases were usually subdivided into blocks, 300 feet long and 600 feet wide, running for six to eighteen months.

The time limits and the exceeding richness of the ore created optimum conditions for highgrading. Leaseholders knew that if they objected to their employees' personal enrichment through "dinner pail shipments," a conflict would quickly develop with the powerful miners' union and all their money-making would stop—while the minutes ticked away toward the end of the lease. As a result, leaseholders often looked the other way and counted on gaining enough through round-the-clock operations to tolerate extensive losses by highgrading. "When the reward awaiting them was counted in millions," one student of Goldfield's boom has written, "the hundred or even thousands taken by the workmen mattered little." Rickard bluntly termed it "an orgy of stealing."[37]

Highgrading in Goldfield soon became a popular activity at all levels—those of officialdom as well as mine levels. The rich ore tempted and usually overcame the scruples of the miner, the lessee, and the claim owner, as well as local brokers and railroad guards. Shift-bosses joined the pick men and muckers in carrying out heavy dinner buckets, while brokers paid repeated visits to obtain "specimens"—one removed an estimated $150,000 worth—and others dipped in to benefit from the bonanza.[38]

Highgrading needed one additional factor to thrive: local acceptance. This it had in good measure in every Western mining camp where owners were distant and reputed to be wealthy. Cornish miners in particular had the notion that highgrading was not a crime. Honest miners, working far from company scrutiny underground, easily developed the idea that there was nothing wrong in picking up a specimen. This continued under the rationalization that, after all, the company was making huge profits from the backbreaking toil of men who were paid only $3 or so a day. Since the owners were so rich, it was argued, they would not miss the amount taken surreptitiously. From such reasoning came "a loose sort of public sympathy" for the "supposedly poor miner" against the "supposedly rich impersonal company."[39]

More than miners and illegal assayers sympathized with highgraders. Goldfield's district attorney testified that "a great many businessmen" there believed "it is a good thing for the town that the miners be allowed to steal high-grade." He recalled one merchant who argued against stopping the practice: "It would kill business." The district attorney charged that the miners' union sanctioned highgrading, although one union member retorted that this was untrue; the union took no action simply because "we are not in the legal business. . . ."[40]

This support for highgrading within the community appeared time and again to frustrate legal prosecution. Goldfield's justice of the peace was on record to the effect that "it would be as much as his life was worth to convict a person for highgrading." Juries—generally composed of local miners and others biased in favor of highgrading—seldom brought forth convictions, either. Goldfield's first highgrading case came before a jury in September, 1901, and was decided in favor of the accused miner. A Cripple Creek judge ruled that ore was real estate and could not be stolen; highgraders, he said, could be prosecuted for trespass but not for larceny. In another Cripple Creek case, three miners caught with ore in their possession escaped conviction by arguing that their bosses had conspired to entrap them.[41]

Employers fought generally losing campaigns against the highgrading evil. The Denver *Post* concluded that it would be "a ridiculous effort" to try to prevent highgrading; keeping it at a minimum was the only course open. But employers kept trying. Their frustration was shown in a letter sent by the attorney for an Aspen mine to company officials in New York:

> For ten days past we have been absorbed in the getting of a jury and trial, in the case of Enfield—one of our late ore-thieving employees. A complete and perfect case was made and ably presented through the best prosecutor in Colorado. The jury

have been out now nearly 48 hours without agreeing. I fear they will "hang"—and feel that they deserve *hanging* if they agree to any verdict except one of conviction against the defendant.[42]

Just as frustration could drive miners to violence, the inability to reduce ore-stealing sometimes provoked extreme measures by management. Various approaches were tried. Sometimes groups of suspects were simply fired without explanation, as Eben Smith decreed for his Cripple Creek operations in 1895: "Discharge all the known thieves. . . . Reduce the number of men in the mine to about 50 to start with. . . . I do not want any talk about ore-stealing at all. If there is any kick or row there telephone me, but I do not think there will be." The district's major mine, the Independence, once fired an entire shift of miners; it soon had to consider other measures when highgrading continued unabated with the new crew.[43]

Further large losses—an estimated 25 percent of the district's miners were participating in highgrading—prompted employers to form the Cripple Creek Mine Owners' Association, to police the mines and the numerous assay shops which specialized in high-grade ores carried in by miners. This act, in turn, led to the organization of the "High-Graders' Association" to combat the employers' group! Eventually the Mine Owners' Association branched out into general opposition to union activities as the district was caught up in labor-management wars around the turn of the century.[44]

Spies were frequently used to locate highgraders also. In one early case, the Cosmos Company in Owyhee County spied on a suspected ore thief for several days in 1866, then saw him carrying a sack when he left work at midnight. His cabin held two hundred pounds of rich ore, but the company decided to allow him to leave without punishment. Many other highgraders were fired across the West after being reported by spies.[45]

Other methods were also attempted in the anti-highgrading campaigns. Because lunch pails were such obvious receptacles for high-grade ore, one Goldfield employer issued an order that all lunch buckets were to be left at the office at the beginning of the shift. The next day there was a sudden change to paper bags for lunches, which were carried below rather than left at the office, since they were not lunch buckets. When the management warned against this subterfuge, the entire crew showed up with paper bags the following day—a confrontation that forced the employer to back down immediately to keep the mine operating as the end of the lease drew near.[46]

But the major all-out method used to foil highgraders was the change room. It arose from a variety of health as well as pecuniary goals, and since change rooms appeared in many districts without high-grade ore, the opposition to them was often splintered—and, to outsiders, irrational.

There were solid health reasons for installing change rooms. These rooms made it possible for miners to come up from a wet shift underground and remove work clothes, clean up, and put on street clothes before going home. Men working in the bowels of the earth usually emerged sweaty and dirty, especially in older mines holding large amounts of decaying timbers and other matter, and in districts where hot water percolated freely underground. A change house was required in such conditions to safeguard miners from pneumonia or other ailments by permitting them to doff their "diggers" and put on dry clothes before heading outside into the cold. In this connection, the change house is discussed in the "sanitation" section of one of the miners' handbooks of the period.

But the handbook adds this significant point: "Where it is necessary to safeguard against ore-stealing, a trusted attendant stands . . . during change of shift, and examines every man as he passes through after stripping." Having a "trusted attendant" inspect naked miners was rankling, particularly in the context of the highgrading controversy.[47]

To many miners, the requirement that they strip and walk up to three hundred feet under the eyes of company guards and other employer representatives symbolized the extremes to which management would go. Outbursts against the system soon spread across the West. The anger spilled over into the community when a mine superintendent in Atlanta, Idaho, in 1877 required the men to strip four times each day in front of his agents. The superintendent argued that he had learned that a group of workers had fled with forty pounds of high-grade ore, selling it for $400 in Boise. As the community became incensed over such treatment in winter, one resident

12. *The change house was often a center of controversy. Few disagreed that it was healthful for miners at the end of a wet shift below, but the employees exploded with wrath when their bosses converted the change house into a center of inspection for stolen ore. Location and date unknown.*

University of Nevada Special Collections photo

asked whether the nineteenth century was coming to the point where honest workmen must submit to "a tyrannical upstart of a superintendent" who was "more abominable" than a Southern slave owner. Some men quit despite the harsh winter weather that made it difficult to leave the mountainous district.[48]

Just as Goldfield marked the pinnacle of Western high-grading, that camp also saw the most vehement attacks on the change room. Charles H. MacKinnon, the miners' union secretary, testified that the three hundred men employed in the Mohawk Mine rebelled when ordered to take off their work clothes and walk some distance to put on their street clothes.

The men would change to their underwear in the change room, he said, "but they refused to parade before the general public which were invited there to witness this changing of the miners." One distasteful aspect was that some of the watchmen were "objectionable, 'particularly obnoxious,' the expression is, to the Union," he emphasized. At the Mohawk, the inspectors in the change room "delved into the mysteries—." Regarding "one man in particular," MacKinnon added, the objection was "that he was unnecessarily particular about searching the men."[49]

Compulsion became the bedrock of the Western hard-rock miner's opposition to change rooms. When erected for health reasons, the change room was a voluntary institution which the miner could use or disregard, as he wished. But when installed to check highgrading, its use became mandatory for all employees, and was made even more onerous by the type of inspection involved. Of course, given the vast amount of highgrading in Goldfield, the union's high-sounding arguments against change rooms must be approached warily. But even the most cynical conclusions do not remove highgrading from its place as a central issue in the struggles for self-protection that accompanied the industrialization of Western metal mining in the latter decades of the nineteenth century.

For the highgrader had found his own answer to delayed paydays, bankrupt employers, and distant owners who let the miners wait while dividends were funneled to stockholders. And to many in the West, the change rooms and other methods used against highgrading symbolized the worst features of the new industrialism's control over its workmen.

CHAPTER IV

Betrayed by the New Technology

A tunnel project in 1870 in Georgetown, Colorado, drew the eyes of the mining world with the anticipation usually reserved for a gold rush. Eastern inventor Charles Burleigh chose Georgetown for the first mining demonstration of his new machine drill, run by compressed air or steam power and capable of striking up to three hundred blows a minute. There had been a crying need for an effective rock drill for years, especially for opening railroad tunnels and mines. In both types of excavation, hammer-and-drill men had to make holes deep in the face of the rock so blasting powder could be inserted and fired. This hand-drilling was laborious, time-consuming, and constituted as much as 75 percent of metal-mining expenses. This situation made a workable machine drill the "great desideratum" of the mining industry. Responding to the call, inventors developed a variety of machine drills, all of them failures until Burleigh's. On the Hoosac railroad tunnel in Massachusetts, some forty drilling machines had been tried, but they produced only a major imbroglio: averaging only eighty hours of life apiece, they clogged the finished portion of the tunnel with an endless procession of runners transporting replacement parts and tools for the broken machines within.[1]

Then came the successful test at Georgetown. Burleigh's

drill used solid pistons and fewer parts than previous machines, and benefited from its predecessors' errors in design. Burleigh "chivalrously selected the most formidable cliff he could find" in Sherman Mountain, and soon his four-man drilling team was pushing forward sixty feet a month—more than five times the speed of hand-drillers in the mountain's exceptionally hard crystalline rock.[2]

As the glowing reports from Georgetown spread across the mining and investment centers of the world, acclaim and thanks poured in. The prestigious *Engineering and Mining Journal* reported that "great jubilation" greeted Burleigh's success, adding that "the event appears to be considered a wonderful thing, not only for Mr. Burleigh, but for the country generally, and for the proprietors of tunnel-claims in particular." After an Idaho demonstration of the Burleigh drill, an excited onlooker remarked, "If hell is below, it wouldn't take long to go there." A correspondent for the local newspaper agreed, condemning critics as "barnacles impeding the Ship of Progress" who had never been forced to use hand drills. And he cheered: "Long life to Burleigh!"[3] Burleigh's drill became, then, a benchmark in the technological development of mining, "the beginning of a new era," as the *Mining and Scientific Press* of San Francisco concluded in 1905.[4]

For all its acclaim, the machine drill was only one of the numerous major technological changes during the decades after 1860 when Western metal mining underwent a near-total transformation and began what one author has called its "salad days." This period saw the development also of the power hoist for deep mining, the invention of dynamite and the safety fuse, the effective employment of electricity in mine operations, the adaptation of wire rope and braided wire belts for deep hoisting, the development of square-set timbering to permit mining amid unstable rock, the creation of new pumps and other machinery for removing water, and a variety of related changes. As early as 1872, the San Francisco *Bulletin* stated that "it is hardly too much to say that mining as a business has been revolutionized in this country within the past few years." In 1908, a professor in the Columbia School of Mines agreed, concluding that "undoubtedly greater progress was made in mining in all its departments during the period of 30 years beginning with 1860 than had been made during the preceding 500 years." Recent writers have agreed with this assessment.[5]

The new technology that was rapidly transforming the industry was in all cases cheered as beneficial for hard-rock miners as well as for company stockholders. For the miners, it was hailed for making work easier and safer. "What precious human life might have been saved," declared one observer, "had these time, labor and money saving machines then been available to lighten the burdens of these hardy, well deserving men!" Other benefits were advertised, including the additional ventilation provided by the machine drill when it released its compressed air underground, and the creation of more jobs through expansion of operations. (The latter was a common argument used by Eastern labor leaders in their praise for the new industrial technology in the 1860s and 1870s.) From such claims one message was predominant: the technological revolution helped the miner at the same time that it increased production and profits.[6]

But after the initial outburst of enthusiasm that greeted these technological changes, the hard-rock miners who used them each day began to encounter less praiseworthy aspects of the mining revolution. As the Burleigh drill was undergoing tests, that realization came dramatically one April evening in 1870, when a blast in the tunnel rumbled across Georgetown. Outside workmen, "overcome with a horrifying sense of the situation, rushed wildly into the long, dark passageway. . . ." They discovered that a premature explosion had killed two miners using the Burleigh drill, seriously injuring a third. "The intelligence spread like a contagion throughout the population" of Georgetown, the local newspaper reported. Six weeks later, the community had another tragedy when a miner was killed and a co-worker injured inside another tunnel, under similar conditions. This news "came down from the tunnel like a fierce, chilling wind from the mountains," reported the local editor, ". . . the tumult of our streets was hushed to a listening silence." While experts disagreed as to the exact cause of the blasts, one general theory blamed sparks jumping to the powder from pipes installed for the machine drills. Some mystification appeared as to how such a tragedy could have occurred in the Burleigh Tunnel, for—as the newspaper noted

—"Mr Burleigh has always exercised the greatest caution as a preventive of accidents to his workmen."[7]

The Georgetown experience with the Burleigh drill—excitement over a new feat of mining technology, followed by tragedy—was in many ways a portent of things to come across the mining West. It constituted the underside of industrialization in the changing frontier, less glamorous than the palaces of the bonanza kings, and not as spectacular as the armed warfare that erupted on occasion in the mining camps. Hard-rock miners were aware of the glamorous and spectacular aspects of mining, but such things were of little consequence in the day-to-day existence of most. An understanding of their lives—and the development of metal mining in the West—is incomplete without also taking into account the workers' day-to-day experience with the new technology.

The starting point in Western hard-rock mining was the hammer and drill. These were the basic tools of the hard-rock miner, and pride in their use was carried out of the mine into the society and folkways of the mining camp. This was especially noticeable during the major holiday in mining communities, the Fourth of July. Annual drilling contests on that day provided the focus of miners' skill, strength, and pageantry, with bets and prizes helping stimulate the activity at the granite block. One Butte miner won over $13,000 in contests across the West. In local competition, the top prizes (usually donated by mining companies) ranged in 1900 from $125 in Stent, Tuolumne County, California, to $400 at Telluride, while winers could take home as much as $5,000 in the Colorado state competition.[8]

Because these annual contests were eagerly awaited, were viewed with excitement, and marked the pinnacle of the hard-rock miner's achievement, they gave way only grudgingly to the advance of the machine drill. Double-hand drilling—"double-jacking"—provided the most spectacular event, for it required the two men to switch positions from swinging the hammer to holding and changing drills every minute or so during the fifteen-minute span. Several times during the event, the drill-holder had to completely remove a piece of steel from the hole and substitute a longer one before the striker could swing down again. The Fourth of July contest in 1906 in Wal-

lace, Idaho, was described as "one of the most exciting athletic events ever witnessed in the Coeur d'Alene," because of the skill shown by two miners when their boulder split during the fourteenth minute: "Quick as a flash the holder of the drill threw away the long steel, grabbed a short one, and in an instant a new hole was being sunk in the remaining portion of the rock." The new depth was added to the first hole's depth to total 35⅝ inches, enough to win first place for the two contestants from the Ajax Mine.[9]

But the machine began to intrude. Former world drilling champion Walter Bradshaw of Butte recalled a challenge issued by a salesman for a machine drill, after Bradshaw and his partner had won the world double-jack championship by drilling fifty-five inches in fifteen minutes. But the salesman immediately conceded defeat without a contest when he saw the Gunnison granite to be used, and realized that his apparatus was made for drilling into coal. Bradshaw later said that even if the salesman had entered a rock-drilling machine, he and his partner would have won in a fifteen-minute contest. But not a longer test—"That's where the machine is better than the man. It can drill twenty-four hours a day, seven days a week, if necessary, without tiring."[10]

The day of the machine had come. Use of the machine drill spread rapidly in large mines, which could afford the compressor, hoses, and related paraphernalia. Conversely, this meant that double-jack skills began to be restricted—to older miners, some immigrant groups, and gradually only to the West's smaller mine operations. The Burleigh drill of the 1860s was joined in the 1870s by the Ingersoll and Rand drills, and later decades added the Leyner piston drill and others. The 1880 census reported that thirty Nevada mines were using 189 machine drills, constituting the bulk of the reported 250 ma-

---

13a and b. The hard-rock miner quickly became a skilled workman, proud of his ability to hammer the drill from all angles and in all conditions. These men practiced at Bull Cliffs in the Cripple Creek District for the 1897 Fourth of July contest—an annual event held on that date throughout the mining West. The big event at Tonopah, Nevada, in 1904 attracted hundreds, who placed bets, watched from precarious positions atop nearby storefronts, and reveled in the skill of the men known as hard-rock miners. But the machine drill was already making this miner's skill obsolete.

a. Denver Public Library, Western History Collection photo
b. Nevada State Historical Society photo

chine drills in use in sixty-five deep mines across the West. By 1892, however, a single mine in Montana—the Anaconda —had 138 machine drills in use, apparently to the exclusion of hand drills.[11]

This conquering of the mining West by machine drills began to turn Fourth of July drilling contests into a collective anachronism—events that were increasingly pointless because the skills they rewarded belonged to an era that was passing. Why should the drilling contests be continued, when "it is only in the smaller mines that this work is done by hand," the *Mining and Scientific Press* asked. The journal ridiculed the traditional contests, arguing that "mine owners would be more interested in a competitive trial of rock-drilling machines rather than men."[12]

The new focus provided a sharp contrast with the days when hard-rock miners were identified by their skill with the hammer and drill, and when reports such as this from Silver City, Idaho, in 1873, bestowed a peculiarly Western sort of sainthood on men recognized as true giants in the earth:

> We challenge the world to beat the wonderful feat of single-hand drilling accomplished this week by a Cornishman, named James Gooey, in the Golden Chariot mine. In one 8-hour shift he drilled 31 feet in very hard rock, and in four 8-hour shifts he drilled 110 feet, being an average of 27½ feet for each shift.[13]

But the new order gave glory not to the man but to the machine, which befitted an industry switching from labor-intensive to machine-intensive technology. One report announced: "From 3 to 4 feet daily is made with the [Champion] drill as against 10 to 12 inches in the same formation by the old method." Another mine averaged 81.5 feet sunk per month, partly because "a large number of machine drills are in use, the Burleigh and Ingersoll being both highly praised." Walter Bradshaw of Butte, James Gooey of the Golden Chariot mine, and other Western single-jack and double-jack heroes were now eclipsed by the inventions of Charles Burleigh and others, whose skills lay in creating machinery rather than in pounding the steel drill.[14]

The miners had been prepared for this change with assurances that the machine drill made work easier and safer, but many began to have doubts about its alleged benefits. Mine owners, they discovered, frequently used the installation of machine drills as an excuse for neglecting to provide extra ventilation equipment. Also, the air pumped below by the machines often smelled of lubricating oils, the combustion of which could create poison gas. Occasionally the air for the machine drill was taken from within the mine itself, providing even less ventilation improvement.[15]

A more insidious problem gradually spread across the mining districts where hammer and drill had been replaced by machine drills. Dan DeQuille, journalist of the Comstock Lode, described it this way:

> Death stalks through the dark chambers of the mines in a thousand shapes. Generally his blows are sudden and terrible. More pitiable, however, seems the living death of the doomed man lingering down to the tomb in the never relaxed clutch of miners' consumption.[16]

This disease—also known by its nickname, "miners' con," and its scientific name, phthisis—appeared on the Comstock Lode in the early 1870s, and apparently was present in other districts following "the inauguration of the machine drill. . . ." Its presence was noted by victims when they felt shortness of breath, developing into a hacking cough, and gradually leading to weakening and debilitation. Lung problems worsened, and surviving hospital records show pneumonia and bronchitis appearing often in doctors' diagnoses of hospitalized miners.[17]

For years the cause of miners' consumption remained unknown, for investigation was often stymied by the fact that miners quit and moved away when the telltale hacking cough appeared; their death records then listed other causes than phthisis.[18]

The search for remedies mounted. Boosters of Colorado decided that climate was the answer, and so the Colorado Legislature in 1889 voted to distribute 50,000 copies of an essay proclaiming the Centennial State to possess the "Preferable Climate" for phthisis. Soon, however, it was discovered that Colorado was preferable for phthisis in a way the boosters did not envision: doctors found that the disease was caused by the sharp-edged dust created by machine drills. This dust, especially abundant in quartz mines, was cutting lung tissues, opening miners to attacks of tuberculosis. Acute miners' consumption, according to a 1904 report, "has only assumed prominence since the introduction of power drills, which produce a far greater amount of dust than when the work is done by hand." This seemed to indicate that metal-mining states—of which Colorado was a leader—were the *least* preferable for anyone who wanted to avoid phthisis.[19]

After the cause of phthisis had been discovered, investigations on prevention still proceeded slowly. The first thorough research was carried out after the turn of the century by S. C. Hotchkiss, a surgeon with the U.S. Public Health Service on assignment for the U.S. Bureau of Mines. Hotchkiss reported that many miners refused to undergo physical examinations, and death reports were inadequate in giving the true cause of death. Despite such hindrances, he determined that phthisis was "the chief or contributory cause" of 30 percent of the miners' deaths in one Colorado district over a nine-year span, while the mortality from respiratory diseases there was 56 percent of the miners' total mortality. Hotchkiss also discovered that the district's miners had a death rate from lung diseases three times that of the remaining adult population. With machine-drill dust definitely established as the cause of miners' consumption, the use of a squirt of water with the drill to block dust formation gained acceptance after 1900.[20]

This meant that the Burleigh Tunnel precedent had been followed again: machinery originally hailed as beneficial for the hard-rock miner had later betrayed him. The experience drew comment by the Montana Inspector of Mines, as he reported the death of two miners using a machine drill in an upraise in a Fergus County mine. Due to an explosion in the air compressor, the work area was filled with poisonous gas, killing the two men and causing two others nearby to narrowly escape death. Noting that machine drills were supposed to ventilate the mine as well as to drill holes, the inspector observed: "It seems that death lurks even in the things which are designed as benefits."[21]

His observation could have served as a slogan for the hard-rock miners' experiences with the new technology. Confronted with drastic changes in machinery and methods, the miners were assured that they, too, would benefit from technological

14. *Windlasses and manways were obviously dangerous for miners, especially as the mine's depth increased and winter iced the rungs of the ladder. Before long, the men at this Cripple Creek District mine circa 1900 would require more than human power to move both ore and laborers.*

Colorado School of Mines photo

progress. But resulting death, injury, or illness often made the promise an empty one.

This proved to be the case in mine transport. As lode mines were first opened in the West, a simple hand-powered windlass was used to lift up buckets of rock; sometimes these were powered by a "whim," a horizontal wheel on top turned by a horse. Miners usually climbed up and down on ladders, either in the shaft or in a separate manway. But this became dangerous as shaft depth increased beyond one hundred feet, for a misstep or ladder failure could send the miner to the bottom. The inefficiency of the windlass for removing ore from larger operations soon brought the introduction of steam hoisting machinery—as early as 1860 in the Ophir Mine on the Comstock Lode when operations had reached the 160-foot level. A mine in Idaho's Owyhee district made the change to steam power in 1868 at a time when thirty men were needed to hoist by windlass the ore broken out by sixteen miners.[22]

Riding up and down the shaft was certainly safer than climbing a tall ladder. Or was it? The miners' frequent use of crossheads—boards lashed to a rope or cable—complicated the question. Crossheads offered speedy transportation, but it would be difficult to invent a more unsafe contraption: "Imagine eight men descending a shaft 4½ feet by 3½ in size, riding on a piece of wood only 6 or 8 inches in width, holding fast to a cable for support. . . . Should a man become dizzy or nervous and fall, or should a jar of the rope cause men to be shaken, what would be the result?"[23]

There were cheers, then, when large buckets were installed on the ropes to allow men to ride to and from work in the shaft, carried by steam power. But instead of improving the accident rate, the change again seemed to point in the opposite direction. Since buckets lacked guywires, they were notoriously unstable, and it was easy for miners to fall while attempting to climb in. Even when standing inside, it was fairly simple to tumble from the bucket, especially when it swung from side to side:

> Morello and two others were descending the shaft and had been lowered 170 feet when the bucket struck one side of the shaft, causing it to tip slightly. The jar and the momentary tendency of the bucket to overturn, as a result of it striking the timbers, caused Morello to lose his hold on the rope and fall down the shaft a distance of 130 feet.

The bucket's swinging could also push men or tools against the rock or timbers lining the shaft, as in a Colorado mishap in 1871 where Henry Jenkinson was caught against a stull: "The engineer, thinking that it was a slight catch of the bucket, put on more steam, when the extra strain on the rope caused it to break, letting Jenkinson fall a distance of eighty feet. . . ."[24]

For economic and safety reasons, then, the bucket was

15. *The horse-drawn whim was often the next step in mine technology. Endlessly circling outside the shaft house, this horse raised or lowered men and ore. Location and date unknown.*

Denver Public Library, Western History Collection photo

inadequate. Its successor was the cage, initially only a plat-form without sides, raised and lowered on a cable or wire rope that was connected to the steam engine on top. It seemed ideal-ly suited both for carrying large amounts of ore and for pro-viding a safer ride for the miners. Held in place by guides along the shaft walls, and providing a stable, flat surface for miners to stand on, the cage quickly became a sensation in the mining industry. When the Eureka Mine in Grass Valley installed its first cage in 1869, a visitor was fascinated with the movement that "glides as smoothly as a sled sliding down hill"—much better than being lowered in a bucket "or pick-ing your way down a dirty, slippery ladder." Formerly it was hazardous and laborious to descend into a mine; "now, it is

16. *These men at the Victor Mine in the Cripple Creek District in 1896 rode the most modern device then known for transporting men in a mine: the cage. But it proved a disaster for hundreds of miners, whose hands, feet, and bodies were ground between the cage and the shaft as the device moved at high speeds. Note the lack of sides on the cages, and the candleholders held by many of the crew—notably the enormous candleholder clutched by the man at lower right.*

Denver Public Library, Western History Collection photo

easier and just as safe as to go down into a ten-foot cellar." Similarly, when the Gold Hill Mine in Quartzburg, in the Boise Basin, installed a cage in 1878, it was predicted that there would be no serious accidents from the breaking of ropes.[25]

The great expectations for a safer future were largely unfulfilled. As with the machine drill, the introduction of the cage into Western metal mines led to thousands of injuries and fatalities. The cage introduced several new variables into the hard-rock miner's life, including high-speed transport, greater reliance on equipment and operators, and the crucial role of uniform signals. It took little time before the new hoisting devices, which had been hailed for the safety they brought to miners, were being condemned as "those infernal traps called 'cages.'"[26]

Eliot Lord, writing of the Comstock Lode in the early 1880s, observed that "the very perfection" of the cage machinery had increased the danger to workmen because of the high speeds involved. This ultimately brought in the geared engines, which increased speed from 300 up to 800 feet per minute. But the introduction of the first direct-acting hoisting engine at the Consolidated Virginia Mine on the Comstock in 1875 brought speeds of up to 2,700 feet per minute. Slower speeds were generally used when carrying men, although Montana's deputy mine inspector stated in 1889 that 1,000 feet per minute was the common speed.[27]

Such speeds hindered the effectiveness of safety devices. By the late 'sixties, devices for automatically stopping cages when cables broke were successfully tested on the Comstock. The frequency of shaft deaths in the ensuing decades is tragic evidence, however, that these were not the ultimate solution their inventors had hoped for. A mining professor pointed out that some of the safety devices could work satisfactorily with geared engines running up to 1,500 feet per minute, but were ineffective with the higher speeds coming into use.[28]

Leaving the depths of the mine for the fresh air above became even more traumatic as cage speeds increased. Frequently the change was so sudden that it overpowered the miners, particularly when they had been working in foul, warm air underground. Two men were killed in Butte's Magna Charta shaft in 1885, after they complained of dizziness as they left the work area to ride to the surface:

When they ascended to the purer air in the shaft, the change seems to have overpowered them; and this, we understand, is generally the effect upon men half asphyxiated with noxious fumes. It is supposed they fell; and there being no guard to hold them in the cage, they dropped between it and the timbers. This produced a heavy strain upon the cable, as there was but eight inches of space between the cage and the shaft, and the former in grinding past them reduced the poor fellows to a pulp.[29]

Compounding the dangers of the mine cage was the fact that up to nine miners were usually crowded into the cage floor, which was often only 3½ by 4 feet, "simply a platform suspended by three iron braces and covered with a bonnet." The miners' main support was the crossbar of the cage, usually two feet above their heads. As the rocky, sometimes timbered walls of the shaft sped by inches away, there were numerous opportunities for accidents (leading to the cage's nickname of "man killer"), for any part of the body extended beyond the cage limits invited disaster. Sometimes only tools were caught, but human appendages were susceptible as well. A crew in the St. Lawrence Mine in Butte was riding up at the end of a shift when one miner put out his shoe to shove his dinner bucket back from the edge. His foot was caught between the rising cage and the shaft and was suddenly drawn and ground through the narrow opening. Although his fellow workers held him on the platform, his leg was pulled from its socket and he died soon afterwards.[30]

When a coroner's jury gathered at Hunt's Undertaking Parlors in Victor, Colorado, on August 27, 1902, they heard testimony of a similar mishap in the Elkton Mine, in which Charles Sullivan had been crushed against the shaft walls when drills he was transporting caught against the timbers. The foreman theorized that when the two riders saw the few drills to be brought up, they held "four or five pieces in their arms and they chanced it." He showed the coroner's jury how they had probably held the long steels, and "in doing so with this long steel projecting out, it caught in the timber, which of course would instantly cause a wreck." A mine carpenter who helped search for Sullivan's body told the jury that at first it was believed that "possibly he had hung on timber. So then we took the cage and came on slowly up and gathered up remains or what parts we could find of them—pieces of skull and brains and old clothes." The rest of Sullivan's body was eventually found in the two hundred feet of water at the bottom of the deep shaft.[31]

Since cages carried more riders than did buckets—especially when double- and triple-deck cages were installed in the larger mines—a single mechanical error created more widows than had been the case in the day of the simple bucket. One of Montana's worst mining accidents occurred when a cable snapped in the Anaconda shaft, sending nineteen men to their deaths. A bucket, on the other hand, could carry no more than two or three miners, while a ladder accident generally brought death to one or two. Increased mechanization also left the hard-rock miner increasingly dependent upon others for his own well-being. The Nevada Inspector of Mines listed some of these danger factors: "defective machinery, flimsy cables, incompetent engineers, dangerous ground, insufficiency of timbers, bad air, poor fire protection . . ."—and said that there were "so many different things the miner must depend on for safety that did he stop to consider them, the mining game would lose thousands of its best men." This complete dependence upon the safe functioning of machinery and other persons, one of the crucial changes introduced into the workplace by the Industrial Revolution, was nowhere better illustrated than with the mine cage.[32]

In relying upon others, signals within the mine suddenly became crucial. Unlike the placer miners' code of laws, which spread across the West with considerable uniformity, a variety of mine signal systems developed. Most used bells rung by miners, informing the hoisting engineer on top what was wanted with the cage—to go up or down, hauling men or rock, to which level, to send down more drills, or similar requests. A California mine engineer noted that even mines within the same district used different signals both for hoisting men and for blasting.[33]

The results were predictable as miners switched from job to job. Men waiting at the top of the Crown Point shaft on the Comstock one day in 1867 suddenly saw a strange form, standing erect, on the upcoming cage. Due to a misunderstood signal, the cage had started rising before the rider was ready, and his face had caught against the timbers: "The top of his nose and the cheeks were literally cut from the bones and hung a bleeding mass over his lower jaw; his front teeth were knocked out, his lower jaw broken in three different places, and a portion of his tongue actually cut off." A miner in the Star of the West mine in Butte mistakenly rang one bell as he and his partner entered the steam-powered bucket; since that signal indicated that dirt, tools, or an empty bucket were to be lifted, the engineer raised it with extreme speed. One of the men leaped, pushing the other rider against the side of the shaft and spilling him, causing fatal injuries. Such cases were legion.[34]

Care of the equipment used for hoisting was beyond the hard-rock miner's scope, again increasing his dependence on others. Ropes, brakes, the new braided wire belts—weak spots in any of these could cause death. This dependence on others was evident also in the miner's relation with the hoisting engineer, who sat at controls in the building at the top of the shaft, pulling levers to raise or lower the cages in response to signals from below. Often his only guide to the depth of the cage at the moment was a string on the passing cable. His was a life-or-death control, playing God with hundreds of lives each shift.

Surprisingly, no lengthy training or testing period appears to have been used in choosing hoist operators. A Lake County, Colorado, miner complained of local hoisting engineers who "cannot prove ever serving apprenticeship. Men toiling hard at the bottom of deep shafts," he added, "are at these fellows' mercy." Licensing was sometimes instituted, but cases are on record of engineers operating the wrong type of hoist for their license, or being "utterly incompetent."[35]

One of the West's most famous cases of suspected engineer error or mechanical defect occurred in early 1904 in the Cripple Creek district, then locked in open warfare between the miners' union and a joint mine owner–state militia force. Fifteen men were killed when the cage went out of control and was pulled up into the sheave wheel, spilling the men into the 1,500-foot shaft of the non-union Stratton's Independence Mine. James Bullock, the sole survivor, told the coroner's jury what happened as the cage began its rise up the shaft. His testimony and that of the engineer are worth quoting at length:[36]

> . . . We kept going right along but it kept slipping; we would go a little ways and then we would slip again; then he took us about six feet above the collar of the shaft, then he lowered us back down.

Q. Did he stop six feet above the shaft?

A. He stopped just for a second or two; then he lowered us and it must have gotten beyond his control, for we dropped about sixty or seventy feet, we were going pretty. We said to each other we are all gone. Then he raised us up about ten feet; then he stopped us and it slipped back again about two feet; then he tried and started us again, and we went to the sheave wheel as fast as we could go. When I was going up there, I began to crouch to save myself from the hard blow. I seen a piece of timber about one foot wide, and I grabbed hold and held myself up there and pretty soon the cage dropped and I began to holler for a ladder to get down.

The hoisting engineer said he discovered the brakes were not working when he tried to connect them as the cage reached the 200-foot level:

> I tried them several times, but that time the cage was at the collar of the shaft. I immediately reversed the engine and sent the cage back 100 feet. I again tried the brakes, reversed the engine, and brought the cage back to the surface. The brake was still stuck; I could not move it. I again reversed the engine and sent the cage back about the same distance and stepped over to the other side and took hold of the other brake, and it was in the same condition. The second time the cage came to the surface, I called three times for the shift boss, for God's sake come and help me put on the brakes. In the meantime, I was reversing the engine backwards and forwards. Mr. MacDonald came and two other men with him. I said come up and help me put on the brakes, and then I discovered the hood of the cage above the collar of the shaft. I immediately reversed the engine, but it was too late.

At that point in the inquiry the engineer broke down.

Many of the jury's questions probed into safety arrangements and the qualifications of hoisting engineers in Stratton's Independence. Why were "chairs" not inserted over the shaft opening to stop the 4,000-pound cage before it plunged downward again? Was there a man on duty at the collar? Why was the engineer alone? Why didn't the brake work? (It had been inspected some six hours earlier, and was found to be working after the accident.) Questioning about another hoisting engineer working for Stratton's Independence revealed that the employer had taken the man's word—nothing more—as to his qualifications. The engineer involved in the fatal accident, however, had been recommended by a former employer.

The jury blamed the management for the accident, charging that the mishap might have been less severe or even avoided if "the usual precautions" had not been ignored: this included having a man present beside the collar of the shaft when hoisting men, use of a safety device to prevent overwinding the cable, installation of "chairs" under the cage when men were being loaded, and use of disc brakes on the hoisting engine (these were found to be "detached from their usual position and useless"). As an extra recommendation, the jury urged that "a competent extra man should stand near the engineer" when men were being hoisted.

Little by little, safety devices and methods were required for the hoisting equipment, and licensing of engineers began, as will be discussed further in Chapter 7. But progress in dealing with industrialism came by trial and error, and the errors often cost workmen's lives. When progress appeared, it was frequently counteracted by some further technological advance which undid the protection provided by new safety devices, as when high-speed direct-acting hoisting engines were introduced.

The complexity of the search for safe procedures amid a radically new work environment was illustrated dramatically by the introduction of electricity into hard-rock mining. Following the Burleigh drill precedent, electricity was brought in on a wave of cheers predicting benefits for both shareholders and workmen. The two major industry journals stressed the advantages: the flexibility of operations made possible through running wires anywhere in the mine, the reduction by half of mine haulage costs through use of electric locomotives, and the general lowering of expenses by substituting machines for some employees. A Coeur d'Alenes mine, for example, was paying a hundred dollars a day for wood fuel, and was frequently forced to close down for lack of wood to run its mill, when it switched to electricity in 1891.[37]

There were benefits for miners, also, chiefly in the realm of working conditions: more light, less heat. Electric lights were installed in 1881 in the Alice Mine and Mill in Butte. "Its success is complete," the Butte *Miner* announced glowingly; "the sixty-stamp mill is so thoroughly lighted up by the Brush light as to enable one to pick up a pin in the remote corners of the mill." When the Butte mines later installed electric power for pumping, hoisting, and compressing, it was found that heat underground was sharply reduced with steam pumping eliminated. Electric firing of dynamite also appeared.[38]

Electrical equipment spread throughout the mining West, especially in the 1890s and early 1900s. Cripple Creek had its first electrical machinery in 1888, with two power companies soon providing electricity from Canon City, twenty-seven miles away, and from a steam plant at nearby Goldfield, Colorado. The mines of Bodie, California, switched to electrical power in 1893, and the Daddy mine in the Coeur d'Alenes generated its own power from a nearby river in 1895. The American Institute of Mining Engineers was informed in 1896 that fifty-two Rocky Mountain mining companies had installed electrical power in the previous eight years, most in the preceding four years. In 1901, the mines of Idaho's Owyhee district began drawing power from a hydroelectric plant at Swan Falls on the Snake River, twenty-seven miles away; and by 1904, most of the Coeur d'Alenes mines received electricity over the 90-mile distance from Spokane Falls. Steam power was then "almost entirely superseded" there. Even the isolated mining districts of Tonopah and Goldfield in southern Nevada began using electric power by 1905, drawn from the Bishops Creek plant ninety-eight miles to the southwest. What was true of Cripple Creek in 1900 was rapidly becoming true throughout the West: "The miner may go up to his work from the town on an electric car, go down in the mine by an electric hoist, operated by electric signals, the shaft being kept dry by an electric pump, do his work by an electric light, talk to the town and thence to the world by an electric telephone, run a drill electrically operated, and fire his shots by an electric blaster."[39]

Of course, not all mines used the new technology to help miners to the utmost. The cost-conscious president of a Montana company cautioned his superintendent to keep the new electric lights fairly dim; otherwise the employees might become accustomed to "excessive illuminations" and use more candles in non-electrified areas of the mine.[40]

But even where electricity was seen as a blessing to workmen, its benefits were often negated by the ignorance that surrounded its use. It was this factor that the Idaho Mine Inspector referred to when he noted in 1903 that "the average miner usually knows as much about volts, ohms and amperes of electricity as he does about Greek." Not only miners were unfamiliar with the dangers of the maze of wires that snaked through the underground shafts and tunnels, however; mine superintendents and managers showed an astonishing lack of knowledge on the subject as well. A study by a Colorado School of Mines student in 1910 found that eight superintendents believed 10,000 volts and up were safe for wet shafts; four believed 1,000 to 6,000 safe; and eight more, 440 to 500. The student concluded that there was "more or less obscurity" on the question. The manager of a Gilpin County mine confessed that neither he nor anyone else in the mine knew enough about electricity to provide details for the student—despite the fact that the mine had employed electricity widely for ten years![41]

The Idaho Mine Inspector reported in 1905 that 500 volts were believed harmless, but this voltage nevertheless had caused the state's first two mine electrocutions. Two years later, a company official in Pittsburgh, Pennsylvania, pondered the question after an Owyhee County miner was electrocuted. "It was thought that the voltage in the mine would not cause death," he stated, "unless the person was in bad physical condition and had a weak heart." It was a strange, dangerous world where neither miners, state inspectors, mine managers, nor company officials understood safe procedures with electricity.[42]

Ranking with the Burleigh drill, power hoists, and electricity in its impact on mining was dynamite, in use in Western mines within two years after it was invented in Europe by Alfred Nobel in 1866. It generally went by the name Giant Powder, after the Giant Powder Company bought patent rights for American production. Tests in California in 1868 showed that it was cheaper than the black powder then in use for blasting by a cost ratio of 51 to 92. A later test determined that the same quantity of dynamite did two and two-thirds the work of black powder. A Columbia University professor in

1908 called dynamite "second to none in its influence on the advancement of mining."[43]

For the miner, Nobel's invention held several improvements over black powder. It was said to be safer, first of all, because as long as it was frozen it could not explode. "They say that unlike nitroglycerine, the giant powder is free from danger in the make and in the handling at the mines," a report claimed in 1868. Complete combustion was promised by manufacturers, removing the smoke and gas problem which the imperfect explosions of black powder created. Tamping was said to be unnecessary, and "the loading is attended with no risk," providing a saving of time and expense. Indeed, the quickness of its preparation and its power meant that less work was required to push a tunnel, sink a shaft, or open a stope. Early opposition occurred partly because it was feared that dynamite would reduce the labor force needed, as at Grass Valley in the 1869 strike. However, the continued expansion of mining largely removed this threat.[44]

But the golden era which dynamite's promoters foresaw did not develop for the hard-rock miner. Without question, many of the mishaps involved carelessness by the miners themselves, such as thawing a frozen dynamite stick over a candle (an issue to be taken up in Chapter 5). But in two major areas, dynamite proved to be a tragic newcomer: premature or delayed explosions, and gases left from imperfect explosions. "Missed holes" were frequent with Nobel's invention, and unexploded sticks of dynamite had to be located among the rubble left by a blast. But when the unexploded sticks could not be found, the way was open for a later workman to encounter them accidentally—and tragically. Two Butte miners were using picks "when the pick of one of the men struck some powder and a terrific explosion occurred. The powder is supposed to have been an old missed hole that had never been discovered. The two men were literally blown to pieces."[45]

Crews took pains to listen for each explosion as a means of keeping track of missed holes. Three hours was a standard waiting period, but longer time spans before dynamite exploded are on record—such as the six-hour lapse after firing in the Elkhorn mine, Montana, which killed a miner searching for the unexploded stick.[46]

The worst lie that the dynamite promoters told, however,

was that dynamite removed the problem of smoke or noxious gases. As the new explosive was being introduced in California in 1869, a mine owner proclaimed that "the bosh as to the powder being injurious is the veriest nonsense in the world." A California company was in agreement in 1885: "The complaint about its being injurious to health turned out to be a mere pretext of the miners, being without any sufficient foundation."[47]

Later reports by mine inspectors were more honest. They noted that dynamite frequently missed complete combustion, filling the stope with carbonic oxide, "one of the most insidious and dangerous of all mine gases," and nitrous gases. Clear-appearing air was no guarantee that these gases were absent, and rock from a blast was often impregnated with the gases so that muckers fell ill as they shoveled it up. The Grass Valley miners who rebelled against the introduction of dynamite in 1869 said that their "only objection" was the danger from noxious gases, "which we inhale into our systems, thereby producing headache and nausea. . . ."[48]

The widely known candle test for unsafe air proved to be no test at all after dynamite was introduced. Traditionally in mining, if a candle flame burned, the air presumably contained enough oxygen for humans. But imperfect explosions sometimes produced carbon monoxide, a colorless, odorless, and tasteless gas that made the candle flame flare up with a pale bluish light.[49]

A string of tragedies followed dynamite's spread across the West. Men were hauled from the Butte mines in 1889 "almost suffocated for want of air to force out the gases produced by the giant powder," and on some days the air became so laden with gas that they could not work. Often the gases made the miners drowsy, bringing an added dimension of danger to the ride up to the surface at shift's end. Dominic McElhenny, a miner leaving the Marie mine near Philipsburg, Montana, in 1891, told his fellow rider in the bucket that he was getting dizzy as they passed the 200-foot level. The partner noticed that McElhenny was getting pale, and tried to tighten his grip on him as they passed the 100-foot level—when McElhenny slipped out and fell to his death 400 feet below. The coroner's jury was told that powder smoke and "bad air" had "pretty near knocked out" the miners before McElhenny got in the bucket to ride to the surface.[50]

Simply returning to the work area after a round of dynamite had been blasted was equally dangerous, because the miner never knew what awaited him in the way of gases. When three Montana miners returned to the bottom of the shaft after lunch—which they ate on top so the blasting gases had time to disperse—they immediately bent down to tighten the four bolts in the water suction pump, "but which they never lived to complete." The foreman later discovered all three face down in the water, drowned. The coroner's jury found that the dynamite in use produced as much as 6 percent nitrous oxide, which would not put out a candle flame and was likely not noticed by the men before it made them unconscious.[51]

From the dynamite, machine drills, electricity, square-set timbering, and other innovations applied to metal mining in the 1860–1910 period, much deeper operations became possible. And with deeper mining, solutions to such problems as poisonous blasting gases became more difficult. Not just ventilation, but dangers from heat, water, sanitation, and fire as well became worse in deep mines. Cave-ins, a perennial mining problem, were also more of a danger in deep mines because adequate timbering was more difficult to install as distances from the outside increased. The air problem, however, was the most common and recurring difficulty involved in the development of deep mining.

As the mines in the Central City district of Colorado pushed below the 100-foot level in 1862, a local editor noted that it was easy to detect miners in town, even when dressed in store clothes, "by the pallid countenance and haggard expression" they possessed from working "where the pure air above never penetrates. . . ." A year later, the same newspaper reiterated that "bad air is causing more trouble than ever before in many of the shafts throughout the country. The ordinary means of ventilation are failing in many instances. We hear complaints of this made by many. . . ."[52]

The conditions of Central City in 1862 were repeated often: a mine would be sunk beyond the shallow depths where ventilation was adequate, miners would be unable to work,

17. *Snowslides periled miners in many districts, especially those working in steep mountains like the ones in the San Juans and other Colorado areas. When the Homestake Mine near Leadville was hit by a snowslide in February, 1885, it took three months before a rescue party (shown here) reached the site—too late to save the ten miners caught in their cabin.*

Denver Public Library, Western History Collection photo

efforts would be made to provide better air, and work would resume until the greater depth and size of the underground working again left the air system inadequate.

The basic problem was that mining was never static; if men were mining, they were expanding their workplace. Goaded by ignorance, or fear, or economic necessity, or bravado, the miners toiled on in badly ventilated stopes. An inspector encountered a Montana miner at work in the bottom of a winze, where his candle was scarcely able to burn: "He requested me to move carefully, as the least motion would quench his light." In a Colorado mine, the men sometimes had to move their candles away from the breast of the drift to find enough oxygen for them to burn. A visitor there tried to light matches, but they sputtered and went out. Some of the men kept both a candle and a carbide lamp available, switching to the latter when foul air was encountered, since the carbide required less oxygen.[53]

Heat—especially hot water—soon joined foul air as a major problem in the Comstock's lower levels, taxing the inadequate ventilation systems further. As early as 1863, the Dardanelles Company, then working at only 265 feet below the surface, encountered hot water which gushed so rapidly that the drill-hole had to be plugged. It was "decidedly a new lead for this district," the Gold Hill *News* reported in amazement. "We are several feet nearer Pandemonium than we had calculated." In 1865, the continued encounters with hot water on the Comstock brought forth the hopeful theory that this was caused by large bodies of "sulphurets"—rich ores—which generated heat when touched by cold water; therefore, hot water made it "unquestioned" that the lode contained wealth. Deeper levels brought increased heat in the ensuing months, especially after the 1,000-foot level was reached by several more mines in 1868. The results in working conditions can be discerned in reports that the superintendent of the Yellow Jacket Mine penned in his daily journal:

> Water in 2,828' level drift continues to increase very hot. Have turned down some cold water from surface which we use in face of drift with a spray or hose—This cools ground very rapidly. (August 23–24, 1880.)
> The temperature of water in mine is as follows—Belcher water at measuring box at shaft, 2,828' level, 138 degrees.

Imperial water at 2,700' level north of north winze, 147 degrees. Same water at Imperial south winze, 154 degrees.

Water standing in our north winze level with 2,700' level, 152 degrees.

Water from our 2,800' level East drift with one inch of cold water from surface mixed with same, 124 degrees. (September 29, 1880.)

North winze very warm; one can scarcely breathe there for the vapor from the water. (May 14–15, 1881.)

Temperature of ground in hole, 167 degrees [3,000' level]. (July 25, 1881.)

Temperature of ground on 3,000' level, 168 degrees. Hole dry—270 feet from shaft. (July 28–29, 1881.)[54]

The State Mineralogist took readings and found men working in the Bullion Mine in temperatures ranging from 130 to 140 degrees Fahrenheit. John Church's 1878 paper on "Heat of the Comstock Mines" stated that "a pretty uniform temperature of 130° Fahrenheit" existed in the Comstock's lower levels; but eight years later, the president of the Yellow Jacket reported that the temperature increased three degrees for every hundred feet sunk below the 1,000-foot level, with water temperatures of 170 degrees and air temperatures of 150 degrees recorded.[55]

Furthermore, on the Comstock the miners had an additional fear besides bad air, heat, and dampness: they worked with the foreboding that they would suddenly be inundated with scalding water. On May 31, 1882, a bulkhead gave way in the Alta Mine, filling the 2,150-foot level with hot water and trapping six men in an upward-slanting drift. Caught in a pocket of foul air, they stayed alive by crowding into the cooling-off house there and hovering over the ventilation pipe bringing in air from the outside. Two men who tried to reach them by boat were later found dead; the first man to get through wore an apparatus that filtered air for breathing through a tin box containing ice. A stronger air current through the ventilation system, and continued pumping of water, made it possible on the third day at midnight for the men to be visited and given stimulants before being taken out to safety. The Alta whistle screamed to announce their rescue, and other companies along the Comstock Lode joined the chorus of steam whistles shrieking into the night air. People rushed into the streets of Virginia City "so full of joy that they could hardly speak."[56]

Work amid such conditions was exhausting—above all, exhausting, according to Comstock records. "Many of men on 3,000 level are troubled with cramps & colic. About every shift one man short," the Yellow Jacket superintendent recorded as temperatures continued to rise in his mine. A miner in the Imperial shaft fell into some water and received a scalded leg when it went over the top of his gum boots. Another Comstock workman slipped to his knees in the Julia Mine's water and jumped out so quickly that it did not enter his shoes—but his legs were scalded so badly that his skin came off. Another Julia miner fell up to his chin in a pool of 158-degree water and was fatally scalded.[57]

This great heat—so great that the men always wore shoes even while removing most of their other clothing—greatly increased existing dangers, such as ascending on the cage, especially in winter. Nausea and dizziness overcame miners as the cage rose to cooler areas; Church termed this "so common that a man who has been working in a hot drift is not allowed to go up alone."[58]

Heat and water increased the suffering of underground laborers in other districts as well, although the extreme temperatures of the Comstock were not known elsewhere. Lead and arsenic poisoning occurred in several districts. Such conditions served to set the hard-rock miners apart, especially as their awareness of inequalities increased in the debates of the early 1900s. Delegates to the Western Federation of Miners convention in 1907 wrangled over their preamble's phrase dealing with "comforts enjoyed by mankind." "The fellow up on top might enjoy them," a Butte delegate argued, "not the fellow who has to pump his shoes out every fifteen minutes to get the sweat out of them. . . ." He added that Butte had "walking skeletons" who labored in "the hot boxes" of the mines.[59]

Laboring in wet mines held additional dangers in winter, especially in the numerous mines without change houses. The problem was indicated in a letter that a Coeur d'Alene miner wrote to his family in 1905: "Three successive nights last week I came off work soaked to the skin, and before reaching home all my clothes were frozen fast on me and I couldn't take them

111

off myself. My hair and moustache were also frozen and I looked a sight." Such working conditions in winter helped cause numerous cases of pneumonia and "La Grippe" in Western mining camps. Those living on the surface were not immune to environmental dangers either, for the fumes from nearby smelters spewed forth constantly. Butte became infamous for the smelter smoke, killing not only grass but also dogs and cats in the vicinity.[60]

Companies attempted to keep up with ventilation needs, but the bulk of the evidence indicates that improvements were usually introduced *after* the miners had suffered. The report in 1867 from the Hays & Ray Mine in the Owyhee District was echoed frequently over the years: "The air in the works is becoming very foul, and an artificial supply will soon be a necessity." A shaft was then planned to connect with the tunnel and improve ventilation. On the Comstock, the superintendent of the Yellow Jacket Mine wrote to the company vice president in 1882 that drifting had gone into "ground containing much clay and foul air, which has retarded work in same. Are preparing a blower and pipe to improve the air." The story was a common one throughout the West: when conditions deteriorated so much that production declined, ventilation equipment was improved.[61]

This is not to deny that extensive improvements in ventilation systems were made. Because the Comstock was the first district with deep mines, it was the first to grapple with the air problem and come up with a variety of solutions. These included wind-sails erected at the top of shallow shafts, described by Dan DeQuille as a cross between a sail and a bag, deflecting breezes downward. A visitor to the Yolo Tunnel on Gold Hill in 1863 found a Chinaman sitting at one end of the tunnel "engaged in the very useful avocation of turning a wheel blowing air through a pipe or box, to supply the miners with fresh air." Another mine's air supply came from a bellows which a man pumped at the mouth of the tunnel. Powerful blowers and fans were installed in the Comstock mines from 1868 onward, with galvanized pipes of from eight to twenty inches carrying air below.[62]

Even when provided with up-to-date ventilation equipment, the mines usually did not provide anything approaching a pleasant working environment. Picture the Comstock system installed by John Church: the air pipe came within twenty feet of the workmen, aimed directly at "their half-naked bodies, assisting in the rapid removal of the streams of perspiration which pour from them in quantities sufficient to soak their garments, fill their shoes, and even moisten the rock under their feet." The men drank ice water as an additional aid to keeping cool, with an allowance of three gallons per man per eight-hour shift.[63]

Greater depth increased the danger of cave-ins as well. The Comstock's soft, crumbly rock made that district a testing ground for this problem also. The early invention of square-set timbering by Philip Deidesheimer met the immediate trouble by building interlocking cribs of square timbers and covering these with lagging. This was later hailed, typically, as "the important event of the year 1860 to the mining world," for it enabled the Comstock companies to proceed deeper in following the rich ore they had discovered. But square-set timbers did not totally remove the problem of cave-ins, for miners could not be covered with timbering at all times. The Coeur d'Alene *Miner*, in a typical report, described how two miners were barring down ground loosened by blasting, "when a large piece of galena, weighing over a ton, fell without warning on Hanley's back, killing him instantly." A talc seam was the frequent cause of cave-ins, too weak to hold the underlying rock after miners removed other supporting rock.[64]

That cave-ins were not widely recognized as a major problem was apparently due to the fact that fatalities came one or two at a time; an explosion drew wide publicity, but the day-to-day deaths of miners caught in cave-ins did not. Idaho's mine accident record from 1903 to 1910, for example, showed that cave-ins were the major cause of mine fatalities in four of the eight years. In Montana, a study of mining fatalities in seven scattered years listed "falls of rock" as the major cause of death, with 28.66 percent of the 321 fatalities. The Colorado state reports, during ten scattered years before 1905 for which classifications were provided, showed cave-ins as the major cause for five years.[65]

Extensive timbering was the solution, but this was one of the costliest items in a mining company's ledger—particularly in relatively treeless areas such as the Comstock—and this led to a tendency to restrict timbering as much as possible. A former miner recalled the results:

> The manager asks the superintendent for tonnage; the superintendent demands ore from the foreman; the foreman tells the shift-boss to get out the rock; and the poor shift-boss goes through the stopes yelling to the machine-men and the muckers, "Rock! Rock! Rock!" Consequently the shift-boss looks upon the timberman as a nuisance who blocks the tracks and the stations with his timbers, thus decreasing the tonnage; and the stope—well, as long as it does not cave, the shift-boss inwardly says: "The stope be damned!"[66]

With large numbers of men working far underground, the greater depth also meant that trips to the top during the shift were out of the question. Elimination of bodily wastes was done in the mine, creating a sanitation problem in any mine with large numbers of workmen. Food discards added to the trouble. The Comstock mines had up to 3,000 men underground in the latter 1870s; Butte had almost 9,000 in 1905. Most of these "never see daylight from the moment they step on the cage until the expiration of their daily work," the Montana inspector commented. "Absolutely no provision is made for the health of these men in a sanitary way."[67]

The issue was presented to the Montana Legislature in 1905, when the governor claimed that in Butte's mines "at least 100% more men die from diseases caused by bad sanitary conditions in the mines than result from all mine disasters." He called (unsuccessfully) for legislation on the subject. A year later, the state mining inspector agreed, terming sanitary conditions "positively injurious to the health of the miners" in some of the larger mines.[68]

This catalogue of tragedies—including machine-drill dust, shaft mishaps, electrocutions, dynamite gases and unexpected explosions, foul air, heat, poor sanitation, increased cave-ins, and lead poisoning—accompanied mining into the deeper levels. All resulted from the application of new industrial technology to metal mining.

The impact of the new technology upon hard-rock miners eventually began to show up in statistics, the black-and-white summaries of the horrors inextricably combined with Western metal mining. Comparisons with metal mining in other countries were decidedly unfavorable to Western hard-rock mining, as shown in the fatality rate per 1,000 men employed:

	Period	Rate
United Kingdom	1899–1906	1.14
Germany	1899–1906	1.07
Belgium	1899–1906	.75
France	1899–1906	2.02
Colorado	1896–1908	2.80
Idaho	1903–1908	2.47
Montana	1894–1908	3.53
South Dakota	1902–1908	2.25
British Columbia	1898–1908	4.23

These averages obscure several disastrous years in American metal mining, however. In 1896, Colorado's death rate was 3.80, and Montana's, 8.28; it was reported that Cripple Creek that year recorded twenty-six mine deaths in a mine labor force of 3,000, "a death rate unparalleled in modern mining." Furthermore, the United States and British Columbia figures are incomplete in that they do not separate the underground miners' rate from that of mine employees in safer areas aboveground, a distinction made in European statistics. The Colorado mine inspector estimated in 1898 that if only underground accidents were included, the state's mine fatality rate would have been 6.0 instead of 3.57. A later survey covering only underground employees put the Colorado record as follows: 1896, 5.966; 1897, 5.876; 1898, 5.458; 1899, 3.743; 1900, 3.823; 1901, 4.919; and 1902, 3.274. Britain's underground rate was 1.67, and France's, 2.49, for the 1899–1906 period. California, Nevada, Arizona, Utah, and New Mexico did not start keeping metal-mining accident records until later.[69]

An insurance company statistician reported that coal mining had an overall fatality rate of 3.13 per thousand employed, compared to 3.09 for metal mines. However, he still claimed that "the mortality of metal miners is higher than the mortality of men in all occupations and at all age periods" because of insufficient data. Coal mining continued to receive more accident publicity, however, largely due to the fact that coal-mine disasters left large numbers of men killed, while metal-mine fatalities usually occurred one or two at a time.[70]

The rapid introduction of new technology and the result-

115

ing greater depth of operations made the miner aware that the line between life and death was a narrow one. The mining camp newspapers that he read gave extensive coverage to accidents, especially in the early days of a district's underground operations. "Mining accidents are becoming alarmingly frequent in this camp," the *Owyhee Avalanche* stated with some astonishment in 1873, an observation that was paralleled in other newspapers across the West. But the same newspaper was soon kept busy chronicling the week-by-week deaths in shaft falls, premature explosions, and cave-ins, giving them little extra comment. The frequent funerals, usually attended by most of the community, reinforced the miner's awareness of the dangers of his calling.[71]

When the Western Federation of Miners founded the *Miners' Magazine* in 1900, the journal repeatedly gave attention to the dangers of underground work, in articles, editorials, letters, and even poetry, whose macabre images could not weaken its obvious authenticity:

The Deep, Black Stope[72]
by Frank Aley

Click,—click,—click, boys, down in the deep, black stope.
    The babies are sleeping, the stars are keeping, vigils
      on those above.
Strike,—strike,—strike, boys, for this is the only hope,
    to sweeten the life, of the faithful wife, who gave the
      world for your love.
It is not so hard to labor, boys, it is not so hard to wait,
    Till sturdy, honest and faithful, we lay by a little store.
It is not so hard to struggle, till the generous smile of fate,
    Shall shed its lustre, on those who cluster, inside the
      miner's door.
But down in the awful blackness, in every tunnel and raise,
    At every shaft and station, about each timber and rope,
The angel of death is lurking, while the faithful mother prays,
    For him who sings, as his hammer rings, down in the deep,
      black stope.
Clean out the holes and load, boys, tend to your business well.
    This is a ticklish matter, where brains with danger cope.
Handle the powder with care, boys, that yellow quintessence
    of hell.
    On every level, you're facing the devil, down in the deep,
    black stope.

Tramp,—tramp,—tramp, boys, to the toll of the old church bell,
  Marching in solemn order, out to the barren slope,
Out to the dead man's city, his ghastly ranks to swell,
  For another soul signed death's pay roll, down in the
    deep, black stope.

The poet's picture was not overdrawn. The "angel of death" was indeed lurking in the metal mines of the West in the turbulent years from 1860 to 1910, as the Burleigh drill and a host of other inventions and methods transformed hard-rock mining from a relatively simple operation into a complex industrial activity. Surveying such developments in various lands, a medical doctor concluded that the process of industrialization in the Western world "was only achieved at a tremendous cost, and an exceedingly large part of this price was paid in the lives and health of the workers." And among workmen most affected by health problems stemming from their work environment, "the miners occupied a prominent position."[73]

This was what happened when the hard-rock miner was put to work with the new technology, in the Burleigh Tunnel and throughout the West—when he learned through tragic experience that death indeed "lurks even in the things which are designed as benefits."

CHAPTER V

The Question of Blame

For Joseph Adams it began as a typical night shift in the Old Bach Mine in Montana that September evening in 1900. He and his partner arrived to start work shortly before 7:30 P.M. and made their way to the end of the tunnel, almost an hour and a half after the day shift had left.

It was unfortunate that the two crews, coming and going, did not cross paths. If they had, Joseph Adams probably would have been told there was unexploded dynamite at the work site. The foreman, he might have learned, had instructed the day crew not to fire the holes, already loaded, so that valuable ore would not be mixed with the "country rock" still scattered about the floor of the drift.

The day shift had followed orders and did not fire the holes. They left behind unfired dynamite and loose rock—but no message to warn the night crew.

As his shift began, Adams began to clean up the country rock, but found many large chunks and decided to use dynamite to break them up further for removal. That was when he began drilling, and then it happened: the impact of his drill set off the dynamite left by the day shift. The blast blinded Adams's left eye and damaged his right eye, fractured his jaw, knocked out most of his teeth, almost totally blew off his left hand, crippled his right hand, fractured his left forearm, and severely bruised his side and chest.[1]

Who was to blame?

Joseph Adams's plight was not unusual across the West, as the industrialization of mining forced new relationships upon laboring men and employers at the same time that the onrush of technology confronted them with strange, powerful inventions. The issue went beyond the narrow one of blame and providing compensation for the injured or survivors, to basic questions involving the human cost of progress and man's ability to change traditions or so-called "natural" laws. The mining West in its years of rapid industrialization thus provides a case study in the modification of custom and law formed years earlier, outside the region. Nowhere is this shown more clearly than in liability for work accidents.

Walter Prescott Webb has eloquently described how Eastern laws, institutions, and customs were modified or overwhelmed in the frontier environment of the Great Plains. Others have probed the diverse ways in which the Industrial Revolution challenged traditions of work and employer-employee relations. But hard-rock miners lived in both worlds. They were first of all pioneers who helped settle a vast frontier and exploit its riches; and at the same time, they were caught up in the dislocations which industrialism forced upon the workplace. Old ways of life and work were strained—both by the migration Westward and by employment in one of the most completely transformed occupations of the new industrial era.[2]

Joseph Adams, of course, was not concerned with such broad issues. Through his lawyer, he argued in Cascade County District Court that the foreman, upon whose orders the dynamite was left unfired, was negligent in not warning the evening crew. Going further, Adams stated that the company should have enforced rules which would assure that miners were systematically notified of such "hidden dangers" as unexploded dynamite.

But the county judge denied Adams's claims. Before his appeal could reach the Montana Supreme Court, Adams died of his injuries, perhaps mercifully.

The high court judges who heard the appeal also showed little sympathy for Adams's case (as argued by the administrator of his estate). No negligence was shown by the company, the court ruled, since negligence is a breach of duty and the employer had no duty to provide a completely safe workplace.

Certainly the company must use "reasonable diligence" to provide a safe work area, but this could not be continuously required in a mining area where workmen "are creating the place of work" and constantly changing it. The company "is never liable for any negligence in carrying out the details of work" if the general workplace is safe, and the job is made dangerous "only by negligence of the men working there," the high court stated.[3]

Joseph Adams, like thousands of other Western metal miners, was caught in a web of legal tradition. This tradition was set down in the common law of liability—a well-developed set of doctrines based on English and American precedents. As one account of Rocky Mountain courts has emphasized, the common law "was perhaps the most deeply rooted" of all the legacies transplanted first on the Eastern seaboard and later in the West. This fact created a host of problems, for the common-law doctrines on accident liability had been developed for workshops less complex and dangerous than those being created under Western bedrock.[4]

There were three major rules in the common law of liability:

Assumed risks

Employees knew, or should have known, how dangerous a job was when they accepted the position. Because of this, they had no legal right to compensation from their employer "if they are injured by exposure to such risks. . . ." This doctrine usually did not cover unsafe or defective methods or machinery, however, except when it could be shown that the workers knew of them in advance.

Several corollaries of this rule had serious implications for hard-rock miners. One stated that if an employee accepted a hazardous assignment unwillingly, because he feared being fired, he still could not receive compensation for injuries received from such work. Employees were expected to refuse unsafe jobs. Another interpretation stated that the worker would not have to assume the risk of a hazardous assignment that he was *ordered* to undertake, "unless the danger was so obvious that no prudent man would have obeyed the order" —and so the question of what a "prudent man" would see as obvious danger was added to the complexities of courtroom imbroglios.[5]

William Kelley, working in 1884 for the Cable Mine in Deer Lodge County, Montana, ran up against the assumed-risks doctrine. He sought $30,000 compensation after a "missed hole" went off as he mucked in the mine: both his eyes were blown out, an ear was torn off, and he received other severe injuries, "rendering him forever incapable of working at his occupation."

But the Montana Supreme Court held that the company had taken all the precautions expected of it, adding:

> Notwithstanding the progress and advancement in the art of mining, it yet remains a hazardous and dangerous occupation, which, in spite of the many obligations of the owner of a mine to the employees, embraces other risks which the servant assumes as incident to the calling.

Kelley's loss, the court added, "is the result of an unforeseen and unavoidable accident incident to the risk of mining."[6]

Contributory negligence

Compensation could also be denied if an employee were injured partly because of his own negligence, even if the major portion of the blame lay with the employer. Since many persons had wide discretion in how to carry out their jobs, the worker was guilty of contributory negligence "if he does not use the safest means, time, and method of accomplishing the work. . . ." Failure to report an unsafe machine, for example, was counted under this heading.

This was the doctrine the Colorado Supreme Court relied upon in 1886 in overturning a lower court decision granting $5,000 to the widow of Robert H. Coe, killed by a bucket that fell down a shaft in a Lake County mine. Coe had been foreman for a week, and was at the bottom of the 200-foot shaft "chinking out the water streak" when the brake-rod on the hoist broke and sent the bucket plummeting down upon him.

Coe, the court stated, had day-to-day control of mine operations and could have had repairs made if he had wanted them. But the court did not probe the question of whether he had sought the employer's aid in fixing the hoist; if the company had used "ordinary care" in providing machinery, it was not liable for injuries resulting from "latent defects not discoverable by inspection, or by the usual and ordinary tests,

121

18. The power hoist epitomized the complex questions of blame and liability which the new technology introduced into hard-rock mining. The miner lost control over his own life by riding in a device operated by someone else—in this case the hoist operator, visible at the rear of this shaft house over a mine in Central City, Colorado. If the company was not liable for "latent defects not discoverable by inspection," how could this miner be responsible? Who would pay his doctor bills? Who would pay his widow?

Denver Public Library, Western History Collection photo

or through defects which the requisite skill and watchfulness have failed to detect. . . ." How a mine foreman could uncover "latent defects not discoverable by inspection" was not revealed. The court limited itself to implying that Coe was guilty of contributory negligence as it sent the case back to district court.[7]

Fellow servant

Persons engaged in the same common pursuit, under control of the same employer, were classed as fellow servants. If the employer had selected them with care and provided suitable equipment, "he is not answerable to one of them for an injury received in consequence of the carelessness or negligence of another. . . ."[8]

The U.S. Supreme Court followed this common-law doctrine when it overturned a lower court award of $2,950 to Patrick Whelan from his employer, the Alaska Treadwell Gold Mining Company. Whelan was breaking rock in the ore pit on November 23, 1891, in the company's mine on Douglass Island, Alaska, when without warning the ore was suddenly drawn into the chute below, carrying him with it and leaving him "severely and permanently injured." The ore dropped because the foreman, Samuel Finley, had ordered the chute gate opened—some thirty feet below where Whelan was working—to load mine cars in the tunnel below.

Was this foreman a fellow servant of Whelan's—thereby freeing the company from liability? The district and appeals courts said he was not. Justice Gray, speaking for the U.S. Supreme Court in 1897, reversed their rulings. Finley, Gray emphasized, was not the company's general manager or superintendent: "he was merely the foreman or boss of the particular gang of men to which the plaintiff belonged." It was immaterial whether Finley could hire and fire employees; he was still a fellow servant with Whelan and the others, "employed in the same department of business, and under a common head." Whelan could not collect.[9]

These three doctrines of the common law of liability—assumed risks, contributory negligence, and the fellow-servant rule—created in the rapidly industrializing America of the Gilded Age what one contemporary authority termed "a region of law-made anarchy so far as the hazards of industry are concerned." For the hard-rock miner of the West, as with thousands of other industrial workers, these doctrines signified that even if he was able to get his injury case into court, the odds against his winning were great, and the odds against avoiding poverty while awaiting appeals were even greater.[10]

The most obvious immediate result of these doctrines in the West was that mining companies won most damage suits brought against them for accidents, at least to the end of the century. Coroners' juries generally followed judicial guidelines, and the usual phrase appearing in their reports was along these lines: "We, the jury . . . find from the evidence, as given, that the occurrence was accidental and the result of carelessness on the part of the deceased, and attach no blame on the part of the owners or managers of the mine." (This case involved a Montana miner knocked from a bucket as it went by a "bend" in the shaft—a bend that the company could have straightened to avoid such an accident.) [11]

From these currents, "law-made anarchy" regarding industrial accidents came into the mining West. It is important to note that these doctrines were not the inventions of company spokesmen or packed juries, but ran through the mining camp populations. They inherited it along with other aspects of the common law. Individual responsibility rather than broad societal responsibility was part of the American tradition, and if no direct cause of an accident could be determined, the search was not pursued to locate indirect causes.

This was shown when even miners' unions agreed that employers were innocent in mine mishaps. The Virginia City Miners Union called a special meeting in 1867 to discuss assignment of blame for the death of Patrick Price, who was killed after being buried by an extensive cave-in, caused by the collapse of an abandoned but unfilled tunnel below. Rather than denouncing the company for dereliction of duty in failing to fill in the lower area, the miners' union followed traditional doctrines and passed a resolution freeing the employer from any feeling of guilt. It noted "a certain rumor current" censuring the mine foreman, and added: "We have fully investigated the above matter, and are very happy to say that, in our opinion and judgment, Mr. Jones and the other officers connected with the mine are fully exonerated from all blame in the premises." [12]

Under existing legal traditions, the company was not to blame in such cases. The juries and the miners' union were not breaking with precedent. But even when a mishap was simply labeled "an accident," thereby removing blame from both victim and employer, the results were the same as if the entire liability had been assigned to the miner. In both cases, he received no compensation.

Many cases could be determined with more certainty, of course. Examining a fatality where a miner had neglected to brace the tunnel timbers and was consequently buried alive, the Montana deputy mine inspector concluded, "It looks to me anything else but an accident." The cause was either "careless-ness in timbering, or else being an incompetent miner," he stated.[13]

But most cases were more complex if blame had to be determined. For example, of the four major causes of mine accidents reported in a Montana survey in 1889, each presented a host of complications to block easy assignment of blame: (1) premature or tardy dynamite explosion, (2) exposure to impure air, (3) miner caught between cage and shaft wall, and (4) cave-ins or rock falls. Each complication could involve cases where the miner or employer was obviously at fault, but within each classification the gray area was enormous: Could the employer be blamed for a delayed dynamite blast? Was the miner expected to know air was bad, especially if it did not affect his candle flame? Were faulty hoisting ropes a sign of poor management or lazy engineers or unobservant miners? Was the miner responsible for knowing whether a hanging wall would continue to hang?[14]

The hard-rock mining experience closely paralleled the Pittsburgh industrial accident record scrutinized by Crystal Eastman in her pioneering 1907–1908 Pittsburgh Survey. In that famous twelve-month study, the blame for almost one-fourth of the job accidents could not be attributed to victim, fellow worker, or employer. Her findings supported a contemporary writer's conclusion that the common law dealt with an imaginary worker who "never relaxes his vigilance under the influence of monotony, fatigue, or habituation to danger, never permits his attention to be diverted, even for a moment, from the perils which surround him, never forgets a hazardous condition that he has once observed, and never ceases to be on the alert for new sources of danger." In refuting the accuracy of this picture for industrial workers in Pittsburgh, Miss Eastman also found that the employee was often goaded into careless or reckless actions by the employer's demands for more production.[15]

Hard-rock miners lived in the same industrial world. Working by the flickering light of candles, breathing an often-strange mixture of gases from dynamite, rotting timbers and human offal, wading in slime and water, listening to the creaking of timbers as the ground shifted, perspiring in the heat or becoming chilled with the cold—such conditions molded the miners into something far different from the perfect servant assumed by the common law.

Men became careless after working in such an environment for months, at up to ten hours a day, seven days a week. They developed "a contempt for small dangers such as the falling of a small rock from the roof," one ex-miner recalled. Carelessness, the common law stated, was the fault of the miner. But what responsibility did this leave with the company, which could enforce strict safety rules through its power of hiring and firing? The former miner just cited above recalled that during two and a half years laboring in "the better mines of the West," he could recall only two occasions when a miner was "called down" for not picking down the back of a drift or stope before it could fall on an unsuspecting workman. And unless companies became strict on the matter of picking down the roof properly, he said, rock falls would continue to kill and maim.[16]

There is abundant testimony of the pressure for more output in Western mines, producing another distortion in the picture portrayed by the common law. The foreman's demand for "Rock! Rock! Rock!" echoed through the stopes in the hard-rock mining regions. One result of this emphasis on speed and output was cited by a South Dakota miner after a co-worker's death in a cage mishap: "He testified . . . that they were not allowed to hold the cage unless they were using it to hoist rock. He also stated that the bosses were always complaining and telling them to hurry up while using the cage."[17]

The Pittsburgh workers studied by Crystal Eastman seldom attempted to obtain compensation for their injuries beyond the amount—usually a pittance, if anything—given freely by the employer, because of a series of hurdles and barriers. These included legal costs, ignorance of court procedures, fear of losing a job, troubles in locating witnesses, and the tremendous length of time it took to bring a case to trial and see it through appeals. Most companies had the time and money to get past these hurdles; few workers did, and the frustrations encountered by one worker could discourage myriads of others. Miners' damage suits "have not resulted so favorably to the plaintiffs as to cause any special effort to be made" by employers to avoid accidents, the Montana Mining Inspector lamented.[18]

Absentee ownership—that great bugaboo of regular pay-days—also frustrated many miners who finally saw their damage suits successfully through the courts. Charles Kelly was left an invalid for life when rock fell on him as he worked in the Fourth of July Mining Company's property in Madison County, Montana, in 1891. He brought suit for $50,000, and was awarded a $15,000 judgment against the company in 1894 by district court. When these funds were not forthcoming, Kelly asked the court to enforce a state law holding that stockholders were indebted to the company for the full amount of their shares—even if they had never paid in full upon purchase. The jury found that the $7.5 million mine of the incorporation papers was worth only $125,000, and in 1898 the Montana Supreme Court ruled that shareholders could not escape liability to creditors for their unpaid balances. No information has been located, however, to indicate whether this decision brought Kelly any more compensation than the earlier rulings.[19]

The multiplicity of lease and contract agreements throughout the mining regions not only increased the dangers of labor underground but also clouded the legal question on assigning blame. It was a double-edged sword held over employees: to turn a profit, leasers usually had to scrimp on all expenses —such as timbering—not intimately connected with producing pay ore. But such workers also found themselves in limbo regarding liability for accidents. The protection this situation provided for the mines' owners was evident in the feeling of relief expressed by the general manager of an Aspen mine in his weekly report:

> This morning, John Strong, a lessee, met with a very painful and serious accident. A box of caps exploded from some cause not yet known, fearfully lacerating his face and tearing out one of his eyes. The leases especially protect the company against claims for damages for personal injuries, so no apprehension need be felt in case of any accidents to lessees.[20]

If things were too dangerous, of course, a workman was expected to quit. To continue working was "what an ordinarily prudent man would not do under the circumstances," accord-

127

ing to one rule of contributory negligence. This was applied in the case of a Colorado miner who obeyed a skip tender's order to get aboard an already overloaded skip, and was killed when one of the guides broke and let the skip scrape against a post. His widow lost her damage suit when the Colorado Supreme Court ruled in 1896 that unless an emergency existed, her husband should have refused the skip tender's order.[21]

Some did quit, such as the crew in the Gem Mine in the Coeur d'Alenes in 1903, when rock falls and cracking noises in the stopes and drifts became intolerable. Another example was Richard Thomas, who was ordered to work in a wet area in the Bunker Hill & Sullivan Mine one day in 1905 when he did not have his rubber boots or jacket along. Thomas recalled that when he complained, the shift boss retorted: "'Who's running this place?' 'Well,' I said, 'you may be running the place but you can't run me. Put another man in there and turn my time in at the office by morning.'"[22]

But men with families to support, or men with financial worries, or men accustomed to living and working among longtime friends could not always be relied upon to refuse orders if conditions were dangerous. When a group of Montana miners protested foul air underground, the company answer was: "Any man who does not care to stand it off can get his check right now." Eleven did. But three of the crew could not quit—they were "poor and with families."[23]

Such instances, becoming more common as the worker's independence weakened, made a mockery of the common law's expectations that employees would not work amid unsafe conditions.

The liability issue also became inextricably tangled with the amounts and methods of voluntary company aid to victims and survivors. When miners did win help from employers, the aid was often such that it could have been of little long-term use to a seriously injured workman or a family in dire straits. Miners' recollections, the files of mining companies, and other sources generally reveal an employer attitude that can most charitably be described as parsimonious. An exception was the case of a militant in the 1880 Leadville strike who said he was receiving $3 per day as a "pensioner" of the Robert E. Lee Mine, having been disabled by a fall. More typically, a Greek immigrant in Bingham Canyon recalled that after his brother was killed in a mine accident "the Company sent my parents three hundred dollars." In 1894, eight years after he was injured in the Maid of Erin Mine in Leadville, Josiah P. Lesher wrote back to the mine owner seeking information that would help him obtain a soldier's pension. The torturously written plea from the crippled miner recalled the assistance he had received after being hurt on the job: "I had worked but a few shifts," Lesher recalled, "when coming off of shift one evening the engineer run the cage up into the sheave and we all jumped off and I struck my ankle on a T Rail at the Mouth of the shaft and broke my ankle and that you had Doctor Heron doctor me for 6 or 7 months after that I went on crutches for 4 or 5 months and at the end of that time you gave me $250.00 and I signed an agreement in your office saying that I would not prosecute the Company for damages. . . ."[24]

At other times even less was provided. One of Frank Crampton's vivid memories of his life as a hard-rock miner was his ten-day entombment after a cave-in, for which the company paid him nothing, not even hospital fees. In numerous other cases, the employers sought to reduce payments to a minimum by a variety of means, including subterfuge. Top officials of the Bi-Metallic Mining Company, writing from their headquarters in St. Louis, instructed their superintendent in Granite, Montana, to deal "with care and ingenuity" when talking with Mrs. Kate Jones, a widow, "so as to relieve the Company from heavy damages" in her husband's death. "We presume that a few hundred dollars will pay all that will be required to settle the claim against this corporation. . . ." Later letters urged the superintendent to "approach Mrs. Jones as a friend, with the representation that you will present her case to the Company, and you being 'a friend at court,' your recommendations would be considered. . . ." He was told to appear not as a company representative (which he was), "but as a friend to Mrs. Jones and name some small amount to her which you think will secure from her and child a release. . . ." Further subverting the concept of liability, the officials in St. Louis instructed the superintendent to tell the widow that since her husband was "a faithful man," the company "might be induced to do something" for the widow and child. Ultimately, the sum of $1,000 was agreed upon. "We are willing to be liberal in this case," the vice president explained, although if Mrs. Jones pressed for more "it will be cheaper for us to stand suit, as we dislike making a precedent of allowing ourselves to be imposed upon."[25]

The widow of an Owyhee County miner faced greater difficulties four years later because she was fighting the company from afar and seeking its benevolence at the same time. The death of Dennis Meehan involved electricity: while leaving a raise in the Trade Dollar mine, an iron pipe he was holding touched a live wire, which electrocuted him as he twisted and became enmeshed in it. Writing to the Trade Dollar manager from her home in Indianapolis, Indiana, Mrs. Meehan used both sympathy and threats in her attempt to win assistance:

May 6, 1907

My dear Sir,

. . . Mr. Meehan's death was indeed a terrible shock to us, and all our friends. It being so sudden it was almost impossible to believe it. As he was our only support we are left entirely helpless. I was always waiting from month to month for his pay, as his wages were the only income.

The children which number five are not of age to leave school yet; God knows what I will do. I cannot use words enough to thank you for your kindness in Dennis' death, and also for sending the remains home so nice. He looked as natural as the day he left home. He looked very nice indeed for coming such a long distance. Poor Dennis was indeed a good and honest man. He will be missed by all. Well Sir, I and the children being left without support, I will ask you to try and help me out, and do your best to raise some money for me that will keep us until the children are able to support. It seems strange to me that if the wire was in good condition a stroke of the pipe could hardly knock the insulation off. It is a terrible loss to me and his family to say such a fine man as he was laying where he is to-day for the sake of those wires. The company ought to at least give the children a pension till the youngest would be of age. Could you please tell me whether it was the Mining Company or the Miners Union that paid the funeral expenses. I feel that it is on the part of the Company to help me as I do not want to bring suit or to sue the Company. If you could do your best I would feel more satisfied to compromise with the Company than to go in the trouble of suing which would be an expense on both parties.

The miners in Pennsylvania were very shocked to hear of Dennis' death, they were all very sorry. He had worked in Williamstown, Penn., for ten years. Dennis was a man that never had an enemy in his life, and was loved by every one.

I would be glad if you could look into the matter at once, and see what they could do. If the miners out there could raise a collection for us I would be very thankful.

Awaiting an answer, I remain

Your sorrowing friend,

Mrs. Dennis Meehan.[26]

Although she pressed for $3,000 as a "compromise" (if the children suffered "it will go pretty hard with the Company"), Mrs. Meehan eventually accepted $1,000 and signed a release. The Trade Dollar also paid $1,000 to survivors in each of two mine fatalities in 1902 and 1905. Beyond such company aid, miners often belonged to benevolent associations that provided funds for injured members; this topic will be discussed in Chapter 7.[27]

One invention born in the Gilded Age focused the complex liability issues most dramatically in the West. This was dynamite, whose arrival in the mining camps suddenly disrupted the simple liability solutions decreed by the common law. Was the miner at fault in blasting mishaps? Or the company, which was in a position to enforce strict rules but did not? Or a co-worker who tamped a charge recklessly? And who was to blame if a fuse burned too slowly, only to go off just as the miner returned to investigate the delay? Could the company be blamed if an imperfect explosion left poisonous gases?

To many observers, it was clear that the blame lay squarely upon the shoulders of just one man: the person setting off the dynamite. This was the logical conclusion, in fact, if the advertising claims for the safety of Giant Powder were accepted. To keep dynamite safe for handling, the sticks were kept below 42° F., and the prescribed method for thawing was to place them on wooden shelves in a room heated to less than 100° F. by steam or hot-water radiators. Smaller devices using containers resting in pans of warm water were also available. Managers of large operations usually did not trust regular miners with explosives, but trained specific persons to unpack, thaw, and deliver the dynamite to the work site. With the Anaconda Company using four million pounds of powder a year by 1909, the necessity for such precautions was compelling from an economic if not a humane standpoint.[28]

But in smaller mines, necessity required that ordinary miners obtain, thaw, transport, load, and fire the Giant Powder themselves. In the process, hundreds of them were mangled by unexpected explosions. Were they ignorant or careless or both? There is much in the historical record to label the hard-rock miner the guilty one. In his travels, the Colorado Inspector of Mines encountered powder being thawed before a hot fire, buried in hot sand, placed in the hot ashes of a blacksmith forge, and even heated with a candle flame. He visited one camp where two boxes (100 pounds) of dynamite were placed on the back plate of a boiler, "so as to keep good and hot for use." They *were* hot—so hot he could not handle them with his bare hands. Ten more boxes sat beneath the boiler. But when ordered to move the powder, the mine manager retorted that he "had done that for four years and never had an explosion."[29]

Some miners' experiences with dynamite could be almost comical. Two Montana miners laid sticks of frozen powder against their open oven door so the dynamite could thaw while the men ate breakfast in their cabin on a frigid winter morning. Suddenly the men realized the dynamite had caught fire and "was blazing and sputtering at a furious rate." Fearing that two full boxes nearby would be detonated, they raced out the door and sat on the opposite slope, expecting the cabin to be blasted to pieces. Instead it burned to the ground—while the pair stood, "half dressed, in the snow and cold, their retreat effectually blocked for more than an hour"—and the thermometer at 40 degrees below zero.[30]

The increasing troubles involving dynamite added to the confusion over liability in the West. This was evident to those whose position enabled them to see beyond the generalizations of "ignorant" or "careless" miners. The deputy mining inspector of Montana was such a person: he emphasized how dangerous it was for miners to thaw dynamite over a candle flame or in their bootlegs—but he went beyond such a simple assignment of blame to argue that "when the company under which they work has no [thawing room] . . . and will not permit them to 'waste' time in order to get ready for blasting, it means to adopt the dangerous method or quit the company's employment."[31]

His comment went to the heart of the issue: was something more than immediate cause to be considered in determining liability?

Where would a search for the *cause* lead, for example, in the case of the Owyhee County miner named Davis, who went to work at 7 A.M. on May 26, 1900, and was told that two shots, a back hole and a lifter, had not been heard during the previous shift's last round? Davis examined the face of the drift, found one unexploded back hole, and saw a pile of debris below, which he assumed covered the lifter (always placed at the bottom). When he drilled, however, the second hole was exploded—not under the debris, but in the breast of the tunnel where it "was not discernible upon a casual examination" because much of it had been broken off in the original blasting. This unexpected explosion killed Davis's two co-workers while leaving him seriously injured.

Davis brought suit against the Trade Dollar Company, arguing that it had failed to keep him accurately informed of the missed holes and could have done so "by exercise of ordinary care and prudence." The circuit court judge disagreed, however, holding that the method of locating missed shots was "uncertain," and that no negligence was shown, since the employer could not maintain an absolutely safe workplace when it was being changed constantly.[32]

Who was the culprit? Could Davis have been expected to locate the hidden charge? How could the employer or his agent have found it? No culprit was ever found, which meant that Davis and the families of his dead co-workers were left to fend for themselves.

What was called "the only proper method" to locate missed shots was described by a Central City miner who lost an eye and most of an ear when a machine drill set off a missed charge. Daniel Hanefin told the court in his damage suit that for safety, the rock and dirt had to be cleared away and the hole located, and then each unfired hole had to be picked clean with a gouger or scraper. Such efforts would require a great amount of time, of course, and this aspect of the safety proposals bothered the highly respected *Mining and Scientific Press*. The journal admitted that it was "difficult to say" how such accidents could be prevented, for "if the men spend several hours" searching for missed and partly exploded charges, "the cost of shaft sinking would become prohibitory, and mining would soon cease." From a "business standpoint," the journal concluded, "the miner must take some risks." [33]

"Some risks" were present in other variations on the dynamite theme. A too-quick or a too-slow fuse could have the same results for a hard-rock miner. In Gilpin County, Colorado, an Austrian miner named Ferdinand Zanini returned twenty minutes after firing his shots: "Just as he came in front of the hole it exploded, killing him; bad fuse was the cause." Such incidents gave logic to another Colorado miner's recommendation that mine inspection also take in the quality of powder, caps, and fuses, "as miners think it cowardice to remain away from a 'missed hole' longer than thirty minutes." [34]

One safe way to avoid injuries from a delayed charge was to remain away from the stope after firing. A Coeur d'Alenes company required thirty minutes' absence; the deputy mine inspector in Montana urged three hours. Technology's major contributions to safety in this area were increasing uniformity in dynamite, caps, and fuses, and the discovery that the use of wooden or copper tamping bars—rather than iron—would prevent sparks that could set off a charge. Also, in 1897 an Upper Michigan company produced a small powder thawer that provided metal tubes to hold the frozen sticks; the tubes were surrounded by water heated by a lamp. *The Engineering and Mining Journal* greeted the device with the accolade that if it could "overcome the predilection of many Colorado miners to thaw dynamite in a kitchen stove, it will have accomplished something in a humanitarian way as well as in a commercial." [35]

Something had to give amid this collision of hoary legal traditions with often-bloody reality. Slowly but inexorably the common-law doctrines eroded—questioned by juries and editors in mining camps, challenged by Western legislators, and bent by discerning judges who realized that the precedents of a simpler day could not stand forever.

Early questioning indicated a growing awareness that the old criteria were perhaps not adequate to cope with the maze of machines, pipes, drifts, and blasting gases that formed the work environment for thousands of hard-rock miners. Relatives of an accident victim were angered when the *Territorial Enterprise* cited "the carelessness of an old miner" in describing a fatal shaft accident. The miner was crossing an open shaft when the cage came from below and struck him. "It can hardly be attributed to that cause," the brother and brother-in-law of the deceased protested, "for to get over from the pump shaft to the cage he was obliged to cross the middle compartment, and while reaching back for his tools the ascending cage struck him." Their argument went beyond the victim's responsibility and raised the broader issue of whether the condition of the workplace itself contributed to the accident.[36]

The theme upon which such questioning began to center was simply that blame in mine accidents was often incapable of being neatly assigned to one side or the other; that it involved a complex of actions taken and not taken, of responsibilities accepted, not realized, or ignored; and that it involved also equipment and management decisions that initially may have seemed the best for job safety. The debate was affected near the century's end by the growing attacks on big business, which gave currency to the concept that employer and employee were not equal in power, and that government and courts could take this into account.

A spokesman finally emerged for this questioning of traditional liability doctrines. This was the state mine inspector, whose appearance in the mining states was one of the responses to the same industrial conditions that spawned challenges of the common law. (Creation of the office will be examined in Chapter 7.) The state inspectors' basic argument was that negligence or carelessness by workmen often reflected laxity by employers in enforcing safety rules. Such cases occurred frequently. When Fred Ames was killed after an overloaded skip (with twelve men) jumped its track, the Colorado mine inspector noted that "the rule of the company is that only six men shall come or go on the skip at a time; but as the company permits employees to violate this rule, it would seem to be, to some extent, responsible for Ames' death." (The state Supreme Court ultimately disagreed, however, and overturned a lower-court verdict for Ames' widow. Its reason was that the judge below had instructed the jury that the company had to exercise care as an "ordinarily prudent" man would do for his own safety "and the safety of those nearest and dearest to him." This would actually constitute more than ordinary care, the court decided, and it held the employer only to ordinary care.)[37]

Several Montana inspectors put the issue more bluntly, condemning employers for poor enforcement of rules and for salving their consciences by saying, "The men should know enough to take care of themselves." An inability to enforce company safety rules, the inspectors argued, suggests that management made mistakes in selecting foremen and superintendents.[38]

This attitude brought some inspectors into confrontation with legislators when the former criticized the politicians for their efforts to protect employers "in the building up of a new industry." Some inspectors also frequently spoke against coroners' juries for following the common law or ignoring contrary evidence in an accident. This conscience or gadfly role by the Montana inspector was evident as early as 1891, when he analyzed the jury's ruling in a case where powder and caps, kept in a blacksmith shop in the shaft house, caught fire and broke a bucket loose in the ensuing blast. The bucket hit Michael Sepp in the Ground Squirrel shaft, fatally injuring him. What angered the inspector in this case was the jury's weak statement that "the death of Michael Sepp should be a warning to mine owners and miners to be more careful in the future."

Why include miners? The inspector saw it as neglect on the part of the company, with no neglect shown on the part of Sepp. "There being no blame attached to any one and no lack of prudence, I fail to see where the warning to mine owners and miners comes in," he added with disbelief. "I consider this Company responsible for the death of Michael Sepp," the inspector asserted, because of the unsafe storage of powder.[39]

Others took up this reasoning, some carrying it even further. The editor of *Engineering and Mining Journal*, an industry spokesman, argued that companies should have full liability for all mine accidents. Only then would the necessary discipline and safe procedures be enforced. An accidental explosion, the journal stated, "should be held as sufficient proof that dangerous conditions existed, and the company should be compelled to show, not that it complied with the letter of the law, but that it tried to make such dangerous conditions impossible."[40]

Increased responsibilities for employers began to appear sporadically in court decisions. Changes on this issue can be charted in the Colorado Supreme Court through opinions handed down in 1886, 1896, and 1906. In 1886, in *Wells et al. v. Coe*, the court required the employer only to provide "ordinary care and diligence"—but he was not liable for injuries produced through "latent defects not discoverable by inspection." Hence, a widow could not recover damages after a faulty hoisting apparatus dropped a bucket on her husband. Ten years later, in 1896, the court still called it erroneous to expect an employer to exercise more care than "an ordinarily prudent man would exercise."

But by 1906, the changes that had transformed hard-rock mining finally were noticed by the Colorado Supreme Court. The court held that "a far higher degree of care is necessary" for an employer "whose employees are far underground with but scant means of escape in case of danger" than for those whose workmen do not face "unseen dangers" or problems of escape. This court—changing its philosophy drastically from twenty years earlier—specifically ruled that employers must provide a workplace safe from "latent" dangers as well as more obvious ones. The 1906 ruling supported Minnie Williams in her damage suit against the Sleepy Hollow mine in Gilpin County for the drowning death of her husband from water pouring in from adjacent mines—a danger known to the employer.[41]

The fellow-servant doctrine came under particularly heavy attack during these challenges to common-law doctrines. This was because the changed conditions underground made it fairly common for a miner to be injured or killed by the acts of another workman both unknown to him and distant. Such relationships differed sharply from those of pre-industrial workshops, where artisans were usually surrounded by fellow workers whose quirks and capabilities they knew well. So many interpretations had appeared by 1894 that the U.S. Supreme Court considered it probable that no part of the law of negligence had brought forth "more variety of opinion" than

19. *These early Comstock Lode miners faced more than poisonous gases and heat as they went underground: they also worked in a legal world of "law-made anarchy" as far as liability for accidents was concerned. The hoist operator held life-or-death control over them—but since he was classed as a "fellow servant," no liability attached to his employer for any accidents he caused as the miners rode the cage.*

Nevada State Historical Society photo

the fellow-servant rule. The Colorado Supreme Court found the rule in "inextricable confusion" by 1895, making it "well-nigh impossible" to decide a case by relying upon it.[42]

Railroading brought major shifts nationally in judicial interpretations of fellow-service. In the West, railroad cases were prominent also, but there was increasing attention paid to underground mining accidents where one employee's misdeeds hurt or killed another. Traditionally, the initial reaction in such cases was to blame the co-worker. But by 1886, confronted with an accident in the Anaconda Mine, a Montana jury took note of the fact that the hoisting engineer was not entirely at fault for running the cage into the sheave wheel, killing one miner and seriously injuring another. It was found that the indicator needle that showed the level of the cage was inaccurate; this forced the hoisting engineer to continually add 200 feet to the level shown on the dial. When he forgot to do this, the cage shot out and spilled the two men. Rather than commenting on the company's responsibility for providing adequate equipment, however, the jury limited itself to the statement that "the accident would not have occurred had the indicator registered 1,000 instead of 800 feet."[43]

Even such mild comments as this pointed to the changing interpretation. For the search into the root causes of industrial accidents could succeed only when those engaged in that search looked beyond the co-worker to the factors that had determined his actions. The search required an examination that did not stop with (for example) the Cripple Creek engineer who hoisted "a trifle too soon" and crushed a miner between the cage and the timbers. Why had he hoisted too soon? Inaccurate signal devices? Overwork? Poor training? Incompetence?[44]

In fact, the new importance given to a "trifle" was indicative of the scope of the transformation brought about by the industrial age. In earlier times, a "trifle" meant little in the workplace; placer miners would value it only if it referred to gold in a prospector's pan. But for hard-rock miners, a "trifle" could be the difference between life and death to men riding a cage, searching out a missed hole, or barring down the ground in a stope. The new era had written a new definition for the word, in the same way that it changed relationships and posed challenges to the fellow-servant doctrine. What if the co-worker should never have been hired? What if he needed more training? Did this shift liability from the engineer's shoulders to those of his employer? And since few hoisting engineers had extensive financial resources, was it any protection for an accident victim to be able to sue this fellow servant?

A company's continued employment of an incompetent hoisting engineer also raised questions. This issue began cropping up frequently, as in the Utah case where Frederick Stoll was injured in the Daly Mine when a hoisting engineer slammed the cage into an obstruction—an obvious danger of which the engineer, but not Stoll, should have known. That hoist operator's record included having caused three deaths in seven years. Citing these facts, the Utah Supreme Court held that a company must use due care not only in hiring a careful and competent engineer, but also in retaining him.[45]

Utah was one of several Western states which abandoned or sharply modified the fellow-servant rule by legislative action in this period. Railroad accidents generally provided the initial impetus, perhaps because of Eastern legislative experience which could be copied easily. But mining cases also prodded Western legislators on the subject. The Colorado and Montana legislatures virtually abolished the fellow-servant rule in industrial accidents by the end of the century.[46]

The courts generally joined the attack on the fellow-servant rule, as shown in two accidents in 1904–1905. In a Montana case, when a miner was injured by the explosion of a missed charge—a charge that his foreman was aware of—the Montana Supreme Court called the foreman a "vice principal" who stood in for the employer; the company had no justification for holding back essential information. And in the famous Stratton's Independence hoisting disaster in Cripple Creek, the coroner's jury completely ignored the fellow-servant rule; its emphasis was entirely upon ways that the company should act regarding safety. And with passage of federal liability acts in 1906 and 1908, the transformation of the fellow-servant doctrine reached from the nation's highest political and judicial levels down to coroners' juries sitting in isolated Rocky Mountain mining camps.[47]

A similar upheaval occurred in the mining regions regarding the "assumed risk" and "contributory negligence" doctrines. It became difficult for hard-rock miners to go along with a common-law concept which stated that when they signed the company payroll they accepted the multitude of unknown dangers waiting below. Was any act short of quitting to be considered contributory negligence, when dangers acquiesced in led to an accident? Applying the common law to these situations increasingly strained the credulity not only of hard-rock miners but also of Western juries, judges, and legislators.

Although many judges diluted and eroded these doctrines, it took the Colorado Court of Appeals to turn the sharp tongue of judicial indignation fully upon them and their continued use in barring compensation to miners from industrial accidents. The case was *Mollie Gibson Consolidated Mining and Milling Co. v. Sharp*, in 1894, and the court's attitude was evident in its opening salvo: "What killed the miner is called an 'accident.' This word does not describe it. It more nearly approaches a crime."

William Sharp's father brought suit seeking damages for his son's death in the Mollie Gibson shaft in 1892. Three weeks before the incident, the company had started to enlarge the shaft opening from 4 by 8 feet to 4 by 12 feet, its size below the fourth level. This expansion was carried out by starting at the surface and working down, blasting dirt and rock into the shaft, where it was stopped by a bulkhead placed across the shaft at the fourth level.

In three weeks, the debris piled up in the shaft to a depth of 75 or 80 feet, and crews were sent in to muck it out. Since it had become impacted, the superintendent ordered the bulkhead removed and a stream of water run on the dirt from above—but news of this was not passed on to the four men going on duty February 15, 1892. In less than two hours after they started work, this column of unsupported, water-impregnated earth suddenly swooshed to the bottom of the shaft, killing three of the four miners, including William Sharp.

The Mollie Gibson Company claimed that the employee assumed all ordinary risks of the job. This argument, the court retorted, "would almost seem like an attempted perversion of good law to bad uses. . . . [It] disturbs our judicial equanimity." The court noted the removal of the bulkhead and the addition of water without informing Sharp, and said the "contributory negligence" claim was destroyed as well by the fact that "no man possessed of his five senses would enter a death-trap like that to which this shift was sent." It ruled in Sharp's favor.[48]

There was a jurors' rebellion underway at least by 1890, when a Colorado report noted that juries in lower-court cases frequently awarded damages to injured workers, "but the Supreme Courts in this and other States have reversed the verdicts. . . ."[49]

It was a gradual, sporadic change. As late as 1897, a report on Montana mine fatalities for the year showed that fifteen were blamed on miners, only three were blamed on the employer or his subordinates, and twenty-six were either termed an "accident" or were silent as to blame. The bi-monthly summaries of court decisions affecting labor presented in the *Bulletin of the Department of Labor* reveal that workmen won some cases and lost others; but most of all, the summaries show that the common law was under attack and in transition.[50]

In the 1902–1904 coroner's jury reports in Cripple Creek, jury decisions against employers were frequent. Employees were also blamed for some accidents, but it is worthy of note that a large number of these Teller County reports pointed the finger of blame at employers. This in itself constituted something of a small revolution in fifty years.[51]

Juries' awards for damages were getting larger also. William Kelley was voted $10,000 damages from the Cable Company after a missed hole exploded, blowing out both his eyes, tearing off one ear, and causing him other serious injuries. This award, however, was overturned in 1889 by the Montana Supreme Court. Ten thousand dollars was also the award to James Harvey in his successful suit against the Alturas Gold Mining Company for injuries to his arms when a Cornish pump fell on them; this lower-court award was upheld by the Idaho Supreme Court in 1893. A South Dakota jury voted $23,000 for William Fullerton in 1895 after both his feet were mangled when he was caught and whirled around by an unguarded revolving machine shaft; this award was affirmed by the higher court. Two years later, a district court jury in Montana awarded $12,000 to a miner whose legs were paralyzed in a rock fall.[52]

A $37,500 award may have been the largest in the mining West during this period. It was voted by a Pitkin County district court to a miner who lost his sight when a foreman improperly used a sand pump and set off a missed charge. The award was overturned in 1895 by the Colorado Supreme Court, however. The court said the amount was "not only much larger than any that has been called to our attention," but the record showed that the jury was "influenced by passion or prejudice," and the evidence "unavoidably aroused the sentiment of pity that every man possesses. . . ."[53]

Employers were aghast at the increasing size of these damage awards to victims. A Colorado mine superintendent warned in an 1892 letter to the company president that within the "last year or two there have been several cases around here, the men invariably obtaining a verdict from $1,000.00 to $5,000.00." The Union Gold Mining Company went to court in 1902 to attack the $15,000 damages it had been ordered to pay a former employee, claiming that if he loaned it at 8 percent interest, he would earn more money than he had ever earned before or ever would be able to earn. The Colorado Supreme Court disposed of this contention by noting that due to the company's negligence, a loaded mine car weighing nearly a ton had fallen on William Crawford, resulting in loss of a leg and fracture of his skull: the company "has made a physical wreck of its employee, and it would now enforce this cruel rule against him. . . ." The jury, the high court added, had seen "the physical condition" of Crawford for itself and voted him $15,000 damages; on the basis of the trial record, the court agreed that this was not excessive.[54]

Fear of court action may be discerned in company officials' statements and in their sudden enthusiasm for liability insurance. No longer could employers count on the courts to decide accident cases by a strict interpretation of the common law. "I think you had better settle this claim for the very best amount possible and not let it go to trial," warned Colorado mine owner Eben Smith after a mine fatality in 1898, "as it will cost considerable to defend the suit and we are liable to get 'stuck' for the $2,000."[55] A top official of an Owyhee mine breathed a sigh of relief when a widow accepted the company's offer of $1,000: "It is not desirable to get into Court," he confided to an aide, "regardless of the results."[56]

An undependable court system forced mining companies to take out insurance to protect themselves against large damage suits. A Georgetown mine superintendent noted in 1891 that his company had escaped damage suits for ten years, but he cautioned that "it is not at all probable that we can work another eleven or twelve years without some damage suit being brought against [us]." In particular, he saw a growing tendency for miners to seek damages, aided by "unscrupulous lawyers." He proposed that the company take out liability insurance, then recoup $1,200 of the $1,650 annual premium by charging the men $1 apiece per month instead of collecting this for the hospital.[57]

From such factors the insurance movement spread rapidly through Western mining camps in the 1890s, often involving English or German insurance companies. Many of these took over a mining firm's liability for up to $5,000 in the death of an employee, and also covered contractors and their employees.[58]

Objections were raised to these policies on several points, such as the requirement that employees pay for the premiums through payroll deductions; the employer, it was charged, was merely passing off his liability to the insurance companies at no cost to the mining firm. Some policies also specified that the company's liability for any accident damages ended when the insurance payment limit was reached. A Coeur d'Alenes company, for example, had a policy that paid $1,500 to survivors and permanently disabled employees, and then "all obligations on the part of the association and the mining company on the account of such injuries or death shall cease." The 1,500 employees each paid $1 per month, and the employers contributed another $750.[59]

From this multiplicity of court decisions, out-of-court settlements, benefit associations, insurance policies, and increasing legislative and union concern (to be discussed in Chapter 7), one major generalization could be made by the end of the century: "There is always an uncertainty as to the outcome in each particular action brought for the recovery of damages for injuries."[60]

This uncertainty disturbed company officials concerned with the profit ledger, and the sudden blossoming of an army of liability insurance salesmen throughout the mountains stemmed directly from that uncertainty. But many companies were moved by more than profits; the string of payments to victims in many cases also bespeaks a humane concern by some employers. Indeed, 66 of the 100 employers surveyed by the Colorado Bureau of Labor Statistics in 1887–1888 agreed that employers should be responsible to their workmen for injuries to the same extent that they would be to non-employees—a belief that contradicted many common-law defenses. Many of these employers were in mining, and they mentioned efforts to help accident victims by continuing their wages, paying medical bills, holding open their positions, and providing other assistance.[61]

But such scattered expressions of sympathy were inadequate for the growing number of victims of mining accidents and their families. It mattered little to them that company officials in distant cities expressed concern for the workers' condition; by the time that sentiment had passed through "the superintendent, foreman, and shift boss to the employee," little feeling was left in the rush for "Rock! Rock! Rock!"[62]

The common law of liability placed much of the blame for mine accidents upon the victim or his fellow worker, neither of whom had the financial resources required for adequate compensation. This served to place the final burden of liability for mining accidents upon the persons least able to handle it—the victim and his family. As legal traditions came under attack, sporadic improvements in court rulings began to appear; the growth of insurance coverage for miners paralleled this trend, although it often had the effect of placing unrealistic limitations on compensation.

What remained by the turn of the century was still "a region of law-made anarchy" regarding industrial accidents, in the mining West as well as in the industrial East. For some, this called for government intervention. But before this happened, hard-rock miners sought other paths to protect themselves.

PART TWO
ORGANIZED RESPONSES

CHAPTER VI

The Union Impulse

The news from Butte was as unexpected as it was disconcerting to the territorial boosters running the Helena *Herald* in 1878. Reports indicated that workers in Butte's developing silver mines had formed a union, Montana's first, and were protesting a wage cut by launching a strike—also Montana's first.

"We are sorry, indeed, to learn that this social and industrial disorder has invaded Montana," the *Herald* announced. "We prided ourselves very much on the fact that our people of all classes were too intelligent to resort to this clumsy and suicidal method of correcting temporary evils." Particularly unfortunate was the impact this would have upon investors: capital, the *Herald* explained, "is always cautious and slow in adventuring to new countries," and needs "much coaxing and constant encouragement to venture so far away from its favorite haunts." Montanans, the editor warned, "could not possibly perpetrate a more insane and harmful act than to do anything to deter capital from coming here."[1]

The shock felt by the Helena editor over the appearance of a labor union and strike in Montana Territory has had latter-day parallels among scholars attempting to explain the phenomenon of industrial labor problems in the middle of a vast frontier. "Individualists do not take to unions," one labor historian has observed, and the West above all has been seen

149

in song, story, and even scholarly studies as the home of in-dividualists. For example, the extremely limited, anemic union impulse among cowboys—those folk heroes usually depicted as the epitome of individualism in America—has been traced to their refusal to follow "proletarian" or organizational dic-tates. One interpretation of the violence that frequently scarred labor-management relations in Western mining in the 1890s and 1900s has been that it proceeded "from the general charac-teristics of the frontier"—that is, a more rough-and-tumble population was more prone to go beyond peaceful methods. But the historians have shown less unity than the miners they study: a more recent appraisal of the origins of miners' unions emphasizes the resemblance of Western mining towns to "their Eastern industrial counterparts," and finds labor violence ap-pearing in the West as well as the East and Europe because of the basic similarities between them. In other words, where the West copied the East it opened the way to unions and labor violence.[2]

While the debate over the appropriateness of union strife in the West is without provable answers—and many of the arguments will be examined in more detail in the discussion of radicalism in Chapter 9—it may be ventured at this point that the search for the birth of unionism becomes more fruitful if it is sought amid industrial conditions. Just as the trade union movement in the East was limited to sporadic local efforts until the rapid industrialization that followed the Civil War, so, too, Western hard-rock miners did not march under the union ban-ner until their occupation had undergone extensive industrial change. The entry of large machinery with the accompanying demand for outside capital, the need for large crews employed by distant owners, the reliance upon external markets—all these factors forced basic changes in the somewhat easygoing ad hoc character of pre-industrial labor-management relations. Workmen in the West as elsewhere found that they could not stand alone to protect themselves against arbitrary pay cuts, wage delays, insecurity of employment, unsafe conditions, and other problems stemming from or worsened by industrialism.

Their organizational response collided head-on, however, with the traditions of American business. The striking Butte miners were pointedly reminded of these traditions ("self-evi-dent truths") by a local Citizens' Protective Association: prop-

erty owners could control their own property and be protected in its use; and each man had the right to dispose of his
labor and services for whatever wages he desired—"with this
right no person or organization has a right to interfere by threats
or by violence." [3]

Against these traditions came the organized miners with
their goals of improving wages and job conditions and, in the
process, challenging the employers' control. As Rodman Paul
concluded after examining two early California strikes, the real
issue was not so much one of employment terms "as of the
implied right of the working men to a voice in the administration of the mines." Similarly, non-Mormon miners attempting
to organize in Logan, Utah, in 1871, were said to be "determined to be governed by the law of their own making." Identical goals—often implied rather than stated—were present in
other campaigns by miners' unions. The clash between these
two sides was not unique to the West. But the rapidity of industrial change on the Western frontier, the juxtaposition of
the primitive beside the technologically complex, and the persistence of the image of the gold rush upon miners' expectations all made the drama of Western unionization different
from what occurred elsewhere. [4]

This chapter will trace that union impulse from its beginnings in Colorado and Nevada, to the rise of the Butte "Gibraltar" and the major Knights of Labor struggle in Leadville,
through the violent clashes of the 'nineties in the Coeur d'A-
lenes, Cripple Creek, and Leadville, and the beginnings of the
Western Federation of Miners. The evolution of such related issues as the flat wage rate and closed shop, the definition
of *miner*, and the unions' attitude toward immigrants will also
be discussed.

The union story began in the earliest lode-mining camps.
Although the Comstock Lode is usually exalted as the site of
the first Western hard-rock miners' union, in fact that initial
attempt occurred in Central City, Colorado, in April, 1863. It
came as placer mining was declining in the district's gulches,
lode mining vigorously expanding, and the high wages of the
"rush" were tumbling rapidly to $2.50 per day for drill men
and $3 for blasters. Shifts were ten hours by day and nine
hours by night. On April 5, the district's miners voted "vocifer-

ously" to quit work and demand $3 per day for miners and $4 for blasters. At least 125 miners signed the resolutions and formed an organization for mutual aid. Some fifty of them then forced employees at the Bob Tail mine to quit work, adding force to their threats by breaking windows and doors at the company offices. A night of wild activity in Central City, sparked by shooting and fights, apparently backfired on the new society, for the organization faded quickly.[5]

Just a month later, some 300 to 400 miners on the Comstock Lode formed a Miners' Protective Association aimed at guarding against a threatened wage cut, defeating "speculative plans affecting their interests injuriously," and creating a mutual benefit fund for the sick and injured and family survivors. Apparently this organization, like the attempt at Central City, did not long survive its birth in 1863, although this may have been because wages remained at the $4 level.[6]

This $4 wage became the keystone of the hard-rock miners' life on the Comstock. From 1863 on, any threat to the $4 wage or any hint of a threat was met with forceful action. But since $4 was considered excessive by mine officials, it was not long before the employees were driven to a collective response again. On March 19, 1864, the crew in the Uncle Sam Mine grabbed John Trembath, a new Cornish foreman who had talked of cutting wages, and sent him up in a bucket, bound with the slogan, "Dump this pile of waste dirt from Cornwall." Trembath was allowed to go free, and the $3.50 wage he had ordered was restored to $4 again. On July 31, the streets of Virginia City and Gold Hill echoed with the shouts, "Four dollars a day!" from the marching miners, after it was learned that new men were being hired on the Comstock at less than the standard $4. Visits by groups of protesters to the mines and mills the next day convinced wavering employers to retain the $4 minimum, and on August 6 the miners took the next step by forming the Miners' League of Storey County. Its $4 goal apparently upheld, the new organization lacked a reason for unity; and when employers began favoring non-League men in hiring, it began to disintegrate. With the Miners' League ineffective and the economy in a slowdown, employers in early 1865 reduced wages on the Comstock to $3.50. The stock-market crash later that year made resistance to the cut unfeasible.[7]

Why had these early Colorado and Nevada attempts at unionization failed? It is probable that company employment was so new in both districts that the non-union tradition remained strong—too strong to be overwhelmed by the minor flareups of 1863 and 1864. The continuous movement of miners away from the district to prospect holes or new rushes also discouraged formation of a lasting union. The situation was hinted at when a doctor in nearby Carson City, Nevada, wrote home to his wife that the region was "only a mining country and nobody expects to stay here longer than to grasp a fortune." When news reached the Comstock a year later of discoveries in Idaho, the Gold Hill *News* noted miners leaving or planning to leave for the new excitement—former placer miners who were willing to desert Nevada, "where the mines are worked only by companies, for a country where every man can work for himself." As late as 1867, a government report found much of the Comstock's population in an "unsettled disposition," and claimed that "the number of those who have come to look upon Nevada as a permanent home are very few, indeed."[8]

Permanency had trouble in such surroundings. In addition, unions were not needed for social purposes; such groups were already present in abundance. A former Comstock resident observed that she did "not think it is possible for any other city to have more different societies than Virginia City" had during those years. A list of groups active in 1870 included the Sons and Daughters of Temperance, Good Templars, Band of Hope, Order of the Red Men, Fenian Brotherhood, Anti-Chinaman, Grand Army of the Republic, the Turnverein, Hebrew Benevolent Society, and German Benevolent Society, plus fire companies and military associations. As will be discussed in Chapter 7, many of these organizations also provided care and benefits for ailing members.[9]

What could the union provide for men who already had easy access to the saloon and to these lodges and social organizations? The answer was protection against the employer, mainly against his power to reduce their pay. Maintenance of high wages would remain the major purpose behind unionization across the mining West. Once unions had succeeded as ongoing institutions, it is true, they could take on some of the social and benevolent functions of the lodges. But to become a permanent institution, an outside threat was required—and as long as a high wage was protected, the threat was weakened. This fact, combined with the transitory nature of much of the labor force, appears in retrospect to have been responsible for the inability of the early unions to survive their own birth pangs.

The Comstock began to change, however. It was a transformation that would occur in many Western mining camps as the frenzy of a new district was replaced by a more settled community, with more permanency of institutions and—quite often—a stronger position held by absentee owners.

On the Comstock, the new strength of distant employers joined with the approach of the Central Pacific Railroad to cast a mood of uncertainty over the district's miners. Would cheaper consumer goods, due to the railroad, remove a major argument behind their high wages? The workmen's weakness was further revealed by severe winters in 1866–1867 and 1867–1868, which paralyzed the district and threw hundreds of miners out of work.[10]

The miners began early to protect themselves in such an environment. The initial organized response came on Gold Hill, whose miners created a union in December, 1866, combining secrecy, benevolent features, and a protest against "the tyrannical oppressive power of Capital." The union further pledged its members to refuse to work underground at less than $4 per day. The following month, four local mine superintendents were warned that unless the $4 was paid, the union would "turn out in force and stop their works until the same is accomplished."

All but one of the superintendents yielded. Greentree of the Imperial, however, rebuffed the Gold Hill union and his comments stung. Soon there were allegations that he was behind the dismissals of union men at various mines. Accordingly, some two hundred union miners appeared one afternoon at the Imperial and forced several employees to quit, leaving behind a warning that Greentree would pay less than $4 "at his peril." The company's shares promptly fell $10 apiece on the San Francisco stock exchange, and in less than two weeks the Imperial's president, William B. Bourn, came to town to talk with union officials.[11]

The synopsis of these talks, copied into the union's minute

book either from the memory of President William Cummings and Recording Secretary Angus C. Hay, or from their notes, shows Bourn to be extremely defensive. The session was especially important in revealing some of the new factors emerging in the changed labor relations picture on the Comstock. Foremost among these was the distance—not only geographical—between employer and employee. "I am a stranger to you," Bourn commented as the meeting opened, and this observation was buttressed by all comments made during the talks. Bourn obviously was unfamiliar with wages and other facts concerning the mine's operation. Cummings, for his part, admitted he had not known Bourn's name before that day— the union minute book misspells it as *Bone*—and added that "your name has never been mentioned in the Union. . . ." These statements showed why the union had turned first to the Imperial superintendent, the company's man on the scene. "Mostly all the other officials of mines reside in San Francisco," Cummings emphasized; the local superintendent was therefore "the only Representative of the mine we could reach. . . ." [12]

The second factor emerging from the talks is the picture of the union as a somewhat unwieldy organization that turned to forceful methods only when left no alternative. Angus Hay, who remained in the background for most of the session, inserted at one point that "we took the only course we saw open" when it seemed to them that Greentree had the final word on the $4 wage at the Imperial. Further pleadings or arbitration were not possible; the "only course" left for the union' was to remove from the mine all men employed for under $4, and warn the company of the danger of continuing to pay below the union scale. Thus did the Gold Hill Miners Union survive its first test and begin a long period of successful defense of the $4 wage.

An untenable situation soon existed on the Comstock, however: there was no counterpart union in Virginia City, the biggest city on the Lode. By midsummer of 1867, however, Virginia City miners began to respond to the jibes of their Gold Hill counterparts—as when the latter union voted on July 2 to admit no Virginia miners to its sessions "until they show by their actions that they will strike for their just rights and maintain a position in Society on an equality with us."

Formation came on July 4, 1867, with Gold Hill union members participating, followed by the first public appearance of the Virginia City Miners Union in the city's Fourth of July parade, "with banner flying, and decorated with badges." Its constitution closely paralleled the Gold Hill document, and it also won a $4 battle—with the Savage Mine—within a month.[13]

The Comstock unions were established, powerful organizations from 1867 on. They became, as a contemporary wrote in 1881, "the head of the organization" of hard-rock miners' unions in the West. As Richard Lingenfelter has shown in his careful tracing of the spread of the Western miners' union movement, the unions which developed over the following six years in the West were largely patterned after the Gold Hill and Virginia City unions, and were usually organized by former Comstock miners. In 1877, all the miners' unions in Nevada were put under the Comstock union's umbrella, with transfer privileges open for all 4,000 members in the expanded association.[14]

Employers soon marked out what would become the major controversy in the growth of Western unions: the payment of wages that were often double those paid to working men outside the region. To miners, the riches of mining properties —trumpeted daily in newspapers and stock brochures—were so great, the work so dangerous, and living expenses so high in the mountains and deserts that high wages were just.

The employers' attack on high wages, like the miners' movement for union organization, began as soon as mining went underground in the West. As lode mining was making its first appearance in Montana amid the boomtime earnings received by men working placer operations in 1866, a mining camp newspaper warned: "If wages continue at their present exorbitant figure, we must hire some kind of foreigners to work our quartz lodes—from $6 to $8 per day for quartz miners is too much of a tax to be long submitted to." Such figures reflected the early scales when competition of nearby placer operations made labor scarce. By the 1880s, however, placer mining was sharply reduced in comparison with the rapid expansion of lode mining; in addition, silver prices were falling while the railroad spread to most major districts. By the Spring of 1885, the *Mining and Scientific Press* observed that "Miners' wages are coming down all over the West. . . ." By then, the

$5–$6 daily wage had generally fallen to $4 or $3.50, and the journal went beyond this to predict that "within a year $3 will be the established price for a day's work in mines of the Pacific Slope."[15]

The prediction was accurate in many cases, and each wage cut correspondingly increased the pressure on Western hard-rock miners to organize for their own protection. Other issues, such as shorter hours, opposition to Chinese, hospital fund payments, and union recognition, were occasionally important, but they paled in significance when compared with the dozens of cases of wage cuts provoking organization among hard-rock miners.[16]

As a result, the Western landscape was dotted with attempts by miners to form unions throughout the 1870s and 1880s. Their efforts began with the new White Pine district in Nevada, where the "boom" wages of $6 a day began falling in 1869 and soon had miners marching in the streets, striking, intimidating non-union men, and giving up in defeat as wages fell to $3.50. A similar pattern was seen in 1872 in the Owyhee district of southwestern Idaho, where the formation of a union, and threats against a wage-cutting foreman, preserved—for a time—the $4 day. Silver Reef, Eureka, and Stockton in Utah were other sites of new miners' unions in the period, with wage cuts providing the initial pressure for organization, followed by violence or the threat of violence leading to the union's demise. This pattern was seen in 1885 in Idaho's new Wood River and Vienna districts, where British and other outside capitalists sought to reduce the wages of $4 to $3.50. Bloodshed was narrowly averted, and the strike in Broadford and Bullion was finally broken by arrests of union men and a change-over to contract work. Union organization followed by defeat also came to miners in Tombstone, Arizona, in 1884, as they fought a wage cut from the prevailing $4 to $3. As in many other wage disputes, violence provided the excuse for troops to break the strike.[17]

This mixed pattern of victories and defeats, with the resulting stimulus or discouragement for union organization, also appeared in Colorado and in the Black Hills of Dakota. The Black Hills rush in the late 1870s sent wages up to $7 in gold dust by February, 1877, but lode mining grew so rapidly that within a year companies were reducing wages, a miners' union was formed in Deadwood, and threats were made against employers who persisted in paying only $2.50. The union was successful, and $3.50 became the standard in the Black Hills. In Colorado, wages were reduced successfully by mine owners in Central City in 1868 despite the united opposition of miners; but when attempts were made in 1873 to cut the $3 daily wage to $2.70 and $2.50, Cornish miners organized the Central City Miners Union. The availability of Irish and other miners who disliked the Cornish helped break the union and sustain the lower rate. In the Caribou mines in 1879, however, the union prevented a reduction below $2.50, and strikes in Telluride in 1883 and Silverton in 1884 also blocked wage cuts. Combining statistics for metal miners and coal miners from 1881 to 1888, the Colorado Bureau of Labor Statistics reported that 6,588 of the 7,163 employees had gone out on strike at some time during the period, marking up thirty-five miners' victories and eleven defeats. In the Coeur d'Alenes of northern Idaho, a wage cut in 1887 spurred organization among miners until unions were active in Wardner, Wallace, Burke, and Gem within two years. Clearly, the drive to preserve high wages was a rocky one in the mining West in the 1870s and 1880s; but even when defeated, the necessity for organization was a lesson driven home forcefully to hard-rock miners.[18]

The origin of the Butte union in 1878 demonstrated how a combination of prosperous mines, united miners, and divided employers could create a strong and lasting organization—in this case, the "Gibraltar of Unionism" in the West.

Butte's rise was spectacular. The camp gained prominence as a silver-mining center in the mid-70s. Late in 1881, the railroad arrived—a fortuitous development because silver ran out the following year and a rich dome of copper ore (valuable only if it could be transported cheaply in bulk) was discovered underlying the district.

Butte was still a silver camp, however, when miners in the Alice and Lexington mines came up from their shifts on June 10, 1878, to receive their monthly paychecks and discovered that wages had been cut from $3.50 to $3. They left work, marched four hundred strong with a brass band through Butte's streets, and that night appointed a committee to draft resolutions. They elected temporary officers the next day, and on June 13 officially created the Butte Workingmen's Union with J. C. Witter as president and with a constitution and by-laws "which are substantially those of the Miners' Union of Nevada. . . ."[19]

On June 19, another procession of miners appeared, this time wending its way to the nearby Walkerville mines to ask manager Marcus Daly to close his Alice Mine until the wage question could be settled. He complied. A. J. Davis of the Lexington made a similar decision after first delivering a lengthy oration to the miners from the balcony of his home. Other mines closed also.[20]

An attempt to break the new Butte union by linking it to violence failed, possibly because union strength and discipline were such that the union leadership was able to control disorderly members. At any rate, on August 13, the Butte *Miner* reported that "the labor troubles were entirely quieted down. . . ."[21]

Thus occurred the birth of the Butte Workingmen's Union, which evolved into the Miners' Union of Butte City in 1881 and the Butte Miners' Union in 1885. By the early 'nineties, it had earned the title "Gibraltar of Unionism," and had organized unions in Philipsburg and other Montana camps. Membership in Butte rose from 65 on the evening it was created, to 800 in 1881, 4,600 in 1893, and 6,213 in 1910. The union maintained the $3.50 base until 1906, when it agreed to a sliding scale based on the price of copper; this immediately raised wages to $4 for several months before the decline in copper prices reduced them again to $3.50.

The union's success in building a strong organization and maintaining the $3.50 wage was aided by two related factors: (1) the fabulous wealth of the "richest hill on earth"; and (2) the struggle between mining companies to control that "richest hill." The employers' struggle was carried out in the courts, in local politics, and at times within the mines themselves, where private armies battled each other. Butte's miners thus found themselves coaxed and courted by companies that sought allies for battles on all three levels. Facing not a single powerful employer but several competing ones, the Butte Miners' Union skillfully made its way to a position of supremacy across the West. The 1878 strike, then, was typical of what would happen in the district: it was marked by a lack of unity among employers, a condition that would remain in the district until Anaconda's rise to supremacy early in this century.[22]

The spread of unionism among the men who toiled for the increasingly large mining enterprises in Butte and elsewhere across the West led to several questions scarcely contemplated at the outset of that movement. One of the issues suddenly rising in importance had originally been so elementary that it was usually ignored: What is a miner? The Gold Hill union on the Comstock gave brief attention to it, initially specifying only that its members had to be "practical miners," a phrase used later by other unions. (The short-lived Silver City, Idaho, union of 1867 said that "none but miners or laboring men" would be enrolled.) But only slightly more than a year after its organization, the Gold Hill union suddenly faced a basic question: "Mr. Williams, a foreman in the Empire Mine, applied for admission to membership. [It was] moved that no foreman be admitted except at the discretion of the union. Motion carried."[23]

In rejecting Williams's application, the union implied that foremen might be admitted if the members so decided. But this was only solving the immediate problem—Williams's application—while ignoring the basic issue of deciding which skills and occupations were eligible for union membership. The inadequacy of its action was obvious three months later as other persons began to knock on the union's door: former miners, now engaged in other occupations, were applying for membership in the Comstock's most powerful citizens' group. The Gold Hill union responded by appointing a three-man committee "to define the word *miner* as regards admissibility." A week later, the committee reported its definition:

> A miner is one who digs for metals or other minerals, but [we] recommend as liberal a construction of the word as possible, and [we] recommend that any party who has been a miner although now engaged in other pursuits be eligible to membership.

But the union members rejected this definition. Decisions continued to be made case by case, although enough problems arose so that in 1873 the secretary was instructed to announce to the community that "mechanics" could not join.[24]

Defining *miner* was no longer simple. This was because

160

lode mining itself was no longer simple; it increasingly involved more than digging for metals. Working in and about the mines were timbermen, carpenters, blacksmiths, pick handlers, water boys, powder men, engineers, hoisting men, cagers, and various types of shift bosses, foremen, and other supervisors. Should these men—most of whom worked closely with those drilling and removing ore—be excluded from union membership?

The policy that gradually evolved over the 1870–1890 period in the West was to limit union membership to all nonsupervisory workmen laboring underground. This policy ran into trouble, however, as the makeup of mine crews changed extensively. The Butte union, for example, voted in 1881 to control wages only for underground miners, but by the 'nineties it was enrolling all company employees, on top and below, including smeltermen. Many other miners' unions made this change also.[25]

These trends in the mining West paralleled what was occurring in the industrial East under the Knights of Labor. Launched in the 1870s in Pennsylvania and preaching the solidarity of all wage earners, the Knights rose on the ashes of weak, isolated craft unions that had shunned cooperation with other laboring groups. By the mid-1870s, many of these craft movements had faded, and groups of workers were seeking an organization. This was especially true of Pennsylvania's coal miners.[26]

When the Knights of Labor went national in 1876, its philosophic bases were somewhat like those already developing in Western mining camps. But soon the organization was not simply paralleling but was beginning to shape Western union development. Rejecting heavy emphasis on political action and benevolent society activities, the Knights of Labor was based primarily upon the organization of all workers regardless of occupation, race, or creed. In later years, politics and benevolent activities would appear among the Knights' activities, but the industrial union approach stressing worker solidarity would remain in the forefront.[27]

The Knights' organizational concepts were apparently carried into the West largely by migrating coal miners—probably out of Pennsylvania's mining districts, from which "twenty-five persons, principally of the mining classes," left for the West on April 3, 1877, the vanguard of an exodus spurred on by wage cuts and spreading unemployment. Numerous groups were reported leaving for the West from the Lackawanna and Wyoming valleys of Pennsylvania that year. Three decades later, a militant WFM leader in Nevada revealed these origins as he was questioned on his introduction to unionism:

Q. When did you come West?
A. I came West twenty-one years ago.
Q. Were you a member of the Knights of Labor in the West, or in Pennsylvania?
A. Pennsylvania.

Others came West through railroad jobs, and it was later concluded that the Knights of Labor "made their way in Utah mainly through the railroad organizations," principally in the early 1880s.[28]

Hard-rock miners were apparently first organized into the Knights of Labor in January, 1879, in Leadville, Colorado. They were preceded in Colorado only by the coal miners of Erie, who formed the state's first Knights of Labor assembly in August, 1878. This was only two years after the organization had expanded from a Philadelphia-Pittsburgh axis into a national grouping. In September, 1879, the Knights named Colorado organizers in Denver, Ft. Collins, and Trinidad; and then on November 22, 1879, Michael Mooney of Leadville was commissioned as an organizer. In the following months, much organizing activity was reported in Colorado coal camps, but hard-rock organizing was apparently limited to Leadville, then undergoing a boom. The only Knights of Labor efforts officially noted in other Western states in 1879–1881 were in San Francisco and in Cheyenne, Wyoming.[29]

Michael Mooney's rise in the Knights' Local Assembly 1005 in Leadville (the "Miners' Cooperative Union") was early evidence of the leadership qualities of this remarkable miner. Information on Mooney's background is scanty, but he stated at one point that he had come to Leadville two years earlier, and he showed some familiarity with Pennsylvania events of the 1870s (although this could have been gained through reading the newspapers). He was frequently accused of being a "Molly Maguire," the reputed death squad of the Pennsylvania coal fields. It is quite possible that he came from Pennsylvania in the exodus of 1877–1878, carrying the Knights' spirit and organizational ideas with him. Whatever his background, when Mooney became a leader in Leadville he possessed, according to one observer, "an almost magical influence over his supporters." He also showed a keen understanding of how to organize a strike.[30]

Trouble between miners and management at the Little Chief Mine began early. Discord was reported in January, 1879, the month the Knights first organized in Leadville, and it is probable the two events were linked. Apparently this involved a company attempt to blame miners for some property destruction, but thirty miners meeting in the Leadville Miners Hall denounced the accusation against them as a "damnable falsehood" and said "drunken men" had caused the damage. Sometime in this period—the records are vague—the union struck the Little Chief, threatening to "shoot any man who went to work for the mine unless the whole of the old crew was put back," according to a letter from the manager to the mine owners. The strike apparently lasted a week, although the manager said nearly forty days of hoisting were lost before the sight of "cold lead" cowed the union.[31]

Other incidents marked the rise of union power in Leadville. In December, 1879, some two hundred miners met on Carbonate Hill to discuss the eight-hour day and formation of a new organization. Two months later, the men in the Chrysolite Mine launched a brief strike, ultimately convincing the company to drop its new policy of deducting doctors' fees from the employees' wages. These events occurred against a backdrop of unrelenting hoopla over the district's mineral riches; in this mine promoter's paradise, the Robert E. Lee Mine became "beyond doubt, . . . the richest mine in the world." Similar praise was showered upon other mines.[32]

The spark that set off the Leadville strike of 1880 came on May 26 in the Chrysolite Mine. It involved several issues, the chief of which were apparently new restrictions on smoking and conversation during working hours, attempts to get more work from the men in the same amount of time, and rumors of an impending wage cut. Shift bosses reportedly refused to enforce the orders, then unloaded their feelings to the miners, and quit. The miners promptly went on strike, demanding the right to smoke and talk underground, plus reinstatement of their shift bosses.

Michael Mooney worked for the Little Pittsburg, but soon joined the Chrysolite strikers and was instrumental in converting the strike into something more than unhappiness over the superintendent's orders. The next day—May 27—the strikers marched and passed resolutions calling for a $4 minimum for all miners (a $1 increase for most), eight hours of work "top and bottom," a ban on strikebreakers, and a pledge to protect members against anti-union discrimination. Two mines that had already been paying $4 "as a precautionary measure" were left open, but others in the Leadville district closed.

With a "small army" on hand to protect the growing numbers of strikebreakers, the strike soon was marred by fighting and intimidation, a situation made to order for unified mine owners confronting a faction-ridden union. State troops arrived at the instigation of the Citizens' Executive Committee of One Hundred, and the remnants of the union eventually voted to accept the pre-strike rate of $4 to $3.50 for eight, nine, or ten hours a day.

Later writers have questioned whether this strike was really launched by miners to improve working conditions. The Leadville strike was "organized rather by certain mine managers than by the miners themselves," according to the editor of the Leadville *Herald*. It was "a sad hoax," according to Richard Lingenfelter, who argues that the strike was triggered to cover up inadequacies in the Chrysolite's supposedly rich veins, enabling major owners to unload their shares before the news got out.[33]

If the miners of Leadville had had a previous record of weakness, lack of militancy, and immunity to organization, a conspiracy view of the 1880 strike would be believable. But such is not the case. On several occasions within previous months—as noted above—the miners had organized and taken forceful action to protect themselves. They had their own Knights of Labor assembly, and their leader—alleged by one local editor to have launched the strike at the behest of mine managers—was a Knights organizer for months before the strike. Such prior developments point to a conclusion that it was a legitimate strike in its basic causes. In Duane Smith's words, it was "apparently unpremeditated." But it is probable also that the Chrysolite group sought to use the strike to its own advantage once it had begun, a pattern not limited to Leadville in 1880.[34]

The Knights of Labor continued to spread through Colorado's hard-rock mining districts—Aspen, Lake City, Eagle, Breckinridge—until the order's membership in the state climbed to 2,736 in 1892, including several coal miners' assemblies. When Cornish and Irish miners rallied in Gilpin County in 1888 to oppose Italians (whom they mistakenly believed to be working as cheap labor), their leader unsuccessfully urged them to join the Knights of Labor, for they would then have 700,000 men back of them in any emergency. The Colorado Bureau of Labor Statistics reported that year that "pretty nearly all" of the local miners' unions in the mountains "have been absorbed by the 'Knights of Labor'. . . ."[35]

The organization spread into Utah, Montana, and Idaho as well. The Loyal League of Park City, a miners' assembly of the Knights in Utah, sought unsuccessfully in 1886–1887 to stop employers from hiring Mormons and Chinese. The Knights began to fade in Utah in the late 1880s, however, pressured by the Mormon Church as well as national trends; and many of the urban skilled tradesmen there began organizing along narrow craft lines, dropping the Knights' philosophy of industrial unionism. Miners in Granite, Montana, however, maintained a Knights assembly for several years starting in 1886; while in Idaho, the Coeur d'Alenes miners organized as late as 1893 as Local Assembly 2462 of the Knights of Labor.[36]

Although it was fading around the nation, the Knights of Labor obviously was still relevant in the mining West. Reports from the Coeur d'Alenes and Montana in the 1890s show the organization not only continuing to grow but also aligning at times with the new Populist movement. Testimony is abundant regarding the influence of the Knights upon men who moved on to other organizations. A Western Federation of Miners member claimed in 1903 that there were "thousands of old-line K. of L.'s in the W. F. of M. . . ." Big Bill Haywood learned about unionism initially from an old miner who was a Knights of Labor member at Haywood's first mining job in Nevada. Haywood never had an opportunity to join, but recalled that from then on, "I was a member in the making." Another radical WFM leader, Ed Boyce, president from 1897 to

1903, spoke proudly of his earlier membership in the Knights; and his successor as president, Charles Moyer, praised these forerunners also. The WFM, said Moyer, "were not the pioneers, for before your organization was even thought of, the Knights of Labor, an industrial organization and the grandest ever launched on the economic field, was fighting the battle for a united working class."[37]

The WFM's inheritance of the philosophy of labor unity from the Knights of Labor was nowhere demonstrated more clearly than in the acceptance of foreigners by the hard-rock miners' unions, as noted in Chapter 2. Only one union encountered in Western records sought to exclude Europeans: a short-lived group in Eureka, Nevada, in 1879, known as the "American Labor Union." As one historian notes, this effort was doomed from the start: "Since there were so many immigrants in the mining camps, this association did not gain much support." With this exception, hard-rock miners' unions were closely identified with European immigrants—ranging from the Irish native Ed Boyce, president of the WFM, to three Cornishmen who were officials of the Butte union at its inception, to "a lot of Italians," presumably union members, who chased strikebreakers away during the 1901 miners' strike in the Coeur d'Alenes.[38]

This welcome to Europeans was intertwined with a philosophy of broad industrial unionism—open to all—which became more firmly implanted as it was carried throughout the West by the hard-traveling miners. Once started, this heterogeneity provided a pool of organizing talent useful in recruiting still more immigrants. This contrasted sharply with the Eastern experience where, as a recent study concluded, the lack of immigrant backing for unions "was largely the A. F. of L.'s own fault, for it refused to admit the flood of foreigners. . . ." Some writers—then and now—have wrongly assumed that the hard-rock miners' unions of the West were made up predominantly of native-born Americans, a conclusion that perhaps stems from the fact that most WFM leaders were American-born. But rather than being "the most purely American of trade unions," as a 1908 article stated and a 1973 study repeated, the WFM was an ethnic hodgepodge. And so it was predictable that the miners' unions in Butte, Leadville, and most other camps of the mining West drew no lines against Europeans; the closest the Butte union came, in fact, was in Cornish-Irish wrangling for leadership.[39]

The pressures which drove these diverse nationalities into miners' unions became more threatening with the economic depression of the early 1890s and the deepening silver crisis —which saw the silver price tumble to sixty-two cents an ounce, half earlier levels. When miners in the Candelaria area of Nevada refused to accept a sliding wage scale based on the price of silver (a system which suddenly gained popularity among mine owners), the Mount Diablo and Holmes Mines closed; and by January, 1892, it was reported, "there are how no miners working in the camp." Layoffs in the Wood River and Coeur d'Alenes districts of Idaho were under way by the end of 1892, and the mines and smelters began to shut down by mid-summer 1893 in Bingham Canyon and the Tintic districts of Utah. David H. Moffatt, Colorado's major mine owner, set the tone when he called his mine managers into Denver and told the press: "Seventy-seven cents for silver mined by men who are paid $3 a day means a loss to the mine owner." Moffatt proposed a wage reduction to $2 a day until silver prices increased, and warned: "If they do not accept such a proposition, I shall be compelled to shut down all my property."

By the end of August, 1893, a Colorado survey showed 435 mines closed, with 45,084 persons unemployed in the state and 22,492 others listed as having left. Six banks failed in Denver on July 18, and three more the next day; while across the state, others were beginning to close their doors also—Ouray, Leadville, Golden, Florence, Aspen, Crested Butte, Greeley. Travelers in the mountains at the end of the summer encountered groups of unemployed miners on "extended picnics," living in groups of twenty or thirty families, surviving by hunting and fishing. In Butte, the major remaining silver mines closed in the summer of 1893, and the prevailing mood made the community receptive to the demands of Coxey's Army. Some 500 of the unemployed left the city in 1894 to join the march on Washington.[40]

Hard-rock miners responded in two major ways to the double blows of the silver price decline and the economic depression of the early 1890s. First—as will be discussed in Chapters 7 and 8—they threw their weight into political battles, initially through the Populist free silver movement. While Populism is usually identified with farmers, in the mining regions it became a working-class creed as well, which often went far beyond monetary arguments. The Idaho People's Party, for example, passed resolutions in 1892 which attacked federal support for mine owners in the Coeur d'Alenes strike, while extending "our hearty sympathy to the Miners' Union in their unequal struggle." The Idaho platform also attacked Pinkerton spies—who by then were being hired to report on hard-rock miners' unions—and called for "the suppression of Chinese immigration," a Western miners' concern that excited little interest elsewhere. In Montana, as Melvyn Dubofsky has shown, miners' union policies and editorials in union newspapers were often indistinguishable from Populist outpourings.[41]

The second major response by hard-rock miners was to fight vigorously against attempts to lower their wages. It is true, of course, that in some cases they meekly agreed to a wage reduction as smelters and mines closed around them throughout the summer of 1893.[42] But in many other areas, the silver price drop and resulting wage reductions of the nineties provoked a determined union response that led to bloody labor-management confrontations. Only the Comstock and Butte, among major camps, held on to former wage scales without a violent strike, and Butte was not a silver district. The Comstock unions received a plea in July, 1893, from the district's mining companies for a reduction from $4 to $3 per day, "in view of the low price of silver," the difficulty in collecting assessments, and troubles in obtaining bank overdrafts. After a series of contradictory votes, the Virginia City and Gold Hill unions balloted jointly and killed the plan, with 229 voting for $4 and 187 voting for a compromise at $3.50. By 1898, it could therefore still be reported that the Comstock daily wage was the same as "a generation ago"—but the district was then in decline, and companies were reported to be less dependent on outside stockholders.[43]

Peaceful solutions were not possible, however, in the Coeur d'Alenes, Cripple Creek, and Leadville. These districts provided the mining West and American labor history with three of their most violent episodes, leaving a "heritage of conflict" in the process. Since each has been extensively treated elsewhere, no effort will be made here to examine them in detail; only an outline of major developments and their impact upon the broader union movement will be discussed.

The Coeur d'Alenes dispute grew out of earlier events as well as the economic crisis of the 'nineties. A local union had been formed in opposition to a wage cut in 1887, followed by creation of a district union in 1890. The following year, employers responded by organizing the Mine Owners' Protective Association, which successfully stood up to a strike against use of non-union miners in the Tiger Mine at Burke. Polarization was well advanced in the Coeur d'Alenes by then. The union was attacking non-union workmen—riding a pair of them out of Wardner on a rail after they had offered to work for $2 a day—while the employers were publicly criticizing the union campaigns. The manager of the Helena and Frisco typified the change: "The greatest thing we have to contend with now," he asserted, "is the miners' union!"

The ostensible reason for the conflict in 1891–1892, however, was the union's demand that the Bunker Hill & Sullivan cease collecting $1 per month from each employee for medical services, and instead earmark this for the new miners' union hospital at Wallace. The resulting strike ended with a compromise, but the major mines suddenly closed with the claim that railroad rates were too high. Within two months, however, the Bunker Hill superintendent revealed the real cause for the shutdown: the owners "cannot afford to operate their mines with wages so high and silver so low as at present." The railroad issue was, in fact, soon resolved.[44]

The union pushed ahead on its demands of $3.50 for all underground workmen—conceded by most mines earlier— and the employment of union men exclusively. These demands were based at least in part upon the use of new drilling and hoisting machines, which were beginning to displace single- and double-jack men and demote them to lower-paid jobs as trammers or muckers. One Coeur d'Alenes resident reported that "when the miners saw this immense boa constrictor approaching in the shape of machines, they wisely took in their fellow laborers and demanded $3.50 a day for all underground men."[45]

Antagonism increased sharply in March, 1892, when the mine owners announced that they would reopen their properties—but only at the old wages of $3.50 for miners and $3 for carmen and shovelers. Strikebreakers soon began to appear in the Coeur d'Alenes, adding to the union's antagonism. During a fight between union members and some guards and strikebreakers at the Frisco Mine on July 11, powder was sent into the mine, wrecking a tramway and old mill. Martial law was declared as the fighting spread, union men were rounded up and held in a bullpen, and military control was instituted for four months. The union was defeated but not crushed.[46]

In 1899, the union again took on the Bunker Hill & Sullivan, because it continued to refuse employment to union men while retaining the split $3.50–$3 scale rejected by other local mines. The management view—as revealed later by the Bunker Hill superintendent—was that the fight "really was for Union control of the district," although it was admitted that wages were "perhaps too low," considering the general prosperity then.[47]

Violence returned to the Coeur d'Alenes on April 28, 1899, when miners converged upon Wardner. Their demonstration was opposed by Bunker Hill guards, and the miners responded by blasting the company mill to smithereens with several hundred pounds of dynamite. This brought in federal troops, inauguration by the employers of a "permit system" that screened out union men, and a general attitude on both sides of "no compromise." To the union newspaper, the Bunker Hill destruction marked "the close of a seven years' war" with the company; the explosion, it said, came from "the spirit of labor driven to desperation and revenge by the disdainful, defiant, contemptuous attitude" of the mine management. In this way the polarization of labor-management relations led to the devastation of the miners' union movement in the Coeur d'Alenes.[48]

Cripple Creek's gold mines drew men in droves after the silver panic of 1893. Unionization was stimulated by the organization efforts of a Scottish immigrant named John Calderwood, as well as by the attempt of several major mines to cut wages or increase the hours of labor. The strike resulting from these company efforts eventually brought a union victory—a victory stemming from the union's total dominance of the district (including elected civil officials) and the presence of Populist Davis Waite in the governor's chair. After the strike for the $3 eight-hour day was launched in February, non-union miners were driven away and deputy sheriffs were arrested by the union. For self-protection, mining company officials brought in outsiders, financing much of the county's law enforcement activities themselves. Mine owner Eben Smith later recalled in a note to another employer that "during the late war at Cripple Creek, you and I bought 100 rifles and ten thousand rounds of ammunition. . . ." Pinkerton detectives were also brought in by the company men. Nursing his wounds at the end of the troubles, Smith confided to a friend that "the only consolation we have is that we hope to elect a decent man as our next governor. . . ." Pressured by Governor Waite to accept the union's demands for the $3 eight-hour day, Cripple Creek mine owners began to prepare for the next conflict (to be discussed in Chapter 8).[49]

At Leadville in 1896, the miners' union demanded a flat $3 per day for all miners. But it was an inauspicious moment for such a campaign, for the economy had not yet fully recovered. One mine owner claimed that if the union struck, "we will have to close all of our properties, as we have not made a dollar in two years." There were other factors which, if known, might have dissuaded the union. Miners were probably not aware that their union was infiltrated with company informers. Further, the legislature later discovered that all companies operating in Leadville were part of an ironbound agreement forcing each to follow majority rule. The union would be unable to play one employer against another, Butte-style.[50]

After the union rejected an arbitration plan featuring a sliding wage scale pegged to silver-lead prices, the companies began importing strikebreakers, mostly from Missouri. The union ordered a hundred rifles and ten or fifteen revolvers, plus ammunition.[51]

Attacks on non-union workers increased as the conflict deepened, and on September 21, 1896, dynamite was thrown into the Coronado Mine and the union attacked the Emmet property. Both mines had been using non-union workers. Three union members and a fireman were killed during the Emmet attack, and troops were soon called in to crush the strike.

"No Union Men Need Apply" became the open motto of the mining firms. The law-and-order argument now shifted completely to their side, bringing with it the open support by government. Systematic attempts to weed out union men began, and by February, 1897, the strike was over and most union members had left Leadville or accepted employment on company terms.[52]

These disputes in the Coeur d'Alenes, Cripple Creek, and Leadville formed the crucible in which the Western Federation of Miners was formed. The Coeur d'Alenes strike of 1892, of course, was the immediate forerunner of these events: Ed Boyce had been incarcerated in the infamous bullpen there; and according to one version, he and thirteen others who were taken to prison in Boise discussed forming a Western miners organization upon the suggestion of their attorney, James Hawley. Immediately after their release, they went to Butte to confer with leaders of the local union there. On May 15, 1893, delegates from across the West met in Butte and formed the Western Federation of Miners.[53]

Taking root in such a strife-torn environment, many activities of the WFM during the next two decades had a certain degree of predictability, as Melvyn Dubofsky has shown. The federation's constitution of 1893 attacked Pinkerton detectives, and called for pay "compatible with the dangers of our employment," in legal money and not tied to use in a company store. Mine safety laws were urged, and also the employment of union over non-union men. Initially, however, the WFM vowed to make an effort for "friendly relations" with employers through the use of arbitration and conciliation to settle disputes.[54]

The WFM's growth was rapid but sporadic. Butte remained the union's nucleus and main financial support, although the sharp increase in Colorado membership eventually helped justify transferring the organization's major offices there. By 1896, it was reported that "nearly every mining camp in Colorado has a branch of the Western Federation," and one estimate was that at least half of Colorado's miners belonged to the WFM at the end of the decade.[55]

The dispersed union movement that the WFM brought together had grown over the preceding three decades primarily to protect wages. This was the central theme for the Central City and Comstock beginnings in 1863, for Butte's first union, as well as for the first unions in Leadville, the Coeur d'Alenes, Cripple Creek, and scores of smaller camps. In this sense, it was a conservative, protective movement, even though broader changes were sometimes pushed, such as the flat rate for all workmen and the closed shop to prevent hiring cheap labor.

The attention paid here to strikes should not leave the impression that more peaceful methods were jettisoned by Western miners en route to their goals. Violence remained the exception. Often union power was so great that it could virtually dictate a decision, as in 1890 at Granite, Montana, where the Bi-Metallic manager received orders from company officials to obey the union's demand that only its members be hired, because "the Miners Union is already really in possession of the Camp. . . ." The Butte union, in a similar attempt, sought to ban the entry into the district of any miner lacking a proper withdrawal card issued by another WFM local.[56]

Other approaches to protect the miners' wages were tried. In Virginia City, the miners' union conducted a "trial" of member Thomas Chappel, who admitted to having worked for $2.50 a day plus an interest in the mine, rather than $4 as decreed by the union. When the Clancy, Montana, Miners' Union was formed as part of the WFM in 1894, it sought to enlist all miners within its ranks and voted that "all underground work" was to be paid $3.50 for ten hours. Committees were sent throughout Clancy and Lump Gulch to learn whether the scale was being followed:

Nov. 10, 1894—Motion made and carried that a committee of three be appointed to wait on Mr. Bell and ascertain if or not he will pay the scale of wages adopted by this union.

Nov. 17, 1894—Carried that an ad be inserted in the Helena Daily Independent for two weeks, warning miners not to go to work at Bell's mine for less than $3.50.

Carried that the men at Bell's mine be notified not to work for less than $3.50 and secretary be instructed to post up a few notices around Clancy in regards to Bell mine.

Dec. 1, 1894—The report of the Committee to wait on Mr. Bell, accepted with applause.[57]

Nonmembers were regarded as a continuing threat to the young Clancy union, as to all miners' unions. In its second month, the union sent a committee to "wait on the miners at Little Nell" and give them "10 days' notice to join the Union." Other committees had more specific orders: "Moved and carried that committee instruct Dan Ruddy to join our Union next Saturday." Mine owners were told to either have all employees at a union meeting or fire the crew, and at one point the exasperated union sent a committee to tell three men at the Little Alma Mine to come to the next union meeting or the committee would "go up there and bring them down."[58]

Actions such as these were more typical than the massive, bloody strikes in Cripple Creek and elsewhere. And they pointed to the fact that miners' unions were rapidly emerging as new centers of political and economic power across the West. This was apparent when John A. Finch, high-ranking official of two Coeur d'Alenes mines, was questioned regarding his charge that the union was setting hours and wages on its own:

Q. Prior to the formation of the union, how were the wages fixed; by the employer or the miners?
A. By the employer. The employer fixed the wages before that time.

Is it not probable, the questioner continued, that the union's new wage actions "arose from the fact that the employer fixed [wages] without consulting them prior to the formation of the union?" "Perhaps that is true," Finch answered.[59]

Much of the transformation of Western mining was summed up in this brief interchange. For above all else, the union movement signified an attempt to share economic power. Some of this change began to be noted in state legislatures and the courts, but much of it came in the undramatic day-to-day relations between hard-rock miners and their employers. Not surprisingly, tensions were often volatile in such a changed setting, and after 1900 the violent conflicts would nearly dwarf the episodes of the 'nineties. But many cases would be handled far short of such extremes.

CHAPTER VII

Responses to the Dangers Below

There was wide awareness across the mining West of the tragic accuracy of Dan Dequille's observation that "Death stalks through the dark chambers of the mines in a thousand shapes." Whether in the passing of a funeral cortege, newspaper accounts of underground accidents, the lowering of a company flag to half-mast, or hospital reports of men with arms blown off, ankles mashed, or pieces of rock in their eyes, residents of the metal-mining districts lived with the constant presence of death and suffering underground.[1]

The impact of miners' funerals was especially profound, not alone for their frequency but also their poignancy: they were removing from life the young, muscular men who hours before were vigorous residents of the community. No cold, emotionless reading of the ritual sufficed for a miner's funeral; more typical was the procession that filed to the Fairview Miners' Union Cemetery in Idaho, one Sunday afternoon in late July, 1874. The three hundred miners sang solemn funeral dirges as they marched with the casket of 21-year-old William Pascoe, a Cornishman who had fallen 600 feet to his death in a shaft, the previous day. Services "of a very appropriate and impressive character" were conducted by a fellow Cornish miner. The event "was of the most solemn description," the local newspaper reported, "and will not soon be forgotten by those who witnessed it."[2]

175

20. The miners' funeral remained a constant part of the mining West despite rapid changes in methods and machinery underground. Fourteen victims of the Sleepy Hollow Mine disaster were bidden farewell in this Central City, Colorado, funeral in 1895.
Denver Public Library, Western History Collection photo

These were community events, leaving a lasting imprint upon the memories of those who lived in the mining camps that dotted the mountains and deserts. "They would walk out to the cemetery. We all go," recalled an Italian widow whose husband once mined in Telluride. Bill Haywood attended a funeral in Telluride also, after twenty-four men were killed in a mine fire. He estimated that there were "about three thousand men in line" in the march to the cemetery, each carrying a sprig of evergreen to place in the open grave.[3]

But funerals end quickly. Remaining when the crowd returned home from the cemetery, and stretching into what seemed to many to be an infinity, was the survivors' struggle for existence. For the attention that mining companies, politicians, and the community at large devoted to a miner's passing did not carry over into providing for those who had depended on him in life. This applied not only to widows and children left helpless by fatal accidents underground, but also to the men crippled but not killed by cave-ins or explosions, or the muckers bent double with "miner's con," or the miners left without arms or legs by cage mishaps. Efforts to alleviate their condition and prevent further accidents will be examined in this chapter.

Company aid for victims and family survivors was generally inadequate. Most company-connected assistance came through one of three major routes: outright donations; medical care financed through required monthly wage deductions; and funds from insurance policies after premiums were paid, also by compulsory deductions from wages. Occasionally a watchman's job or similar position would be given to a disabled miner, and sometimes other employees were invited to help support the victim, too. A Comstock Lode foreman wrote of receiving "Orders from Supt. P. Kervin" to take up "a collection of $1.00 from all the men to send to Pat Ward's family who are in destitute circumstances." The inadequacies of this approach were apparent in the totals collected: $26 from men in two major Comstock mines, plus $10 from the superintendent. That company aid was neither extensive nor common is apparent from the dearth of comments on it and the paucity of such donations in company ledgers. A miner in Colorado's Clear Creek district probably summed up the majority view of injured workmen: "I never heard of them receiving assistance from employers."[4]

Compulsory deductions for hospital care often drew criticisms also. Their obligatory nature rankled, and the quality of care frequently failed to meet needs or expectations. A Colorado miner voiced the common complaint: "Nearly all companies deduct a dollar a month from each man's pay for doctor's services. It would be better, in well-established mining towns, for miners to have and maintain a hospital."

Compulsory insurance systems were also resented. With premiums of $1 to $1.50 per month deducted from employees (sometimes joined by a company contribution of 50 cents), such plans began to appear in larger mines by the end of the century. Coverage was severely limited, however. Bill Haywood attacked this feature of the insurance plan required of employees involved in the 1903 Colorado City smelter strike. The workmen, he noted, paid compulsory premiums of 3 percent of their wages, plus hospital and physician's payments, but this "only protected a person during working hours, and the fees for medical attention, etc., did not provide hospital and nurses for the employees nor professional attention for his family."[5]

These weaknesses left workers with one realistic alternative: to assist themselves. The brutal truth of this fact emerged —perhaps unintentionally—in 1867, when a Comstock superintendent retired and gave a final speech to his workmen. The Chollar-Potosi employees, Charlton Beckwith said, had always rushed to care for their fellow workers who were injured, and had provided for the victims' families. "Never would these workmen have permitted such neglect as the Trustees of the Ophir manifested toward Dixon, who was killed in the Ophir mine, and whose grave to this day is unmarked by any suitable sign, even of a burial spot. [Cries of 'shame.']" Beckwith added that among Chollar-Potosi workmen, "A man hurt in their mine became their charge, of their own motion." They were noble and gave aid even though their wages were not large, and "'charity' with them necessarily is a direct and heavy tax upon their hard earnings." What Beckwith neglected to mention was that when workmen were forced to provide such financial assistance to injured fellow employees, it demonstrated that companies such as his were not caring for their own men.[6]

Because self-help was the sole realistic alternative, in the decades from 1860 to 1910 hard-rock miners attempted a variety of approaches to care for both their injured fellows and the families left fatherless by mine fatalities. Money was a prime requirement, of course, but in countless cases the miners gave more than money. In the process they often found themselves in conflict once again with the traditional prerogatives of their employers. Along with the rest of the nation—and for the same general reasons—hard-rock miners also turned increasingly to government for aid in preventing mine accidents and ultimately as a source of uniform compensation for victims. Through such activities, the Western miners moved another giant step away from the individualism of the frontier.

The miners' efforts to deal with the causes and results of mine accidents, then, cannot be simply described in terms of man's benevolence to man. Rather, the story is a complex one that includes national trends, the clash of harsh industrial reality with tradition, and an often frustrating search for the most desirable pathway among several alternatives.

Western miners' campaigns placed them within the broad working men's movement that had originated in Europe at least by the early nineteenth century. Mutual aid societies soon appeared in the West, sometimes as separate bodies, frequently as part of local lodges, but increasingly as a function of the hard-rock miners' unions. The unions, in fact, usually turned to these concerns immediately upon their formation.[7]

This was true of the West's first two unions of hard-rock miners, in Central City, Colorado, and the Comstock Lode, both in 1863. The call for the Central City meeting that produced a short-lived union emphasized the "DANGER of working lodes," as well as the need for higher wages, and the miners voted to "provide for those who, either from sickness or accident, are not able to work, their employer having—with only a few honorable exceptions—neglected to do so." Weeks later, the brief initial Comstock organization listed as one of its three objects, "the providing of aid and comfort for [the men] in times of sickness and adversity."[8]

Although the demand for the $4 day received the most publicity in 1866 when the Gold Hill Miners' Union was formed on the Comstock, the new union's first bylaws also provided for $10 weekly payments to victims of sickness or accident,

179

and a funeral payment of $100. This pattern was followed in 1867 when the Virginia City union was born, and it was repeated throughout the mining West for the next five decades, with some exceptions.

Union records reveal that although funerals attracted community attention, enormous amounts of time were spent caring for injured members away from the public view. The Gold Hill union, for example, worried about injured miners who were still working; it sent a committee in 1868 to the Eclipse Mine to "ascertain the cause that Mr. Sheridan was allowed to remain so long in the Mine after his being injured." But most union attention dealt with tangible assistance. Medicine, crutches, transportation to distant hospitals, and nursing care were often provided, and the membership was kept informed of needs through a visiting committee.

The union "visiting committees" deserve special mention, for they played a crucial role as the direct contact between the ailing miner and his union brothers. The Gold Hill union records are instructive. The visiting committee reported at one meeting in 1868 that it found "Mr. Lyons as being very weak but improving very fast," Mr. Fitzpatrick "doing well but not able to work," Mr. Fraser with a sprained ankle, Mr. Duffey "improving very slowly [but he] will not be able to work for some time," and Mr. Collins "not doing very well—the small bone of leg is broken, and he needs attention." But the intangible importance of simply having union brothers stop by was of value also. Word came from one recovered Gold Hill member that "he expressed his gratitude to this Union for their kind consideration and attention," and was returning $10 to the union for its building fund. But another Gold Hill miner, Elisha Hawkins, sent word that "as none of the members nor visiting committee had been to see him during his illness, he felt and thought that he had been neglected." The apologetic committee tried to explain its difficulties in locating him, and a special emissary was sent to soothe Hawkins's feelings. Two other injured members sent word that they "were doing well, and wished no assistance, thanking the Union for their sympathy."[9]

The processes involved in these obligations were extremely time-consuming, if union records bear relation to time actually expended. For example, it took portions of six meetings

for the Clancy union to handle the case of "Brother Sparring."
On February 4, 1896, members learned that the president and
vice president had taken Sparring to the hospital in Helena,
and "funds collected during the week" were used to defray
expenses; the union voted approval. A week later, a bill of
$30 for medicine and doctor's care for Sparring was received
and ordered paid. On February 18, a $22 hospital bill arrived
and was paid by the union, but on February 25 the union was
informed that it had paid $99 on Sparring's "illness," which
was $29 beyond the union maximum of $70 allowed. Sparring
was told to pay back the $29 "as soon as practicable"—reveal-
ing the union's additional function as a lending agency. On
March 3, however, the union received another doctor's bill
covering fifteen visits to Sparring, and the members voted that
it be paid. On March 10, still another communication from
the doctor was reported, reducing his previous bill by $5; this
new bill of $25 was then ordered paid, and the union's six-
week concern with Brother Sparring was over, at least until he
suffered another injury or illness.[10]

Other functions grew out of the union's power in the community. The Silver City union even used its dominance to
regulate doctors' fees: no doctor could charge more than $2.50
for all cases involving married miners and their families, and
this fee included "all medicines required."[11]

The union's position as the major source of aid for the
injured also made it the focus of wrangling over the level of
assistance and even whether benefits should be provided at all.
In the Gold Hill union's second year, it heard a report on the
illness of a Mr. Collins, who owed an attendant $40. Collins
"thought he was entitled to the benefit as long as he was sick
and that he had a right to use the money as he liked." This
set off a debate over whether the money should be earmarked
only for the helper's pay, but in the end the union gave in
and approved "the usual benefit." Two other miners who were
reported "sick" were denied benefits, however: one of them
had not paid dues for nine months, and no record could be
found that the other had ever been in the union. The Silver
City union denied funds to P. T. Donnelly "as benefits cannot
be allowed in chronic cases," and the Gold Hill union demanded that W. H. Lester return money appropriated earlier "as
he was receiving sick benefits when he was not entitled to

them." Apparently Lester resisted, for five weeks later the membership voted that he "be expelled from this Union forever. . . ."[12]

The financial outlay was a heavy burden to miners' unions, as is evident in surviving financial records. For example, for three months ending in September, 1903, the Telluride Miners' Union showed funeral expenses of $498 and sick benefits of $476. In Owyhee County, Idaho, the 150-member De Lamar union paid $4,000 in disability and survivors' benefits from 1896 to 1898, while the nearby 525-member Silver City local paid $6,000 for the same period. From 1890 to 1900, the Granite, Montana, union paid funeral benefits of $4,500 and "sick benefits" of $18,640. Among larger unions, the Virginia City Miners' Union gave out over $400,000 in death and injury payments in its first forty-five years, and the Butte Union claimed $155,000 paid out by the time it marked its twenty-first anniversary in 1899. Butte's one-year totals were enormous; in 1910, for example, it reported sick and injured benefits during the previous year of $64,159, and funeral payments of $14,130. For Western Federation of Miners locals as a whole, the one-year totals for 1910 were $146,532.18 for sick and injured payments and $34,497.40 in funeral payments.[13]

The totals were impressive, but not in a manner to be boasted of by the local chamber of commerce. For the drain on union treasuries provides a grim measure of the enormous toll taken by mine accidents; it also makes understandable the continuing efforts by unions to crack down on unjustified claims. Hard times in the Depression of the early 'nineties even reduced the Gold Hill Miners' Union to dropping benefits entirely, and one ailing member had to be informed "that no sick benefits [have] been paid for some time & [we] don't know when they will."[14]

Several unions, usually those most pressed by large-scale disasters, set up their own hospitals. This was the response by miners' unions in Telluride, Colorado, and Tonopah, Nevada, after each lost many members in 1901 and 1902. The Smuggler Union fire on November 21, 1901, burned buildings over the mine tunnel and injured dozens, killing twenty-four members of the Telluride Miners' Union. Only three months later, the nearby Liberty Bell Mine was swept by three snowslides on one day, killing eighteen men. Almost a tenth of

21. *Wagons with caskets, the union leading the march to the cemetery—these were frequent events in the history of hard-rock mining across the West. This union funeral in Tonopah, Nevada, in 1911 was for fourteen men buried in the Tonopah-Belmont disaster.*

Nevada State Historical Society photo

the Telluride union's members were lost in these two disasters. In Tonopah, an epidemic (the disease is not identified in union reports) carried away twenty union members; a newspaper reported that the others "cared for the sick, and administered to the dying, and gave financial assistance to the widows and orphans." Miners' union hospitals soon appeared in both Telluride and Tonopah, the former spending $30,000, helped by a $3,000 loan from the WFM. Other miners' unions built their own hospitals in Park City, Utah; Silver City and Wallace (Coeur d'Alenes), Idaho; Ymir and Sandon, British Columbia; Goldfield, Nevada; and Judith Mountain, Montana.[15]

Unions also took the lead in the sporadic attempts to provide a separate home, hospital, or asylum exclusively for disabled and injured miners. Grass Valley, California, was apparently the scene of the first effort, launched in 1871 with a lottery to provide funds. It "evoked a feeble response," ac-

183

22. *Just as miners' unions were conspicuous in caring for injured members, they also devoted much time and money to laying to rest the remains of deceased fellow workers. Funerals were usually conducted by unions, as in this Tonopah procession in 1911. One hundred dollars was the common union provision for widows.*

Nevada State Historical Society photo

cording to one writer. Within ten years, however, the California Legislature voted to erect "a public hospital and asylum for the reception, care, medical and surgical treatment and relief of the sick, injured, disabled, and aged miners. . . ." But no appropriations were made to allow further work, despite occasional goading editorials.[16]

In the early 1890s, the idea met renewed interest, however, when the printers' unions began work on a national
home in Colorado Springs, Colorado, for the aged and disabled
members of their crafts. The Cigarmakers' Union sent a committee to investigate the possibilities of constructing a similar
establishment in the state; and in 1891, the Colorado Legislature asked the U.S. Congress to donate the abandoned Fort
Crawford military reservation in Montrose County for a home
for disabled miners. But this effort came to naught.[17]

A new wave of enthusiasm for the plan began in 1896. At
the Western Federation of Miners' convention that year, delegates voted unanimously that "the time has arrived when the
combined efforts of the miners of the West can do something
for the alleviation of the sufferings of our unfortunate brothers." To build the proposed home, union donations and private contributions were to be solicited, and matching amounts
sought from Congress and Western state legislatures. "Old
age, permanent injuries of any kind, incurable diseases, or the
dreaded miners' consumption" were to be sufficient to admit
"any miner" to the WFM's home.[18]

With this spark, interest in the idea appeared elsewhere.
Two hundred and fifty Owyhee County voters sent a petition
calling on the state to erect a home for "the old and broken-
down mining prospectors" of Idaho. No further action occurred, however. Across the border in Utah, the legislature
approved a measure to create a "Branch of the State Miners'
Hospital" in Park City, upon donation of $5,000 and a suitable
site. Funds eventually were provided by Mrs. Mary Judge of
Salt Lake City, in memory of her deceased husband who had
grown wealthy in mining. Soon, Congress was petitioned for
twenty acres of land from the Fort Douglas Military Reservation in Salt Lake County. The U.S. Senate approved the land
grant, but no action was taken in the House and the measure
died.[19]

The WFM's drive also met with little long-term enthusiasm. A target of $50,000 was set, and Carson City or Virginia
City, Nevada, were proposed as sites, but the call for aid from
member locals prompted an uneven response. The Gold Hill
Miners' Union discussed the call for funds in 1896, then voted
"that it be postponed indefinitely." The Silver City, Idaho,
local, on the other hand, began paying a yearly assessment of

$1 per member for the home in 1898. The WFM Executive Board admitted in 1900 that "some unions did not allow their share of the miners' home fund to remain in the treasury," and so the assessments were being returned to those unions "that acted so generously. . . ." When the Tuolumne, California, Miners Union urged the 1902 WFM Convention to "create a miners' home," the convention's Organization Committee voted against the proposal and the majority of delegates agreed. The plan surfaced again briefly among Anti-Trust Democrats in Butte the following fall, but other approaches to assisting disabled miners were in the air by then. It was clear that, as a solution for caring for lode mining's victims, the miners' home was an idea whose time had not come.[20]

Paralleling these campaigns to take care of victims and survivors was a slowly spreading movement to reduce accidents by improving mine safety. Some efforts were carried on by unions alone, and it appears probable that the sudden popularity of the "safety cage"—protected by an iron "bonnet" on top, with devices attached to stop the cage quickly if a rope or cable should break—was encouraged by unions in the 1860s and 1870s. Other types of attention were also given to the problem. In 1895, the Clancy Miners Union corresponded with the Montana mine inspector regarding the "condition of Bell Head mine." After the turn of the century, the WFM sought to impose a uniform bell signal system on the West, petitioned for federal investigation into mine safety in the Treadwell mines in Alaska, and publicly scolded its locals through the *Miners' Magazine* for neglect of their members' safety and health. Possibly goaded by this scolding, the WFM local in Sutter Creek, California, went on strike in 1903 after men were fired for refusing to ride a cage held up by a damaged rope.[21]

Unions were conspicuous also in their support for legislation to reduce the accident toll. As elsewhere, this trend made slow headway in the West throughout most of the Gilded Age, picked up speed in the late 'eighties, and gained prominence as a major part of miners' activities by the century's end. European (especially British) precedents and recent enactments by such Eastern mining states as Pennsylvania paved the way for Western legislatures to enter the field.[22]

Somewhat hesitantly, as befits a newcomer in a strange

land, mine safety legislation began to appear in the mining West. In 1872, California required mines deeper than 300 feet to provide a second exit; in 1877, the first Colorado Constitution gave the General Assembly broad powers over ventilation, escape shafts, and other health and safety measures for underground miners; and two years later, Nevada required mines deeper than 450 feet to be equipped with iron-bonneted safety cages. These were the tentative beginnings of Western mine safety legislation; they were also the first fruits of a new philosophy that sought government assistance for labor's dealings with employers.[23]

Few changes were more fundamental in this trend than the creation of the post of state mine inspector. Appearing in hard-rock mining states from the late 1880s on, this early, broadly conceived position was born in the realization that mine safety needed an outsider as overseer. Anguish over the lack of such an inspector was evident by then among many hard-rock miners. "Quartz mines should have inspectors as well as coal mines," a miner from Ouray County wrote to the Colorado Bureau of Labor Statistics before the legislature had acted. "In fact," he added, "they need them more, as more men are employed in this branch." Others voiced similar requests. "Please send down a mine inspector. In silver mines there are none," pleaded a Pitkin County miner. A Clear Creek miner claimed that most mines were "too dangerous for men to enter"; and a San Juan miner urged the appointment of an inspector who would force companies to erect buildings safe from the district's snowslides, "which throw several out of work and many to eternity."[24]

Encouraged by such mining sentiment, supporters of the inspection plan launched their Colorado legislative campaign in 1887. They could build upon an 1877 state law creating a coal mine inspection system, which apparently passed with little difficulty because of the Pennsylvania precedent in 1870 and the weak position of coal mine owners in state politics. Frustrations developed early in the metal mine inspection fight, however. The 1887 bill was amended extensively, then indefinitely postponed by the Senate mining committee, then defeated 22–21 in the House. During the 1889 legislative session, miners in Leadville, Garfield County, and other districts actively supported the bill; Leadville's workmen even dispatched two men to Denver "to insist on the passage of the mine inspection bill." The success of the bill in the Colorado Legislature that year did not ensure a successful system, however; for in 1892 it was reported that the office had been inoperative for two years, since the 1891 legislature had made no appropriations for it.[25]

The legislative halls of Montana also became a battleground over the issue in 1889. Employers there—as in Colorado and elsewhere across the region—feared the system because of government intervention in a hitherto sacred sphere, with untold possibilities for adding to mine owners' expenses. The employers' chief spokesman claimed that "if there was water in a mine, the inspector could demand that it be pumped out for the simple reason that he might go and take a look at the mine. . . ." The opposition even scored an initial victory—later overturned—in requiring miners' signatures to appear on the safety complaint given to their employer. Mine owners descending on Helena for the debate claimed the system gave "too much liberty and authority" to the inspector.

But the bill survived its first Montana test. Perhaps this was because the majority Democrats had urged it in their election platform; perhaps it was because of continuing underground tragedies; or perhaps it was because someone noted the contrast between the $2,500 proposed for the inspector's salary and the $20,000 authorized for squirrel bounties.[26]

South Dakota created the office of mine inspector the following year, in 1890, but Idaho's miners ran into a gubernatorial roadblock in their attempts to pass such a bill in 1891. Despite overwhelming legislative support (32–2 in the House, 13–2 in the Senate), the measure was vetoed by Idaho Governor Norman B. Willey. Willey admitted that inspection was needed in coal mines, but contended that "totally different conditions exist" in metal mines. During thirty-three years spent in lode mining, he asserted, "I have not observed any mining accident involving peril to the life or limb that could have been avoided or mitigated in any way by the system of inspection provided in this bill." His conclusion was that the bill "merely aims at a legal extortion of fees from mine owners without any resulting benefit to any one." The system was also attacked by the Wallace *Press*, which charged that the inspectors in neighboring Montana "have a good time annually at the expense of the taxpayers. . . ." The *Press* noted that an attempt was being made to "saddle a similar luxury on the Idaho people, in order to provide a berth for some broken-down politician," and the editor was thankful it had been defeated.

Mine inspection finally made it through the Idaho Legislature and past the governor in 1893.[27] Other Western states followed, their tardiness reflecting mainly the strength of opposition from mine owners. Utah passed a coal mine inspection act in 1896, but efforts to provide metal mine inspection were unavailing for years. One mine official in 1900 termed these proposals "premature," but a Salt Lake City labor journal in 1905 lamented that "conditions in the mines are onerous in the extreme, the Legislature having repeatedly refused to furnish inspectors. . . ." British Columbia—which in labor matters was often closely linked to the Western states—passed a mine inspection bill in 1897. The California legislature approved a similar measure that year also, but the governor killed it with a pocket veto, beginning a long string of defeats for mine inspection there. Wyoming passed a metal mine inspection law in 1903, but its lode-mining operations were tiny compared to those of its Rocky Mountain neighbors. Congress in 1908 provided for inspection of metal mines in Alaska—under Congressional jurisdiction because Alaska was still a territory. The following year, Nevada passed an inspection law, and Arizona created a commission to come up with a measure; the Arizona law was finally passed in 1912 by the first legislature under statehood. As late as 1910, therefore, the *Engineering and Mining Journal* could report that no appropriations were made for metal mine inspection in California, Arizona, New Mexico, and Utah. Mine inspection, without a doubt, had an uneven road to travel through the West.[28]

In actual operation, the system had many shortcomings. Sometimes these stemmed from impotence born of legislative compromise, at other times from financial impoverishment. For years the Montana inspector was limited to merely inspecting mines; if owners "feel disposed to make the changes, they will do so; if not, the Inspector's power ceases. . . ." By 1898, however, the powers of the office had increased enough so that suit was filed against Anaconda for violating a requirement on cage doors; and in 1903, the Legislature ordered that the inspector "shall have access to any mine and all parts thereof," with criminal prosecution for any recalcitrant mine owner.[29]

From the beginning, the Colorado inspector worked under a stronger system than this, for the 1889 law empowered him to "enjoin or restrain the owner, agent, manager, or lessee from working the mine until it is made to conform to the provisions of this act. . . ." Mine operators faced a fine of $50 to $500 for blocking the inspector's visit, and were required to assist him as necessary.

Through the years, the Colorado inspection law was steadily strengthened. In 1895, the methods to use in penalizing an uncompromising mine owner were spelled out further by permitting the inspector to turn to "any court of competent jurisdiction" in going after an unsafe condition. In 1896, Harry A. Lee, Colorado Commissioner of Mines and the man in charge of the inspection system, issued a detailed list of safety recommendations covering everything from candles and tamping bars to sanitation and the need for surveys underground; the recommendations carried the strong implication that they were to be followed. While the broad impact of these orders fell on the shoulders of mine owners, the commissioner did not subscribe to the view that the hard-rock miner was completely innocent. Any worker caught using wrong signals "should be discharged," Lee wrote, and companies should enforce strict safety rules, which should be "as inexorable as in the regular army." Failure to comply, "however trivial" the infraction, should bring "loss of position, without recourse."[30]

State mine inspectors repeatedly attacked the heartless basis of much so-called mine safety, and quickly emerged as the conscience of the West on the subject. Dangerous cage conditions were tolerated, the deputy Montana inspector lamented; and if a fatal accident occurred, a jury would convict company officials—but "this would not restore life, nor bring comfort to the comfortless, nor bread to widows and orphans who had been deprived of their main support." Three years later, the Montana inspector attacked the inadequacies of mine ventilation in the state, and argued that "it seems to me to be a God-given right to all men to breathe pure air." By 1902, the inspector termed the existing mining law "heartless in its terms which applied to a human being," because conviction of a mine

owner for gross negligence could only occur after—not before
—a fatal or near-fatal accident.[31]

Colorado's chief inspector, Harry Lee, argued in his 1896
list of recommendations that most accidents came from the
desire to first "strike it rich and then make safe"—while he
contended these should be reversed. Lee asked in 1900:

> Why are more men killed in mining than in any other industrial
> pursuit of the state? Why does Colorado proportionately lead
> the list of fatal accidents as compared with all other states or
> provinces?

Lee said he felt that almost all unsafe conditions could be eliminated, although this might lower profits. This led him to a
perturbing question: "How far should an industry be permitted
to advance its material welfare at the expense of human life?"
In discussing a specific problem—the dangers of riding in wobbly buckets—Lee said he "still entertains the hope that the
consideration of expense and comfort may not continue to
overbalance the value of human lives."[32]

This was the conscience role of the Western mine inspector. But it had other, less inspiring results, for it helped drive
men who were truly concerned with the plight of hard-rock
miners into despondency. Colorado's Harry Lee was worried
that the use of statistics showing the high rate of mine fatalities was breeding fatalism rather than a recognition that accidents were avoidable.

This frustration overcame the Montana inspector in his
1908 report. He looked back over nearly two decades of metal
mine inspection and concluded that most efforts had "in the
main, proved futile." Furthermore, he had no doubts that the
same would be said someday of his own efforts. He urged
an entirely new look at metal mine safety by a commission
which would specify both duties and responsibilities of miners
and employers.[33]

Not all mine inspectors, however, carried concern for the
safety of hard-rock miners to such a degree. The Idaho inspector's office, in particular, was frequently occupied by men more
interested in promoting the state's mines than in promoting
mine safety. One inspector even praised Idaho's safety conditions by noting that his office had received no legal complaints
on dangerous mines for seven years. This interpretation avoid-

ed an alternate, more embarrassing, and probably more accurate explanation: Idaho miners felt it was useless to complain.[34]

They had some reason not to bother with complaining to their state inspector. From the beginnings of Idaho's mine inspection in 1893 down through the passage of a strong inspection law in 1909, the office was occupied by men who saw their major responsibility as puffing the state's mineral riches. The suspicion began early that the miners' well-being underground was being ignored. Shortly after the first inspector took office, a coroner's jury in the Coeur d'Alenes investigated a cave-in that killed three miners in the Bunker Hill & Sullivan Mine, and asserted:

> We earnestly and emphatically call upon Mine Inspector Haskins to visit these mines immediately and demonstrate that he is willing to enforce the law if there should be any infraction thereof, and that he wears not the collar of any individual or corporation. . . .[35]

Jay A. Czizek was state mine inspector in 1899 when the state's first annual report was published, and he had nothing to say about injuries, health, or mine safety, but much to say about the wonders of Idaho's minerals. A mining journal noted at the time, however, that Czizek was "a large stock holder" in the Mount Clemens & Idaho Company mines near Warren, and this may have colored his outlook. For his second report, covering 1900, Czizek devoted one page to mine safety and nineteen pages to extolling Idaho's mineral riches and justifying a larger appropriation for his office. His approach served as a precedent for later mine inspectors in Idaho.[36]

The possibility of more ominous results from this type of mine "inspection" was raised in letters written by Inspector Martin Jacobs in 1903, found among papers of the Trade Dollar Mining Company of Owyhee County. They reveal that Jacobs solicited financial aid from mining company officials to fight legislative proposals aimed at increasing taxes on mines—which in the Coeur d'Alenes had not exceeded $5 per acre for at least ten years. In the process of defending these companies, Jacobs showed a close relationship with men he was supposedly independent of. "The large mining companies in the North are going to assist some in this matter," he wrote, "and they asked me to take it up with the mining Mgrs of

Southern Idaho." He urged the Trade Dollar manager to contact Owyhee employers and legislators, adding: "There is also,
of course, a question of expense connected with this matter,
which is perfectly legitimate, and if your company and the
others can contribute thereto, we will greatly appreciate it."

Jacobs used the term *we* frequently in discussing the mine
owners' efforts, as when he wrote: "We have the matter in
pretty good shape, and I believe there will be no trouble about
our success if we do not delay on getting our men properly
lined up."

These comments reveal much. But in a hand-written letter,
characterized by poor spelling and grammar—in contrast with
the neatly typed letters usually sent out—Jacobs was even
blunter:

> Now the Northern mine owners, of course, have put ther mon-
> ey a good many thousand, but it has ben used on the five North-
> ern Co or nearly all of it. The Co in the South East are the
> hard ones, as they think a mine owner is mad of money and
> they want to make him pay more than is just in taxes. I have
> things in good shape, but I need sum money as soon as posible
> to get certain people to work. You people do the best you can
> and send it as soon as posible, and I will see that it is put to
> good use.

Trade Dollar officials apparently gave reluctantly if at all to
this project. Jacobs asked them for $500, which he had already
"promised out," but company letters show considerable opposition to committing funds. The tax law that ultimately passed
provided for taxation at the price paid to the federal government for the land, rather than at the level of company profits.
It was a victory for Jacobs and his allies. He also fought to
shorten the statute of limitations for mine accident compensation claims.[37]

Reasons for the contrast between the Idaho inspectors and
those of other states are difficult to uncover with certainty.
One possibility is the earlier domination of much of Idaho mining by large companies, at a time when Montana's mine magnates were still feuding among themselves. A major constitutional difference was that Idaho elected its inspectors, while
in other states they were appointed. Although Idaho's Inspector Robert Bell pointed with pride in 1904 to his re-election

—he contended that "the splendid majority vote" showed his efforts were appreciated—when he stepped down after six years in office he urged that the position be made appointive. His successor was well qualified, he stated, "but his nomination at the last Republican convention was an accident due to a political trade," and good candidates had to "plead for the support of a lot of dickering delegates largely from farming communities. . . ."[38]

The overall results of mine inspection for hard-rock miners are difficult to assess. Examples abound on both sides of the question—inspection was a farce, inspection was worthwhile. The manager of the Bunker Hill & Sullivan called Idaho's system of yearly visits to his mammoth enterprise "rather a perfunctory affair" which accomplished little because, he claimed, economic considerations kept an employer from running an unsafe mine. This may be dismissed as self-serving, but it is clear that the great expectations for mine inspection were frequently frustrated.[39]

In Montana, powerful companies such as Anaconda proved a recurring obstacle to the inspector's work, as when he was neither notified nor allowed to investigate after a fire suffocated two men in early 1898. This came at a time when the inspector was trying unsuccessfully to force Anaconda to abide by a hoisting-cage law, and the county attorney refused to bring suit against the company. The failure to penalize Anaconda, the inspector stressed, came "through no want of endeavor on the part of this department." The Western Federation of Miners noted this case and concluded that "this company has proved to be superior to the law" after two years of efforts by the inspector to bring Anaconda in line. A WFM militant attacked the Montana system in 1907, criticizing the inspectors' salaries, arguing that "they never go down in the mine to see that the place is fixed up," and adding that the governor "will appoint men favorable to the company every time."[40]

Another problem was the impossibility of inspecting all the mines and all areas within every mine. A Colorado workman testified that in ten years as a hard-rock miner—beginning at the time of the state's first mine inspection law—he had seen only one mine inspector. Harry Lee, Colorado's inspector from 1895 through 1903, complained that travel took as much time as investigation for him and his two assistants, and he admitted that "at no time since the establishment of the bureau have its officers been able to take up a camp, district, or county and finish it up systematically."[41]

But human error weakened the inspection system as well. Failings revealed in testimony after the 1904 disaster at the Independence mine in Cripple Creek—in which fifteen men were killed when a cage shot up into a sheave wheel—led one observer to condemn "the wretched manner in which mine inspection is conducted in Colorado," with political appointments singled out for blame. The critic referred to deputy inspector M. J. McCarthy's testimony on his visit to the Independence some seven months before the hoisting disaster, and McCarthy's follow-up actions regarding unsafe equipment:

A.   . . . I believe that I recommended to the bureau of mines office that there was not a safety clevis on the cable as is usually used on some cables. . . .

Q.   Did you make any recommendations to those in charge of the Independence Limited at that time?

A.   I do not think that I did at that time.

Q.   Did you at any time since?

A.   No sir, I do not think so. . . .

Q.   I would like to ask you if when [the state inspector] finds something that he considers worthy of reporting, does he not make any recommendations to the management of the property where he finds this lacking?

A.   I usually make a recommendation where I find any thing of that sort lacking both to the management of the mines and to the office. At that time I did not, for the simple reason that the blanks that we used at the time we went into office were lacking along these lines.

Q.   Could you not call the attention of the management to it even without the blanks?

A.   I presume that I could, but in that case I do not remember that I did. . . .

Q.   Is there no state law in regard to cages where men are handled not being run without safety dogs?

A.   That I cannot tell you, I am not a lawyer and therefore I cannot say.

McCarthy's boss, State Mine Inspector E. L. White, then testified that only safety clutches—not safety "dogs"—were required by law. "The only reason for not making the report [to the mine's managers regarding safety "dogs" on the hoist] was because the blanks used [were] lacking," he said; the law's requirements had been met.[42]

Despite such obvious failings, there is much evidence to indicate that mine inspection had value—even if only as a potential threat to employers. The Colorado inspector forced several mines to improve safety in 1896, filing suit against the Dillon Mine and winning an injunction blocking its operation until several dangers had been corrected. Mine owner Eben Smith apologized to a Boston investor that mine output had declined, partly because "the mine inspector, after the Anna Lee disaster, made a thorough investigation of the mines in Cripple Creek and had a great many of them go to work and put their properties in a safe condition for the men to work in." Following the Stratton's Independence tragedy, orders were issued which affected some 150 Colorado mines, requiring them to make specific improvements in hoisting equipment.[43]

Furthermore, after more than a decade of metal-mine inspection across the West, declines began to appear in mine fatality rates. Colorado's rate, for example, dropped from almost six deaths per thousand men employed in the mid-1890s to a low of 1.96 by 1908, although the charge was made that these statistics were inaccurate because they included men working in safe areas outside the mine. Montana's rate fell from its high of 8.28 in 1896 to 1.45 in 1908, although it rose again to 3.6 deaths per thousand by 1910, a level fairly common across the region.[44]

Another possible measure of success should be noted: the abundance of enemies of inspection, especially among mine owners, which might indicate that the system was accomplishing something positive in the way of mine safety. But the clearest indication of the value of the mine inspector came from hard-rock miners themselves. The newly formed Western Federation of Miners came out in 1893 in support of mine inspection, and listed as one of its ten objectives: "To labor for the enactment of suitable mining laws, with a sufficient number of inspectors, who shall be practical miners, for the proper enforcement of such laws." The WFM remained steadfast in its support for mine inspection. When a bill to abolish the mine inspector's office began advancing through the Idaho Legislature in 1897, the Silver City Miners' Union rallied to oppose it. In a resolution sent to the legislators, the union stressed the inspector's "vast importance in protecting miners against the negligence of incompetent mine management," and emphasized that "the fact that we have such an office is in itself a potent factor in impelling mine owners to the utmost care in looking to the safety of miners." Among the signers was William D. Haywood, then recording secretary of the Silver City union, soon to rise as one of the WFM's most radical leaders. After this resolution was received, the Idaho State Senate indefinitely postponed action on abolishing the office of mine inspector.[45]

Mine safety campaigns usually moved on to focus upon specific legislation, once the office of mine inspector was established. But hard-rock miners—like automobile and motorcycle drivers of a later day—did not always support in practice the measures enacted for their own safety. This was particularly true of the safety cage regulations appearing in the 1890s in Montana. In 1897, the Montana Legislature heard pleas for requiring protective gates on cages, a proposal pushed by Representative W. J. Evans of Butte, a miner. Evans noted that most mine cages were "simply a platform suspended by three iron braces and covered with a bonnet," which permitted a multitude of accidents when miners' arms or legs touched the uneven sides of the shaft. Drawing on ten years' experience in the state's mines, Evans claimed that "it is the unanimous opinion of the miners who day after day are raised and lowered in these cages, that they are the most dangerous implements now in use in our mines."

Passed on March 1, 1897, the Montana safety cage law made side gates obligatory on cages containing more than two riders and operating in shafts more than 300 feet deep. The mine inspector reported soon thereafter that "with few exceptions the law has been complied with," although he admitted that "certain prejudices" among "a considerable number of employees" and "a few" mine owners caused him to exercise "reasonable leniency" in putting the requirement into effect.[46]

Evidence of the unpopularity of the law began to appear. In the Diamond Mine in Butte on November 6, 1897, a miner riding in a cage without the required gates was killed when it started up as he stooped to pick up the lid of his dinner bucket, crushing him against the shaft wall and propelling him to the bottom of the shaft. Comments on the mishap by other miners indicated the disfavor with which the new side gates were held, one miner admitting that "he would just as soon ride without them and had heard others say the same thing." Another miner who agreed was asked whether it was "the general opinion of the men that they are safer without them." "Yes, sir," he replied. Pressed on this point, another said "it was because the men would have a better show to get off if the cage went into the sheaves." The jury blamed the victim's carelessness for the accident, but the Butte *Bystander* quoted a local miner as saying that "the fact is that the last six fatalities of the nature in Butte" involved cages lacking the required gates. This case was not isolated, for the inspector received a petition opposing the cage law signed by 450 employees of the Anaconda, Never Sweat, and Mountain Con mines.

Troubles with the Anaconda Company on this law were noted above: the company refused to install safety cages, the inspector was unable to prod the county attorney into prosecuting, and in 1899, Anaconda tried unsuccessfully to have the measure repealed. When the law was finally brought to bear against the firm, it was fined $300 in district court, whereupon it appealed the matter to the State Supreme Court and lost.[47]

Many of the other mine safety laws passed across the West in the 1890–1910 period also focused upon the mine shaft, scene of countless accidents. These included uniform mine signals, prohibitions on carrying workmen in buckets, the employment of a man known as a "cager" at all levels to give signals and assist loading, and maximum cage speeds. Hoists were required to have level indicators, and engineers faced licensing exams, a prohibition on drinking intoxicants, and an 18-year age minimum. Increasingly stringent laws regulated ventilation, safety exits, tamping bars, dynamite storage, and even the screws on shaft collars.[48]

The shift to state legislation occurred as well in the realm of compensating accident victims. As noted in Chapter 5, the common-law barriers that blocked injured miners from winning damage suits began to erode as the nineteenth century closed, and legislation soon completed the breakup. Colorado's 1901 law typified the trend: a company was now held responsible for injuries or death caused by one of its employees to another—overturning the fellow-servant doctrine. Railroad workers were the focus of much early Western legislation on the subject, following a pattern established in the East and Middle West. But miners were soon covered also.[49]

As with mine inspection bills, the debates over liability changes were frequently filled with acrimony, as old arguments over driving away investors were revived. One Idaho solon called a 1907 employer's liability bill "too drastic to be other than a vicious piece of legislation," because it would "put nine-tenths of the companies out of business in case they should have one accident each."[50]

Despite such attacks, the common-law doctrines soon were toppled. A change then appeared quite suddenly among employers: they began to push for further legislative intervention. If liability laws were not completely satisfactory for workmen because lengthy, costly court action was still required, it was also true that employers were not secure either. Courts were increasingly supporting the claims of accident victims and awarding large compensation totals to them. As a result, mine owners and other employers saw their insurance premiums rising as they faced an increasingly unpredictable world.[51]

From across the sea came what seemed a better answer. Germany in 1884 and England in 1897 had instituted state-operated systems of compensation for victims of industrial accidents, which dismissed all debate over blame. Instead, this system provided specified amounts for each accident victim and set premiums for employers. Maryland was the first American state to pass such an act, creating a cooperative insurance fund covering workers in several industries in 1902. This was declared unconstitutional in 1904, however.[52]

America's true inauguration of the European philosophy of a compulsory state-run insurance system providing automatic compensation regardless of blame came in a major hard-rock mining state rather than in an Eastern industrial commonwealth. Montana, in 1909, enacted workmen's compensation for all coal miners, covering some 3,300 workmen. Apparently the relatively small size of the coal-mining force led to their selection for initial coverage. The head of the Montana Federation of Labor explained that this was done "in order to simplify [the law's] construction and prevent undue criticism and antagonism which might develop if made to embrace all employers and employees in the State. . . ." Perhaps, as with the early enactment of coal mine inspection laws, the relative weakness of coal companies was significant also. Anaconda's power was so great in Montana by 1909 that an attempt to cover hard-rock miners would have led to a vicious political and economic battle—which the miners' unions were in poor shape for at that time. The Montana act provided for compensation of $1 for each workday missed by injured coal miners, with an automatic $1,000 for loss of an arm or eye, and $3,000 in case of death. It was financed by a levy of one percent of each coal miner's wages and one cent per ton of coal mined in the state.[53]

Montana's pioneering act was declared unconstitutional in 1911, on grounds that it denied the employer equal protection, because he could still be sued at the option of the victim despite his payments into the fund. But by that time the movement was unstoppable. New York passed a system of general application, and the system spread rapidly until, by 1915, thirty-three states had passed workmen's compensation laws.[54]

Workmen's compensation in Montana provided a fitting, perhaps even predictable, close to the pioneer period of Western hard-rock mining. One of the major problems of that period from 1860 to 1910 was to develop a system to protect hard-rock miners from the dangers they faced underground, to aid them when injured, and to care for their survivors. Benefit plans were started by unions and did much to meet the need, but the search for a better system led eventually to state legislation. There was a progression: mutual benefit activities by unions, creation of the office of mine inspector, detailed safety laws, employer's liability, and finally workmen's compensation —all showing the growth from self-help to calling on state assistance. As with other industrial workers around the nation, hard-rock miners discovered that only governmental intervention could provide the breadth and uniformity of protection needed. Their success with safety and health legislation would not be equaled in certain other areas, however. The eight-hour day campaigns, especially, would reveal that government could be an enemy as well as a friend. From these differing experiences would grow a dilemma that would split the Western miners' union movement.

CHAPTER VIII

The Dilemma
of Political Action

Meeting in convention as the movement for the eight-hour day entered a crucial stage across the West in 1902, the Western Federation of Miners boldly asserted that "the strike has failed to secure to the working classes their liberty," and called upon workers to seek their liberties instead "at the sacred shrine of American freedom, the ballot box."[1]

It was not an untested course for the WFM. The ballot box had frequently served hard-rock miners well, especially in the realm of safety legislation, where state after state in the West had established and strengthened mine inspection and other protections during the previous decade. On the local level, increased political activity by miners had produced a spate of elected officials from the ranks of mine labor. Butte's county election in 1900, for example, brought a long list of present and former WFM members into office, including both the new county sheriff and treasurer (the latter held the same position with the miners' union); all but five of the victors, in fact, were members of local labor unions. Reports such as this from the miners' union in Black Hawk, Colorado, were typical of the times:

> We have elected two out of three aldermen and one of our candidates was defeated by only one vote. In caucus we came

within six votes of nominating the mayor. We have started to take an active part in politics and we will have candidates at the next election that will make the race for the Senate and House of Representatives.[2]

Perhaps hard-rock miners had an incentive to political action that was missing with most other occupational groups: they were dominant in many Western districts, and even where not dominant they often possessed considerable political muscle. Miners formed 29 percent of Colorado's working population in 1880, for example, and although this declined to 13.7 percent in 1900 and 8 percent in 1910, the numbers remained impressive in several localities—almost 8,000 in Teller County (Cripple Creek) in 1900, the same year in which a writer was amazed that there were over 4,000 miners in Leadville. The 1900 census reported that miners and quarrymen formed the following percentages of the gainfully employed in the major metal-mining states and territories: Montana, 15.1 percent (17,387 miners and quarrymen); Arizona, 14.9 percent (7,947); Nevada, 13.8 percent (2,741); Colorado, 13.7 percent (29,957); Idaho, 11.7 percent (7,318); Utah, 8.3 percent (7,028); New Mexico, 6.8 percent (4,548); and California, 4.2 percent (26,891). Relatives, merchants, and others dependent upon miners could swell these totals, adding to the miners dominance of their own districts. They were increasingly less formidable statewide as other settlers poured in, however. In this regard, the miners may have turned to concerted political action at the wrong historical moment—the time when their comparative advantage was waning.[3]

But now they were aware of their political muscle, aware that they were a slowly stirring giant rising in the mountains. This marked a change, for the hard-rock miners' previous political activity as a separate group was usually sporadic and short-lived—a "Workingmen's Independent Party" in Butte, or an uprising to legally exclude the Chinese. As the turn of the century neared, however, an increasing proportion of the American population was caught up in the belief that reforms could best be achieved through the political system, and miners joined—and led—this crusade in the West. Soon their own concerns were drawn into the political system, as occurred with the mine safety issue examined in Chapter 7. But there were many others, including the company store and boardinghouse controversies, the mechanic's lien, liability of stockholders for unpaid wages, the importation of strikebreakers, the blacklist, bi-weekly pay, and the shorter workday. Bills dealing with all of these appeared in the hoppers of Western legislatures during the 1890–1910 period, and in most cases the record shows progress for hard-rock miners. Setbacks occurred, however, and on several issues they were frequent and frustrating. From these Western political controversies arose some of the most violent episodes in the battle-scarred chapters of American labor history. Because of the eight-hour day's importance in this, and because of its role in the evolution of political philosophies among Western hard-rock miners, it is singled out for emphasis in this chapter.[4]

The eight-hour day ranked with wage disputes as a major source of labor-management discord in the mining West. It was called "one of the most absorbing topics of the day" in Montana by the early 'nineties, and by 1900, "the subject of greatest public interest" across the nation.[5]

There was, however, a basic difference between the eight-hour day and most other legislative controversies involving miners. The fight for shorter hours threw hard-rock miners into a blunt, direct confrontation with employers on a dollars-and-cents issue. Mine owners could concede that better safety practices were economically sound as well as ethically preferable, and the boardinghouse and company store might be transferred without loss to other hands. But reducing the workday to eight hours always meant a greater expense if wages remained unchanged (as they usually did). And miners' wages were already considered excessive.

The eight-hour day had an extensive history in the West by the 1890s, but usually not as a result of legislation. It appeared in scattered districts, with no obvious pattern. Eliot Lord wrote that eight hours' work "had become a uniform requirement" on the Comstock Lode by 1866, and ten years later the Con Virginia and "all other leading mines" there were reported still using the eight-hour shift. Strikes for the eight-hour day failed in Unionville, California, in 1869, and Pioche, Nevada, in 1872, but the eight-hour system was in effect in Idaho's Owyhee district in 1873, in the Boise Basin in 1876, at Rocky Bar and Atlanta, Idaho, in 1877, at Central City and some Leadville mines before 1880, in the Green Mountain Mine in Butte in 1888, and in the Tiger Mine in the Coeur d'Alenes in 1889. A miner in Pitkin County, Colorado, claimed in 1888 that "hereabouts the rule of eight hours has been very generally recognized."[6]

National as well as regional trends appear to have been responsible for this. Eastern working men from the Civil War onward had conducted eight-hour campaigns, with Congress showing support for requiring the system for government employees, while the urban building trades achieved significant hour reductions throughout the period. San Francisco working men held a mass meeting in 1865 to seek legislative backing for the eight-hour day, leading to the enactment in 1868 of shorter hours for California public employees, and in 1876 for other workers (although the latter law was ineffective). This campaign spilled over into Nevada, where the Legislative Assembly passed an eight-hour measure 25–0 in 1869, but the State Senate killed it 12–4. Competing mine owners, trying to win Nevada's U.S. Senate seat in 1872, instituted the system voluntarily in their Comstock properties as they courted miners' votes.[7]

By the early 'nineties in the West, there was considerable local success but little statewide legislative success in the eight-hour campaigns, which raises questions regarding the miners' sudden shift during that decade to political action. Four developments appear important in this turnabout:

1. Although many Western hard-rock miners were working eight-hour shifts, many others were not and the latter's chances of success appeared to be diminishing as corporation power increased. Longer hours for these mining company employees became intolerable, furthermore, when public employees and building trades workers—such as Denver's by 1890 —were under the shorter workday.

2. Smelter workers and other non-miners were being taken into the Western Federation of Miners in large numbers by the latter 'nineties, and few of these were permitted the luxury of the eight-hour day. Ten or twelve hours a day was common for smelter workers and engineers; by 1896, for example, all hoisting engineers in the WFM's locals in Cripple Creek, Leadville, and Red Mountain were working twelve-hour shifts. Admitting in 1903 that "the majority" of West-

ern miners were working eight-hour days, WFM President Charles Moyer stressed: "We must not forget our brothers who are compelled to toil twelve long hours per day in mills and smelters." These workers were now in the WFM, Moyer reminded his audience, and they "are entitled to your undivided support. . . ."

3. Considerable success in passing mine safety and other protective legislation for miners had been recorded in many Western states and territories, paralleling developments elsewhere.

4. Health conditions underground were worsening as mines went deeper, and the connection between illness and excessive labor in poor conditions was increasingly recognized. In Colorado, it was reported that six hours' labor was considered enough work in an upraise, where ventilation was usually poor. A former manager recalled, "I have worked men four hours and paid them for the day. That would be where the water was dripping down." As legislators gave attention to other health matters, such as meat inspection, it was a logical next step to examine the hours of labor amid unhealthful occupations. The connection seemed obvious to a Utah employer. Asked what was "exceptional" in smelting and mining to warrant passage of an eight-hour law as "a sanitary measure," he replied: "Arsenic, sulphur, and lead."[8]

The seven-day week made these conditions even worse. Only one Butte mine was granting Sunday off to its employees in 1889, and a miner's letter home in 1905 shows that the seven-day workweek was still prevalent in the Coeur d'Alenes:

> Today we have a shift off and it's bad weather, so there is nothing to do but stay in doors and look pleasant. . . . I'm not sorry to lay off today because working every day is too much. As a rule we work 29 or 30 days each month, but this month I have full time put in with only 27½ shifts.[9]

Although the drive to obtain the eight-hour day for Western hard-rock miners differed in several respects from Eastern working men's campaigns—most notably in the absence of the "create more jobs" argument in the West—in at least one aspect the two sections of the country were similar: in both, a major early focus of legislation was upon workmen holding life-or-death powers over others. For such employees, alert-

23. *Early Western legislation for shorter hours concentrated on this man: the hoisting engineer, the individual with more life-or-death power than anyone else in Western hard-rock mining. Illness, drunkenness, inattentiveness, fatigue—any of these present in the hoist operator could bring disaster to men riding the cage.*

Denver Public Library, Western History Collection photo

ness and good health proved crucial both for their own and for others' longevity. In the East, the occupations most readily fitting this category were railroad engineers and streetcar operators, who were consequently singled out early for hours restrictions; many persons could be killed by their inattentiveness. In the West, it was the hoisting engineer who fitted this description: he sat at the top of the mine shaft, pulling levers and handles and moving men and ore up and down at great speeds.[10]

Some Western hoisting engineers refused to endanger the lives of others by remaining long hours at their posts. After several cases where engineers ran cages "into the sheaves" on the Comstock Lode in the late 1870s, the local Society of Engineers sought to prove that the twelve-hour day was excessive, and some mines reduced the hoist operator's hours to eight. Such occurrences were rare, however, and long hours for hoisting engineers became a fixture of mine life. Only fourteen years later, when the major Coeur d'Alenes mines were expanding rapidly and the stress on hoist operators was increasing correspondingly, two engineers quit work at the Tiger Mine "for the alleged reason that they considered twelve hours too long to work at an occupation of that kind." Their work was especially dangerous, they claimed, because men were working at the bottom of the shaft just below the dropping cage. Their employer refused to grant them the eight-hour day, however. Not surprisingly, Montana's first hours legislation for working men, passed in 1893, restricted the daily labor of just one group: hoisting engineers.[11]

With this background, the situation in the mining West in the mid-'nineties may be briefly recapitulated. Talk of the eight-hour day was widespread. Wyoming had included eight-hour coverage for coal miners in its 1889 constitution, and it had been proposed for metal miners in Montana and Colorado. While many workmen had gained shorter hours on their own initiative, many others—especially smelter workers and hoisting engineers—had not. The WFM had been born, and despite the economic doldrums of 1893–1894, it was beginning to grow and flex its muscles. The populist movement gave additional spur to Western reform legislation.[12]

Utah was first to respond to these diverse influences by enacting the eight-hour day for hard-rock miners and smeltermen in 1896, as the polygamy controversy cooled and Congress permitted the territory to join the Union. Much of the credit for the successful bill must rest with Thomas Kearns, a former hard-rock miner, by 1896 a mine owner in Park City with much sympathy for his workmen. Kearns and his partner had refused in 1892 to follow other mine owners in cutting wages; at Utah's Constitutional Convention in 1895, he supported his employees' request to seek an hours limitation clause in the new document. He was unsuccessful, for the first Utah Constitution specified instead that eight hours be the daily limit for workers on government projects. But it added this pregnant phrase: ". . . the legislature shall pass laws to provide for the health and safety of employees in factories, smelters, and mines."[13]

The wording and linkage were crucial. This phrase channeled the movement for the eight-hour day through the legislative corridors of Western capitols as a health measure rather than as a plan to create more jobs or simply to strike a blow for the working man. Given the worsening work environment of lode mining, use of the health argument was a natural route for the shorter-hours campaign to take. Further, as a health measure the eight-hour day could fit within the police powers that every state government possessed as a basis for protecting its citizens.

This provision in the Utah Constitution did not remain unused for long. A clamor for legislation soon went up from miners and smelter workers, most of whom worked the ten-hour day, seven-day week, although both longer and shorter workdays could be found. House Bill No. 11, the eight-hour bill, was soon wending its way through the first legislative session under statehood, in 1896. The measure was boosted at every turn by petitions sent in from the laborers in Park City, Sandy, Mingo, and elsewhere, whose workdays it proposed to shorten—namely, "working men in all underground mines or workings, and in smelters and all other institutions for the reduction or refining of ores or metals. . . ."[14]

The bill's travels through this first Utah Legislature under statehood were stormy at times. The House Judiciary Committee recommended rejection of the measure, arguing that it needed a provision "that any laboring man allowing himself to be employed more than eight hours a day be declared guilty of a misdemeanor." Wage reductions would follow the bill's passage, one legislator warned, adding that it "would result in strikes and hard feelings between employers and employees." The *Deseret Evening News* came out against the bill on the eve of the Senate vote, contending that "any law which abridges the freedom of making contracts or impedes their due execution is unconstitutional." The Mormon-controlled newspaper worried also that Utah might become so "law-ridden" that investors would stay away—reviving the dilemma over the sacredness of capital. The House Labor Committee fought back and finally guided the measure to 26–10 approval in the House and 14–0 in the Senate.[15]

A test came quickly. Albert F. Holden made special contracts of ten hours a day for miners and twelve hours a day for smeltermen at his Old Jordan Mine in Bingham Canyon. Pushed by the WFM and Utah labor organizations, authorities fined Holden fifty dollars and sentenced him to fifty-seven days in jail. He appealed.[16]

Holden was unsuccessful. Despite claims by his attorneys that the Utah law was class legislation, violating the freedom of contract of employers and employees, the Utah eight-hour law was approved as constitutional by both the state Supreme Court and the United States Supreme Court. The latter's ruling established the Utah law as the major pillar of support for the eight-hour-day movement across the mining West. If the legislature determined that shorter hours were needed as a health measure, and reasonable grounds existed for believing this, Utah's eight-hour law was valid, Justice Henry Billings Brown asserted. He also noted that mining and manufacturing had changed so drastically, and the worker's comparative strength had declined so sharply, that special legislation for workmen was valid.[17]

While Utah was breaking new legislative and judicial ground on the eight-hour day, such uses of government were being blocked in Montana. The frustrations began during the 1889 Constitutional Convention, when clauses limiting government workers to the eight-hour day were defeated 21–19 and 37–26. A year later, in 1890, the Butte miners sought unsuccessfully to reduce their ten-hour workdays on their own. They were goaded in this by the success of the newly formed Carpenters' Union, which had just forced contractors to reduce their workday in Butte from ten to nine hours. Returning to the legislature for the 1891 session, the Butte Miners' Union needed only three days to collect 3,050 signatures on a petition calling for an eight-hour-day law. Petitions also came from the Granite Knights of Labor, from Cascade County miners and laborers, and from workers in Elk Horn and Camp Barker. Only one petition opposing the measure was reported, from the superintendent of the Butte and Boston Mining Company "and twenty-five others," presumably employers.[18]

Despite the abundance of petition signatures, a rocky path confronted the eight-hour bill introduced by the union's Peter

Breen. Limited to mine employees, the measure's narrow 4–3 victory in the House Labor Committee presaged later difficulties. In the House debate, the fact that only miners were covered prompted considerable discussion. One member offered an amendment to include "all classes of labor in the state," arguing that he wished to treat each group alike. Breen, however, answered that "the other classes of labor had not asked to be included" in the eight-hour coverage, "and until they did so he saw no reason for so doing." Breen's success was only temporary, and the final bill failed to pass, 21 to 30. Except for a brief attempt in 1897, Montana miners abandoned the legislative route and waited until a better opportunity and method for achieving the eight-hour day appeared.[19]

That opportunity came in the Spring of 1900. Butte's miners were then working ten hours on day shift and nine hours on night shift. A union committee was authorized by the membership to present the mine managers with a request for the eight-hour day.

The union's timing was propitious. Copper was as high as 18 cents per pound, up from 11 or 12 cents months earlier. And although there had been a slight slackening in the bitter competition between local mine owners, they were still at odds with each other and still solicited miners' votes for their candidates in local elections. The union skillfully planned its actions in this setting. The major contenders in 1900 were Marcus Daly, the longtime head of the Anaconda holdings, who was weakened by his own failing health and the company's takeover by the Amalgamated (Standard Oil); William Scallon, Daly's replacement as the Amalgamated's man in Butte; William A. Clark, who had extensive holdings throughout the district and who was a foe of Daly's since 1889; and F. Augustus Heinze, a rising entrepreneur and an ally of Clark's for the 1900 campaign.[20]

Clark had unceremoniously resigned his U.S. Senate seat several months earlier under the cloud of suspicion raised by a Senate investigation, which concluded that he had purchased his seat by bribing Montana legislators. Now, in the early summer of 1900, he was planning his moves for re-election in the next legislature. Heinze was also preparing for future victories, for he had been blocked by Anaconda in his last major contest with the firm in 1898. Clark and Heinze employed some

2,000 miners and ran their Butte mines directly, while the Amalgamated, with some 5,000 employees in the district at that time, was managed by local agents who had little control over basic policies. The union challenge was based upon the expectation that the Amalgamated, Clark, and Heinze would each yield on the eight-hour question to win points against the others.[21]

It was a shrewd plan. Before a startled crowd on Miners' Union Day, June 13, the union president announced that Heinze and Clark had agreed to reduce their employees' workdays to eight hours. The celebration was long and exuberant, and spilled over into the election that Fall. Campaign oratory revealed that politics—as much as the miners' health—was involved in the Heinze-Clark decision, as Democrats linked the opposition Republican Party with the Amalgamated, which had held back on granting its employees the shorter workday. But with the Democratic, Fusionist (Democrats and Populists), and Republican platforms all endorsing the eight-hour day in some form, passage in the 1901 legislative session was assured.[22]

Introduced by Representative John J. Quinn, a trustee of the Butte Miners' Union and delegate to the previous WFM Convention, the Montana bill duplicated the successful Utah law. To taunts about the bill's lack of coverage of other workmen, the Helena *Independent* warned that under a general eight-hour law, the federal government would be drawn in to intervene in some dispute of railway or telegraph employees "on the ground that the law interferes with interstate commerce. . . ."

Others charged that the measure was "practically a seven-hour bill," because by custom the men traveled within the mine and also lunched on company time. But to exclude such time from the eight-hour day—as some proposed—would give the shift boss "the power to tyrannize over the miners," warned Senator Connolly from the mining camp of Granite. This would occur, he warned, because shift bosses would make miners arrive early and wait until he permitted them to descend. "For God's sake, I ask you, don't do this!" he pleaded. Connolly was successful in blocking the amendment, and the final measure passed both houses without dissenting votes. By then the Amalgamated had yielded to the eight-hour requirement.[23]

The critics were correct in predicting misunderstandings

over the meaning of the new eight-hour-day requirement, for disputes arose over both the length of actual work time and the amount of wages. The union charged that Clark quickly turned against his former backers and installed a 9½-hour day in his mines—apparently meaning that his employees used their own time to descend into the mine, eat their lunch, and ascend. The Amalgamated and some other companies adopted the same requirements in their mines, the Amalgamated allegedly saving $1,430 a day under the system. While most enterprises apparently continued previous pay levels, the East Helena smelter cut wages from the former $2.50 for twelve hours to $2.20 for eight hours, provoking an unsuccessful strike.[24]

A nagging thought remained in the background as Montanans hailed their new eight-hour-day law. Although virtually a copy of the Utah measure that had withstood a constitutionality test, Utah had something Montana lacked: a constitutional provision empowering the legislature to pass laws for the health of workmen. The specter of some future legislature or judge eliminating the eight-hour law led its supporters to seek a constitutional amendment matching Utah's. With all political parties endorsing the plan, the 1903 legislature approved it, and the voters gave the amendment overwhelming support in 1904: it passed 29,237 to 2,394. This event caused the Amalgamated to relent and permit its by then 10,000 employees to go to work on company time. Only then did the company concede the eight-hour day in all its workings.[25]

As frustrating as the Montana eight-hour-day campaigns appeared to participants, these campaigns were eclipsed by struggles over the issue in Colorado and Idaho. Open, blatant government aid to employers amid extreme polarization became prominent features in the latter two states, and feuds between mine owners—so common in Butte—were supplanted by the employers' close cooperation and joint action.

By 1894, Colorado's public employees were covered by an eight-hour law, and miners in Cripple Creek and several other districts also worked eight-hour shifts. The newly formed Western Federation of Miners then launched a campaign to win the eight-hour day by legislation for the rest of the state's metal miners, coal miners, smeltermen, and mill workers. When a bill was passed in 1895, it also covered factory employees and included a request that the state Supreme Court first rule on whether such a law would be constitutional.[26]

The court's ruling against the bill was portentous. It pointed toward the frustrations Colorado miners would face over the following decade—frustrations that would lead to widespread violence. The Colorado justices termed the new eight-hour law unconstitutional because it was class legislation; the legislature could not "single out" miners, smeltermen, and factory workers and impose restrictions "from which other employers of labor are exempt." This ruling was cited by opponents of the plan as a reason for rejecting a similar WFM-supported bill in 1897.[27]

Then came the 1898 *Holden v. Hardy* ruling by the U.S. Supreme Court. The decision breathed new life into the movement in Colorado, where in 1899 pro-labor legislators helped pass "a verbatim copy" of the Utah eight-hour law, adding only a penalty clause. The bill faced an immediate onslaught from company spokesmen, however; unsuccessful in the legislative halls, they found support in the Colorado Supreme Court. In 1899, the court unanimously ruled in *In re Morgan* that the new eight-hour law was class legislation, violated the right of contract, and was not a valid exercise of the state's police power. The Utah case was no precedent, the Colorado justices ruled, because Colorado lacked a constitutional provision specifically permitting legislation for the health and safety of mine and smelter workers; the Utah Constitution, on the contrary, possessed such a clause.[28]

Disbelief greeted the *In re Morgan* decision, but not only among miners. Legal experts noted the spectacle of a state court overturning a law that was copied from one which the U.S. Supreme Court had previously upheld as a valid exercise of a state's police power. The Colorado court's attitude was termed "certainly novel" by the *American Law Register*; the journal said the case was the first it had seen where the national court "has intimated that a law would fall within the police powers, and the state court has thereupon decided that it would not."[29]

The ruling also brought a hardening of attitudes on both sides, as miners decided that they had been wronged by a pro-employer state court, and mine owners felt emboldened by the judicial assistance they had received. These divisions worsened when the smelter trust flatly rejected a strike-ending recommendation put forward by the State Board of Arbitration. The board's recommendation was that the smeltermen's workday be reduced to eight hours and that their wages be increased above their $2.50 per day. After holding out for three more weeks, the smeltermen gave way. Now polarization moved toward previously unknown extremes in Colorado.[30]

At this point, the miners tried to examine their alternatives. Throughout the summer of 1899, the Colorado labor movement, dominated by the WFM, debated whether further legislative attempts to achieve the eight-hour day were justified—or whether strikes held better hope for success. Despite the recent setbacks, the bulk of organized labor in Colorado came down on the side of continued political action. In June, 1900, the State Federation of Labor endorsed passage of a constitutional amendment similar to Utah's empowering the Colorado Legislature to enact an eight-hour law. The campaign appeared on the road to success when all political parties supported the plan that Fall. The constitutional amendment—ratified by the 1901 legislature—won the approval of the state's voters in 1902 by a lopsided 72,980 to 26,266 margin. Political action seemed nearing the payoff.[31]

There was still one hurdle: legislative action was required for the constitutional amendment to be translated into an eight-hour day. This proved not to be automatic. The 1902 election, which showed public support for the amendment and for sympathetic candidates, also brought into office a new governor who had been evasive on the eight-hour day. He was James H. Peabody, former mayor of Cañon City, successful businessman, and a Republican in that year of heavy Republican victories. And Peabody, along with many other Coloradoans, was disturbed by the growing power of the WFM; he viewed it as a violent, revolutionary, un-American organization.[32]

There was some evidence for his view. Intimidation of non-union men had been a frequent activity during WFM strikes in Colorado since the 1894 Cripple Creek conflict, and as recently as 1901, WFM members had surrounded a mine in Telluride, exchanged shots with the non-union employees inside, and forced eighty-eight of them to hike over the mountains with a warning never to return. Non-union men were driven from Cripple Creek that year, and the assassination in

1902 of a mine manager in Telluride was widely believed to have been the work of the WFM. Further, the increasingly socialistic utterances of such WFM leaders as Ed Boyce and Big Bill Haywood added to the impression that the federation represented an alien growth amid American free institutions. These and similar incidents brought home to Colorado's new governor the conclusion that the WFM constituted a serious threat to the state, a worsening threat that had to be removed. Although written in 1904, the following opinion by Governor Peabody matched his views at the time he took office in early 1903, and was apparently shared by many in the business community:

> For ten years this Federation has stopped at nothing to accomplish its purpose—threats, intimidation, assaults, dynamite outrages, murders, have everywhere characterized its policy. . . . It has never had a strike that has not been bloody. The catalogue of its crimes affright humanity. . . .

This was the man elected to lead Colorado in the 1903–1905 period when miners and smeltermen confidently expected passage of the long-delayed eight-hour-day proposal.[33]

With miner-legislators such as WFM official Max Morris of Arapahoe County leading the drive, eight-hour bills began to advance through the Democratic-controlled Senate and the Republican-controlled House early in 1903. But the employers, backed by a fund alleged to total $50,000, launched their counterattack. Largely silent during the 1902 state campaign, they now began arguing through anonymous bulletins that less than half of the state's voters had bothered to cast ballots on the eight-hour-day proposal, destroying its validity as a directive for legislative action. These spokesmen claimed that a job would be unhealthy for eight hours as well as nine or ten, making shorter hours illogical as a health measure. Passage of the bill, they warned, would drive low-grade mines out of existence, and would violate the employee's right to contract for longer hours if he wished.[34]

The WFM responded vigorously to such claims, mainly through J. C. Sullivan, a hard-rock miner who was president of the State Federation of Labor, and Representative Morris. Morris noted that the San Juan district had been under the eight-hour system for four years and none of its low-grade

215

mines had been forced to close. Sullivan contended that the smelting corporations were overcapitalized and had made enormous profits, "largely on the labor of those who work twelve or sixteen hours for starvation wages. When 17,000 men are paid half wages, or work double time for one wage, it is a natural sequence that the capital they save would double every few years."[35]

This debate—which should have been conducted in front of the voters six months earlier—ended in a legislative imbroglio. Each branch of the legislature passed its own bill by overwhelming margins, then stubbornly refused to compromise. Conference committees were unable to end the impasse, and time ran out on April 6, 1903, with no eight-hour day on the statute books. A special session in July had similar results.[36]

The legislature's failure led to a series of strikes in Colorado in 1903–1904 which may accurately be termed a labor-management war. Union recognition was a key issue in most such wars, but the eight-hour-day issue lay at the base of this strife, for the frustration provoked by legislative inaction laid the groundwork for confrontation. This was clear to the Denver *Post* early in the conflict, when it surveyed the growing violence and observed that "while there is seemingly no connection between the various strikes and labor troubles, all are traceable in a general way to this failure on the part of the Legislature" to pass the eight-hour bill. Bill Haywood, writing in 1904 as violence mounted, admitted that many questions were involved in the spreading conflicts, but called the eight-hour day "the main issue."[37]

To be sure, the strike in February, 1903, against the Colorado City ore processing companies was mainly over discrimination against union men and wages; the eight-hour day was already a fixture there. But this strike fit into the statewide confrontation because of the distrust generated by the major employer's rigidity and the governor's willingness—even eagerness—to send troops against the WFM. A recent study by George Suggs of Peabody's term in office supports the view that the WFM conceded much to bring about a settlement, but the head of the smelter trust remained unbending and reneged on earlier agreements. The Colorado City strike was a turning point, Suggs concludes, "because it helped place the resources of the Peabody administration at the disposal of forces destined to break the miners' union in the name of law and order."[38]

That the corporations were prepared to use the eight-hour deadlock to crush the WFM became more apparent with each passing month; in their view, the time was past for yielding to the WFM. The smelter trust's general manager asserted, for example, that "the real issue" facing the people of Colorado was "the control of the Western Federation of Miners over the mining and smelting industry of Colorado. . . ." And when smeltermen in Denver struck for the eight-hour day in June, 1903, an executive of the trust asked, "What is the use of giving in? The Western Federation of Miners now want eight hours. If we grant them that it will be only a question of time before they are striking for six. And if it should get that it will be clamoring for four." Giving in would be disastrous in such circumstances.

Events in Idaho Springs, Colorado, in the late spring and early summer of 1903 served to convince mine owners of the correctness of their views. On April 10, 1903, the miners' union in Idaho Springs—where nine-hour shifts were in force—presented a notice to mine managers announcing that its members would go on the eight-hour day on May 1 because it was "apparent to us that we cannot hope to secure an eight-hour day through legislation." Some 250 miners struck when employers rejected their demand. They scored some early victories in some mines, but on July 28 an explosion ripped through the transformer house of the Sun and Moon Mine, one of the holdouts that had resumed operations with strikebreakers. The only death was of one of the dynamiters, an Italian union member. Frenzied local businessmen held a rally the next day at which one of them propounded the major question: "Shall the people of Idaho Springs or a few outsiders run this city?" Moyer and Haywood, the WFM leaders, "are the arch anarchists of this country," one speaker proclaimed. Another argued that "if it is good law for the Western Federation of Murderers at Victor to walk five Austrians out of town, it is good law for us citizens to adopt here tonight." Soon the newly formed Citizens' Protective League deported nineteen WFM members. Although Peabody responded rapidly elsewhere to even a hint of violence affecting mining or smelting property, in this case he refused to intervene to stop the deportations until "the civil power has been exhausted. . . ."

Cripple Creek provided the next defeat for the WFM. Angered over the smelter trust's refusal to raise wages to match those at other smelters in Colorado City, the federation launched a strike in August against the Cripple Creek mines that supplied ore to the trust's smelters. This strike did not center on the eight-hour day, but was an integral part of that campaign because the WFM had just launched a statewide eight-hour drive for all workers in its jurisdiction. As Suggs has emphasized, "the success of the millworkers became imperative if the union's prestige in Colorado was to be maintained."

On September 2, the Cripple Creek Mine Owners and Operators' Association, noting frequent cases of assault, arson, and gunslinging, pleaded with Governor Peabody to send in troops despite the refusal of Sheriff Robertson—a WFM member—to request them. Since the WFM began the strike, the owners' telegram stated, "they have pursued the policy of threats and intimidation, to prevent men from going to work on the property, going to the extent of backing their threats by the display of guns." The WFM and allied local officials denied the union's complicity in lawlessness, but the mayor of Victor backed up the mine owners' plea and also requested that troops be sent.

The response came rapidly. On September 4, more than 1,000 National Guardsmen were brought in by train to preserve peace in the district. Ordered to Cripple Creek only after the mine owners' association agreed to provide funds for their support, the soldiers found their arrival protested by local meetings and petitions.

Even without martial law, the military's harassment of the union soon became blatant in Cripple Creek: strikers were arrested as vagrants, a pro-union newspaper was silenced, and local authorities were warned about supporting the strike. An attempted train derailment and a mine explosion that killed two men provided continued justification for military occupation, although the strike quieted enough by January, 1904, so that troop withdrawals began. But on June 6, violence erupted again when an explosion killed thirteen non-union men waiting for a train at the Independence station of the Florence and Cripple Creek railroad. The resulting uproar set off new rumors and charges that the WFM had resumed its attacks, although no evidence linking the union to the explosion was produced. Leaders of the mine owners' association and the local Citizens' Alliance then forced Sheriff Robertson to resign, and other city and county officials were removed from office. The troops returned as mine owners took control of the district.

All the employers' and the National Guard's hatred of the WFM then boiled to the surface. Union men were assaulted, their headquarters stormed, and their stores looted. Deportations began. Refusal to resign from the WFM warranted exile; twenty-five men were sent from the district on the first day after the Independence blast, and more than two hundred were eventually forced to leave by the military or the citizens' group. A complete blacklist was instituted. The victory of the mine owners was total in Cripple Creek by the end of the summer.

The situation across the state in Telluride was similar. Millmen had been omitted in 1901 from an eight-hour-day settlement between the union and the district's mining companies, and tensions had increased due to the violence of that strike, the 1902 assassination of the Smuggler-Union manager, and editorial attacks. This cold war ended and open hostilities resumed in Telluride with the close of the frustrating 1903 legislative session. The initial spark was provided when the WFM's San Juan District Union demanded an eight-hour day for all millworkers by September 1, 1903. This was quickly rejected by the employers' group, the Telluride Mining Association.[39]

The resulting eight-hour-day strike soon broadened to include other issues, as the WFM charged that mining companies were discriminating against union men. Telluride business leaders sought National Guard protection, and despite the lack of rioting or insurrection, Governor Peabody yielded to their request on November 20, 1903. As in Cripple Creek, the business community was required to underwrite the costs of the 400-man military expedition; mining companies also provided the troops with sleeping quarters, meals, and similar accouterments. Before the strike faded across the San Juans in 1904, WFM members had been arrested, beaten, blacklisted, deported, and their organization finally subdued. As in Cripple Creek, the mine owners were in control in the San Juans.[40]

The federation continued to lose on the eight-hour-day controversy in Colorado. A law passed in 1905 was so limited that smelter workers were not covered unless they were "directly attending" furnaces or other machines and "in contact with noxious fumes. . . ." The WFM later claimed that the law covered "about twenty percent of those employed in the production and reduction of ores and coal." Not until 1911 was a broad act passed to give Colorado's miners and smelter workers the eight-hour day, and then opponents were able to delay its effectiveness another two years by a ruse to require voter approval. Thus, eleven years after voters balloted 72,980 to 26,266 in 1902 for the eight-hour day for miners and smelter workers, the system was finally established by Colorado law.[41]

The WFM's troubles in Colorado paralleled its frustrations in Idaho after 1900. The 1889 Idaho constitution placed an eight-hour limit on daily labor for state and municipal works, and the eight-hour shift appeared in scattered mining camps during the nineties. Many major mines such as the Bunker Hill & Sullivan, however, employed the ten-hour day, seven-day week. Unlike Colorado, in Idaho the WFM had already been crushed—during the 1899 Coeur d'Alenes strike—and this severely reduced the federation's effectiveness in pressing the eight-hour campaign in 1900.[42]

In its 1901 session, the Idaho Legislature, joining the movement then surging through the Rockies, voted to submit to voters a constitutional amendment empowering the legislature to pass laws for the health and safety of employees in "factories, smelters, mines and ore reduction works"—phrasing almost identical with the 1896 Utah Constitutional provision that had become crucial in court tests. As in Colorado and Montana, Idaho voters in 1902 gave overwhelming support to this amendment—20,096 for, 835 against. In Shoshone County in the Coeur d'Alenes the vote was 2,049 to 70; in Owyhee County it was 710 to 9. Noting the lopsided margins throughout the state, the Idaho Statesman concluded: "If ever there was a vote of direction to a legislature that vote was such a one."[43]

Although both parties had supported the eight-hour plan during the 1902 campaign, leading Republicans in the new legislature—their party in control for the first time since 1895—lost interest quickly. The Republican floor leader in the House,

Francis Jenkins of Latah County, formerly headed the Bunker Hill & Sullivan interests, and warned that the state's mining industries "could hardly stand" a reduction from the ten-hour workday to eight hours. Jenkins reversed the usual argument on labor amid difficult conditions, claiming that a poor labor environment slowed the work and "it was unfair to limit the working day to eight hours, when perhaps the workmen were doing nothing half the time." He noted that less than a third of those voting in the election had cast ballots on the eight-hour-day amendment. Representative Owen of Bingham, a vocal opponent of the plan, drew hisses from the gallery when he proclaimed that since workmen spend much of their leisure time in saloons, to "shorten the hours of labor would be to lengthen the hours of dissipation."

One Idaho Republican vigorously supported the eight-hour day. This was William E. Borah, just beginning what would become a lengthy career in the U.S. Senate, and there-fore not a member of the legislature during the debates of 1903. Borah emphasized the *Holden v. Hardy* decisions by the Utah and the United States Supreme Courts, and observed that "there was little reason to suppose that the Supreme Court of Idaho would reverse these tribunals." If any Republican had claimed in the 1902 campaign that the plan was unconstitution-al, Borah wondered, "what would have become of the 7,000 majority given the party last November?"

But as in Colorado, a majority other than the voters was suddenly gaining strength under the polarized conditions de-veloping across the strife-torn mining West. The power of the mining companies was apparent when the bill was attacked by Senator O'Neil, elected from Shoshone County where the eight-hour provision had passed 2,049 to 70. O'Neil explained that "the mining interests up there are opposed to the eight-hour measure. That settles it for me. I am here to represent the people of my county." With the farm counties' representatives joining those who sympathized with mine owners, the eight-hour bill was blocked in the Idaho Legislature in 1903; the vote was 23 to 18 in the House and 22 to 17 in the Senate.

The momentum of the movement in Idaho was further slowed by the publicity given to the bloody events in Colorado in the ensuing months. When the bill came up again in the legislature in 1905, warnings of violent upheavals if the status quo were upset dominated much of the debate. Representative France of Shoshone County contended that reduction in hours would necessitate a wage reduction, and this "might result in conditions such as have existed in Colorado for the past two years. Do you want that in Idaho?" He also noted that the Republican candidates—despite the party's actions in the 1903 session—had swept Shoshone County during the previous election, and the leading opponent of the eight-hour proposal was re-elected. France asserted flatly that "the votes of the miners of Shoshone County are already recorded against this bill."

More significant was the opposition of Adam Aulbach, a Democrat from Murray, also in Shoshone County. As former owner of the Wallace *Press* in the 1890s, Aulbach had been a close observer of the Coeur d'Alenes strife. He told a reporter during an interview as the session opened, "I have not lived there since the labor troubles," speaking in a tone which the *Statesman* reporter said "denoted some significance." Despite his pro-labor background, when the eight-hour bill came up in the House in 1905, Representative Aulbach voted against it. "The Coeur d'Alenes were now at peace," he said in defense of his vote, "and it would be wrong to disturb such conditions and unfair to the miners, who had never petitioned for an eight-hour law." Aulbach advocated "standing pat" on existing conditions "rather than go back and stir up revolution." The bill was defeated, 30 to 15.

What the WFM and its political campaigns and strikes could not accomplish, a labor shortage brought about in Idaho in 1906 and 1907. Faced with inadequate crews—with "piratical small operators" luring miners away from large companies by offering higher wages—the major mining interests suddenly became enamored of the eight-hour principle. The large Coeur d'Alenes mines shifted to the eight-hour system while maintaining the former rate of wages, and Republicans were transformed into eight-hour men for the 1906 campaign. When the issue came up in the next session of the legislature, the Idaho House wasted few hours in approving the plan, but the other chamber was even faster. The Senate took five minutes.[44]

Frustrations were fewer elsewhere in the U.S. and Canadian West, but eight-hour-day legislation had difficulties everywhere. And as conflicts over the issue multiplied, Western miners became more open to considering avenues for change outside of party politics.

An eight-hour law was passed in British Columbia at the end of the 1899 session of the provincial legislature, under the prodding of the WFM, which had recently begun organizing miners north of the border. Mine owners were incensed at the suddenness of the bill's appearance and passage, and blamed "the scum of American camps" coming north into Rossland, Slocan, and other Kootenay mining communities. Due to the higher wages in Slocan—$3.50 rather than the $3 elsewhere —employers there argued that they could not economically abide by the law. Representatives of American mining firms operating in the district simply ignored the new measure.

Other companies gave in, however, providing an enlarged foothold for the WFM in British Columbia. Soon two types of "outsiders" were arriving in the Kootenay: Italians, Missouri-ans, and other strikebreakers on the one hand; and WFM mem-bers driven from the strife-torn Coeur d'Alenes, on the other. Attempts to use the Canadian Alien Labour Act against either group immediately led to demands that it be used on the other. Because of this, and because the Canadian government feared upsetting relations with the United States over its enforcement in the Eastern provinces, the Alien Labour Act was of little im-portance in the British Columbia eight-hour troubles. This cleared the way for the union to keep out strikebreakers by various forms of persuasion, which largely succeeded. The WFM was consequently able to win the major strikes over the issue in British Columbia, and could announce in 1900 that the eight-hour law was in effect there despite the mine owners' continued opposition.[45]

Although the eight-hour day had been in force on the Comstock earlier, it had fallen by the wayside by the late 'eight-ies, when the Gold Hill Miners' Union began discussing the system again. A bill to enact the eight-hour plan in Nevada was not passed until 1903, covering miners and employees of smelters and refining works. In an early test case brought against a cyanide plant owner, the act was overturned by a district judge on grounds that by affecting two types of workers it un-constitutionally covered two separate measures. The WFM won a reversal in the case of *In re Boyce* before the Nevada

Supreme Court in 1904. A strike erupted at Searchlight, Nevada, in the dispute over enforcement of the new eight-hour law.[46]

The year 1903 saw Arizona, Nevada's neighbor, also pass an eight-hour law following an extensive political campaign by miners' unions. A legislative compromise excluded smelter and mill employees, however, from the final measure. The territory's copper mine operators then sought to reduce wages as well as hours, prompting an employee walkout. The Arizona Rangers arrived at Morenci on June 6, 1903, in response to the employers' pleas. Five days later, President Theodore Roosevelt sent in federal troops, and a court injunction ordered the miners back to work. The strike leader was sentenced to two years' imprisonment and fined $2,000, and nine of his assistants also received heavy penalties. The WFM's *Miners' Magazine* complained that federal troops were sent "to aid the corporations in trampling under foot" the new law. A stronger, broader eight-hour bill was not passed in Arizona until after statehood in 1912.[47]

The eight-hour day for miners in the Black Hills of South Dakota was not achieved through legislation during the 1890s and early 1900s, but was granted in 1906 to employees of the Homestake Mine at Lead, the district's major mining enterprise. Contemporary speculation considered this a political move designed to tarnish other local mining companies. When "a large majority" of the smaller operators rejected shorter hours, the WFM launched a lengthy strike which finally brought the eight-hour shift to the rest of its members in the Black Hills.[48]

This left California alone without eight-hour-day coverage for hard-rock miners among the major Western metal-mining states. Despite its role as the pioneer of Western mining, California had not given birth to a miners' union movement capable of more than limited success. There was considerable evidence, then, to support the assertion by the president of the Tuolumne Miners' Union in 1900 that California was "the poorest organized state in the West," resulting in a variety of wage scales and "more poorly paid men than any other Western state." California "practically offers no protection to the miner," he added—no mine inspector, no hours limitation, no ban on compulsory hospital fees. In 1908, the criticism was repeated by another California WFM member, who claimed that "ours is the only state in the West without an eight-hour law" for mining company employees, and he urged the dispatch of more union organizers to agitate the issue. A year later, in 1909, the California Legislature passed an eight-hour law covering miners, smeltermen, and millworkers. Its constitutionality was upheld, for by then the day was past when a Western court could prevent hard-rock miners from achieving the eight-hour day.[49]

When he looked back on these struggles from 1910, WFM President Charles H. Moyer took pride in the success of the miners' eight-hour-day movement. "To organized labor," he stated, "must be given the credit for the reduction in the hours of toil." Because of the union's agitation through both politics and strikes, he explained, "we have the eight-hour workday in almost every state and territory in our jurisdiction."[50]

There was much that was unsaid in Moyer's benediction on the eight-hour day. He undoubtedly could still recall the bloody campaigns in Colorado, when he was imprisoned for using the flag in a poster, and when he had scornfully commented that "after ninety days' session, capital has gained another victory and labor once more realized that their franchise had accomplished nothing." Success had come, but at an extremely high cost. For many disillusioned miners, the struggle over the eight-hour day in the century's opening years first eroded and then destroyed the links of trust and support that bound them to their government. They became cynical about the effectiveness of the political system. Not surprisingly, these men began to search for other solutions to the problems of the Western hard-rock miner.[51]

CHAPTER IX

Radicalism and the "Red-Hot Revolutionists"

Kindled by defeats in the eight-hour-day and other campaigns, and nourished and sustained by the antagonism of increasingly powerful corporations, radicalism began to spread across the transformed Western landscape.* The pioneer era of Western hard-rock mining thus appeared to be closing with a large portion of the labor force endorsing the overthrow of existing economic and political systems. These miners appeared to be moving toward a syndicalist philosophy which advocated extensive strikes to gain control of production. In Melvyn Dubofsky's succinct phrase, they were among those who "opted for an alternative to the capitalist order."[1]

The radicalism that emerged within the Western Federation of Miners and its offspring, the Industrial Workers of the World (IWW), has received extensive examination. Various conditions have been discovered in the development of Western lode mining that helped encourage radical approaches. Frontier isolation, it is argued, made social polarization more facile because of the absence of intervening, moderating groups in the community. Or the rapid growth of industrial centers

---

*As used here, *radicalism* means seeking sweeping changes in the principles of society. In the case of Western miners, radicalism was an attempt to create an entirely new basis for the existing economic and political systems.

created disruptive, Pittsburgh-like conditions that quickly imposed patterns of Eastern labor-management conflict on the new urban islands of the frontier. Or the failure of earlier reform groups such as the Knights of Labor and the Populists drove the frustrated miners to make their own attempt at changing the system. Such developments, it is argued, caused miners to seriously question the existing basis of society and, in the process, to come up with plans for a vastly different order.[2]

These explanations are compelling, for all can be shown to have played some part in the WFM's shift to the left during the turn-of-the-century years. But taken together or separately they are insufficient. As William Preston has pointed out, these conditions existed in other areas as well without leading to radical labor programs.[3]

The sweep of hard-rock mining history from the start of deep mining at Central City and the Comstock Lode leads to a different conclusion. Radicalism, viewed in the context of the long-term experiences of hard-rock miners across the West, stemmed most immediately from a mounting sense of desperation among workmen who felt that they were suddenly losing their capacity to protect themselves in a world dominated by trusts and corporations that could count on government allies. Sensing this, they clutched at alternatives.

There was much evidence to support their worst fears. Corporate power had, without doubt, grown sharply in many areas of the West in the 1890s and early 1900s. Moreover, many of the new industrial giants were highly visible and were absentee-owned, such as the American Smelting and Refining Company, which was taken over by the Guggenheim interests in 1902 and "practically includes all the silver-lead smelting interests in the United States." Standard Oil gained control of the Amalgamated (Anaconda) operations in Butte as the Heinze-Clark-Daly feuds were ending, and it rapidly enlarged the 55 to 60 percent of U.S. copper production that it already controlled by 1902. Soon the Amalgamated owned banks, newspapers, hotels, water and electric plants, and railroad yards across Montana. Giant firms also dominated other areas. In Bisbee, Arizona, it was Phelps Dodge; in the Coeur d'Alenes, it was the Bunker Hill & Sullivan; and at Goldfield in the Nevada sagebrush, all the operating mines but one fell under the control of two men within a year after the district opened in 1906.

Even the new Alaskan mining frontier was invaded in 1908 by the Morgan-Guggenheim interests, which soon controlled copper and gold mines, the Alaskan Steamship Company, a railroad, and fish canneries. The "vampire which has already started its blood sucking operation," the Nome *Gold Digger* warned, "is laying its plans for the complete subjection of the country to its will."[4]

Even where a dominant firm did not emerge, employers in many areas ceased their traditional feuding and drew together in mine operators' associations which—aided by the use of spies—often aimed at blocking miners' unions. The 1891–1904 period was prolific in the formation of such alliances—the Coeur d'Alenes Mine Owners' Protective Association in 1891 ("almost simultaneous" with the birth of the first miners' union), the Northwest Miners' Association, the Colorado Mine Operators' Association, the Idaho State Mining Association, and several others across the West. The *Mining and Scientific Press* applauded the moves: mine operators, it observed, "alone have made no consolidation of interests and naturally have become the bird to be plucked." In Colorado, this development was carried another step with the growth of local citizens' alliances, which soon merged with mine owners' associations to challenge union power.[5]

Responding to union threats, unity began to replace the quarrels and feuding once common among mine owners. A clue to the motivation behind this growing cooperation is provided in a letter from the head of the Goldfield Mine Owners' Association to his counterpart in Cripple Creek, during the WFM trials in Boise in 1907:

> Matters here have taken such a form in the struggle with the labor situation that we have been obliged to organize. . . .
> What I really wish to bring to your attention is the fact that the cause of operators in Goldfield is now practically identical with yours, and I should like for my personal information, to be posted as to the progress of the Idaho cases. It may be that we can assist you. . . .

The head of the Cripple Creek association agreed, and quickly wrote back:

> Am very glad to hear that you are getting your organization in working shape and sincerely hope that you will be able to avoid

trouble but am afraid you will not as long as the Federation have a hold there. . . .

While Idaho is carrying on this fight the people there as well as here feel that this is a fight that vitally concerns all metal-mining operators in the West and that they should all work together.[6]

Sensing profitable opportunities, new detective agencies entered the field of Western mining, as indicated in this letter received in 1906 by the manager of the Trade Dollar mine in Owyhee County, Idaho. It was sent by the Manufacturers Information Bureau's office in Denver:

Dear Sir:

Considering the status of labor conditions (the redoubled effort to organize all mining camps since the arrest of the WFM officials), we believe as an employer of labor you are naturally desirous of keeping your mines clear of agitators and trouble breeders.

Our Inspection System, embracing educational features, now operated on a large scale, international in scope, promptly and unfailingly uncovers employees who are dishonest, incompetent, extravagant, or disloyal to your interests. . . .

We furnish PRACTICAL MEN, educated in this work, who report daily and cover all meetings. . . . [They are] a quiet, peaceful, subtle influence; an exigency devised to meet a condition. . . .[7]

The formation of employers' alliances, the increased use of "spotters" hidden among the crews, and the frequency of government intervention to protect corporation property—these began to produce a new world for workmen who had known life under the smaller, feuding, litigation-beset operations of earlier days. Many miners became convinced that their world was under seige. WFM oratory from the turn of the century onward is heavily laced with this fear. An era was passing—but the new era arrived bearing a yoke for working men. William D. ("Big Bill") Haywood, the one-eyed WFM leader, wrote that the miners he encountered in the Coeur d'Alenes in the late 'nineties "were in a fever of revolt. There was no method of appeal; strike was their only weapon." And, he added, soon other Western miners saw that "the legislature, the courts, and the army were against us. . . . If this dreadful thing happened in Leadville, in the Coeur d'Alenes, how long before it happens in Butte, in the Black Hills, in Nevada? What is to stop it happening in the camp where I live?" The WFM's *Miners' Magazine* warned in 1903 that "never before in the history of the West have the mining corporations presented a more arrogant front than now. . . ." "Annihilation" was viewed as the purpose of the newly organized employers, and the federation's executive board read a clear lesson from it all: "It is our firm conviction that the days of our privilege to strike for better conditions or to resist tyranny are about over."[8]

It was this sense of desperation that propelled the WFM into radicalism as the Colorado tragedy ran its course. References to a past happier time now became frequent. Ed Boyce, WFM president from 1896 to 1902, looked back to the federation's beginnings in 1893 and saw no improvement since then in the miner's independence. At that time, he explained, many districts were still unprospected, so that a discharged or blacklisted miner "could become his own employer, and in many cases did better than he could working for a day's wage. . . ." But by 1903, he stated, the industry had fallen into the hands of a few men whose power was such that no WFM member could truthfully say "he is more secure in the employ of the trust today than he was in the employ of the individual ten years ago," and the opportunity for a job outside the trust's control "is almost impossible." Further concentration of capital would bring the end of the WFM, Boyce warned ominously, "for the money wrung from the earth by the miners will be used to destroy their organization. . . ."[9]

Several major strands of radical thought began to appear in the oratory and writings of the WFM's leadership. Boyce called in 1897 for the membership to obtain rifles, and he repeatedly attacked the wage system as "slavery in its worst form." He warned that there could be no harmony between organized capitalists and organized labor, for employers wanted long hours and low wages, and workers wanted short hours and high wages. Boyce complained to the 1902 WFM Convention that the federation had faced over fifty lockouts in nine years, "and in all instances the forces of government have been used against us." This polarization evident in Boyce's denunciations, the belief in the irreconcilable nature of labor-management relations, became the cornerstone of the hard-rock miners' radicalism.[10]

Haywood, who would eventually jump bail and flee to the Soviet Union during the post–World War I "red scare," became

the proponent of a plan for the WFM to create a system of cooperative mines, waiting for the day (not expected "for at least ten
years") when the government would operate the mines. Others,
such as President Charles Moyer (who succeeded Boyce in
1902), attacked time contracts because workers had "to be free
at all times to take advantage of any opportunity to temporarily
better our condition." Despite a WFM prohibition on them,
however, time contracts were in force in several districts, including such union strongholds as Butte and Tonopah.[11]

Closely tied to this was the WFM's growing estrangement
from the American Federation of Labor and the entire philosophy of trade unionism—that is, of confining organization to
skilled workers mainly concerned with protecting themselves,
with little attention to the unskilled even if working for the same
employer. The WFM had affiliated with the AFL in 1896, but
Boyce became angered at the latter's conservatism and lack of
aid to the WFM during the Leadville strike that year. Boyce and
AFL President Samuel Gompers began a duel through the mails,
which led to the WFM's withdrawal from the AFL in 1897.
Hostility increased as the miners created the Western Labor
Union and the American Labor Union to compete for the allegiance of other workmen in the AFL's jurisdiction. Western
working men, Boyce wrote, "are one hundred years ahead of
their brothers in the East," and he added that he "never was
so much surprised in my life" as at the 1896 AFL convention
when delegates talked of "conservative action when 4,000,000
idle men and women are tramps upon the highway. . . ." He
blamed the "vicious system of government" for this, and said
it would continue until workers "have the MANHOOD TO
GET OUT AND FIGHT WITH THE SWORD or use the ballot with
intelligence."[12]

The WFM leader took the lead in proselytizing socialism
among hard-rock miners before he resigned his office in 1902.
Boyce had apparently been converted sometime in the 'nineties, possibly during the Leadville strike of 1896, when he is
known to have been with Socialist leader Eugene V. Debs. In
1900, the WFM Convention, under Boyce's leadership, declared first in its list of principles: "We believe that the wage
system should be abolished and the production of labor be distributed under the co-operative plan." Number seven in the
list proclaimed: "We regard public ownership and operation

of the means of production and distribution as the logical solution of the industrial problem," and urged workers to "give the subject the thoughtful consideration its importance deserves." Boyce's final speech to the WFM, in 1902, called for members to "adopt the principles of Socialism without equivocation. . . ." The 1903 convention reiterated the previous year's stand and pledged not to pause "in a determined effort to bring about such a change in our social and economic conditions as will result in a complete revolution of the present system of industrial slavery." The delegates defeated a plan, however, that would have barred members from running for political office as Democrats or Republicans.[13]

Although the WFM majority shifted sharply away from the regular parties in this move into socialism ("Does anyone believe for one moment that the moneyed class of this country will relinquish their power over the dominant political parties?", Moyer asked in 1905), it should be noted that the organization did not abandon its belief in the political route for protection. In 1904, the WFM executive board painted a bleak picture of workmen's conditions but still recommended that "independent political action be the slogan of the wage earners, as we see in this alone the solution of the problem." A year later, President Moyer stressed a two-pronged attack: "Industrial unionism on the industrial field, class-conscious political action on the political field, are weapons still in the hands of the masses."[14]

And it did seem that politics might pay off. That was the first reaction in November, 1904, when Colorado voters rejected Governor Peabody's bid for re-election—the same Peabody who had helped to block the eight-hour day, who upheld deportations of union men, and who rushed to the aid of businessmen whenever they felt threatened by the WFM. It was a successful use of political action by working men and their allies. *The Miners' Magazine* was elated.

Within weeks, however, rumors began to appear that mine owners and their friends were concocting a scheme to overturn the election results. Each new allegation, each hint that such a coup would be attempted, brought a corresponding weakening of faith in the electoral process among WFM leaders. Rumor soon became fact. The Colorado Supreme Court upheld claims that the Democrats had won through vote fraud, and ordered the victory given to Peabody in March, 1905; as prearranged, he resigned so that the Republican lieutenant governor could become governor. This act ripped away the WFM's lingering faith in obtaining protection through voting strength: "Our boast that the ballot is the potent weapon through which wrongs may be redressed has received a jolt. . . ."[15]

The "jolt" from these events of 1903–1905 proved to be the final blow in propelling the federation away from supporting political action and into the formation of revolutionary demands supporting socialism, the general strike, and direct action to seize control of the means of production.

In retrospect, then, the formation of the Industrial Workers of the World in 1905 can be regarded as the culmination of the WFM's frustrations from the 1896 Leadville strike onward, as the organization tried various avenues to protect itself from being overwhelmed by the growing power of employers. Strikes, politics, cooperative mining, educating the membership, joining with other groups such as the Populists—all these strategies had fallen short of the goal, in the minds of WFM leaders.

But one approach, gradually developing over previous years, still seemed to hold out the possibility of success. This was the attempt to build a massive, broad-based organization of working men, not limited to mine and smelter employees, to drastically augment union strength and overpower adversaries. Thus, the WFM created the Western Labor Union and enlarged it to form the American Labor Union; the WFM also sent organizers into metal mining regions outside the West, such as Minnesota, Michigan, and Missouri; and President Boyce in 1902 called for the WFM to invite other labor organizations "to meet in convention for the purpose of outlining a plan by which they can unite for political action." Two years later, more definite steps were taken when the 1904 convention instructed the WFM executive board to plan "for the amalgamation of the entire working class into one general organization." A meeting was held under WFM and ALU auspices on November 6, 1904, in Chicago, resulting in a call to some thirty supporters of industrial unionism to convene there early in

1905. This second session prepared for the June 27, 1905, gathering that founded the Industrial Workers of the World.[16]

The new organization was the child of the WFM. Hard-rock miners authorized the planning sessions, played the crucial role in organizing the first convention, and represented the only significant labor union present among a conglomeration of so-called "leaders" who claimed to speak for large groups but in fact had been chosen only by the WFM and ALU representatives who sent out invitations. A final boost from the miners came when the WFM convention voted overwhelmingly in favor of the federation participating in the new labor body's activities. Haywood later recalled that in the first IWW session "it was the miners' delegates that decided every important issue. They had come with the definite purpose of organizing an industrial union."[17]

Students of the IWW have continued to give heavy emphasis to the WFM's role in its creation. "In a quite real sense," Paul Brissenden has written, "the IWW was born out of the Western Federation." He cites the financial and physical support of the "militant miners union," the heavy proportion of the IWW's membership (one-third) that came from the WFM, and the fact that the bitter WFM fights in Colorado and elsewhere "prepared the ground and spread the sentiment for the extension of revolutionary industrialism." Melvyn Dubofsky agrees: the major IWW characteristics, he states, were already present in the WFM by 1903—industrial unionism, labor solidarity, political nonpartisanship, direct economic action, and syndicalism. And these came not from Socialist intellectuals or Europeans but from "the experiences Western workers had lived through in America. . . ."[18]

The initial enthusiasm of hard-rock miners for the philosophies of the IWW lasted into 1907, even though the two organizations' leaders were already backing off from each other by then. That the WFM still sought radical change was apparent in the new preamble to the federation's constitution, which was substituted that year:

1. We hold that there is a class struggle in society and that this struggle is caused by economic conditions.
2. We affirm the economic condition of the producer to be that

he is exploited of the wealth that he produces, being allowed
to retain barely sufficient for his elementary necessities.
3. We hold that the class struggle will continue until the producer is recognized as the sole master of his product. . . .
4. We assert that the working class, and it alone, can and must
achieve its own emancipation.
5. We hold, finally, that an industrial union and the concerted
political action of all wage workers is the only method of
attaining this end.

The new preamble also referred to WFM members as "wage
slaves."[19]

This document closely paralleled the original preamble of
the IWW. Declaring that "the working class and the employing class have nothing in common," the IWW predicted that
a struggle between the two classes would continue until workers "come together on the political, as well as on the industrial
field, and take hold of that which they produce by their labor
through an economic organization of the working class, without affiliation with any political party." The concentration of
industry, the IWW's preamble stated, could not be changed
by divided trade unions but by an organization that combined
all employees within one industry "or in all industries if necessary," so that they could all strike together.[20]

Much emphasis has been given to the personality clashes
that brought about the estrangement between the federation and
its offspring. Especially noted are the role of Daniel De Leon
and his abrasive tactics that helped drive some WFM delegates from the IWW hall in 1906. The arrest early that year of
Haywood, Moyer, and George Pettibone for the murder of
Idaho's ex-Governor Steunenberg has also been cited as depriv-
ing both organizations of the radical dominance of Haywood.
The Idaho trials—although ultimately resulting in freedom for
the three men—left control of the federation's relations with
the IWW in the hands of less radical officers, and also allegedly
convinced Moyer that the WFM could be destroyed unless it
managed to discard its reputation for violence.[21]

While leadership and personalities—and egos—were obviously important, the basic philosophical differences should
not be lost sight of in examining the split between the WFM
and its offspring. Political action became the first fundamental

stumbling block to long-term unity when the IWW's anti-politics faction gained dominance in 1906 and 1907 and eradicated their preamble's call for workers to join politically. Moyer and Haywood also began to drift apart; by the end of the first trial, Moyer had aligned himself with moderates while Haywood was leaning toward the IWW's anti-politics faction. Haywood's stance was apparently based partly on his friendship with Vincent St. John, a WFM veteran of Telluride who later became the IWW's secretary-treasurer.[22]

But it is also clear that the reconstituted IWW of 1906 was too radical and visionary to be accepted by the bulk of the hard-rock miners. These were men who, despite several crushing defeats, had won many legislative and economic victories over the previous decade. Suspicions grew as WFM members began to realize that their control of the IWW had been sharply reduced although they provided a large part of its membership and finances. Moyer apparently sensed this growing incompatibility quickly, for he wrote from his Idaho prison cell on October 2, 1906:

> If the reports in the *Daily People* are correct, I want to serve notice on those calling themselves revolutionists that their program will never receive my endorsement, nor that of the Western Federation of Miners, if in my power to prevent it. By the gods, I have suffered too much, worked too hard to ever tamely submit to the Western Federation of Miners being turned over to Mr. Daniel De Leon, to take the place of his defunct trades and labor alliance. . . . Centralization of power with De Leonites at the helm, and the final landing of the organization in the ranks of the Socialist Labor Party is the object. . . .

This critique was supported by the editor of the *Miners' Magazine*, who condemned the attempt to make the federation give up its autonomy "to a mushroom combination of revolutionary shouters. . . ."[23]

At the heart of the debate was the action of the De Leon faction in forcing out the IWW's president, a WFM delegate, during the 1906 IWW session. Moyer labeled the proceedings as unconstitutional, "damnable acts," and drove his point home in a letter to the WFM membership: "Let us be consistent," he stated; if the federation condemned government officials "for trampling under foot the constitution" to imprison Moyer, Haywood, and Pettibone, "let us not spare those who follow in their footsteps, applying the same methods" to illegally oust the elected president of the IWW. And he made it clear whom he was condemning: the "revolutionists."[24]

One historian has put January 1, 1907—shortly after Moyer's letters were sent—as the real end of the WFM's connections with the IWW. This was well before the miners' stormy convention in June and July, 1907, when the question of ties to the IWW was debated. Following that tumultuous session, feeble attempts were made to sponsor a meeting aimed at reestablishing the IWW, but the rigidity of the opposing sides blocked compromise. For example, despite Haywood's importance within the union, his enthusiasm for the IWW made him unwelcome to other federation leaders, who abruptly terminated his appointment as a WFM field representative. When Haywood stood to address the 1908 WFM convention, Charles Moyer rose and left the hall, according to Haywood's later recollection. By that time, the federation had given up cooperating with what a union organizer termed the "red-hot revolutionists."[25]

Events outside the convention hall gave further impetus to anti-IWW sentiment within the Western Federation—in such far-flung outposts as Alaska's Tanana and Nome districts; Goldfield, Nevada; and Butte. In each, radical activities brought divisions that weakened the miners' union movement. Much of this radicalism originated with IWW members, and negative community reaction paralleled a rise of anti-"revolutionist" feeling among WFM members.

The IWW-WFM dispute spread rapidly to Alaska. There, Tanana district (Fairbanks) miners who had surged into one of the continent's last major gold rushes became angered at their employers' cost-cutting and formed a union in early 1907. They launched a strike in April to obtain the eight-hour day —which prevailed in other Alaskan employment—and made some success under the WFM's Yukon organizer in developing community support. His attempt to prevent the growth of a radical or violent image was upset, however, when union militants provided the evidence sought by critics who claimed "socialist agitators and anarchists" were present in the organization. When strikebreakers were being marched in from the coast, union militants ambushed them on the trail, spurring reports of "anarchy" and convincing Fairbanks citizens to form three rifle companies for anti-union duties. Martial law was declared, a union-patronized saloon was closed, and the union newspaper was slapped with libel charges. The strike was finally crushed after some union men shot at a train transporting strikebreakers to the mines. The Tanana union soon joined with the WFM's local in Nome—then wracked with an IWW-WFM struggle—to back a candidate in the upcoming election for territorial delegate to Congress. The opposition campaign tarred the union candidate as an "anarchial socialist" because of his WFM support; he lost. Whether accurate or not, the image of the WFM as a radical organization was proving a burden.[26]

In Goldfield, Nevada, during the same period, the IWW captured WFM Local 220 and attempted to gain complete dominance over the district. Many miners in Goldfield had been deported from Colorado and held a cynical attitude toward both government and employers. Vincent St. John, for example, went to Goldfield late in 1906 after being freed from a Colorado jail, and was soon rising as a leader in the new district. At a celebration to commemorate the St. Petersburg massacre in Russia, the Goldfield workmen under St. John and other IWW militants approved resolutions condemning the President of the United States and the U.S. Supreme Court, as well as lambasting Idaho authorities for holding Moyer, Haywood, and Pettibone. St. John later recalled with enthusiasm the IWW's control in Goldfield:

> The highest point of efficiency for any labor organization was reached by the IWW and WFM in Goldfield, Nevada. No committees were ever sent to any employers. The unions adopted wage scales and regulated hours. The secretary posted the same on a bulletin board outside of the union hall, and it was the LAW. The employers were forced to come and see the union committees.[27]

On October 22, 1907, the Goldfield WFM local passed a resolution urging the federation to maintain its ties with the IWW rather than breaking them as top WFM officials were then advocating. The IWW dominance was revealed in other events as well. AFL carpenters were instructed to join the WFM or quit their jobs, and this dispute led to a restaurant shoot-out. IWW supporters won control of a mass meeting originally called to reassert WFM strength, and a pro-WFM vote at another meeting was quickly overturned by the IWW. The IWW was, it seemed, supreme in Goldfield.

In late November, 1907, however, a strike over the use of scrip to pay employees provided mine owners with the opportunity to destroy both the WFM and the IWW in the district. A Business Men's and Mine Operators' Association had been formed after the earlier strikes, and this group became convinced that the local WFM was dominated by the radical IWW element. To break the union, they closed their mines until the nation's financial crisis lifted, smelter charges declined, and labor conditions improved. Governor Sparks was then prevailed upon to call for federal troops. The soldiers' presence after December 6, 1907, was instrumental in crushing the union, although the troops were soon recalled. With this backing, however, employers were able to adopt the notorious "rustling card"—a note required of each job applicant which showed that he was without a radical past and which promised no union activities. Soldiers and the rustling card soon left the district, but they had served their purpose. The union abandoned the strike in April, 1908.

After examining the complex Goldfield situation, Vernon Jensen has concluded that "internal dissension in the union was as much responsible as the opposition of the employers" for the union defeat. The Goldfield Miners' Union, he stated, "was the first casualty" in the war between the WFM and the IWW. Delegates to the 1908 WFM convention were informed by one of their leaders that because of the "bitter, insane, factional fight" at Goldfield, "the strongest, most progressive and advanced local union of the federation was soon torn into warring elements." A major reason for this was the IWW's attempt to gain total dominance over the entire community, a goal which the WFM had not sought; this led only to a bitter reaction against the unions in Goldfield and severely eroded local support.[28]

Divisions based on the WFM-IWW feud also created "warring elements" in Butte's Local Number One, the "Gibraltar of Unionism." After the show of power by the Amalgamated in 1903—when it closed its enterprises, threw 20,000 men out of work, and forced the Montana Legislature to bow to its demand for a change of venue law—the corporation continued to increase its dominance over the union as well as over the state's economy. Under this pressure, the union's local leadership became more conservative at the same time that the federation was shifting leftward with the creation of the IWW. When the company offered a higher wage in 1906, pegged to fluctuations in the price of copper, the local union leadership accepted it as part of a five-year contract. This flew in the face of the federation's prohibition against signing time contracts, and brought a storm of abuse from within the Butte local as well as from other WFM groups. This controversy added to the tumult of the 1907 WFM convention. During the same period, rumors began to appear of Amalgamated influence within the ranks of Local Number One. Allegations were further stimulated when the copper price fell, causing a wage reduction in Butte under terms of the recently signed contract. An economic downturn in late 1907 brought the discharge of some 6,000 Amalgamated employees.

Soon the feuding between factions within the Butte organization took a more violent turn. That the IWW was present as well as Amalgamated agents is not questioned; the closeness of the IWW's ties to some of the events of 1908–1914 is not clear, however. These ranged from the disruption of a union meeting in 1908 when Moyer was present, to turmoil that forced the WFM executive board to take control of the local on June 19, 1914, followed by the dynamiting of the Butte Miners Union hall four days later. Moyer was convinced that the IWW was the instigator of Butte's troubles; the Socialist mayor of Butte, however, declared that the IWW did not take part in the 1914 bombing. But when a new union was formed, a majority of the twenty-man executive committee were known IWW members.

Counterattacks by Moyer and others were of no avail. Butte was put under martial law after another dynamiting, and troops took control of the district for several months. And suddenly, on September 9, 1914—eight days after the National Guard's arrival—the Amalgamated announced that it would no longer deal with the miners' union. This meant, as Melvyn Dubofsky has stated, that "what had once been the strongest miners' union in the West was no more. Indeed, union domination of Butte had been completely terminated."[29]

But long before these events in Butte, many WFM members had become convinced that the IWW was out to take over their organization or tear it apart in the process. The major concern of these members became, as Moyer phrased it in 1908, to "first preserve our own organization" in order to lead the way to industrial unionism. Only brief years before, preserving the WFM had meant an all-out attack on mining and smelting corporations and their governmental allies—but by 1908 the immediate threat to the federation was the IWW. When saving the WFM required abandoning the IWW, most members chose to maintain their ties to their own federation.[30]

Other WFM decisions growing out of this disenchantment with the IWW's brand of radicalism included the growing realization that few working men supported the leap into industrial unionism; that political action held out more hope than syndicalism for improving the life of the working class; and that attempts to dominate employers completely (as at Goldfield) were hopeless and should give way to reason and justice in seeking "an amicable adjustment" of difficulties. Also, the federation's leaders realized that, more than ever, the WFM needed allies.

President Moyer in 1908 and 1909 struck out at proposals to bring all American workmen to industrial unionism. This was "undertaking the impossible," he warned, for most workers were content with capitalism. The Knights of Labor had failed, the American Railway Union was crushed, and industrial unionism "is by no means popular; . . . it is not wanted by the working class of the United States." What should the WFM do? Here the co-founder of the IWW revealed the discouragement of preceding years: "Let us continue our efforts, for the time being, in bringing into our ranks these people over which we claim jurisdiction" in the metal mines.[31]

Accompanying this aspect of the retreat from radicalism was the call for a return to political action, a philosophy spurned amid the flush of creating the IWW. It is clear in retrospect, however, that the WFM membership had never fully accepted the rejection of politics, for across the West large numbers of hard-rock miners had continued to participate in state and local election campaigns. The bitter debates at the 1907 convention revealed that many WFM delegates did not share the IWW rejection of both major parties and of politics in general. They

241

even turned down a plan to prohibit their union officers from accepting nominations of non-Socialist parties. The road to political action, they affirmed, was to remain open.[32]

The miners also refused to jettison traditional approaches to improving working conditions. This became clear from the debates and reports in yearly WFM conventions, and it apparently formed part of the backdrop to Moyer's plea in 1908 that the union should meet employers "in a straightforward, businesslike manner," using facts and being firm but "ready to listen to the other side. . . ." Rather than pushing the membership into the class struggle, Moyer urged them to "meet the employer halfway. . . ." The contrast with IWW rhetoric—and with the WFM's own rhetoric just two or three years earlier—was enormous, and was additional testimony to the reaction against the IWW's revolutionary methods.[33]

Beyond his concern for the reactions of employers, Moyer was extremely worried about the growing isolation of his federation. Old and potential allies were no longer willing to lend support, as a WFM organizer discovered when he received a frosty reception in a meeting with AFL carpenters in Spokane in early 1908. He soon learned that "the treatment handed to the carpenters of Goldfield by some of our red-hot revolutionists was the cause of the icy atmosphere I encountered that evening. . . ." After similar receptions in Portland, Tacoma, and Everett, the organizer reported back to the WFM: "Our chickens are coming home to roost."[34]

There were many other occasions when miners' unions became aware that one of the major costs of revolutionary agitation was isolation. Sometimes this price was too high to pay. A WFM leader in Index, Washington, implied as much when he responded to criticism in the *Miners' Magazine* of a conciliatory speech he had given in his community. The Index leader argued that because of the depressed state of the district's mines, some local companies would be glad for an excuse to shut down, "so you see we cannot afford to be arrogant." He added that he had spoken "to suit conditions that exist now," before a varied audience which he did "not propose to alienate. . . . The success of a union in a small place like this depends not a little on its social standing."[35]

This growing fear of isolation produced renewed interest in establishing ties with unions that had been insulted or treated coolly by the WFM during the swing to radicalism. This paralleled the need to keep doors open to political allies as well. Such actions were encouraged by the fact that unions across the nation had provided crucial financial aid to the WFM during its troubled days of court actions and lockouts. For example, despite the WFM's jibes at the conservatism of the United Mine Workers of America, coal miners' locals from the East and Midwest sent large amounts of financial support in 1903–1904, and the *Miners' Magazine* was moved to acknowledge this loyalty gratefully in early 1904. The launching of the IWW a year later precluded the development of close ties between the WFM and the more conservative UMWA. But after the federation broke with the IWW, both the UMWA and the United Brewery Workers were invited to send delegates to the 1909 WFM convention, and hard-rock miners visited the UMWA at its Indianapolis convention in 1910.[36]

The next step away from isolation was to re-establish ties with the American Federation of Labor. Since the AFL still included many industrial unionists (such as the UMWA) and socialists, this move was not a surrender but rather another attempt to seek allies; the possibility of reforming the errant AFL still remained open as well. In January, 1910, representatives of the WFM and the AFL met to discuss establishing closer ties, and these steps toward reconciliation were approved by the WFM convention delegates, 265 to 35. In May, 1911, the WFM formally rejoined the AFL.[37]

These constituted the major policies emerging from the WFM's break with the IWW. All had roots in the union's earlier experiences, but they were shaped as well by a melange of current and historical factors within the membership—ranging from the hard-rock miners' expectations, to their support for private ownership and the established political parties, to a variety of personal characteristics noted below. These factors had only been submerged, not eliminated, when the series of crushing defeats at the hands of corporations drove the miners into a frantic quest to prevent the destruction of their movement. As months went by, however, the rising concern over the IWW's embrace enabled these latent anti-radical pressures to emerge again. The result was not a conservative Western Federation but an organization seeking to protect its members without endorsing revolt. The WFM after 1908, as before, took in a variety of philosophies, but those that fit IWW ideals were weakened, while the anti-IWW tendencies were strengthened by the experiences of the previous three years.

One of the basic factors underlying the refusal by many miners to march under the IWW's banner was that the suffering and frustrations of the Colorado labor wars were not shared by the bulk of the WFM membership. Writers have long assumed that the WFM's defeat in Cripple Creek was merely the experience of Tincup, Silver City, Lump Gulch, and Tonopah writ large—that the pitched battles and employer victories, though only the tip of the iceberg of labor-management relations in Western hard-rock mining, accurately revealed the makeup of the entire iceberg. Recent studies have continued this interpretation: a book on Alaska mining takes note of the WFM's experiences to the south and concludes: "In every western mining camp, the operators fought the union bitterly." Another book draws on previously published accounts and generalizes that "extreme violence . . . characterized virtually all the conflicts, both major and minor, which took place in the metal mines from the 1880s right through to the 1920s and beyond." Vernon Jensen's pioneering study was entitled *Heritage of Conflict*, which accurately reflected its contents.[38]

Because these studies were limited mainly to the well-publicized bloody defeats of the WFM, their conclusions are inaccurate for the whole of Western hard-rock mining. There were violent strikes, from the Coeur d'Alenes through Cripple Creek and Telluride, and they were accorded great attention. But they were not typical of labor-management relations in most mining camps over several decades. And because crushing defeats were not the usual outcomes for unions in their disputes with mining companies, radicalism had difficulty becoming broadly established among Western hard-rock miners.

Idaho in the 1890s provides a good illustration. While the bloody strife of the Coeur d'Alenes received massive publicity, the companies involved in those strikes employed only a third of the miners of Idaho. At the other end of the state during the same period, the Silver City Miners' Union was maintaining good relations with several employers in Owyhee County, even while winning disputes with them. But no wide publicity —in contemporary newspaper reports or in later historical

244

studies—has described the Owyhee County experience. Bill Haywood was a member of the Silver City local during part of this period, and his published recollections depict miners and superintendents who tolerated and even had respect for each other. The Silver City union minute book reveals this as well, as in this account of the union's attempt to raise daily wages above the $2.50 level (to which they had sunk during the 1893 depression):

> [David Farmer] reported he had performed the duty assigned him, and Mr. Irwin [a superintendent] assured him that [he] had given orders to his Foreman at the time to pay all men that were to work underground $3.00 per day. Mr. Irwin requested that all men be reported to him that won't join.[39]

Several of the factors that worked in favor of the miners were evident when an Aspen mine manager admitted that he favored yielding to the employees' request for the eight-hour day while maintaining the $2.50 wage. The town's merchants unanimously favored the shorter workday, he explained to the company president, and miners were "having the sympathy of almost the entire community." The manager added:

> Should the miners finally be forced to accept less wages, they will go to work in an ill-natured way, and it would be a very long time before they overcame the feeling that they had been forced to accept something which they should not have accepted, and we would not get as much work out of them during ten hours as they have given us during eight.[40]

There remained limits to an employer's power, in Aspen as elsewhere.

Even after the turn of the century, when large companies were gaining dominance in many districts, reports in the *Miners' Magazine* frequently belied the charges made by Haywood, Boyce, and others concerning the inevitability of capitalists crushing their workers. "[A] feeling of good fellowship exists between our union and the mine managers," wrote a WFM member from Gilman, Colorado, in 1900. "We have an eight-hour work day and everything is going along harmoniously." The magazine reported that the Rossland Miners' Union in British Columbia had presented a mine manager with a gold-mounted ebony cane "in appreciation of his friendly relations towards the members of the Western Federation of Miners."

While strife was brewing in Goldfield, labor-management relations in nearby Tonopah were cordial. Goldfield mine operators were rebuffed, in fact, when they sought the aid of Tonopah employees to oppose the IWW. The Tonopah operators said they intended to uphold their contract with the union and wanted to avoid the spread of Goldfield's troubles to their own camp. And when an Alaskan WFM organizer denounced some operators along Prince William Sound, he admitted he was "pleased to find" that other employers were "sensible men who recognize the right of the workers to organize for fair conditions."[41]

That labor-management relations on the whole were good

24. Small mining operations, such as the Grizzly Bear Mine in isolated Ouray County, Colorado, pictured here, remained plentiful across the Western landscape down through the turn of the century. Labor relations were often more amicable in such mines than in the larger ones, for it was more common for the owners to be local folk, open to local pressures.

Denver Public Library, Western History Collection photo

25. *Large mines were the setting for most labor-management strife. The investment required in an enterprise the size of the Rawley Mine in Saguache County, Colorado, pictured here, was enormous—mine and mill equipment, buildings, transportation expenses—and this frequently meant that distant capital was required. With so much money involved, owners were frequently less willing to share economic decision-making with a union of workmen.*

Denver Public Library, Western History Collection photo

in Western metal mining is the conclusion of a recent study by Richard Peterson. He argues that this stemmed primarily from the fact that many Western mine owners and superintendents were former hard-rock miners. Marcus Daly of the Anaconda was one; the WFM's major troubles with the company began only after his death. John Mackay, the Comstock magnate, maintained the support of his employees largely because of his own background as a miner and his insistence upon maintaining good relations with them. When other Comstock mine owners sought to reduce wages to $3.50, Mackay refused. "I always got $4 a day when I worked in these mines," he said, "and when I can't pay that I'll go out of business." These men were not unique. And frequent cases of mine owners seeking public office from an electorate dominated by hard-rock miners provided yet another reason to cater to the wants of workmen.[42]

Employers had economic inducements as well to seek better relations rather than confrontation with their miners. Labor supply was one. A serious shortage of workmen across the West in 1906 meant that mine owners were forced to lure employees or reduce output: wages went up twenty-five cents a day at such widely divergent points as Butte, Owyhee County, Bisbee, and the Coeur d'Alenes. Shaft men in Butte, ordinarily paid $3.50, were raised to $5 per day, while "the piratical small operators" offered higher wages and "Shanghaied" many good miners from the large employers. If low wages help build support for radicalism—a pattern noted by John Laslett during America's recurring depressions from 1873 to 1896—then the wage increases of 1906 may have helped cool the miners' ardor for the IWW just as that organization was seeking a foothold across the West. And the labor shortage would have provided additional pressure on employers to avoid the "soulless corporation" image if they expected to maintain a full crew.[43]

The case of the Homestake Mine in the Black Hills during the pre-1910 period provided another reason for employers to seek the good will of their workmen. As documented by Joseph Cash, the company—often at the urging of owner George Hearst's wife—went far to maintain high wages, the eight-hour day, good medical service, and other attributes of a benevolent employer. The benefit for the Homestake owners was admitted in a 1908 WFM report:

> Owing to the fact that comparatively fair conditions exist in the jurisdiction of the Lead City Miners' Union, a large number of the men employed in that camp, believing that these conditions will continue indefinitely, have, through indifference, neglected the opportunity to become members of the Union. . . .[44]

On the other hand, it was generally true that maintaining good relations with employees was less important for the trusts that began to appear near the turn of the century. It must be noted, however, that while trusts were dominant in smelting, they controlled only pockets of lode mining and never even half of hard-rock mining employment. Strike reports in WFM records usually involved smaller operations; in 1907, the WFM claimed victory in eight of the eleven significant strikes during the previous year, most involving smaller mines.

Taken as a whole, such evidence suggests that while violence occurred in Western mine labor disputes, it reaped publicity—then and now—all out of proportion to what was experienced by the vast majority of hard-rock miners. For the bulk of the employers of Western mine labor, Richard Peterson's opinion is probably more accurate: "Their attitudes and practices suggest that labor exploitation and instability in the industry have been overemphasized."[45]

In addition to the conservative influence of generally peaceful labor-management relations, the shift to radicalism was also cooled by several attributes and customs of miners' unions. These locals had often been formed over a specific job problem and had centered their activities upon a variety of day-to-day concerns of the membership. Revolution was not one of these. Union records indicate that an enormous amount of time was devoted to the benefit system for the victims of mine accidents. That miners showed continuing concern as well for mine safety, irregular wage payments, and similar problems is also amply demonstrated in records of the period. But these concerns scarcely appeared in IWW rhetoric, for the new organization was championing other more utopian causes. Further, many of the basic complaints of hard-rock miners were best solved when employers were prosperous—enabling companies to raise wages and pay them on time, to install adequate timbering, to hire more men, and to be generous with aid for injured employees. Hopes for company prosperity ran counter to the IWW's philosophy, however. Two recent studies of the IWW have noted the contradictions forced upon the organization on the occasions when it attempted to meet workmen's needs for "bread-and-butter unionism" while also seeking revolution. This contradiction soon became painfully evident.[46]

There is some evidence that many hard-rock miners supported another goal that depended on company success: a rise in stock values. From the development of the Comstock Lode onward, employees purchased shares in local mines, often in companies for which they worked. An 1867 report claimed that many Comstock workmen received stock dividends worth three times their wages each month. The impact of the Owyhee troubles of 1875 was worsened because many miners had stocks in the district companies. "As high as 12,000 shares, at one time," were owned in a single mine by workmen "who watch every movement in San Francisco with jealousy." Their knowledge of the mine's wealth made them alert to stock manipulation schemes.

The major example of hard-rock miners as participants in the stock market occurred in the "Gibraltar of Unionism." The Butte local voted in 1901 to use $50,000 of its surplus funds to purchase shares in the Amalgamated. This may have been a factor in the union's reluctance to go on strike against the company later. In the Goldfield strike of 1907–1908, charges were made that union leaders used their control over the membership to cause fluctuations in mine stocks for their own benefit.[47]

Although politics became unpopular for many miners as a result of frustrations in the eight-hour-day campaigns, it is clear that support for regular party politics continued for most through the period of revolutionary rhetoric. Whatever their ineptness in meeting the miners' needs in Colorado in 1903–1904, the political parties often took up issues that reflected genuine concerns of working men. "We have gained more up there by the unions being in politics for the last three or four years," announced a British Columbia WFM member, "than we did for fifteen or twenty years previous to that by not being in politics. . . ." He spoke on behalf of the Socialist Party, but his claim also indicated the success to which members could point despite the bloody eight-hour debacles.[48]

Continuing allegiance by miners to the major parties reveals something of the accomplishments of those parties, for it is doubtful that miners would have blindly followed Democratic and Republican politicians if these had turned a deaf ear to requests for safety laws, anti-blacklist legislation, and similar measures. When the WFM's state organizer for Nevada came under fire in 1903 for campaigning in support of a Democratic candidate for governor, the Wedekind Miners' Union defended his actions by pointing out that the aspirant for office was a supporter of the Western Federation of Miners, ran a closed shop in his mine, and supported the miners' eight-hour-day drive. In Arizona during the same period, the Chloride Miners' Union proudly reported its support for the territory's Democratic Party and the party's pro-labor platform.[49]

Within the union, Marxian socialism was not met with overwhelming enthusiasm by large numbers, despite their anger at Peabodyism or the Amalgamated. Although the WFM's annual conventions passed pro-Socialist or pro-revolution resolutions, the opposition to these was always substantial, and the majority's dedication to socialism often seemed of questionable durability.

Actions of the Butte union in 1903 may be indicative. One of the federation's most vocal groups in denouncing capitalism, the local accepted an invitation to send six representatives to dine at the White House with President Theodore Roosevelt —the same man whose name former WFM head Ed Boyce had slightly earlier refused to toast at a banquet. The White House dinner drew criticism from various sources, directed at various targets. *The Engineering and Mining Journal* took Roosevelt to task for consorting with a group that it compared with the Mafia in Italy. At the opposite extreme, the WFM executive board attacked Local Number One for accepting an invitation from the man who had recently sent troops to crush a WFM strike in Arizona. Although Butte was closely involved with the early IWW, the president of the local in 1906 called his union "just as conservative as ever" when he explained the need to accept a wage cut because the contract was tied to changes in the price of copper. The shift to radicalism was not clear-cut among hard-rock miners.[50]

Opposition to radicalism within the WFM membership was revealed in many instances, especially during the heated debate of the 1907 WFM convention. Participants included one delegate who also served as secretary of his local chamber of commerce, another who announced, "I don't want to have any hot air about your revolutionary convention at all," and a patriot who attacked a speaker for identifying the U.S. flag's red stripes with "the blood that was spilled in the Coeur d'Alenes" —this in a union whose president three years earlier had been arrested for "desecrating the flag" in a poster with printed statements on its stripes!

Concern for the federation's radical image was evident when a report referred to miners as "dynamiters." A delegate from Jerome, Arizona, quickly asked that the word be stricken from the record. When a Butte member demanded to know why, the Arizonan explained: "We as miners among ourselves call ourselves thugs, scamps and dynamiters; among ourselves we understand what that means, in that sense, but when this

251

is going to the outside, people do not understand it and might put an improper construction upon it."* A further clue on membership feelings came in a request from the Crown King Miners Union in Arizona for two dozen WFM buttons. "We have plenty of Industrial Workers of the World buttons," the letter stated, "but no one seems to care to wear them."

To a delegate from southwestern Idaho it was all too much. Rebelling at continued efforts by pro-IWW spokesmen to align the Western Federation with Marxist programs, he proclaimed: "I am no Socialist; . . . you can't legislate socialism into me no more than you can legislate religion into a hog."[51]

If personal feelings and characteristics played a large role in determining the federation's rejection of IWW radicalism, these were also important in guiding the miners' enthusiasm for unionization itself. (Generalizations are difficult, however: up to 200,000 men were employed in Western metalliferous mines.) For some men, the squalor of the mine camp may have stimulated a desire to overthrow the system; however, this cause of encouragement may have declined as conditions began to improve in many mining communities by the turn of the century. And there is some question whether squalor produced large numbers of militants. Drinking ranked especially high among the worst-off miners, and a WFM organizer confessed after traveling through his region that "the measure of despair . . . that is finding solace in the flowing bowl, is simply appalling." Another report lambasted the dismal bunkhouse conditions that had a deadening effect upon miners: "They continue in the same rut, never realizing that there is anything elevating and grand in life, and when they visit the nearby town the saloon is the only place where they are welcome. . . ." Some unions provided reading rooms for their members, but a WFM spokesman in Chloride, Arizona, admitted that not over five members would read the literature he provided them on scientific government. "I am going to try a bunch of dime novels," he wrote in disgust. This was hardly the stuff of which militant agitators were made.[52]

Such conditions helped stimulate the high rate of mobility

*The motion to delete *dynamiters* from the report lost, 30 to 60, although it is probable from delegates' comments that some persons voting against the deletion wished only to avoid the precedent of censoring the verbatim transcript of the convention's debates.

discussed in Chapter 2. Union records abound with reports of members seeking transfers or traveling cards, and the foot-loose miner's neglect to transfer membership was termed "the hardest problem many weak locals have to contend with." Mobility could spread unionism, but it also presented enormous hurdles for any organized movement seeking a better world. The impact that excessive mobility could have on maintaining an organization was indicated in a report from Needles, California:

> Owing to the fierce conditions which prevail at the Gold Road Mine, this has become what is known as a ten-day camp, and experience has taught us that in camps of this kind it is almost impossible to keep intact an organization worthy of the name of a Labor Union.

High rates of mobility as a discouragement to radicalism have been cited by scholars comparing the conservatism of American labor movements to those of Europe. If true, then the extreme mobility of hard-rock miners must be added to the list of factors that helped turn the federation away from the IWW.[53]

These conditions continually tried WFM organizers. The account of one of these men, L. W. Callahan, reveals the extreme dedication of the WFM's servants in the field but also raises questions as to how the federation managed to exert much force at all. Callahan addressed the 1908 convention on his organizing trips through the Pacific Northwest, and although he claimed to be "much gratified at the uniform success," his description of the year's activities casts doubt on the magnitude of some of these accomplishments, although not on his personal steadfastness.

At the smelter in Everett, Washington—"a little industrial hell controlled by our arch enemies, the Guggenheims" —Callahan found the workmen divided by nationalities with no feeling of unity. Only forty of the 150 employees showed up for his organizing session; when he returned to hold a meeting several weeks later, he found, "if possible, a more inaccessible bunch" than encountered earlier: only a dozen attended.

Callahan next went into the Cascade Mountains to the Slate Creek country, traveling by train, steamboat, stagecoach, and foot, "the last 75 or 80 miles being so rough and inaccessible that I was obliged to walk." Pockmarked with tiny mines, none having more than fifteen employees and with no building in the area large enough for a meeting, the district was "too badly scattered to admit of organization."

In a trip through Idaho and Oregon, Callahan also failed when he attempted to form unions in Idaho City, the Seven Devils country, and Granite Pass. He was successful, however, in launching the Atlanta Miners' Union with twenty-four members and the Cornucopia Miners' Union with twenty-eight (despite the "vicious opposition" of a mine manager at the latter site). He crossed to the Blue Ledge district in northern California, where he found some 150 miners working in a "very crude" camp. After arranging a meeting in a hotel—the only structure in the camp not located on company property—Callahan "went after the boys." He found them to consist of "'weak knees,' old Federation renegades, and natural good fellows," and persuaded forty to meet and form the Blue Ledge Miners' Union.

Isolated camps proved impossible to organize in the Skykomish mining district in Washington, while a bitter IWW–WFM wrangle at the Tacoma smelter convinced Callahan to leave and "let matters rest easy for awhile." When he formed a new local at Loomis in Okanogan County, the manager of the major mine attended but "gracefully retired when we were ready for initiations."

Callahan's year recorded considerable success in securing donations to the federation's defense fund, but before it was over he had one more major frustration, at Chesaw, Washington. There, the frosty atmosphere at the organizational session surprised even this battle-hardened veteran. Upon investigating, he explained, "I found I had been wasting my eloquence on a brilliant assemblage of straw-bosses, shift-bosses, assistant superintendents, superintendents, general managers, and the whole weary list with a small sprinkling of wild-eyed miners." Callahan termed the event "an awful shock. Heaven preserve me from another one like it." During a year in which rebuffs and apathy often seemed dominant, Callahan's experience at Chesaw was perhaps an accurate, if undeserved, symbol of his labors for the WFM across the Pacific Northwest.[54]

That Callahan's record with hard-rock miners was not unique is shown in reports of WFM locals during the period of the federation's shift to radicalism. These reports present a picture that was often considerably at variance with that projected by prosecuting attorneys, Pinkerton agents, and editorial writers. Local unions complained frequently of their inability to reach a quorum, to convince more than 63 of the 400 members to vote in a union election, or to collect dues, let alone sell subscriptions to the *Miners' Magazine*. A member in a small Montana camp lamented in 1902: "I am sick at heart to see unions in the condition they are. They are honeycombed with petty jealousies. One brother and another will get miffed at some trivial affair and then he will not come to the union meetings, and perhaps he will not pay his dues." In the WFM's annual list of "Defunct and Disbanded Unions," large numbers of locals left simply "no interest" as their epitaph.[55]

Such members made poor union material and doubtful radicals. The Cloud City Miners Union in Leadville claimed that eighty-eight former members were working as strikebreakers although the union had given each of them aid during the 1896 strike. A scab list from the Searchlight union in Nevada included the local's first president, secretary, and warden, as well as an ex-vice president and an ex-financial secretary. Repeated cases are chronicled in WFM records of union officers who absconded with the local's funds.[56]

This record of unmilitant union members, of loyal unionists whose overriding concern was for solving immediate problems, and of miners who maintained traditional party allegiances must be placed in the balance when examining the failure of radicalism among Western hard-rock miners. While some of these characteristics may have helped develop a spirit of alienation from society—fitting in with the famed "Wobbly" estrangement—they could also work against a movement that required dedication to a distant, utopian tomorrow at the cost of bread-and-butter sacrifices today. Certainly there were many in the WFM prepared to build that utopian future. But many others were not.

CHAPTER X

Epilogue: End of the Pioneer Era

As the pioneer era of hard-rock mining drew to a close, during the opening decade of the new century, Westerners who knew portions of that history suddenly became aware that the old ways were vanishing. At that elbow of history, each saw what was most dramatic from his own point of view, of course. What drew the attention of Western journalists was often different from what struck hard-rock miners as significant. Later historians, viewing events with the advantage of hindsight and seeking to fit the miners' experiences into the sweep of American history, would in turn come up with other conclusions.

A common symbol of the pioneer era had been the lone prospector—independent and motivated by dreams of wealth —but by 1910 it was evident that he had almost passed from the scene. A contemporary writer recalled that for years the prospector and his mule had set out from "every city, town, and village" in the West, grubstaked by local businessmen; but by 1910 this had "all ceased." Some blamed land law changes, but one observer said the prospector was passing on because luck was no longer enough: knowledge of geology and engineering was now equally important before the earth would reveal its mineral bounty. Residents of mining communities might comment further on the outward changes in mine operations, especially the new electrical installations that sent aerial

256

tramways across mountain valleys and railroad cars up from town to transport the men to their work.[1]

Miners recognized that they lived in a vastly different world also, but their experiences made them aware of other developments than these. The enormous power of the Amalgamated and other mining and smelting corporations by 1910 struck WFM President Charles Moyer, and he looked back almost wistfully to earlier times when "we could treat with our individual employer or representative of a company. . . ." Small mines remained, but the shift to technologically-intensive (rather than labor-intensive) mining aided the expansion of large enterprises, with their ability to bring together great aggregations of capital. It was this growth that concerned Moyer, who feared the power of such combinations to arbitrarily set workmen's wages.[2]

This change had ominous implications. One of these was the broad influence of these new corporations: they now reached across wide expanses of territory and probed into local and personal matters hitherto untouched. It was a trend aided by communications improvements, the growth of employers' associations, and the need for information on employees as the new medical assistance programs appeared. In earlier days, miners came and went and their employers scarcely knew even their names or cared to. The new Anaconda hiring form in 1901 revealed the trend: it requested data on each employee's birth, nationality, employment record, literacy, marital status, and property ownership, among other topics. The WFM, both angered and worried, condemned the form and asked: "How long will the American workingmen continue to be slaves instead of freemen?"[3]

Recurring economic crises—such as the 1907 panic that tumbled copper prices, brought the layoff of over 5,000 men in Butte, and reduced the wages of those still employed— drove home a further lesson to hard-rock miners. This was their dependence upon the fluctuations of world metal markets. More than the early years had ever known, remote mining camps were now in close touch with world financial centers, and the railroad and the telegraph ranked with the maze of new equipment underground in their impact upon the lives of workmen.

To a latter-day historian, both the contemporary observers

and the miners overlooked other significant changes as the pioneer era ended. True, the departure of the prospector was important, but no more so than the fact that the common law of liability, in its harsh form of 1860, had all but disappeared as well, emasculated by both judicial decisions and legislation. Mine-safety laws were also far advanced by 1910, as was the statutory eight-hour day for workmen in mines and other private employment. And the meteoric rise of workmen's compensation—a trend given its biggest impetus in Montana—was further testimony to the fundamental nature of the changes. Nothing like these protections existed when miners began their first probes below bedrock, five decades earlier. Taken together, they constituted a revolution as far-reaching as dynamite or the machine drill.

The transformation—judicial, legislative, but most of all in public opinion—arose from many sources, but a basic stimulus was the rise of the miners' union movement, especially the growth of the Western Federation of Miners after 1893. Union agitation helped draw attention to the necessity for change, and unions also functioned to direct complaints into effective channels.

And yet, the union movement was just one aspect—albeit the most important single aspect—of the miners' never-ending quest for protection. The oft-noted mobility of the miners was part of that quest; low wages or foul air underground became reason enough for a worker to ask for his pay and head over the ridge. Highgrading and threatening (or kidnaping) company officials were also attempts to seek security in a frontier that basically lacked it. And then there was politics.

In retrospect, it should be noted that the rising tide of political activity by miners from the early 'nineties onward focused most insistently on measures to give protection: mine safety, the eight-hour day, prohibitions upon blacklisting and compulsory store patronage—these appeared in the statute books as miners first became aware of, and then used, their numerical importance in the Western states and territories.

To point out that none of these statutes made the mine stope a perfect workplace is not to assess them as failures. Hard-rock miners recognized these laws as improvements. What judges said about the constantly changing nature of the underground workplace was true of the entire industry, however. Not only was the stope undergoing constant change, but also the machinery, technology, crews, systems of ownership, and dynamics of local politics were seldom constant for long.

These factors made progress difficult for hard-rock miners, and contributed to the weakness of their union movement by 1910. (The union would be almost enfeebled in the aftermath of the First World War, and would not return to strength until the 1930s and 1940s.) But the troubles within the WFM as the pioneer era closed should not obscure the fact that hard-rock miners had played a crucial role in transforming the Western frontier to protect its human inhabitants.[4]

The WFM's achievements stand out when compared to most other labor groups in the industrializing world of the nineteenth century. For hard-rock miners were dual pioneers, confronting a hostile Western environment while challenging the worst aspects of the Industrial Revolution as it spread over the region. More than simply enduring, these miners won changes that would be adopted and accepted as commonplace by later generations. Their story was an epic—a hard-rock epic, created from often-agonizing chapters by the men who drilled and blasted, mucked and trammed, on the dual frontiers of the American West and the Industrial Revolution.

NOTES

I: Machinery on the Route to the Mines

1. San Francisco and Sacramento newspapers quoted in *Gold Hill News* (Nev.), Feb. 26 and 29, 1864.

2. Hubert H. Bancroft, *History of Washington, Idaho, and Montana—1845–1889* (San Francisco, 1890), Vol. XXXI, p. 728n. *Idaho World*, Aug. 26, 1865. *Daily Alta California*, Feb. 27, 1869, p. 2. Grass Valley (Calif.) *National*, Feb. 25, 1869, p. 3; March 1, 1869, p. 3.

3. Industrialism is here defined as the adoption of machinery and power other than manpower or animal power to carry out a job, and the resulting social organization that this creates. It usually involves great speed of production compared to hand-tool methods, complex and large-scale operations, and a division of labor into specialized tasks. The West discussed throughout this book is the region of the United States between the Great Plains and the Pacific Coast, including adjacent provinces of Canada.

4. Herbert G. Gutman, "Work, Culture, and Society in Industrializing America, 1815–1919," *American Historical Review*, LXXVIII:3 (June, 1973), 540 –541.

5. U.S. Bureau of the Census, 10th Census (1880), part 13: *Statistics and Technology of the Precious Metals*, pp. 122, 133, 136–137. Definitions included at the bottom of the page are drawn principally from the following: Robert L. Romig, Idaho Historical Society; C. G. Warnford Lock, *Miners' Pocket-Book* (New York, 1901), pp. 219, 401–413; D. C. Davies, *A Treatise on Metalliferous Minerals and Mining* (London, 1888), pp. 405–432; and Otis E. Young, Jr., *Western Mining* (Norman, Oklahoma, 1970), pp. 103–105, 293–302.

6. Material on Sanford quoted here and discussed in the following paragraphs is drawn from Albert Byron Sanford diary, July 28, August 3, 10, 22, 1881.

7. *Gold Hill News*, Jan. 9, 1866.

8. J. Ross Browne, *A Report upon the Mineral Resources of the States and Territories West of the Rocky Mountains* [39th Cong., 2d Sess., House Ex. Doc. 29, Jan. 8, 1867], p. 20. *Idaho World*, Aug. 31, 1867. Bancroft, *History of Washington, Idaho, and Montana*, p. 549n. *Idaho Tri-Weekly Statesman*, May 16, 1878, p. 2.

9. Frank A. Crampton, *Deep Enough—A Working Stiff in the Western Mine Camps* (Denver, 1956), p. 42. Cf. *The Engineering and Mining Journal*, Feb. 4, 1873, p. 72 [hereafter cited as *E/MJ*]. Rossiter W. Raymond, *Statistics of Mines and Mining in the States and Territories West of the Rocky Mountains* [42d Cong.,

2d Sess., House Ex. Doc. 211, 1872], p. 43. A recent work offers the clearest and most complete description of hard-rock mining methods: Young, *Western Mining*, pp. 187–191.

10. Mrs. Speranza Pangrazi, interview, Telluride, Colo., July 22, 1972. Ernest Ingersoll, "Ups and Downs in Leadville," *Scribner's Monthly*, XVIII (May–October, 1879), quoted in Don L. and Jean Harvey Griswold, *The Carbonate Camp Called Leadville* (Denver, 1951), p. 45. Crampton, *Deep Enough*, p. 42. Virginia City (Nev.) *Territorial Enterprise*, Jan. 21, 1869, quoted in *Alta California*, Jan. 25, 1869, p. 1.

11. A good description of the variety of occupations in and around the Comstock mines is found in Dan DeQuille, "The Silver Miner of the Comstock," *E/MJ*, Jan. 9, 1892, p. 85.

12. Ralph Emerson Mann, II, "The Social and Political Structure of Two California Mining Towns, 1850–1870" (unpublished doctoral dissertation, Stanford University, 1970), p. 112.

13. *Gold Hill News*, Jan. 20, 1866. Browne, *Mineral Resources* for 1866, pp. 60–61.

14. On unemployment problems, see *Idaho Statesman*, March 15, 1877, p. 2; April 24, 1877, p. 2; March 23, 1878, p. 2; April 6, 1878, p. 2. Wallace (Idaho) *Press*, Dec. 20, 1890, p. 1. *The Mining and Scientific Press*, May 16, 1885, p. 314 [hereafter cited as *M/SP*]. *Idaho World*, June 9, 1876, p. 2. *E/MJ*, May 10, 1879, p. 336. Gold Hill (Nev.) Miners Union minute book, May 4, 1891, p. 185 (communication from Butte City Miners Union). The shutting down of Granite is described by Rev. A. C. McMillan, "A Young Clergyman Looks at Granite's Glittering Glory," *Montana—The Magazine of Western History*, XIV:3 (July, 1964), 72–73.

15. *Gold Hill News*, Feb. 15, 1864. *Montana Post*, Jan. 13, 1866, p. 3; Dec. 1, 1866, p. 6. *Idaho World*, Sept. 29, 1870, p. 2. Joseph H. Cash, *Working the Homestake* (Ames, Iowa, 1973), p. 85. *Territorial Enterprise*, May 24, 1867, p. 3.

16. *Territorial Enterprise*, June 2, 1867, p. 3; June 7, 1867, p. 3; Sept. 11, 1867, p. 3. "Letter from White Pine," *Alta California*, March 31, 1869, p. 1. D. E. Livingston-Little, *An Economic History of North Idaho, 1800–1900* (Los Angeles, 1965), p. 102.

17. *Montana Post*, Nov. 19, 1864, p. 2. Owyhee Avalanche Publishing Co., *A Historical, Descriptive, and Commercial Directory of Owyhee County, Idaho* (Silver City, 1898), p. 29. *Butte Miner* (Mont.), July 30, 1878, p. 4; also edition of April 21, 1886, quoted in *M/SP*, May 1, 1886, p. 297.

18. Robert B. Merrifield, "Nevada, 1859–1881: The Impact of an Advanced Technological Society upon a Frontier Area" (unpublished doctoral dissertation, University of Chicago, 1957), p. 33. Grass Valley *National*, June 20, 1868, p. 3. *Alta California*, Feb. 4, 1869, p. 2. Leadville, (Colo.) *Weekly Herald*, May 1, 1880, p. 1. For a summary of the thriving Western theater in this period, see Ray Allen Billington, *America's Frontier Heritage* (New York, 1966), chap. 4, especially pp. 85–87.

19. J. Ross Browne, *Mineral Resources of the States and Territories West of the Rocky Mountains* [40th Cong., 2d Sess., House Ex. Doc. 202, 1868], p. 385. Also see Rossiter W. Raymond, *Mineral Resources of the States and Territories West of the Rocky Mountains* [40th Cong., 3d Sess., House Ex. Doc. 54, 1869], p. 141. *E/MJ*, Jan. 14, 1873, p. 25. Lynn Irwin Perrigo, "A Social History of Central City, Colorado, 1859–1900" (unpublished doctoral dissertation, University of Colorado, 1936), pp. 398–402, 406. Rodman Wilson Paul, *Mining Frontiers of the Far West, 1848–1880* (New York, 1963), pp. 125–126. Livingston-Little, *Economic History*, pp. 74–78. *M/SP*, Aug. 14, 1886, p. 98. *Alta*

California, May 8, 1869, p. 2. U.S. Geological Survey, *Mineral Resources of the United States* (Washington, D.C., 1884), pp. 325–326.

20. Sacramento (Calif.) *Union,* Sept. 6, 1856, cited in Rodman W. Paul, *California Gold—The Beginning of Mining in the Far West* (Cambridge, Mass., 1947), p. 171. Gold Hill *News,* Jan. 15, 1864.

21. See Browne's two *Mineral Resources* reports, for 1866: pp. 73, 78, 100–101, and 105; and for 1867: pp. 348–349 and 353. Eliot Lord, *Comstock Mining and Miners* (Washington, D.C., 1883; reprint 1959), p. 124. Grant H. Smith, *The History of the Comstock Lode, 1850–1920* (Reno, 1943), pp. 32, 85.

22. Joseph Edward King, "'It Takes a Mine to Run a Mine': Financing Colorado's Precious-Metals Mining Industry, 1859–1902" (unpublished doctoral dissertation, University of Illinois, 1971), pp. 319–320. Browne, *Mineral Resources* for 1867, p. 523. *Rocky Mountain News,* Jan. 19, 1889, p. 1; Feb. 3, 1889, p. 14; Feb. 12, 1889, p. 1. Paul, *Mining Frontiers,* p. 99. *E/MJ,* Sept. 5, 1871, pp. 153–154; Jan. 5, 1905, p. 19. Rodman W. Paul, "Colorado as a Pioneer of Science in the Mining West," *Mississippi Valley Historical Review,* XLVII:1 (June, 1960), 38–39, 42–43, 49. Colorado Mine Inspector, *Report, 1907–1908,* p. 29. U.S. Geological Survey, *Mineral Resources of the United States, 1892,* pp. 46–49.

23. Gold Hill *News,* March 12, 1864. King, "It Takes a Mine," p. 13. White Pine *News,* quoted in Carson City (Nev.) *Daily Appeal,* July 14, 1869, p. 2.

24. Dan Cushman, "Cordova Lode Comstock," *Montana—The Magazine of Western History,* IX:4 (October, 1959), 17–18. *Montana Post,* Nov. 19, 1864, p. 3; June 17, 1865, p. 2; March 3, 1866, p. 3. King, "It Takes a Mine," p. 16. Bancroft, *History of Washington, Idaho, and Montana,* XXXI, 430–431. *Owyhee Avalanche,* Aug. 26, 1865, p. 2. *Idaho World,* Nov. 18, 1865; May 6, 1868. Frank Hough diary, June 13 and 17, 1901.

25. Colorado *Laws, 1887,* pp. 24–25.

26. Clark C. Spence, *British Investments and the American Mining Frontier, 1860–1901* (Ithaca, N.Y., 1958), pp. 3, 7 ff., 230–231. Duane Smith, *Silver Saga —The Story of Caribou, Colorado* (Boulder, 1974), pp. 26–37. Bancroft, *History of Washington, Idaho, and Montana,* XXXI, 579n. K. Ross Toole, "When Big Money Came to Butte: The Migration of Eastern Capital to Montana," in Michael P. Malone and Richard B. Roeder, eds., *The Montana Past—An Anthology* (Missoula, 1969), p. 183. See discussion of this issue in the following: King, "It Takes a Mine," pp. 285–288, 300, 301n. Melvyn Dubofsky, "The Origins of Western Working Class Radicalism, 1890–1905," *Labor History,* VII: 2 (Spring, 1966), 134.

The 1880 Census revealed the changes occurring in outside investment. The leading base of absentee mine owners was New York, whose residents controlled 148 deep mines outside their state, 68 of them in Colorado. California —showing San Francisco's continuing role as a source of mine investment —ranked second with 105 mines owned beyond its own borders, 68 of them in Nevada. Only 16 percent of Nevada's mines were owned by Nevadans. U.S. Census, 1880, *Statistics and Technology,* pp. 111–112.

27. T. A. Rickard, *A History of American Mining* (New York, 1932; reprint 1966), p. 110. Ed. Werner, Saguache, Colo., to Leonard Gow, Glasgow, Scotland, 1891 (date unclear), in Dr. Ed. Werner letterpress book. *E/MJ,* Sept. 23, 1882, pp. 160–161. (Throughout the early 1880s both *E/MJ* and *M/SP* carried news items and warnings on investing in fraudulent mine stocks.) Eben Smith, Denver, to C. B. Patrick, Pocatello, Idaho, Sept. 1, 1894, Eben Smith letterpress book.

28. Twain letter to *Evening Post* (New York?) reprinted in *E/MJ,* Sept. 25,

1880, p. 202. *Kelly v. Fourth of July Min. Co.*, 53 Pacific 959, 971 (Montana Supreme Court), July 5, 1898.

29. Melvyn Dubofsky, *We Shall Be All—A History of the Industrial Workers of the World* (Chicago, 1969), p. 23. For evidence showing the varied pattern of corporate control, see: Spence, *British Investments*, pp. 92–93; and Joseph H. Cash, "Labor in the West: The Homestake Mining Company and Its Workers, 1877–1942" (unpublished doctoral dissertation, University of Iowa, 1966), pp. 69–70.

30. McKaig to Hutchinson, May 20, 1898, Trade Dollar Co. papers (Idaho files). Ernest Le Neve Foster, Georgetown, Colo., to Secretary J. J. Humphreys, Fletcher Mining Co., New York, March 5, 1887, Ernest Le Neve Foster papers.

31. Secretary Edward T. Wastrell, La Crosse Gold Mining Co., to H. A. Hoffmann, Denver, June 3, 1897, La Crosse Gold Mining Co. letterpress book.

32. The dilemma of the sympathetic owner and unsympathetic foreman is discussed in the autobiography of Alice Hamilton, *Exploring the Dangerous Trades* (Boston, 1943), pp. 15–16. Gold Hill *News*, Oct. 24, 1863; Jan. 2, 1866. *Territorial Enterprise*, July 4, 1867. Grass Valley *National*, July 21, 1868, p. 3.

33. *Owyhee Avalanche*, Nov. 3, 1866, p. 2.

34. William C. Miller and Eleanore Bushnell, eds., *Reports of the 1863 Constitutional Convention of the Territory of Nevada—As Written for The Territorial Enterprise by Andrew J. Marsh and Samuel L. Clemens and for The Virginia Daily Union by Amos Bowman* (Carson City, 1972), pp. 80–81, 85–86, 89, 126–128. Merrifield, "Nevada," pp. 174–175.

35. *Idaho Statesman*, May 23, 1874, p. 2. President Edward Boyce, quoted in Western Federation of Miners journal, *The Miners' Magazine*, I:3 (March, 1900), pp. 39–40. The development of this philosophy will be discussed in Chapters 8 and 9.

36. Clancy (Mont.) *Miner*, July 25, 1896, p. 1.

37. Gold Hill *News*, Dec. 11, 1863.

38. Ibid., Feb. 27, 1864. Salt Lake City (Utah) *Tribune*, quoted in *Idaho Statesman*, May 9, 1878, p. 2. *M/SP*, Oct. 3, 1891, p. 213.

39. *M/SP*, Jan. 23, 1886, pp. 63–64; Nov. 22, 1902, pp. 300–301. Wallace *Press*, June 11, 1892, p. 1.

40. For an examination of the 1869 Grass Valley strike, see Richard E. Lingenfelter, *The Hardrock Miners: A History of the Mining Labor Movement in the American West, 1863–1893* (Berkeley, Calif., 1974), pp. 84 ff.; and Paul, *California Gold*, pp. 327 ff.

41. *Alta California*, Feb. 9, 1869, p. 2.

42. *Territorial Enterprise*, June 11, 1867, p. 3; July 27, 1867, p. 3.

II: Who Will Work?

1. *Gilpin County* (Colo.) *Observer*, Jan. 11, 18, 25, and Feb. 1, 8, 15, 1888. Also see discussion in Lynn Irwin Perrigo, "A Social History of Central City, Colorado, 1859–1900" (unpublished doctoral dissertation, University of Colorado, 1936), pp. 595–596.

2. John R. Commons and John B. Andrews, *Principles of Labor Legislation* (New York, 1936), pp. 348–349. Selig Perlman, *A History of Trade Unionism in the United States* (New York, 1923), p. 89.

3. *Gilpin County Observer*, Jan. 25, Feb. 1, 8, 15, 1888. *The Mining and Scientific Press*, April 8, 1899, p. 371 [cited hereafter as *M/SP*].

4. The type of success story that spurred miners on involved John Beck, a German immigrant who came to Utah's Tintic district in the late 1860s. Working mainly alone on a small underground claim, his initial $20 stake eventually made him a millionaire. Such incidents occurred frequently enough to keep the dream alive across the West. Beth Kay Harris, *The Towns of Tintic* (Denver, 1961), pp. 38–41. By 1899, when the corporation was dominant in Western mining, it was still reported that some miners held down wage jobs only to aggregate enough capital to develop their own claims. Testimony of Harry A. Lee, Colorado Commissioner of Mines, July 13, 1899, in U.S. Industrial Commission, *Report . . . on the Relations and Conditions of Capital and Labor Employed in the Mining Industry* (57th Cong., 1st Sess., House Doc. 181, 1901), vol. XII, p. 233.

5. Horace W. Mathews, Homestake Mine, Leadville, Colorado, to Miss Bessie Charles, Eaton, Ohio, Feb. 23, 1885, printed in Leadville (Colo.) *Herald*, "Extra" edition, May 3, 1885, p. 2. The letter was found after a snowslide killed Horace W. Mathews.

6. Wage data were drawn from a wide range of newspaper accounts, contemporary reports, and later studies. The major ones are: T. A. Rickard, *Interviews with Mining Engineers* (San Francisco, 1922), pp. 311–312. Eliot Lord, *Comstock Mining and Miners* (Washington, 1883; reprint 1959), pp. 182, 190. Robert L. Romig, "The South Boise Quartz Mines, 1863–1892: A Study in Western Mining Industry and Finance" (unpublished master's thesis, University of California, Berkeley, 1950), p. 44. Montana Mine Inspector, *Report, 1889*, p. 75. *M/SP*, March 21, 1885, pp. 190–191; April 15, 1899, p. 406; Sept. 1, 1906, p. 253; Dec. 1, 1906, p. 1040. More detailed information on wages will be covered in Chapters 3 and 6.

7. Paul H. Douglas, *Real Wages in the United States, 1890–1926* (Boston, 1930), pp. 137, 140, 143. Clarence D. Long, *Wages and Earnings in the United States, 1860–1890* (Princeton, N.J., 1960), pp. 27–28, 98, 109. Stanley Lebergott, "Wage Trends, 1800–1900," in Bureau of Economic Research, *Trends in the American Economy in the Nineteenth Century* (Princeton, N.J., 1960), pp. 462, 491–492. *The Engineering and Mining Journal*, Jan. 17, 1874, p. 37; July 25, 1874, p. 51; Jan. 9, 1875, pp. 20–21; March 6, 1875, p. 148; Feb. 17, 1877, p. 101; April 14, 1877, p. 239; April 28, 1877, p. 281; Oct. 8, 1898, p. 422 [hereafter cited as *E/MJ*]. Illinois Bureau of Labor Statistics, *Statistics of Coal in Illinois —1893* (Springfield, 1894), p. xxxvii. Duane A. Smith, "Colorado's Urban-Mining Safety Valve," *The Colorado Magazine*, XLVIII:4 (Fall, 1971), 313. These East-West wage differences helped propel many coal miners westward, including organized groups fleeing hard times in Pennsylvania in the 1870s and a young Illinois coal miner named John Mitchell in 1886 and again in 1891. Mitchell—later to become president of the United Mine Workers —labored in metal mines across the West before returning home to the lower wages of Illinois coal mining. See Elsie Glück, *John Mitchell—Miner—Labor's Bargain with the Gilded Age* (New York, 1929; reprint 1969), pp. 14–15, 20–21.

8. Alexander MacDonald, *Report . . . to the Members of the Miners' National Union on the Conditions and Prospects of Labour in the United States* (n.p., apparently 1877), passim. Mrs. Ermira Visintin, interview, Telluride, Colorado, July 22, 1972. E. H. Phelps Brown, with Margaret H. Browne, *A Century of Pay—The Course of Pay and Production in France, Germany, Sweden, the United Kingdom, and the United States of America, 1860–1960* (New York, 1968), pp. 30–46. These statistics give ample support to an economist's conclusion that "although advice may have brought some men to go West, the impact of

wage rates and incomes probably attracted many more" (Lebergott, "Wage Trends," p. 452).

9. N. P. Hulst, in *Trans. Lake Superior Mining Institute* (1894), quoted in Walter R. Crane, *Gold and Silver* (New York, 1908), pp. 11–12.

10. Gold Hill (Nev.) *Daily News*, March 23, 1864; Jan 10 and 14, 1865. *Idaho Tri-Weekly Statesman*, May 22, 1873. *Owyhee Avalanche*, July 19, 1873. T. A. Rickard, *A History of American Mining* (New York, 1932; reprint 1966), p. 212.

11. Carson City (Nev.) *Daily Appeal*, May 1, 1868, p. 2; Aug. 12, 1869, p. 2. *Daily Alta California*, May 22, June 17, 1869, quoted in Alexander Saxton, *The Indispensable Enemy—Labor and the Anti-Chinese Movement in California* (Berkeley, Calif., 1971), p. 58. Gunther Barth, *Bitter Strength—A History of the Chinese in the United States, 1850–1870* (Cambridge, Mass., 1964), pp. 1–3. Gerald E. Rudolph, "The Chinese in Colorado, 1869–1911" (unpublished master's thesis, Denver University, 1964), p. 1.

12. *Owyhee Avalanche*, June 9, 1866, p. 3. *Montana Post*, Nov. 2, 1866, p. 5. *Idaho Statesman*, Sept. 24, 1874, p. 3.

13. Carson *Morning Appeal*, 1886, quoted in Gary P. Be Dunnah, "A History of the Chinese in Nevada: 1855–1904" (master's thesis, University of Nevada, 1966), pp. 57, 79. Adolph Sutro, Virginia City, Nev., to Joseph Aron, n.p., Oct. 1, 1869, apparently published by Aron in Paris, France, on March 15, 1889. Lord, *Comstock Mining*, pp. 355–356, 204, 253. *Idaho Statesman*, March 1 and 6, 1873. Rudolph, "Chinese in Colorado," pp. 20, 81, 85. Leadville (Colo.) *Chronicle*, March 8, 1879, quoted in Don L. and Jean Harvey Griswold, *The Carbonate Camp Called Leadville* (Denver, 1951), p. 96. Wallace (Idaho) *Press*, April 11, 1891. Russell Elliott, "The History of the White Pine County" (unpublished paper in possession of the Nevada State Historical Society), p. 67. *M/SP*, Jan. 2, 1886, p. 1; July 16, 1898, p. 55; Nov. 21, 1903, p. 332; Dec. 12, 1903, p. 382. John Rowe, *The Hard-Rock Men—Cornish Immigrants and the North American Mining Frontier* (New York, 1974), p. 225. *Hum Fay, Dear Yick, Hum Tong, and Huie Pock v. Frank Baldwin et al.*, 9th Circuit Court, District of Montana, 1898, testimony, vol. II, pp. 222 ff.; vol. III, pp. 211 ff.

14. Fumio Ozawa, "Japanese in Colorado, 1900–1910" (unpublished master's thesis, University of Denver, 1954), p. 40. *Miners' Magazine*, March, 1902, pp. 34–35.

15. Colorado Bureau of Labor Statistics, *Report, 1889–1890*, p. 55. Governor's message to Montana House, Dec. 11, 1869, Montana Territory House *Journal*, 6th Sess., p. 32. Barth, *Bitter Strength*, chap. 6. Betty Derig, "Celestials in the Diggings," *Idaho Yesterdays*, XVI:3 (Fall, 1972), 18.

16. "Chinese skilled miners are quite equal to those of any other race," asserted the government's 1870 report on Western mining. Rossiter W. Raymond, U.S. Commissioner of Mining Statistics, *Mining Statistics West of the Rocky Mountains* (42nd Cong., 1st Sess., House Ex. Doc. 10, 1871), pp. 3–6, 28. *E/MJ*, Aug. 13, 1872, p. 108; Dec. 17, 1881, p. 407; June 9, 1877, p. 400. Saxton, *Indispensable Enemy*, chap. 3. *M/SP*, May 21, 1904, p. 341. Edward C. Kirkland, *Industry Comes of Age—Business, Labor, and Public Policy—1860–1897* (Chicago, 1967), p. 329.

17. *Miners' Magazine*, July, 1901, p. 28. Idaho tax law printed in *Idaho World*, Feb. 3, 1866. This law was overturned by the territorial district court, and a similar act passed in 1869 was disapproved by Congress as well as the territorial Supreme Court. *Idaho World*, March 24, 1866, and Sept. 2, 1869. 16 Stat. 366 (1870). Nevada *Laws, 1879*, p. 105. British Columbia *Statutes*,

1884, pp. 3–12; and *Statutes, 1897*, p. 275. The latter ban was overturned by the Privy Council in London in 1905. *M/SP*, Sept. 16, 1905, p. 186.

18. Robert G. Athearn, *Westward the Briton* (New York, 1953), pp. 187–202. Wilbur S. Shepperson, *Restless Strangers—Nevada's Immigrants and Their Interpreters* (Reno, 1970), pp. 13–14. Dana Evans Balibrera, "Virginia City and the Immigrant" (unpublished master's thesis, University of Nevada, 1965), p. 70. Ralph Emerson Mann, II, "The Social and Political Structure of Two California Mining Towns, 1850–1870" (unpublished doctoral dissertation, Stanford University, 1970), p. 120. U.S. Ninth Census *Compendium* (1870), pp. 376, 396, 425. U.S. Tenth Census *Compendium* (1880), pt. 1, pp. 332, 492–493.

19. Rickard, *Interviews with Mining Engineers*, p. 395. U.S. Works Projects Administration, *Copper Camp* (New York, 1943), pp. 121, 133. *E/MJ*, March 3, 1894, p. 193.

20. Grass Valley (Calif.) *Daily National*, Nov. 10, 1868, p. 2. Helena (Mont.) *Independent*, Feb. 20, 1889, p. 4. The Montana office was ultimately opened to naturalized citizens as well as the native-born.

21. Butte (Mont.) *Miner*, Aug. 29, 1876. *M/SP*, June 2, 1888, p. 345. *E/MJ*, Jan. 25, 1879, p. 57; April 19, 1879, p. 278. Andrew F. Rolle, *The Immigrant Upraised—Italian Adventurers and Colonists in an Expanding America* (Norman, Oklahoma, 1968), pp. 170–171. Rowland T. Berthoff, *British Immigrants in Industrial America, 1790–1950* (Cambridge, Mass., 1953), pp. 51–52, 59.

22. *Copper Camp*, p. 121. Arthur Cecil Todd, *The Cornish Miner in America* (Glendale, Calif., 1967), pp. 59, 61, 229, 256. A. C. Todd, "Cousin Jack in Idaho," *Idaho Yesterdays*, VIII:4 (Winter, 1964–1965), 4–5. Rowe, *Hard-Rock Men*, pp. 196–197. Joseph Harper Cash, "Labor in the West: The Homestake Mining Company and Its Workers, 1877–1942" (unpublished doctoral dissertation, University of Iowa, 1966), pp. 62, 62n. Otis E. Young, Jr., *Western Mining* (Norman, Oklahoma, 1970), pp. 151, 151n. London *Mining Journal*, quoted in *E/MJ*, Feb. 4, 1904, p. 200. A. K. Hamilton Jenkin, *The Cornish Miner—An Account of His Life Above and Underground from Early Times* (London, 1927, 1948), p. 322.

23. Mrs. Albina Clementi, Mrs. Speranza Pangrazi, and Mrs. Ermira Visintin, interviews, Telluride, Colorado, July 22, 1972.

24. Colorado Bureau of Labor Statistics, *Report, 1887–1888*, pp. 255–270. *The Age*, Feb. 26, 1890, p. 2. Testimony of James T. Smith, Denver, Colo., July 13, 1899: U.S. Industrial Commission, *Report*, XII, 222. *Reveille*, Aug. 28, 1902, p. 3; March 2, 1906, p. 4; and Butte *Miner* quoted in *Reveille* of May 8, 1903, p. 1.

25. Mann, "Two California Mining Towns," p. 62. *Gilpin County Observer*, Feb. 1, 1888, p. 4. *M/SP*, March 22, 1884, p. 206. Ronald Conklin Brown, "Hard-Rock Miners of the Great Basin and Rocky Mountain West, 1860–1920" (unpublished doctoral dissertation, University of Illinois, 1975), p. 363. Carroll D. Wright, ed., *A Report on Labor Disturbances in the State of Colorado. . . .* (58th Cong., 3d Sess., Senate Doc. 122, 1905), p. 149. Western Federation of Miners, 17th Convention *Proceedings* (1909), pp. 23, 262–263. *Copper Camp*, pp. 133–137.

26. Gold Hill (Nev.) Miners' Union Records, Vol. I (March 16, 1867), p. 93.

27. The Immigration Commission in 1908–1910 found that most Mexicans and Italians working in Arizona metal mines got less than the $3.50 paid to other miners. See U.S. Immigration Commission, *Reports: Part 25, Japanese and Other Immigrant Races in the Pacific Coast and Rocky Mountain States* (61st Cong., 2d Sess., 1909–1910), pp. 130–132. An excellent study of the Chinese

issue in the context of the West's labor development is Saxton, *Indispensable Enemy*.

28. Testimony of Robert C. Chambers, Salt Lake City, Aug. 2, 1899: U.S. Industrial Commission, *Report*, XII, 588. Marshall Sprague, *Money Mountain —The Story of Cripple Creek Gold* (Boston, 1953), pp. 134–136.

29. Rodman W. Paul, *California Gold—The Beginning of Mining in the Far West* (Cambridge, Mass., 1947), pp. 326–327. W. Turrentine Jackson, *Treasure Hill—Portrait of a Silver Mining Camp* (Tucson, 1963), p. 169. Todd, *Cornish Miner*, pp. 163–167.

30. Merle W. Wells, "The WFM in British Columbia: The Eight Hour Statute, the Alien Labour Acts, and the Recognition Issue in the Kootenay Mines, 1899–1902" (paper presented on May 14, 1976, before the Pacific Northwest Labor History Association, Seattle, Wash.), pp. 6, 8–9, 12. Emma F. Langdon, *The Cripple Creek Strike—A History of Industrial Wars in Colorado 1903–4–5* (Denver, 1904–1905), pp. 118–120.

31. "Coeur d'Alenes Mining Troubles" (56th Cong., 1st Sess., Senate Doc. 24, 1899), p. 13. Wright, *Labor Disturbances in Colorado*, p. 107. George G. Suggs, Jr., *Colorado's War on Militant Unionism—James H. Peabody and the Western Federation of Miners* (Detroit, 1972), p. 21. *Miners' Magazine*, August, 1902, pp. 36–45. T. A. Rickard observed the Barthell monument on his ride through the San Juans in 1902, and condemned the final quotation from Longfellow as "the prostitution of poetry!" Rickard noted that no one was punished for "murdering" non-union miners, "while the one murderer, killed in the act, is commemorated in marble and in poem!" (T. A. Rickard, *Across the San Juan Mountains* [New York, 1903], p. 40).

32. Recent studies as well as more traditional works generally uphold the view that the New Immigration was non-union and/or anti-union in the Eastern industrial centers. This was true until the late 1890s in the Pennsylvania coal fields, according to Victor R. Greene, *The Slavic Community on Strike— Immigrant Labor in Pennsylvania Anthracite* (Notre Dame, 1968), pp. 210–213. The same was true in the steel mills until approximately 1901, concludes David Brody, *Steelworkers in America—The Non-union Era* (Cambridge, Mass., 1960), pp. 135–137. Typical of turn-of-the-century views are those of Frank Julian Warne and John R. Commons, in Commons's *Trade Unionism and Labor Problems* (New York, 1905), pp. 339–340, 343–344.

33. Colorado Bureau of Labor Statistics, *Report, 1895–1896*, p. 19. *M/SP*, April 8, 1899, p. 371. Wright, *Labor Disturbances in Colorado*, pp. 102–105, 152, 155.

34. Testimony of Joseph MacDonald: U.S. Industrial Commission, *Report*, XII, p. 485. Joplin (Mo.) *Daily Globe*, March 27, 1901, p. 2. Suggs, *Colorado's War on Militant Unionism*, p. 134. Wright, *Labor Disturbances in Colorado*, pp. 151–158. Two of the four persons charged in the Idaho Springs incident had Italian names.

35. Rickard, *Across the San Juan Mountains*, p. 41. Langdon, *Cripple Creek Strike*, p. 212.

36. *Miners' Magazine*, Dec. 3, 1903, p. 8. Russell R. Elliott, *Nevada's Twentieth-Century Mining Boom—Tonopah, Goldfield, Ely* (Reno, 1966), pp. 254–258. More Italians appear to have gone into lower-paying coal mining jobs in the West than was true of other European groups. Here, too, however, they often became active union members and gained a reputation for militancy in Colorado coal mine strikes in Gunnison County in 1891 and Las Animas County in 1903–1904, as well as for leading the Chandler Mine boycott in

1902 after Japanese were hired. *E/MJ*, Dec. 26, 1891, p. 732. Wright, *Labor Disturbances in Colorado*, pp. 341–342. Ozawa, *Japanese in Colorado*, p. 44. Rolle, *Immigrant Upraised*, pp. 173–178. WFM 17th Convention, *Proceedings* (1909), pp. 325–326.

37. Handersohn's name indicates that he may have been a Scandinavian immigrant, as were many Upper Peninsula miners. Missoula (Mont.) *Gazette*, reprinted in Wallace (Idaho) *Press*, May 21, 1892. *Gogebic Advocate*, May 7, 1892. *The Menominee Range*, May 19, 1892, p. 1. Duluth was the nearest railhead for connections to the West.

38. It is not possible to tell, of course, whether the telegram sent to the Michigan newspaper was influenced by the man's new employer. *Menominee Range*, May 19, 1892, p. 5. Testimony of Emil Peterson, Sept. 19, 1904, reprinted in Langdon, *Cripple Creek Strike*, p. 119.

39. Eben Smith, Denver, to S. W. Dorsey, London, England, Oct. 6, 1896, Eben Smith letterpress book.

40. Joseph P. Gazzam, "The Leadville Strike of 1896," *Bulletin of the Missouri Historical Society*, VII:1 (October, 1950), 89–94. Many of Gazzam's statements in this recollection do not ring true, however, and his claims must be considered suspect. Also see Wright, *Labor Disturbances in Colorado*, p. 92.

41. William Anderson, Commissioner, Missouri Bureau of Labor Statistics and Inspection, to AFL President, Samuel Gompers, June 1, 1903, American Federation of Labor Files, Series 7, Box 77: United Mine Workers Correspondence. Joplin's lack of unionization may have stemmed in part from the region's geology. Because its lead and zinc veins lay horizontal and at shallow depths, individuals and small groups of men could mine with little machinery, and were not required to seek extensive financing. As a result, large operations did not appear in the Joplin district. See Joplin *Globe*, Feb. 5, 1901, p. 3. This issue is examined in Arrell M. Gibson, *Wilderness Bonanza—The Tri-State District of Missouri, Kansas, and Oklahoma* (Norman, Oklahoma, 1972), pp. 3–4, 67–69, 79, 152, 196, 198–199, 201, 203, 205–208, 259–260, 262–265.

42. Merrill Hough, "Leadville and the Western Federation of Miners," *Colorado Magazine*, XLIX:1 (Winter, 1972), pp. 29–30. Carthage (Mo.) *Press*, Nov. 19, 1896, pp. 6–7; Dec. 10, 1896, p. 3; Dec. 17, 1896, p. 3; Dec. 24, 1896, p. 8. Colorado Legislature, *Report of the Joint Special Legislative Committee of the Eleventh General Assembly on the Leadville Strike* (1896), pp. 21–22, 36.

43. *Miners' Magazine* (January, 1902), p. 46.

44. Wells, "WFM in British Columbia," p. 15. Testimony of John A. Finch, Secretary-Treasurer, Standard Mining Co. and Vice-President and Treasurer, Hecla Mining Co., Wallace, Idaho, July 27, 1899: U.S. Industrial Commission, *Report*, XII, p. 494. *E/MJ*, July 8, 1899, p. 47; Feb. 23, 1901, p. 255.

45. David L. Lonsdale, "The Movement for an Eight-Hour Law in Colorado, 1893–1913" (unpublished doctoral dissertation, University of Colorado, 1963), pp. 216–217. *M/SP*, Sept. 19, 1903, p. 180. *Miners' Magazine* (August, 1903), p. 20; Jan. 14, 1904, pp. 6–7. WFM 15th Convention, *Proceedings* (1907), p. 203. Cash, *Working the Homestake*, p. 94.

46. Testimony of Frederick Burbidge, Manager, Bunker Hill & Sullivan Co. Mine, and Joseph MacDonald, Wallace, Idaho, July 27, 1899: U.S. Industrial Commission, *Report*, XII, 452, 484–485. *E/MJ*, March 3, 1894, p. 193.

47. *E/MJ*, Jan. 19, 1901, p. 92; Jan. 5, 1905, p. 13. *M/SP* April 9, 1904, p. 251; Sept. 19, 1903, p. 180. *Idaho Laws*, 1897, pp. 5–6. U.S. Immigration Commission, *Reports: Part 25, Japanese and Other Immigrant Races . . .* , p. 97.

48. James Reid, letter printed in *Carthage Press*, Dec. 24, 1896, p. 8. Testimony of James T. Smith, deputy labor commissioner, Denver, July 13, 1899: U.S. Industrial Commission, *Report*, XII, 215.

49. *Miners' Magazine*, May 1901, p. 6.

50. Ibid., Feb., 1902, p. 15. Also see Jan. 14, 1904, pp. 6–7; and Nov., 1901, pp. 5–6.

51. WFM 18th Convention, *Proceedings* (1910), p. 28.

52. *Miners' Magazine*, Nov., 1901, pp. 5–6.

53. Grass Valley *National*, May 22, 1869, p. 3. *Alta California*, June 7, 1869, p. 1; Aug. 7, 1869, p. 2. WFM 15th Convention, *Proceedings* (1907), p. 162.

54. *Idaho World*, June 30, 1866. MacDonald, *Report to Miners' National Union*, p. 8.

55. Nevada Mining Inspector, *Report, 1912*, pp. 7–8. Gold Hill Union Records, vol. 1, 74 (Feb. 16, 1867); 97 (March 23, 1867); 147 (Sept. 12, 1867); and 154 (Oct. 10, 1867). Victor Miners Union No. 32, Ledger Book, 1894–1903, passim. "Leaving the country" did not, of course, mean leaving the United States; it simply meant leaving that area or mining district.

56. Andrews N. Rogers, Central City, Colo., to R. H. Rickard, Treasurer, Republic Gold Mining Co., New York, May 29, 1880, Andrews N. Rogers letterpress book. Gen. Mgr. William J. Cox, Camp Bird Co., Ltd., Ouray County, Colorado, 1905 Report, in "Mine Engineer Reports," unpublished compilation by Colorado School of Mines Library, Golden.

57. *Reveille*, Oct. 21, 1902. Testimony of Charles H. MacKinnon, *Goldfield Consolidated Mines Co. v. Goldfield Miners Union No. 220, W.F.M.*, January, 1908, Testimony Record, pp. 136–141.

III: Payday—Perhaps

1. Two months later, the Seligmans won a court order requiring the other stockholders to repay them $65,650 of the amount. The Gregory story is taken from the following: Helena (Mont.) *Independent*, Jan. 28, 1887, p. 4. Butte (Mont.) *Miner*, Jan. 29, 1887, p. 1; March 12, 1887, p. 3. *The Engineering and Mining Journal*, Jan. 29, 1887, p. 84 [hereafter cited as *E/MJ*]. *The Mining and Scientific Press*, Feb. 5, 1887, p. 90 [hereafter cited as *M/SP*]. Montana Mine Inspector, *Report, 1889*, pp. 106–107.

2. Robert L. Romig, "The South Boise Quartz Mines, 1863–1892: A Study in Western Mining Industry and Finance" (unpublished master's thesis, University of California, Berkeley, 1950), p. 71.

3. *M/SP*, Jan. 30, 1897, p. 89. William C. Miller and Eleanore Bushnell, eds., *Reports of the 1863 Constitutional Convention of the Territory of Nevada. . . .* (n.p., 1972), p. 86. John Rowe, *The Hard-Rock Men—Cornish Immigrants and the North American Mining Frontier* (New York, 1974), pp. 234–235.

4. *Thompson v. Wise Boy Min. & Mill. Co.*, 74 Pacific 958 (Idaho Supreme Court, 1903).

5. *Owyhee Avalanche*, Nov. 10, 1866.

6. *Idaho Statesman*, Nov. 23, 1875. Theodore B. Comstock, letter, *E/MJ*, March 26, 1881, pp. 214–215. Eben Smith, Denver, to Arthur Nichols, Leadville, July 31, 1894, Eben Smith letterpress books.

7. *Owyhee Avalanche*, Oct. 20, 1866. Rowe, *Hard-Rock Men*, p. 233. *Daily Pioche Review* (Nevada), Sept. 26, 1872. *Deseret Evening News*, March 20, 1896, pp. 1–2. For other information on the scrip problem, see Richard E. Lingenfelter, *The Hardrock Miners: A History of the Mining Labor Movement in*

the American West, 1863–1893 (Berkeley, 1974), pp. 29–30. Western Federation of Miners 16th Convention, *Proceedings* (1908), pp. 257 ff.

8. *Idaho Statesman*, Feb. 26, 1876; Oct. 28, 1875; Feb. 22, 1876; July 15, 1876.

9. *Coeur d'Alene Miner*, Oct. 14, 1893, p. 2. WFM 15th Convention, *Proceedings* (1907), p. 291.

10. Charles P. Flinn, Holy Moses Mine, to Eben Smith, Aspen, Colo., April 22, 1891, Eben Smith letterpress books. Idaho Mine Inspector, *Report, 1903*, pp. 128–129. Also see *Coeur d'Alene Miner*, March 11, 1893, p. 1; *E/MJ*, June 29, 1895, p. 613; and U.S. Industrial Commission, *Report . . . on the Relations and Conditions of Capital and Labor Employed in the Mining Industry . . .* , XII, pp. 465, 525.

11. *Miners' Magazine*, March, 1901, pp. 12–14.

12. Wage information is drawn from the following: Romig, "South Boise Quartz Mines," p. 44. *Montana Post*, Aug. 27, 1864; May 20, 1865; June 30, 1866. Rowe, *Hard-Rock Men*, pp. 249–250. *E/MJ*, April 19, 1866, p. 339; April 14, 1877, p. 239; July 24, 1880, p. 57; Nov. 20, 1880, p. 337; Dec. 17, 1881, p. 407; Oct. 22, 1892, p. 399; May 10, 1884, p. 355; March 20, 1886, p. 216; Nov. 6, 1897, p. 541; Nov. 17, 1906, p. 930. Gold Hill (Nev.) *Daily News*, March 23, 1864. Eliot Lord, *Comstock Mining and Miners* (Washington, D.C., 1883; reprint 1959), p. 182. Lingenfelter, *Hardrock Miners*, pp. 69–75. Russell Elliott, "The History of White Pine County" (unpublished paper in possession of the Nevada State Historical Society), pp. 66–67. *M/SP*, Aug. 11, 1906, p. 162. Joseph H. Cash, "Labor in the West: The Homestake Mining Company and Its Workers, 1877–1942" (unpublished doctoral dissertation, University of Iowa), pp. 74–75. South Dakota Mine Inspector, *Report, 1897–1898*, p. 21. Sheelwant B. Pawar, "An Environmental Study of the Development of the Utah Labor Movement: 1860–1935" (unpublished doctoral dissertation, University of Utah, 1968), pp. 68–69. Montana Mine Inspector, *Report, 1889*, p. 75. Colorado Bureau of Labor Statistics, *Report, 1891–1892*, p. 35. Colorado Mine Inspector, *Report, 1897*, p. 158. Charles Merrill Hough, "Leadville and the Western Federation of Miners," *Colorado Magazine*, XLIX: 1 (Winter, 1972), 21. Hough, "Leadville, Colorado, 1878 to 1898: A Study in Unionism" (unpublished master's thesis, University of Colorado, 1958), p. 31.

13. *M/SP*, Dec. 10, 1892, p. 378.

14. Richard Thomas in Burke, Idaho, to his parents in Cornwall, April 13 and 23, 1905, quoted in A. C. Todd, "Cousin Jack in Idaho," *Idaho Yesterdays*, VIII:4 (Winter, 1964–1965), p. 10.

15. Miners' budgets and expenses quoted in Rowe, *Hard-Rock Men*, pp. 151, 165n. *M/SP*, Jan. 30, 1897, p. 89. U.S. Industrial Commission *Report*, XII, p. 465.

16. Leasing information is drawn mainly from Rowe, *Hard-Rock Men*, chap. 5. *E/MJ*, Sept. 19, 1891, p. 329; March 4, 1893, pp. 193–194; Dec. 15, 1904, pp. 941–942. *M/SP*, Aug. 22, 1885, p. 132; April 24, 1886, p. 275; Sept. 16, 1899, p. 310; Nov. 10, 1900, p. 516; Aug. 15, 1903, p. 95.

17. *E/MJ*, July 2, 1898, p. 17. U.S. Industrial Commission, *Report*, XII, pp. 352, 356.

18. R. H. Reid, Denver, to C. W. Martin, Colorado Springs, Sept. 18, 1895, Smith letterpress books. Ernest Le Neve Foster, Denver, to James Portland, Leadville, Jan. 8, 1894, Ernest Le Neve Foster Papers, Vol. III. George F. Crane, Secretary, New Gregory Mining Company, New York, to John H. Kemp, agent, Central City, Colo., Feb. 9, 1897 (two letters), John H. Kemp correspondence file. Dr. Ed. Werner, Saguache, Colo., to unknown,

apparently 1891, Dr. Ed. Werner letterpress book, in Gold and Silver Extraction Co. file.

19. The development of the mechanic's lien is discussed in John R. Commons and John B. Andrews, *Principles of Labor Legislation* (New York, 1936), pp. 337–338. The 1864 law has not been located. It is referred to in *Idaho World*, Jan. 26, 1865. *Owyhee Avalanche*, June 8, 1867. Idaho *Laws, 1868–1869*, p. 125. Idaho *Laws, 1874–1875*, pp. 616–617. *Owyhee Semi-Weekly Tidal Wave*, Dec. 25, 1868. *Smith v. Sherman Min. Co.*, 31 Pacific 72, 73 (Montana Supreme Court, 1896).

20. *Owyhee Avalanche*, Oct. 20, 1866, p. 3. *Idaho Statesman*, May 15, 1877, p. 3; May 17, 1877, p. 3; May 19, 1877, p. 3.

21. Grass Valley (Calif.) *National*, Aug. 25, 1868, p. 3. Clancy (Mont.) *Miner*, March 20, 1897, p. 1; May 1, 1897, p. 1; May 15, 1897, p. 1; Oct. 9, 1897, p. 1.

22. Butte (Mont.) *Bystander*, Dec. 31, 1892, p. 3. Colorado *Laws, 1893*, pp. 315–326. Colorado *Laws, 1895*, p. 202. *Davidson v. Jennings*, 60 Pacific 354 (Colorado Supreme Court, Feb. 5, 1900). *Schweizer v. Mansfield*, 59 Pacific 843 (Colorado Court of Appeals, Jan. 8, 1900). *M/SP*, Dec. 7, 1901, p. 241; Feb. 7, 1903, p. 83.

23. Montana *Laws, 1872*, pp. 727–728. Colorado *Laws, 1877*, pp. 150–151.

24. *Owyhee Avalanche*, Sept. 15, 1866, p. 2. J. Ross Browne, *Mineral Resources of the States and Territories West of the Rocky Mountains* (40th Cong., 2d Sess., House Ex. Doc. 202, 1868), p. 522.

25. *E/MJ*, May 30, 1896, p. 526; Nov. 10, 1904, p. 761. Denver (Colo.) *News*, July 1, 1898. Denver (Colo.) *Times*, July 12, 1902. Colorado Bureau of Labor Statistics, *Report, 1895–1896*, p. 18.

26. The WFM frequently encouraged its members to form cooperatives. See *Miners' Magazine*, July, 1901, pp. 8–9; February, 1902, pp. 7–8; March, 1902, pp. 12–13. Cooperative mining ventures are described in the following: *Coeur d'Alenes Miner*, Oct. 6, 1894, p. 3. U.S. Industrial Commission, *Report*, XII, 447. *M/SP*, Oct. 20, 1894, p. 243; Dec. 29, 1894, p. 413. *E/MJ*, Oct. 13, 1894, pp. 337, 348–349; Oct. 27, 1894, p. 398; Nov. 17, 1894, pp. 457, 470; Dec. 1, 1894, p. 517; Dec. 8, 1894, p. 541; Dec. 29, 1894, p. 613.

27. *E/MJ*, June 13, 1885, p. 411. Clancy *Miner*, March 20, 1897, p. 1.

28. *Idaho Statesman*, Oct. 26, 1875, p. 1.

29. Colorado Bureau of Labor Statistics, *Report, 1887–1888*, pp. 312–313. Romig, "South Boise Quartz Mines," p. 39.

30. Owyhee Avalanche Publishing Co., *A Historical, Descriptive, and Commercial Directory of Owyhee County, Idaho* (Silver City, 1898), pp. 27–28. *Idaho Statesman*, July 4 and 11, 1876.

31. Smith, *Silver Saga*, pp. 32–34, 96, 164–166. Lingenfelter, *Hardrock Miners*, p. 137. *E/MJ*, Feb. 23, 1889, p. 193; Oct. 17, 1896, p. 383. *M/SP*, Feb. 8, 1896, p. 111; Feb. 22, 1896, p. 151; March 21, 1896, p. 231; Oct. 17, 1896, p. 315.

32. *M/SP*, June 6, 1908, p. 775. Russell R. Elliott, *Nevada's Twentieth-Century Mining Boom—Tonopah, Goldfield, Ely* (Reno, 1966), p. 116. Marshall Sprague, *Money Mountain—The Story of Cripple Creek Gold* (Boston, 1953), p. 69. Grass Valley *National*, June 1, 1868, p. 3. *Daily Alta California*, June 7, 1869, p. 1.

33. *Owyhee Avalanche*, Nov. 3, 1866, p. 3. Beth Kay Harris, *The Towns of Tintic* (Denver, 1961), pp. 136–137. *M/SP*, Oct. 6, 1900, p. 404. Helena *Independent*, Jan. 31, 1903, p. 1. *E/MJ*, Aug. 5, 1905, p. 222.

34. Otis E. Young, Jr., *Western Mining* (Norman, Oklahoma, 1970), pp. 219–223. Jim Sterrett, interview, Cripple Creek, Aug. 6, 1972.

35. *M/SP*, June 6, 1908, p. 774.

36. Ibid., p. 774. Frank P. Tondel, "As I Remember Goldfield," *Nevada Historical Society Quarterly*, III:3 (Summer, 1960), p. 16. Byrd Sawyer, "Labor Conditions in Tonopah and Goldfield" (unpublished master's thesis, University of California, Berkeley, 1931), chap. 5, pp. 3–6. Sprague, *Money Mountain*, pp. 203–204. Phyllis F. Dorset, *The New Eldorado—The Story of Colorado's Gold and Silver Rushes* (London, 1970), p. 369.

37. Sawyer, "Labor Conditions in Tonopah and Goldfield," chap. 5, pp. 3–4. *M/SP*, June 6, 1908, pp. 774–775. Gene M. Gressley, ed., *Bostonians and Bullion—The Journal of Robert Livermore, 1892–1915* (Lincoln, Nebr., 1968), pp. 115–116. *Reveille*, Nov. 30, 1906, p. 1.

38. *M/SP*, April 7, 1900, p. 374; June 6, 1908, p. 776.

39. Dorset, *New Eldorado*, p. 369. *E/MJ*, Oct. 17, 1903, pp. 572–573. The Cornish view that highgrading was no crime was brought out repeatedly in the 1869 strike in Grass Valley, where the Cornish were a major group in the population. See Rossiter W. Raymond, *Statistics of Mines and Mining in the States and Territories West of the Rocky Mountains* (41st Cong., 2d Sess., House Ex. Doc. 207, 1870), p. 54.

40. Testimony of A. H. Swallow and Charles H. MacKinnon, *Goldfield Cons. Mines Co. v. Goldfield Miners Union*, record of testimony, p. 46. For benefits to local businesses, also see *M/SP*, Sept. 22, 1906, p. 332.

41. Elliott, *Nevada's Twentieth-Century Boom*, p. 115. Raymond, *Statistics of Mines and Mining* for 1869, p. 54. Sprague, *Money Mountain*, pp. 205, 312. *E/MJ*, Oct. 17, 1903, pp. 572–573.

42. Denver (Colo.) *Post*, reprinted in *M/SP*, April 7, 1900, p. 374. Thos. Hy. Edsall, Aspen M. & S. Co., to J. B. Wheeler, New York, Nov. 20, 1889, D. R. C. Brown letterbook.

43. Eben Smith, Denver, to Chas. A. Keith, Cripple Creek, May 20, 1895, Smith letterpress books. *M/SP*, April 7, 1900, p. 374.

44. *M/SP*, Oct. 6, 1900, p. 404. Sprague, *Money Mountain*, p. 312.

45. *Owyhee Avalanche*, Sept. 8, 1866, p. 3. Sprague, *Money Mountain*, p. 203. Eben Smith, Denver, to W. S. Jackson, Colorado Springs, March 10, 1898, Smith letterpress books.

46. *M/SP*, June 6, 1908, p. 775.

47. C. G. Warnford Lock, *Miners' Pocket Book—A Reference Book for Engineers and Others Engaged in Metalliferous Mining* (New York, 1901), p. 341.

48. *Idaho World*, Jan. 23, 1877, p. 2; Feb. 20, 1877, p. 3.

49. MacKinnon testimony, *Goldfield Cons. Mines Co. v. Goldfield Miners Union*, record of testimony, pp. 9–12, 20–21, 177, 236–237. *M/SP*, June 6, 1908, p. 776. Elliott, *Nevada's Twentieth-Century Mining Boom*, pp. 116, 125.

IV: Betrayed by the New Technology

1. *Engineering and Mining Journal*, April 18, 1871, p. 249; April 2, 1872, p. 209; Aug. 22, 1874, p. 113 [hereafter cited as *E/MJ*]. Walter R. Crane, *Gold and Silver* (New York, 1908), p. 356. Rossiter W. Raymond, *Mines and Mining of the Rocky Mountains, the Inland Basin, and the Pacific Slope* (New York, 1871), pp. 503, 506.

2. Raymond, *Mines and Mining*, pp. 507–508. *E/MJ*, April 18, 1871, p. 249.

3. *E/MJ*, April 18, 1871, p. 249. *Owyhee Avalanche*, Jan. 30, Feb. 6, 13, and

20, 1875. On use of the Burleigh drill, see the following: Rossiter W. Raymond, *Statistics of Mines and Mining in the States and Territories West of the Rocky Mountains* (41st Cong., 2d Sess., House Ex. Doc. 207, 1870), p. 507, and Raymond's report of the same title published in 1872 (42d Cong., 2d Sess., House Ex. Doc. 211), pp. 487–492. *Browne v. King et al.*, 100 Fed. 561, 563 (Eighth Circuit Court of Appeals, 1900).

4. *Mining and Scientific Press* (July 15, 1905), p. 38 [hereafter cited as *M/SP*].

5. Otis E. Young, Jr., *Black Powder and Hand Steel—Miners and Machines on the Old Western Frontier* (Norman, Oklahoma, 1975), p. 32 and passim. San Francisco *Bulletin*, quoted in *E/MJ*, Jan. 30, 1872, pp. 74–75. Crane, *Gold and Silver*, p. 353. For recent scholars' conclusions, see: Otis E. Young, Jr., *Western Mining* (Norman, Oklahoma, 1970), p. 204. Rodman Wilson Paul, "Colorado as a Pioneer of Science in the Mining West," *Mississippi Valley Historical Review*, XLVII:1 (June, 1960), passim. Paul, *Mining Frontiers of the Far West* (New York, 1963), p. xii. Melvyn Dubofsky, *We Shall Be All—A History of the Industrial Workers of the World* (Chicago, 1969), pp. 19–20.

6. Risdon Iron and Locomotive Works, *Gold Mines and Mining in California —A New Gold Era Dawning on the State* (San Francisco, 1885), p. 161. Dr. G. W. King, "First Aid to the Injured in Mining Accidents," reprinted in *M/SP*, Sept. 13, 1902, p. 146. *Owyhee Avalanche*, Feb. 13, 1875. Herbert Thomas, *Cornish Mining Interviews* (Camborne, England, 1896), p. 94. Testimony of Frederick Burbidge, Manager, Bunker Hill & Sullivan Mine, Wallace, Idaho, July 27, 1899: U.S. Industrial Commission, *Report . . . on the Relations and Conditions of Capital and Labor Employed in the Mining Industry* (57th Cong., 1st Sess., House Doc. 181, 1901), XII, pp. 458–459. The support for technology shown by Eastern labor leaders is discussed in Irwin Yellowitz, *Industrialization and the American Labor Movement, 1850–1900* (Port Washington, N.Y., 1977), chap. 1.

7. *The Colorado Miner*, April 28, June 2, 1870.

8. Works Projects Administration Writer's Program, *Copper Camp* (New York, 1943), p. 223. Western Federation of Miners, *Miners' Magazine*, September, 1900, pp. 41, 44. Victor I. Noxon (as told to Forest Crossen), "Hard Rock Drilling Contests in Colorado," *Colorado Magazine*, XI:3 (May, 1934), p. 84. John Rowe, *The Hard-Rock Men—Cornish Immigrants and the North American Mining Frontier* (New York, 1974), pp. 274–275.

9. *Copper Camp*, p. 222. *M/SP*, July 14, 1906, p. 41.

10. *Copper Camp*, p. 221.

11. Arthur J. Hiester, E. S. Geary, and E. H. Murchison, "Air Drills and Modern High Explosives" (unpublished graduation thesis, Colorado School of Mines, 1912), pp. 3–4. U.S. 10th Census (1880), Part 13: *Statistics and Technology of the Precious Metals* (Washington, D.C., 1885), p. 151. James A. MacKnight, *The Mines of Montana—Their History and Development to Date* (Helena, 1892), pp. 21–22. *M/SP*, Oct. 13, 1900, p. 432.

12. *M/SP*, Aug. 6, 1892, p. 90

13. *Owyhee Avalanche*, Oct. 18, 1873.

14. *E/MJ*, Jan. 31, 1891, p. 150. John A. Church, *The Comstock Lode—Its Formation and History* (New York, 1879), p. 14.

15. *Owyhee Avalanche*, Feb. 13, 1875. *E/MJ*, June 27, 1903, pp. 958–959. S. C. Hotchkiss, "Occupational Diseases in the Mining Industry," *American Labor Legislation Review*, II:1 (February, 1912), p. 137.

16. Quoted in *M/SP*, Feb. 18, 1893, p. 106.

17. Miners' consumption was mentioned in 1874 by Adolph Sutro, "Lec-

ture on Mines and Mining . . . ," printed in supplement to *The Daily Independent*, Oct. 31, 1874, p. 4. Nevada Mine Inspector *Report, 1912*, p. 10. Hospital records consulted were St. Peter's Hospital, Helena, Mont., Registers, vol. I (1884–1893) and vol. II (1893–1907); and St. Vincent's Hospital, Leadville, Colo., Registers, vol. I (1891–1901) and vol. II (1901–1918). Also see 1865–1880 records of Storey County Hospital and Coroner on the Comstock Lode, summarized by Eliot Lord, *Comstock Mining and Miners* (Washington, D.C., 1883, reprint 1959), pp. 436–437, 440–441.

18. *M/SP*, Feb. 18, 1893, p. 106. Hotchkiss, "Occupational Diseases," pp. 133–134.

19. Colorado *Laws, 1889*, p. 293. *E/MJ* June 2, 1904, p. 871.

20. Hotchkiss, "Occupational Diseases," pp. 133–134, 137–138. *M/SP*, Sept. 5, 1903, pp. 152–153. *E/MJ*, Dec. 5, 1903, pp. 854–855; June 23, 1904, p. 994. That this was not a cure-all was shown in the Homestake Mine at Lead, S.D., which installed wet drilling in 1923 but by 1936 could still find silicosis (phthisis) in 161 of its 1,140 miners. See Joseph H. Cash, "Labor in the West: The Homestake Mining Company and Its Workers, 1877–1942" (unpublished doctoral dissertation, University of Iowa, 1966), pp. 97, 236–237.

21. Montana Mine Inspector, *Report, 1889*, p. 121.

22. By 1866, the forty-six companies on the Comstock had forty-four steam engines in use. Lord, *Comstock Mining*, pp. 220–221, 227. Dan DeQuille, *The Big Bonanza* (Hartford, Conn., 1876; reprint 1947), p. 89. *Owyhee Avalanche*, quoted in *Idaho World*, Feb. 26, 1868.

23. Montana Mine Inspector, *Report, 1889*, pp. 83–84, 123–124.

24. Gold Hill (Nev.) *News*, March 27, 1864. Coroner's Jury Report No. 119, death of Freeman Hunt, May 25, 1904, Teller County District Court files, Cripple Creek Colo. Montana Mine Inspector, *Report, 1889*, p. 121; and *Report, 1900*, pp. 79–80. *Boulder County News* (Colo.), Aug. 5, 1871.

25. Grass Valley (Calif.) *Daily National*, March 30, 1869, p. 3. *Idaho World*, Dec. 24, 1878.

26. *Daily Alta California*, July 14, 1868, p. 2.

27. Lord, *Comstock Mining*, pp. 367, 402. James D. Hague, *Mining Industry*, in Clarence King, *Report of the Geological Exploration of the Fortieth Parallel*, Professional Papers of the U.S. Army Engineer Dept., No. 18 (Washington, D.C., 1870), vol. III, pp. 122–123. Church, *Comstock Lode*, p. 16. Alfred C. Watts and Herbert E. Badger, "Hoisting and Haulage in the Cripple Creek District" (unpublished graduation thesis, Colorado School of Mines, 1902), pp. 15, 17, 19–20. Montana Mine Inspector, *Report, 1889*, p. 120. Modern elevators commonly travel at 800 feet per minute.

28. Raymond, *Statistics of Mines and Mining* for 1869, pp. 591–600. Prof. Robert Peele, quoted in *E/MJ*, June 16, 1906, p. 1148.

29. Butte (Mont.) *Miner*, Jan. 7, 1885.

30. Helena (Mont.) *Herald*, reprinted in Butte (Mont.) *Weekly Tribune*, Jan. 30, 1897. Montana Mine Inspector, *Report, 1889*, p. 120.

31. Coroner's Jury Report No. 91, death of Charles Sullivan, Aug. 27, 1902, Teller County District Court files.

32. *E/MJ*, Nov. 7, 1891, p. 538. Nevada Mine Inspector, *Report, 1910*, pp. 6–7.

33. *E/MJ*, Feb. 23, 1905, p. 382.

34. Virginia City (Nev.) *Daily Territorial Enterprise*, July 2, 1867, p. 3. Butte *Miner*, Jan. 14, 1885.

35. Colorado Bureau of Labor Statistics, *Report, 1887–1888*, pp. 303, 306–308. Montana Mine Inspector, *Report, 1891*, pp. 22–23; and *Report, 1897*, .p. 52.

36. Material on the Stratton's Independence disaster is drawn from Coroner's Jury Report No. 115, Jan. 27–30, 1904, Teller County District Court files. For comments on the jury's findings, see *MISP*, Feb. 6, 1904, p. 91. Also see Carroll D. Wright, ed., *A Report on Labor Disturbances in the State of Colorado, from 1880 to 1904* (58th Cong., 3d Sess., Senate Doc. 122, 1905), pp. 220–223. It should be kept in mind that the jury's findings were probably colored by the miners' union's anger at the company, against which it was then striking.

37. *EIMJ*, March 1, 1902, p. 307. *MISP*, March 5, 1904, p. 159. Wallace (Idaho) *Press*, April 4, 1891.

38. Miner's candles were still used in work areas of most mines; electric lights were generally installed at loading points by the shaft. Butte *Miner*, March 1, 1881. Montana Mine Inspector, *Report, 1909–1910*, p. 116.

39. *EIMJ*, July 13, 1895, pp. 37–38; Sept. 26, 1896, p. 292; March 1, 1902, p. 308; Nov. 7, 1903, p. 714; Jan. 5, 1905, p. 13. *MISP* Jan. 19, 1900, p. 47; Sept. 22, 1900, p. 348; April 20, 1901, p. 194; Feb. 15, 1902, p. 94; March 12, 1904, p. 186. Frederick L. Ransome, *Preliminary Account of Goldfield, Bullfrog, and Other Mining Districts in Southern Nevada*, U.S. Geological Survey Bulletin 303 (Washington, D.C., 1907), pp. 23–24.

40. President Charles Clark, St. Louis, Mo., to Supt. James B. Risque, Granite, Mont., Feb. 28, 1889, Bimetallic Min. Co. files.

41. Thos. B. McKaig, secretary-treasurer, Pittsburgh, Pa., to Supt. W. J. Hutchinson, Silver City, Idaho, Oct. 29, 1896, Trade Dollar Co. papers (Idaho files). Idaho Mine Inspector, *Report, 1903*, p. 10. Vincent F. Vacek, "A Study of Electrical Installations in Colorado Mines" (unpublished graduation thesis, Colorado School of Mines, 1910), pp. 52A–55A, 1A, 41–43. The topic was more complicated than the students, mine superintendents, or inspectors guessed. Modern electrical experts know that more than voltage must be known to determine safe levels of electricity. Amperage, the rate of current flow, is crucial, as is the presence of water or other metal conductors. The National Fire Protection Association sharply reduces protection requirements for electrical use below 50 volts. Requirements are much more severe for over 600 volts; at that point, entrances to exposed conductors must be kept locked or guarded, and signs must be installed proclaiming "Warning—High Voltage—Keep Out." "Qualified persons" are exempt from these bans, but miners would generally not rank as qualified in this field, especially before 1910. See National Fire Protection Association, *Handbook of the National Electrical Code* (New York, 1972), pp. 636–646.

42. Idaho Mine Inspector, *Report, 1905*, pp. 10–11; the 1903–1910 totals are summarized in *Report, 1910*, p. 5. McKaig to Manager Frederick Irwin, Silver City, April 22, 1907, Trade Dollar Co. papers (Idaho files).

43. Crane, *Gold and Silver*, pp. 131, 356. Lord, *Comstock Mining*, p. 366. *EIMJ*, Feb. 18, 1873, p. 104; May 18, 1878, p. 346.

44. *Alta California*, Jan. 5, 1868, p. 2. Risdon, *Gold Mines and Mining*, pp. 176–177.

45. Helena (Mont.) *Independent*, Jan. 15, 1900. The accident raised Butte's toll from blasting deaths to four in ten hours.

46. Montana Mine Inspector, *Report, 1897*, p. 55.

47. Grass Valley (Calif.) *Union*, quoted in *Alta California*, May 24, 1869, p. 2. Risdon, *Gold Mines and Mining*, p. 176.

48. Montana Mine Inspector, *Report, 1905–1906*, pp. 24–25. *M/SP*, Feb. 13, 1904, p. 108. Grass Valley *National*, April 28, 1869, p. 2.

49. *M/SP*, Sept. 13, 1902, p. 146.

50. *M/SP*, Sept. 30, 1905, pp. 224–225. Montana Mine Inspector, *Report, 1891*, pp. 21–22.

51. Montana Mine Inspector, *Report, 1900*, pp. 78–79.

52. Central City (Colo.) *Daily Miners' Register*, Aug. 25, 1862; July 25, 1863.

53. Montana Mine Inspector, *Report, 1891*, p. 38. Hotchkiss, "Occupational Diseases," pp. 136–137.

54. Gold Hill *News*, Oct. 27, 1863; Dec. 11, 1863; Jan. 6, 1865. Lord, *Comstock Mining*, pp. 390–391. J. E. Jones, journal, dates indicated. Jones was superintendent of the Yellow Jacket Mine, Gold Hill, Nev.

55. John A. Church, "The Comstock Lode," in William R. Balch, comp., *The Mines, Miners, and Mining Interests of the United States in 1882* (Philadelphia, 1882), pp. 185–186. H. L. Slosson, Jr., *Deep Mining on the Comstock* (San Francisco, n.d.), pp. 12–13.

56. John A. Church, "Accidents in the Comstock Mines and Their Relation to Deep Mining," in Balch, *Mines, Miners, and Mining Interests*, p. 802.

57. Church, "The Comstock Lode," p. 186; "Accidents in the Comstock Mines," p. 799. Jones journal, Sept. 11–13, 1881; Feb. 16, 1882.

58. Lord, *Comstock Mining*, p. 313. Church, "Accidents in the Comstock Mines," p. 799.

59. *Territorial Enterprise*, quoted in *E/MJ*, April 4, 1874, p. 213. William D. Haywood, *Bill Haywood's Book—The Autobiography of William D. Haywood* (New York, 1929, reprint 1966), p. 32. *M/SP*, Sept. 1, 1900, p. 254. Western Federation of Miners, 15th Convention, *Proceedings* (1907), p. 379.

60. A. C. Todd, "Cousin Jack in Idaho," *Idaho Yesterdays*, VIII:4 (Winter, 1964–1965), p. 9. Doctors in Leadville held a debate in 1879 on the pneumonia problem, which one doctor called "more prevalent here than at any other place he had ever practiced, and more fatal." See Leadville (Colo.) *Weekly Herald*, Nov. 22, 1879, p. 1. On Butte's troubles with smelter smoke, see Haywood, *Bill Haywood's Book*, p. 82.

61. *Owyhee Avalanche*, April 13, 1867. Tho. G. Taylor, Gold Hill, Nev., to R. H. Follis, San Francisco, n.d. [1882], Yellow Jacket Mine, Gold Hill, Nev., letterpress book.

62. DeQuille, *Big Bonanza*, pp. 385–388. Gold Hill *News*, Dec. 10, 1863; March 28, 1864. Grass Valley *National*, May 26, 1869, p. 3. Church, "The Comstock Lode," pp. 16–19, 185–186; and *The Heat of the Comstock Mines* (paper presented to the American Institute of Mining Engineers, Chattanooga, Tenn., May, 1878), pp. 1–4. George J. Young, *The Ventilating System at the Comstock Mines, Nevada* (paper presented to the American Institute of Mining Engineers, Spokane, Wash., September, 1909), reprinted in University of Nevada *Bulletin*, III:4 (Oct. 1, 1909), pp. 1000 ff.

63. Church, "The Comstock Lode," p. 186.

64. Grant H. Smith, *The History of the Comstock Lode, 1850–1920* (University of Nevada *Bulletin*, XXXVII:3 [July 1, 1943], pp. 23–24. Hague, *Mining Industry*, pp. 103, 105, 112. Coeur D'Alene *Miner*, reprinted in *M/SP*, Sept. 1, 1894, p. 139. Montana Mine Inspector, *Report, 1892*, pp. 12, 19.

65. *E/MJ*, July 9, 1898; Jan. 14, 1904, p. 79 (on accidents in 1893, 1895, 1897–1898, and 1900–1902). Idaho Mine Inspector, *Report, 1910*, p. 5. Colorado Mine Inspector, *Reports* for 1889–1890, pp. 10, 22, 45; for 1893–1894, p. 12; for 1898, p. 18; for 1899–1900, p. 35; for 1901–1902, pp. 246–247; for 1903–1904, pp. 22–23.

66. Montana Mine Inspector, *Report, 1902*, pp. 13–14. *E/MJ*, Feb. 6, 1909, pp. 301–302.

67. Church, "Accidents in the Comstock Mines," p. 801. *M/SP*, Dec. 9, 1905, p. 403. Montana Mine Inspector, *Report, 1907–1908*, p. 18.

68. *M/SP*, Jan. 18, 1905, p. 54. Montana Mine Inspector, *Report, 1905–1906*, p. 22.

69. Frederick Hoffman, "Fatal Accidents in American Metal Mines," *E/MJ*, March 5, 1910, p. 512. (1904 omitted from South Dakota figures.) *E/MJ*, Jan. 2, 1897, p. 8. Colorado Mine Inspector, *Reports* for 1898, p. 22; and for 1901–1902, p. 250.

70. See opinion of Ontario Inspector of Mines, quoted in *E/MJ*, March 5, 1910, p. 512; also issues of Jan. 14, 1904, p. 79; and June 25, 1910, pp. 1321–1324. Young, "Ventilating System at the Comstock Mines," pp. 1002–1005.

71. *Owyhee Avalanche*, July 12, 1873.

72. *Miners' Magazine*, February, 1900, p. 13.

73. George Rosen, *The History of Miners' Diseases—A Medical and Social Interpretation* (New York, 1943), p. 188.

V: The Question of Blame

1. *Shaw v. New Year Gold Mines Co.*, 77 Pacific 515–519 (Montana Supreme Court, 1904).

2. Walter Prescott Webb, *The Great Plains* (New York, 1931, 1972), passim. A recent scholarly study of the clash between industrialism and tradition in the workplace is: Herbert G. Gutman, "Work, Culture, and Society in Industrializing America, 1815–1919," *American Historical Review*, LXXVIII:3 (June, 1973), 531–588.

3. *Shaw v. New Year Gold Mines Co.*, 77 Pacific 515–519.

4. John D. W. Guice, *The Rocky Mountain Bench—The Territorial Supreme Courts of Colorado, Montana, and Wyoming, 1861–1890* (New Haven, 1972), p. 3.

5. Common-law summaries are mainly drawn from Victor H. Olmsted and Stephen D. Fessenden, "Employer and Employee Under the Common Law," *Bulletin of the Department of Labor*, I:1 (November, 1895), pp. 103, 106–107. Origins of these doctrines are summarized in *Dryburg v. Mercur Gold Min. & Mill. Co.*, 55 Pacific 367, 368–369 (Utah Supreme Court, 1898).

6. *Kelley v. Cable Co.*, 20 Pacific 669, 671–672 (Montana Supreme Court, 1889). Helena (Mont.) *Independent*, Jan. 20, 1889, p. 4.

7. Olmsted and Fessenden, "Employer and Employee," pp. 102–103. *Wells and Others v. Coe*, 11 Pacific 50–54 (Colorado Supreme Court, 1886).

8. Olmsted and Fessenden, "Employer and Employee," pp. 104–105.

9. *Alaska Treadwell Gold Min. Co. v. Whelan*, 64 Federal Reporter 462, 463 (9th Circuit Court of Appeals, 1894). *Alaska Mining Company v. Whelan*, 168 U.S. 86–89 (U.S. Supreme Court, 1897).

10. Paul U. Kellogg, in Crystal Eastman, *Work-Accidents and the Law* (New York, 1910), p. v.

11. Lump City (Mont.) *Miner*, Oct. 5, 1895, p. 5. This newspaper moved during the following January to nearby Clancy, Mont. Also see *Deep Mining & Drainage Co. v. Fitzgerald*, 43 Pacific 210, 214 (Colorado Supreme Court, 1895). Montana Mine Inspector, *Report, 1898*, pp. 46–47, and *Report, 1889*, p. 108. Coroner's Jury Report No. 101, death of Westley McChesney, Aug. 31, 1903, in Teller County District Court files, Cripple Creek, Colo.

12. Virginia City (Nev.) *Daily Territorial Enterprise*, Oct. 6, 1867, p. 3. See

comments on this type of situation in Western Federation of Miners, *Miners' Magazine*, December, 1901, p. 2.

13. Montana Mine Inspector, *Report, 1889*, pp. 109–110.

14. Ibid., p. 6.

15. Eastman, *Work-Accidents*, pp. 86, 100. E. H. Downey, *History of Work Accident Indemnity in Iowa* (Iowa City, 1912), p. 53, quoted in Roy Lubove, "Workmen's Compensation and the Prerogatives of Voluntarism," *Labor History*, VIII:3 (Fall, 1967), 257.

16. *Engineering and Mining Journal*, Feb. 6, 1909, pp. 301–302 [hereafter cited as *E/MJ*].

17. Ibid., pp. 301–302. South Dakota Mine Inspector, *Report, 1897–1898*, pp. 10–11.

18. Eastman, *Work-Accidents*, pp. 186–187, passim. Montana Mine Inspector, *Report, 1902*, p. 18.

19. This case is discussed in *E/MJ*, Nov. 24, 1894, p. 494; July 16, 1898, p. 78; and Nov. 12, 1898, p. 580. Also see Lump City *Miner*, Sept. 7, 1895, p. 1.

20. Olmsted and Fessenden, writing in 1895, said the common law removed liability from a person who employed an independent contractor when the former did not control means and methods of work. Olmsted and Fessenden, "Employer and Employee," p. 99. Fred Bulkley, general manager, Aspen Mining and Smelting Co., report to Pres. J. B. Wheeler, Feb. 13, 1893, D. R. C. Brown Papers. Gene M. Gressley, ed., *Bostonians and Bullion—The Journal of Robert Livermore, 1892–1915* (Lincoln, Nebr., 1968), p. 162.

21. Eastman, *Work-Accidents*, p. 183. *Last Chance Mining & Milling Co. v. Ames*, 47 Pacific 382, 383 (Colorado Supreme Court, 1896). A skip is a cartlike device pulled on a track when the shaft is off the perpendicular; it usually travels on a very steep incline.

22. *E/MJ*, Sept. 19, 1903, p. 444. A. C. Todd, "Cousin Jack in Idaho," *Idaho Yesterdays*, VIII:4 (Winter, 1964–1965), p. 9.

23. Montana Mine Inspector, *Report, 1889*, p. 123.

24. Leadville (Colo.) *Weekly Herald*, June 5, 1880, p. 1. Zack Talas, quoted in Helen Zeese Papanikolas, "Life and Labor Among the Immigrants of Bingham Canyon," *Utah Historical Quarterly*, XXXIII:4 (Fall, 1965), p. 293. Josiah P. Lesher, Butte, to Eben Smith, Cripple Creek, Sept. 12, 1894, Eben Smith letterpress books.

25. Frank Crampton, *Deep Enough—A Working Stiff in the Western Mine Camps* (Denver, 1956), p. 120. Letters of top officials of the Bimetallic Mining Company (President Charles Clark, Vice President Paul A. Fusz, and Secretary Alf. H. White), St. Louis, Mo., to Supt. James B. Risque, Granite, Montana, Jan. 7, 9, 22, Oct. 4, and Nov. 15, 1889, Bimetallic Mining Company files.

26. Mrs. Dennis Meehan, Indianapolis, Indiana, to General Manager Frederick Irwin, May 6, 1907, Trade Dollar Co. papers (Idaho files).

27. Mrs. Meehan to Irwin, July 1, 1907; Secretary-Treasurer Thomas B. McKaig, Pittsburgh, Pa., to General Manager Frederick Irwin, Dewey, Idaho, Oct. 7, 28, 1904; May 2, 1907; Charles R. Leonard, Butte, to General Manager James Hutchinson, Silver City, June 21, July 19, 1902; Johnson & Johnson Attys. to Irwin, Feb. 2, 1905, Trade Dollar Co. papers (Idaho files). *Idaho Statesman*, April 23, 1907, p. 8. Ed. Nicholls, Butte, to Hutchinson, Nov. 14, 1902, Trade Dollar Co. papers (Bancroft files).

Records of several Colorado mine managers indicate that they customarily paid wages and doctors' bills for miners recovering from injuries. Colorado Bureau of Labor Statistics, *Report, 1887–1888*, pp. 219–233. Dan DeQuille wrote of the Comstock in the mid-1870s: "When men are hurt in the mines the companies always render them assistance" (DeQuille, *The Big Bonanza* [1876] (New York, 1947), p. 340). Lodge assistance is cited in Lynn Irwin Perrigo, "A Social History of Central City, Colorado, 1859–1900" (unpublished doctoral dissertation, University of Colorado, 1936), pp. 540–542.

28. Montana Mine Inspector, *Report, 1905–1906*, p. 25. *E/MJ*, March 2, 1907, pp. 428–429. Colorado Mine Inspector, *Report, 1899–1900*, pp. 29–30, 48–49. Montana Mine Inspector, *Report, 1909–1910*, p. 118.

29. Colorado Mine Inspector, *Report, 1893–1894*, pp. 18, 22–23, 32; *Report, 1899–1900*, p. 48. *E/MJ*, Jan. 18, 1896, p. 68; Sept. 4, 1897, pp. 272–273; May 18, 1905, p. 972.

30. Clancy *Miner*, April 1, 1899, p. 1.

31. Montana Mine Inspector, *Report, 1889*, pp. 121–122.

32. *Davis v. Trade Dollar Consol. Min. Co.*, 117 Federal Reporter 122, 122–124 (Ninth Circuit Court of Appeals, 1902).

33. *Browne v. King et al.*, 100 Federal Reporter 561, 564 (Eighth Circuit Court of Appeals, 1900). *Mining and Scientific Press*, Dec. 27, 1902, p. 364 [hereafter cited as *M/SP*].

34. Colorado Bureau of Labor Statistics, *Report, 1887–1888*, p. 300.

35. *M/SP*, Feb. 20, 1904, p. 128. Montana Mine Inspector, *Report, 1889*, pp. 6, 113. Otis E. Young, Jr., *How They Dug the Gold* (Tucson, 1967), p. 80. The Rundle Powder Thawer is discussed in *E/MJ*, Dec. 18, 1897, p. 731.

36. *Territorial Enterprise*, July 17, 1867, p. 3; July 18, 1867, p. 3.

37. Colorado Mine Inspector, *Report, 1893–1894*, p. 17. *Last Chance Mining & Milling Co. v. Ames*, 47 Pacific 382, 384.

38. Montana Mine Inspector, *Report, 1897*, pp. 5–6; and *Report, 1900*, pp. 11–12.

39. Montana Mine Inspector, *Report, 1891*, pp. 19–21; *Report, 1902*, p. 18; and *Report, 1907–1908*, pp. 17–18.

40. *E/MJ*, June 22, 1901, p. 776.

41. *Wells and others v. Coe*, 11 Pacific 50, 51. *Last Chance Mining & Milling Co. v. Ames*, 47 Pacific 382, 384. *Williams v. Sleepy Hollow Mining Co.*, 86 Pacific 337, 340.

42. *Northern Pacific Railroad Company v. Hambly*, 154 U.S. 349, 355 (U.S. Supreme Court, 1894). *Deep Mining & Drainage Co. v. Fitzgerald*, 43 Pacific 210, 213.

43. *M/SP*, April 3, 1886, p. 224.

44. Coroner's Jury Report No. 87, death of Andrew Kippie, Oct. 10, 1902, in Teller County District Court files.

45. Stoll lost the case, however, because his injury occurred before passage of an 1896 law holding employers liable for a co-worker's negligence unless the victim and co-worker were working jointly on the same project. *Stoll v. Daly Min. Co.*, 57 Pacific 295–300 (Utah Supreme Court, 1899). An historical survey of the development of the fellow-servant rule is provided in *Dryburg v. Mercur Gold Min. & Mill. Co.*, 55 Pacific 367.

46. For the importance of railroad cases in these changes, see summaries in Olmsted and Fessenden, "Employer and Employee," pp. 433–434. Also see *Frost v. Oregon Short Line Railroad*, 69 Federal Reporter, 936–943 (U.S. Circuit Court, District of Montana, 1895). Stephen D. Fessenden, "Present Status of Employers' Liability in the United States," *Bulletin of the Department*

of Labor, No. 31 (November, 1900), pp. 1174–1177, 1188 ff. Legislative attacks on the safety problem are discussed in Chapter 7.

Colorado modified the fellow-servant rule in 1877, then almost totally eliminated it in 1901. For discussion, see court opinion in the case that upheld the latter law: *Vindicator Consol. Gold Min. Co. v. Firstbrook*, 86 Pacific 313–317 (Colorado Supreme Court, 1906). For judicial emasculation of earlier law, see the following: Colorado Bureau of Labor Statistics, *Report, 1887–1888*, pp. 209–210. Colorado *Laws, 1901*, p. 161. Montana *Laws, 1903*, pp. 156–157; *Laws, 1905*, p. 52.

47. *Allen v. Bell*, 79 Pacific 582–584 (Montana Supreme Court, 1905). Coroner's Jury Report No. 115, Stratton's Independence disaster, March 17, 1904, in Teller County District Court files.

48. *Mollie Gibson Consolidated Mining & Milling Co. v. Sharp*, 38 Pacific 850–853 (Colorado Court of Appeals, 1894).

49. Colorado Bureau of Labor Statistics, *Report, 1889–1890*, p. 9.

50. Montana Mine Inspector, *Report, 1897*, passim. See decisions in *Bulletin of the Department of Labor*, vol. 1, nos. 1–4 (1895–1896).

51. Coroner's Jury reports, nos. 64–121, 1902–1904, in Teller County District Court files.

52. *Kelley v. Cable Co.*, 20 Pacific 669. *Harvey v. Alturas Gold Min. Co.*, 31 Pacific 819, 820. *Homestake Min. Co. v. Fullerton*, 69 Federal Reporter 923–925 (Eighth Circuit Court of Appeals, 1895). Clancy *Miner*, April 24, 1897, p. 4.

53. *Deep Mining & Drainage Co. v. Fitzgerald*, 43 Pacific 210, 214–215.

54. Supt. Ernest Le Neve Foster, Georgetown, Colo., to President Paul Lichtenstein, n.p., Jan. 9, 1892, Ernest Le Neve Foster papers. *Union Gold Min. Co. v. Crawford*, 69 Pacific 600, 605 (Colorado Supreme Court, 1902).

55. Eben Smith, Denver, to J. E. Rockwell, Colorado Springs, Colo., Dec. 2, 1898; R. H. Reid, Denver, to Smith, Los Angeles, April 15 and 25, 1901, Eben Smith letterpress books.

56. McKaig to Irwin, Feb. 18, 1904, and July 27, 1907, Trade Dollar Co. papers (Idaho files).

57. Foster to Lichtenstein, Dec. 9, 1891, and Jan. 9, 1892, Foster papers.

58. Testimony of James Doyle, Denver, Colo., July 18, 1899, and Robert Chambers, Salt Lake City, Utah, Aug. 2, 1899, in U.S. Industrial Commission, *Report . . . on the Relations and Conditions of Capital and Labor Employed in the Mining Industry* (57th Cong., 1st Sess., House Doc. No. 181, 1901–1902), XII, pp. 368–369, 585. U.S. Immigration Commission, *Japanese and Other Immigrant Races in the Pacific Coast and Rocky Mountain States* (61st Cong., 2d Sess., Senate Doc. 633, 1909–1910), pt. 25, pp. 107, 121.

59. Testimony of President D. C. Coates, Colorado Federation of Labor, Denver, July 14, 1899: U.S. Industrial Commission, *Report*, XII, 258–259. The Coeur d'Alenes policy covered the Federal Mining and Smelting Co., the Morning Mine, and the Hecla Mining Company. *M/SP*, Feb. 4, 1905, p. 77.

60. Fessenden, "Present Status," pp. 1209–1210.

61. Colorado Bureau of Labor Statistics, *Report, 1887–1888*, pp. 219–223.

62. The problem of translating top-level concern into practice on the job is discussed in Colorado Mine Inspector, *Report, 1899–1900*, pp. 29–30. It parallels the Pittsburgh situation, as discussed in Eastman, *Work-Accidents*, pp. 98–104.

VI: The Union Impulse

1. Helena (Mont.) *Herald*, June 24, 1878, p. 2.

2. Vernon H. Jensen, *Heritage of Conflict—Labor Relations in the Nonferrous Metals Industry up to 1930* (Ithaca, N.Y., 1950), p. 10. William H. Hutchinson, "The Cowboy and the Class Struggle (Or, Never Put Marx in the Saddle)," *Arizona and the West*, XIV:4 (Winter, 1972), 321–330. Selig Perlman and Philip Taft, "Labor Movements," vol. IV in John R. Commons et al., *History of Labour in the United States, 1896–1932* (New York, 1935), p. 169. Melvyn Dubofsky, "The Origins of Western Working Class Radicalism, 1890–1905," *Labor History*, VII:2 (Spring, 1966), p. 135, passim.

3. Butte (Mont.) *Miner*, Aug. 6, 1878, p. 4.

4. Rodman W. Paul, *California Gold—The Beginning of Mining in the Far West* (Cambridge, Mass., 1947), pp. 328–330. Salt Lake City (Utah) *Tribune*, March 24, 1873, p. 2, quoted in Sheelwant B. Pawar, "An Environmental Study of the Development of the Utah Labor Movement: 1860–1935" (unpublished doctoral dissertation, University of Utah, 1968), pp. 64–65.

5. Central City (Colo.) *Tri-Weekly Miner's Register*, April 1, 1863, p. 3; April 6, 1863, p. 2; subsequent issues showed the absence of union activity. Also see Lynn Irwin Perrigo, "A Social History of Central City, Colorado, 1859–1900" (unpublished doctoral dissertation, University of Colorado, 1936), pp. 345–347.

6. Eliot Lord, *Comstock Mining and Miners* (Washington, D.C., 1883; reprint 1959), pp. 181–183.

7. Ibid., pp. 183–190. Gold Hill (Nev.) *Daily News*, March 21, 1864; this version reported the slogan as "This is Cornwall dirt." The Comstock union story is detailed in the following: Richard E. Lingenfelter, *The Hardrock Miners: A History of the Mining Labor Movement in the American West, 1863–1893* (Berkeley, Calif., 1974), pp. 33–42; and Grant H. Smith, *The History of the Comstock Lode, 1850–1920* (Reno, Nev., 1943), p. 99.

8. Dr. Charles L. Anderson, Carson City, Nev., to his wife in Minnesota, April 8, 1863, quoted in Robert B. Merrifield, "Nevada, 1859–1881: The Impact of an Advanced Technological Society upon a Frontier Area" (unpublished doctoral dissertation, University of Chicago, 1957), p. 27. Gold Hill *News*, Feb. 27, 1864. J. Ross Browne, *Mineral Resources of the States and Territories West of the Rocky Mountains* (40th Cong., 2d Sess., House Ex. Doc. 202, 1868), p. 384.

9. Mary McNair Mathews, *Ten Years in Nevada* (Buffalo, N.Y., 1880), p. 180, quoted in Merrifield, "Impact of an Advanced Society," p. 36.

10. It was predicted in 1867 that the Central Pacific would reduce lumber and firewood costs by 35 percent for the Comstock mines. In 1871, the president of the Hale & Norcross argued that wages should be reduced because of the falling prices for consumer items. Browne, *Mineral Resources* for 1866, p. 385. Lord, *Comstock Mining*, p. 361. Gold Hill *Daily News*, March 22, 1867, p. 3; July 8, 1867, p. 3. Smith, *Comstock Lode*, p. 102. Virginia City (Nev.) *Daily Territorial Enterprise*, Feb. 2, 1867, p. 3.

11. Gold Hill *News*, Feb. 12, 1867, p. 3; Feb. 13, 1867, p. 3. Gold Hill Miners Union Minutes, Jan. 3 and 17, Feb. 7, 11, 21, and 28, 1867.

12. This discussion appears in Gold Hill Miners Union Minutes, Feb. 28, 1867. Also see report in Lingenfelter, *Hardrock Miners*, pp. 47–49.

13. Gold Hill Miners Union Minutes, July 2, 1867. *Territorial Enterprise*, July 6, 1867, p. 1; Aug. 6, 1867, p. 3. Lingenfelter, *Hardrock Miners*, pp. 49–50. *Constitution, By-Laws . . . of the Miners' Union, of Virginia, Nevada—Or-*

ganized July 4th, 1867. Constitution, By-Laws, Order of Business, and Rules of Order of The Miner's Union, of Gold Hill, Nev.

14. *Engineering and Mining Journal*, March 26, 1881, p. 220 [hereafter cited as *E/MJ*]. Lingenfelter, *Hardrock Miners*, pp. 66, 128–129.

15. *Montana Post*, June 30, 1866, p. 3. *Idaho Statesman*, Aug. 16, 1870, quoted in *E/MJ*, Sept. 13, 1870, p. 164. *Mining and Scientific Press*, March 21, 1885, pp. 190–191 [hereafter cited as *M/SP*]. Lingenfelter, *Hardrock Miners*, p. 134.

16. *E/MJ*, June 20, 1885, p. 420; April 25, 1885, p. 275; Nov. 11, 1893, p. 492. Wage information drawn from contemporary newspapers and weekly reports in *E/MJ* and *M/SP*.

17. Carson (Nev.) *Daily Appeal*, July 14, 16, 21, 30, and 31; Aug. 3, 5, 8, and 14, 1869. Also *Alta California*, Jan. 13, 1869, p. 1; July 13, 1869, p. 1; July 14, 1869, p. 1; July 15, 1869, p. 1; July 16, 1869, p. 1; July 29, 1869, p. 1; and Aug. 3, 1869, pp. 1, 2. W. Turrentine Jackson, *Treasure Hill— Portrait of a Silver Mining Camp* (Tucson, 1963), pp. 128 ff. Lingenfelter, *Hardrock Miners*, pp. 69–75, 161–176. *Owyhee Avalanche*, March 23 and 30, April 6, and May 4, 1872; March 27, 1875. Pawar, "Environmental Study," pp. 65, 69–70, 90–92. J. Kenneth Davies, "Utah Labor Before Statehood," *Utah Historical Quarterly*, XXXIV:3 (Summer, 1966), p. 211. Idaho Historical Society, *Mining in Idaho*, n.d. *M/SP*, May 10, 1884, p. 320; Dec. 20, 1884, p. 386; Feb. 21, 1885, p. 129; March 21, 1885, p. 193; March 28, 1885, p. 212. *E/MJ*, March 7, 1885, p. 158; March 14, 1885, p. 180; March 21, 1885, p. 187; April 4, 1885, p. 232; May 30, 1885, p. 377.

18. *E/MJ*, Feb. 17, 1877, pp. 108–109. *Idaho World*, Feb. 29, 1878, p. 2. Butte *Miner*, April 23, 1878, p. 4. Lingenfelter, *Hardrock Miners*, pp. 103–105, 132. Perrigo, "Social History of Central City," p. 347. Duane A. Smith, *Silver Saga—The Story of Caribou, Colorado* (Boulder, 1974), p. 94. Colorado Bureau of Labor Statistics, *Report, 1887–1888*, pp. 118–129. Edward Boyce, "Coeur d'Alene Mining Troubles" (56th Cong., 1st Sess., Senate Doc. No. 25, 1899), pp. 1–2. Discussed in Jensen, *Heritage of Conflict*, p. 27, and in Robert M. Smith, "The Idaho Antecedents of the Western Federation of Miners—Labor Organization and Industrial Conflict in the Coeur d'Alene Mining District of Idaho, 1890 to 1893" (unpublished doctoral dissertation, University of California, Berkeley, 1937), p. 33.

19. Butte *Miner*, May 28, 1878, p. 5; June 11, 1878, p. 8; June 18, 1878, p. 5. U.S. Works Projects Administration, *Copper Camp—Stories of the World's Greatest Mining Town: Butte, Montana* (New York, 1943), pp. 15–19.

20. Butte *Miner*, June 25, 1878, p. 5.

21. Ibid., Aug. 13, 1878, p. 5.

22. Ibid., June 18, 1878, p. 4; Aug. 6, 1878, p. 5; Aug. 13, 1878, p. 5; Oct. 15, 1878, pp. 4, 5; Oct. 22, 1878, p. 4; Oct. 29, 1878, pp. 1, 14. Jensen, *Heritage of Conflict*, pp. 17, 289n. Smith, "Idaho Antecedents," pp. 25–26. Western Federation of Miners, 18th Convention *Proceedings* (1910), p. 200. *The Reveille*, Nov. 1, 1907, p. 1.

23. "Constitution & By-Laws, Pledge and Minutes of the 'Miners' Union' of the town of Gold Hill—State of Nevada." Fairview Miners Union Constitution, reprinted in *Owyhee Avalanche*, March 30, 1872, p. 3; Oct. 5, 1867, p. 2. Gold Hill Miners Union Minutes, Feb. 27, 1868.

24. Gold Hill Miners Union Minutes, May 21 and 28, 1868; July 20, 1873.

25. Lingenfelter, *Hardrock Miners*, p. 185. Helena (Mont.) *Independent*, April 11, 1887, p. 1. *E/MJ*, May 24, 1890, p. 598. WFM 10th Convention *Proceedings* (1902), p. 156; 11th Convention *Proceedings* (1903), p. 94. Pawar,

"Environmental Study," p. 173. Testimony of James Gann, Wallace, Idaho, July 27, 1899: U.S. Industrial Commission, *Report . . . on the Relations and Conditions of Capital and Labor Employed in the Mining Industry . . .* (57th Cong., 1st Sess., House Doc. No. 181, 1901), vol. XII, p. 487. WFM 16th Convention *Proceedings* (1908), p. 17. The WFM organized smelter workers in the late 1890s. Jensen, *Heritage of Conflict*, pp. 109, 119. *Constitution and By-Laws of San Juan District Union*, p. 13.

26. Norman J. Ware, *The Labor Movement in the United States, 1860–1895—A Study in Democracy* (New York, 1929), pp. 28–35.

27. Ibid., pp. 40, 42.

28. *E/MJ*, Feb. 17, 1877, p. 101; April 14, 1877, p. 239; April 28, 1877, p. 281. Testimony of Charles H. MacKinnon, *Goldfield Consolidated Mines Co. v. Goldfield Miners Union No. 220*, WFM (January, 1908), transcript of testimony, p. 136. Pawar, "Environmental Study," pp. 93–95.

29. By August, 1880, a Knights of Labor assembly existed in Georgetown, also a Colorado lode-mining center. Carroll D. Wright, ed., *A Report on Labor Disturbances in the State of Colorado, from 1880 to 1904 . . .* (58th Cong., 3d Sess., Senate Doc. No. 122, 1905), p. 35. Knights of Labor, *The Journal of United Labor*, May 15, 1880, pp. 3, 5–6, 15; Aug. 13, 1880, p. 5; May 15, 1881, p. 118; July 15, 1881, p. 131. Jensen, *Heritage of Conflict*, p. 22.

30. Leadville (Colo.) *Herald*, June 5, 1880, pp. 1, 2. Lingenfelter, *Hardrock Miners*, p. 146. Mooney then disappeared from prominence in Western hardrock mining until 1902, when an M. J. Mooney, "who is known from the Missouri River to the Pacific coast," gave the major address for the twenty-fourth anniversary of the founding of the Butte miners' union. And at the WFM convention that summer, he was described as "the unapproachable wit of the convention," nominating himself for president, among other oratorical high jinks. This is quite possibly the same Michael Mooney who led the Leadville strike. *Miners' Magazine*, July, 1902, pp. 12, 15.

31. George H. Holt, undated report to Little Chief Mine executive committee [circa 1879]; Holt Business papers #13, Jan. 15, 1879, in George H. Holt papers.

32. Leadville *Herald*, Dec. 6, 1879, p. 3; May 29, 1880, p. 4; June 5, 1880, p. 1. Charles Merrill Hough, "Leadville, Colorado, 1878 to 1898: A Study in Unionism" (master's thesis, University of Colorado, 1958), pp. 45–46. Duane A. Smith, *Horace Tabor—His Life and the Legend* (Boulder, Colo., 1973), p. 132.

33. Information on the Leadville strike is drawn principally from the following: Leadville *Herald*, issues of April, May, and June of 1880, passim. *Rocky Mountain News*, May 28, 1880, p. 4. Jensen, *Heritage of Conflict*, pp. 19–24; Lingenfelter, *Hardrock Miners*, pp. 143–156; Wright, *Labor Disturbances*, chap. 5; and Don. L. and Jean Harvey Griswold, *The Carbonate Camp Called Leadville* (Denver, 1951), pp. 180–199.

34. Lingenfelter, *Hardrock Miners*, p. 146. Smith, *Horace Tabor*, p. 134.

35. Colorado Bureau of Labor Statistics, *Report, 1887–1888*, p. 83; and *Report, 1891–1892*, p. 59. *Gilpin County Observer*, Feb. 8, 1888, p. 1.

36. Pawar, "Environmental Study," pp. 103, 105–107. *Coeur d'Alene Miner*, April 22, 1893, p. 1; Sept. 23, 1893, p. 1. *Miners' Magazine*, February, 1900, pp. 28–30.

37. Dubofsky, "Origins of Western Working-Class Radicalism," p. 140. WFM 16th Convention *Proceedings* (1908), p. 18. William D. Haywood, *Bill Haywood's Book—The Autobiography of William D. Haywood* (New York, 1929; reprint 1966), pp. 30–31. Boyce, "Coeur d'Alene Mining Troubles," p. 1.

38. The "American Labor Union" of 1879 is obviously no relation to the later WFM creation of the same name. Gary P. Be Dunnah, "A History of the Chinese in Nevada: 1855–1904" (master's thesis, University of Nevada, 1966), p. 54. Melvyn Dubofsky, *We Shall Be All—A History of the Industrial Workers of the World* (Chicago, 1969), p. 66. John Rowe, *The Hard-Rock Men—Cornish Immigrants and the North American Mining Frontier* (New York, 1974), pp. 245–246. Joplin (Mo.) *Daily Globe*, March 27, 1901, p. 2.

39. Leon Wolff, *Lockout—The Story of the Homestead Strike of 1892* (New York, 1965), pp. 17–18. Victor R. Greene, *The Slavic Community on Strike—Immigrant Labor in Pennsylvania Anthracite* (South Bend, Indiana, 1968), pp. 212–213. John R. Commons, "Is Class Conflict in America Growing and Is It Inevitable?," *American Journal of Sociology*, XIII (May, 1908), p. 762, quoted in Gerald Rosenblum, *Immigrant Workers—Their Impact on American Labor Radicalism* (New York, 1973), pp. 161, 176. Lingenfelter discusses some Cornish-Irish disputes within the Butte union; Lingenfelter, *Hardrock Miners*, pp. 186, 190–193. The use of native-born Americans as strikebreakers was examined in Chapter 2.

40. This information on the Western impact of the Depression is drawn from: *M/SP*, Jan. 9, 1892, p. 18; Dec. 24, 1892, p. 410; Dec. 31, 1892, p. 438; July 1, 1893, p. 2. Forest Lowell White, "The Panic of 1893 in Colorado" (master's thesis, University of Colorado, 1932), pp. 24–27, 60–62. Donald L. McMurry, *Coxey's Army—A Study of the Industrial Army Movement of 1894* (Seattle, 1968), pp. 199–206. *The Mineral Industry* (supplement to *E/MJ*), 1893, vol. II, pp. 311–312.

41. John D. Hicks, *The Populist Revolt* (Lincoln, Nebr., 1961), pp. 265, 291–299. Wallace (Idaho) *Press*, June 11, 1892, p. 1. Dubofsky, "Origins of Western Working-Class Radicalism," pp. 140–142.

42. Hough, "Leadville," pp. 75–76. White, "Panic of 1893," p. 14. Fred. Bulkley, Aspen, Colo., to President J. B. Wheeler, Oct. 9, 1893, and Nov. 6, 1893, in D. R. C. Brown papers. *E/MJ*, Nov. 11, 1893, p. 503. Colorado Bureau of Labor Statistics, *Report, 1895–1896*, p. 21.

43. Gold Hill Miners Union minutes, July 31 through Oct. 23, 1893. Also see *M/SP*, July 22, 1893, p. 50; Sept. 30, 1893, p. 210; Oct. 21, 1893, p. 258; March 12, 1898, p. 282.

44. Information on the Coeur d'Alenes strike is taken mainly from the following: T. A. Rickard, *A History of American Mining* (New York, 1932; reprint 1966), pp. 324–336. Smith, "Idaho Antecedents," pp. 23–39, 50–54, 71–73, 247–248. Jensen, *Heritage of Conflict*, chaps. 4 and 7. *E/MJ*, Jan. 10, 1891, p. 72. Wallace *Press*, Aug. 22, 1891, p. 4; Feb. 13, 1892, p. 3, citing Anaconda (Mont.) *Standard*, n.d. B. Goldsmith, acting manager, Bunker Hill & Sullivan Mine, to Simeon G. Reed, June 6, 1887, cited in Richard H. Peterson, "Conflict and Consensus: Labor Relations in Western Mining," *Journal of the West*, XII:1 (January, 1973), p. 4.

45. Letter to *Idaho Statesman*, June 4, 1892, reprinted in Wallace *Press*, June 11, 1892, p. 4. On this subject, also see letter from "Pioneer," in ibid., p. 1, and Burke correspondence on Feb. 13, 1892, p. 2. Smith, "Idaho Antecedents," pp. 72–73. *Coeur d'Alene Miner*, June 4, 1892, p. 4. Haywood, *Bill Haywood's Book*, pp. 80–81.

46. Rickard, *History of American Mining*, pp. 329–332. Jensen, *Heritage of Conflict*, pp. 32–37.

47. Testimony of Dr. F. P. Matchette, Frederick Burbidge, and John Finch, Wallace, Idaho, July 26 and 27, 1899: U.S. Industrial Commission, *Report*, XII, pp. 437, 441, 451, 498. *M/SP*, Oct. 21, 1893, p. 270; Aug. 25, 1894, p. 123;

Dec. 8, 1894, p. 354; July 29, 1905, p. 79. *Coeur d'Alene Miner*, June 24, Sept. 2 and Oct. 21, 1893. Smith, "Idaho Antecedents," pp. 247–248. Jensen, *Heritage of Conflict*, pp. 74–75. *E/MJ*, May 6, 1899, p. 539. T. A. Rickard, *Interviews with Mining Engineers* (San Francisco, 1922), pp. 99–100.

48. This account is based on Jensen, *Heritage of Conflict*, pp. 74–77, and on Rickard, *History of American Mining*, pp. 333–336. Brig. Gen. H. C. Merriam, "Coeur d'Alene Mining Troubles" (56th Cong., 1st Sess., Senate Doc. No. 24, 1899), Dec. 11, 1899, pp. 15, 20. Boyce, "Coeur d'Alene Mining Troubles," p. 3.

49. Wright, *Report on Labor Disturbances*, p. 75. Marshall Sprague, *Money Mountain—The Story of Cripple Creek Gold* (Boston, 1953), pp. 135–136, 149–150, and Part II, passim. The governor's crucial role is shown in Wright, *Report on Labor Disturbances*, pp. 75–85; and Jensen, *Heritage of Conflict*, chap. 5. Eben Smith, Denver, to Wm. Trevorrow, Barry, Colo., July 9, 1894, Smith letterpress books.

50. Smith to John Canning, Leadville, May 29, 1896, Smith letterpress books. "Reply of Mine Owners of Leadville, Colo., area to Miners Union Thanksgiving Statement," Leadville, Dec. 15, 1896, 13. John A. Campion, Leadville, telegram to Smith, June 1, 1894 ("Confidential"), Smith papers. Wright, *Report on Labor Disturbances*, 88.

51. Wright, *Report on Labor Disturbances*, p. 96. Colorado State Legislature (11th Session, 1896), *Report of the Joint Special Legislative Committee . . . on the Leadville Strike*, pp. 21–22.

52. Wright, *Report on Labor Disturbances*, pp. 92–93, 97, 101. Perlman and Taft, "Labor Movements," pp. 182–183. Colorado Legislature, *Report on Leadville Strike*, p. 9. Jensen, *Heritage of Conflict*, p. 41.

53. Jensen, *Heritage of Conflict*, p. 74, chap. 6. Smith, "Idaho Antecedents," p. 234. Haywood, *Bill Haywood's Book*, pp. 62–63.

54. See Dubofsky, "Origins of Western Working-Class Radicalism," passim. Western Federation of Miners Constitution, May 19, 1893. The issue of radicalism versus conservative trade unionism will be examined in Chapter 9.

55. Colorado Bureau of Labor Statistics, *Report, 1895–1896*, pp. 8–9; and *Report, 1899–1900*, pp. 20–21:

56. President Paul A. Fusz, St. Louis, Mo., to Supt. James B. Risque, Granite, Mont., Feb. 12, 1890, Bimetallic Mining Co. papers. *Jefferson County Sentinel* (Mont.), Jan. 16, 1890. *E/MJ*, Nov. 6, 1897, p. 541. *M/SP* April 12, 1902, p. 210; May 24, 1902, p. 289. WFM 16th Convention *Proceedings* (1908), pp. 276, 280–281, 292.

57. Copy of Virginia City Miners Union report, Oct. 13, 1901, contained in Gold Hill Miners Union records (Yale Collection). Clancy Miners' Union No. 30 (WFM) minute book, Oct. 24, Nov. 3, 10, 17, and 24, and Dec. 1, 1894; March 31, 1896.

58. Clancy Miners Union minute book, Nov. 24, Dec. 8 and 15, 1894; Feb. 2 and Sept. 3, 1895.

59. Testimony of John A. Finch, Wallace, Idaho, July 27, 1899: U.S. Industrial Commission, *Report*, XII, p. 494–495.

VII: Responses to the Dangers Below

1. *Mining and Scientific Press*, Feb. 18, 1893, p. 106 [hereafter cited as *M/SP*]. *The Colorado Miner*, June 2, 1870. Anaconda lowered its flag when a death occurred in a company mine. Butte (Mont.) *Miner*, Jan. 10, 1885,

p. 1. Hospital records taken from St. Peter's Hospital, Helena, Mont., Register, vol. I (1884–1893), passim.

2. *Owyhee Avalanche*, Aug. 1, 1874, p. 2.

3. Mrs. Albina Clementi, interview, Telluride, Colo., July 22, 1972. William D. Haywood, *Bill Haywood's Book—The Autobiography of William D. Haywood* (New York, 1929; 1966), p. 98.

4. Heber Holman, diary, Jan. 23, 1895. Colorado Bureau of Labor Statistics, *Report, 1887–1888*; other comments on pp. 255–270.

5. Comments on hospital deductions appear frequently in responses by miners reprinted in Colorado Bureau of Labor Statistics, *Report, 1887–1888*. *MISP*, May 9, 1896, p. 375. Joseph Harper Cash, "Labor in the West: The Homestake Mining Company and Its Workers, 1877–1942" (unpublished doctoral dissertation, University of Iowa, 1966), p. 167. Haywood is quoted in Carroll D. Wright, *A Report on Labor Disturbances in the State of Colorado, from 1880 to 1904 . . .* (58th Cong., 3d Sess., Senate Doc. 122, 1905), p. 44. Also see *Engineering and Mining Journal*, July 2, 1887, p.12; Dec. 24, 1887, p. 474; Feb. 16, 1905, p. 352 [hereafter cited as *EIMJ*]. The Drum Lummon Mine at Marysville, Mont., was a pioneer in this system, paying $1.50 per day to victims undergoing treatment, and $1,000 in case of death; this served as a model for some of the mines in the Coeur d'Alenes. See W. Turrentine Jackson, "The Irish Fox and the British Lion—The Story of Tommy Cruse, the Drum Lummon, and the Montana Company Limited (British)," *Montana —The Magazine of Western History*, IX:2 (April, 1959), p. 35–36.

6. Gold Hill (Nev.) *Daily News*, July 5, 1867, p. 2.

7. Miners often went together in ad hoc groups to assist a fellow worker, as Bill Haywood discovered when his hand was mangled in a Silver City, Idaho, accident. His fellow workers took up a collection "and presented me with a purse of money that tided us over this emergency very well" (Haywood, *Bill Haywood's Book*, p. 61). For the European background of mutual benefit groups, see Sidney and Beatrice Webb, *Industrial Democracy* (London, 1902), vol. I, chap. 2. Also Maurice F. Neufeld, *Italy: School for Awakening Countries—The Italian Labor Movement in Its Political, Social, and Economic Setting from 1800 to 1960* (Ithaca, N.Y., 1961), pp. 60, 174–175.

8. Central City (Colo.) *Miner's Register*, April 1, 1863, p. 3; April 6, 1863, p. 2. Eliot Lord, *Comstock Mining and Miners* (Washington, D.C., 1883; reprint 1959), p. 183.

9. Gold Hill (Nev.) Miners' Union minutes, Jan. 16 and 23, June 4 and 18, 1868; March 21, 1867. Also see Clancy (Mont.) Miners' Union minutes, Feb. 4, 1896. Apparently the term *sick* covered injuries also. The Silver City minutes contain such references as this: "Bro Own Reil reported sick [with a] broken leg" (Silver City [Idaho] Miners' Union minutes, April 19, 1897).

10. The nature of Sparring's injury or illness is not revealed in the minutes. Clancy Miners' Union minutes, Feb. 4, 11, 18, 25, and March 3 and 10, 1896.

11. Silver City Miners' Union minutes, Nov. 8, 1897; Jan. 24 and Feb. 3, 1898.

12. Gold Hill Miners' Union minutes, June 28, 1868; Sept. 19, 1867; July 1 and Aug. 12, 1889. Silver City Miners' Union minutes, March 1, 1897.

13. Telluride (Colo.) Miners' Union papers, 1903 financial records. Owyhee Avalanche Publishing Co., *A Historical, Descriptive, and Commercial Directory of Owyhee County, Idaho* (Silver City, Idaho, 1898), pp. 39–40, 61. *Miners' Magazine*, March, 1900, p. 39; April, 1900, p. 29. *45th Anniversary Program*

—Virginia Miners Union—July 4th, 1912 (Virginia City, 1912). Western Federation of Miners, 18th Convention *Proceedings* (1910), pp. 200–203.

14. Gold Hill Miners' Union minutes, Feb. 3, 1873; May 1 and 15, 1893; Feb. 8, March 26, Sept. 24, 1894. Cf. Silver City Miners' Union minutes, Jan. 11 and 25, 1897. San Juan District Union (WFM), local bylaws, Article VII, Sept. 5, 1898.

15. Colorado Mine Inspector, *Report, 1901–1902*, p. 252. Charles W. Henderson, *Mining in Colorado—A History of Discovery, Development, and Production* (U.S. Geological Survey, 1926), p. 223. *Miners' Magazine*, December, 1901, pp. 1, 3; July, 1902, p. 28; November, 1901, pp. 45–46. *The Nevada Miner*, July 1, 1902, p. 53. WFM 10th Convention *Proceedings* (1902), pp. 107–108. Wright, *Labor Disturbances*, p. 43. Mother Mary Agnes, Goldfield, Nev., to Charles Moyer, Denver, June 2, 1913, Goldfield (Nev.) Miners Union (WFM) No. 220, papers. Wallace (Idaho) *Press*, May 30, 1891, p. 2.

16. John Rowe, *The Hard-Rock Men—Cornish Immigrants and the North American Mining Frontier* (New York, 1974), p. 289. California *Laws*, 1881, p. 81. See discussion in *M/SP*, Jan. 2, 1897, p. 2.

17. Colorado Bureau of Labor Statistics, *Report, 1891–1892*, pp. 118–119. Colorado *Laws, 1891*, p. 416.

18. *M/SP*, May 23, 1896, p. 415.

19. Idaho House *Journal, 4th Session* (1897), p. 48. Utah *Laws, 1897*, pp. 241–243. *M/SP*, Jan. 11, 1902, p. 16. U.S. Senate Committee on Military Affairs, "Home for Miners" (57th Cong., 1st Sess., Senate Report No. 877, 1902), p. 1. *Congressional Record* (57th Cong., 1st Sess.), vol. 35, pt. 4, pp. 3549 and 3701 (April 2 and 4, 1902).

20. *M/SP*, April 30, 1898, p. 462. Gold Hill Miners Union minutes, Aug. 10, 1896. Silver City Miners' Union minutes, May 31, 1897; Feb. 14, 1898. *Miners' Magazine*, December, 1900, p. 22. WFM 10th Convention *Proceedings* (1902), pp. 76–77. Butte (Mont.) *Reveille*, Oct. 4, 1902, p. 8.

21. The Gold Hill union discussed joint action with the Virginia City union to have safety cages installed in the Comstock mines. The matter was "indefinitely postponed" after a short examination, however (Gold Hill Union minutes, July 16 and 30, 1868). Grass Valley's Eureka Hoisting Works obtained a safety cage in late 1867, and within a year the devices were reported in use on the Comstock also. Other information indicates that these early safety cages were inadequate to offer assurances of an accident-free ride. See Grass Valley (Calif.) *National*, Oct. 28, 1867, p. 3; March 31, 1868, p. 3; March 30, 1869, p. 3. Also see *Idaho World*, Dec. 24, 1878, p. 3. WFM 11th Convention *Proceedings* (1903), pp. 202–203; 16th Convention *Proceedings* (1908), p. 398; 17th Convention *Proceedings* (1909), pp. 25–26. *Miners' Magazine*, January, 1901, pp. 10–11; Dec. 3, 1903, p. 8. Clancy Miners' Union minutes, June 25, July 9, 1895.

22. George Rosen, *The History of Miners' Diseases—A Medical and Social Interpretation* (New York, 1943), pp. 424–425, 438–441. Grass Valley *National*, April 16, 1869, p. 3. Pennsylvania *Laws, 1870*, p. 3.

23. California *Laws, 1871–1872*, p. 413. Colorado Constitution included in Colorado *Laws, 1877*, pp. 71, 126. Nevada *Laws, 1879*, p. 55.

24. Colorado Bureau of Labor Statistics, *Report, 1887–1888*, pp. 300–302.

25. Colorado *Laws, 1877*, pp. 126–130; *Laws, 1883*, pp. 102–111; *Laws, 1889*, pp. 254–255. *Rocky Mountain News*, Jan. 3, 1889, p. 8; Jan. 11, 1889, p. 6; Jan. 12, 1889, p. 2; Feb. 12, 1889, p. 1; Feb. 15, 1889, p. 7; March 3, 1889, p. 2; March 10, 1889, p. 3; March 13, 1889, p. 7; March 19, 1889, p. 2; March 24, 1889, p. 6. Colorado House *Journal, 6th Session* (1887), pp. 382,

1307–1309, 1802–1803, 1829. Colorado Senate *Journal, 6th Session* (1887), pp. 161, 1495. Colorado Bureau of Labor Statistics, *Report, 1891–1892*, p. 37.

26. Information on the controversy in Montana is taken from the following: Helena (Mont.) *Independent*, Feb. 20, 1889, p. 4; Feb. 21, 1889, p. 4; Feb. 27, 1889, p. 4; Feb. 28, 1889, p. 4. Montana Mine Inspector *Report, 1889*, pp. 122, 124. Montana Territorial Council, *Journal, 1889*, p. 281. Montana Territorial House, *Journal, 1889*, p. 249. Montana Territory *Laws, 1889*, pp. 160–164.

27. South Dakota *Laws, 1890*, pp. 263–267. Idaho House *Journal, 1890–1891*, pp. 28, 132–133, 141, 160. Idaho Senate *Journal, 1890–1891*, pp. 139, 143, 148. Wallace *Press*, Feb. 6, 1892, p. 4. Idaho *Laws, 1893*, pp. 152–154.

28. Utah *Laws, 1896*, p. 346. U.S. Industrial Commission, *Report . . . on Relations and Conditions of Capital and Labor Employed in the Mining Industry . . .* (57th Cong., 1st Sess., House Doc. No. 181, 1901), vol. XII, p. 636. *The Crisis*, n.d., quoted in *Miners' Magazine*, Jan. 19, 1905, p. 13. British Columbia *Laws, 1897*, pp. 273–284. *M/SP*, April 10, 1897, p. 303. Wyoming *Laws, 1903*, p. 31. *U.S. Statutes at Large* (60th Cong., 1st Sess., May 23, 1908), vol. 35, pt. 1, p. 226. Nevada *Laws, 1909*, pp. 167, 218. Arizona *Laws, 1909*, pp. 112–115; *Laws, 1912*, pp. 87–111. *E/MJ*, Dec. 3, 1910, p. 1090.

29. *M/SP*, Jan. 26, 1895, p. 49. Montana Mine Inspector, *Report, 1889*, p. 77; *Report, 1892*, pp. 5–6; *Report, 1900*, pp. 13–14. *E/MJ*, Dec. 31, 1898, p. 797. Montana *Laws, 1903*, pp. 179–183.

30. Colorado *Laws, 1889*, pp. 256–257; *Laws, 1895*, pp. 213–214. *M/SP*, Feb. 8, 1890, p. 92. Colorado State Mining Bureau, *Recommendations for Safety Appliances in Mining*, pp. 7, 13. The orders issued by the inspector are instructive of his attitude; see Colorado Mine Inspector, *Report, 1897*, pp. 157–158; and *Report, 1905–1906*, p. 18.

31. Montana Mine Inspector, *Report, 1889*, pp. 83, 120, 122; *Report, 1892*, p. 6; *Report, 1902*, pp. 10–11, 18.

32. Colorado Mine Inspector, *Report, 1899–1900*, pp. 26–27, 44–45. Discussed in *E/MJ*, Feb. 8, 1896, pp. 129–130. Also see early arguments by the Colorado assistant inspector, in *M/SP*, Feb. 8, 1890, p. 92.

33. Colorado Mine Inspector, *Report, 1899–1900*, pp. 26–27. Montana Mine Inspector, *Report, 1907–1908*, pp. 9–10, 16–17.

34. Idaho Mine Inspector, *Report, 1906*, p. 11; *Report, 1908*, p. 19.

35. *Coeur d'Alene Miner*, Feb. 24, 1894, p. 1.

36. Idaho Mine Inspector, *Reports* for 1899, 1900, 1901, 1902, passim; see especially pp. 4–5, 21–22, in 1900 *Report*; also *Report, 1903*, pp. 6–7; *Report, 1905*, p. 8; *Report, 1906*, pp. 7–8, 10–11, 14–15, 19, 149. *E/MJ*, Nov. 24, 1900, p. 618.

37. Martin H. Jacobs, Boise, to Mgr. Frederick Irwin, Silver City, Idaho, Jan. 8, 13, 15, 19, and Feb. 2, 1903; also intercompany letters discussing this: Sec.-Treas. Thos. B. McKaig, Pittsburgh, Pa., to Irwin, Jan. 19 and Feb. 3, 1903, Trade Dollar Co. papers (Idaho files). Tax fight is discussed in *Idaho Statesman*, Jan. 20, 1903, p. 5; and *E/MJ*, June 13, 1903, p. 907.

38. WFM 15th Convention *Proceedings* (1907), p. 379. Montana Mine Inspector, *Report, 1909–1910*, p. 29. Idaho Mine Inspector, *Report, 1904*, p. 137; *Report, 1908*, pp. 15–16.

39. Testimony of Frederick Burbidge (Wallace, Idaho, July 27, 1899): U.S. Industrial Commission, *Report*, XII, p. 459.

40. *E/MJ*, Jan. 15, 1898, p. 82. Montana Mine Inspector, *Report, 1898*, pp. 5–6. *Miners' Magazine*, August, 1900, p. 6. WFM 15th Convention *Proceedings* (1907), p. 379.

41. U.S. Industrial Commission, *Report*, XII, pp. 228, 358. Colorado Mine Inspector, *Report, 1898*, pp. 17–18.

42. *E/MJ*, Feb. 11, 1904, p. 228. Coroner's Jury Report No. 115, Independence Mine disaster, Jan. 26, 1904, in Teller County District Court files, Cripple Creek, Colo.

43. *M/SP*, March 14, 1896, p. 203. Eben Smith, Denver, to J. Parker Whitney, Boston, Mass., March 25, 1896, Eben Smith letterpress books. *E/MJ*, Feb. 18, 1904, p. 291.

44. *E/MJ*, March 5, 1910, pp. 511–512. Colorado Mine Inspector, *Report, 1907–1908*, p. 5. Montana Mine Inspector, *Report, 1910*, p. 41.

45. Montana House *Journal, 1895*, p. 367. Montana Mine Inspector, *Report, 1902*, p. 11. Nevada Mine Inspector, *Report, 1910*, p. 6. Colorado Mine Inspector, *Report, 1889–1890*, pp. 6–7. Western Federation of Miners Constitution, May 19, 1893. Idaho Senate *Journal, 1897*, pp. 125–126.

46. Helena (Mont.) *Herald*, n.d., quoted in Butte (Mont.) *Weekly Tribune*, Jan. 30, 1897, p. 1. Montana Senate *Journal, 1897*, pp. 223, 232, 240. Montana *Laws, 1897*, pp. 245–246. *E/MJ*, March 20, 1897, p. 290; June 12, 1897, p. 611. Montana Mine Inspector, *Report, 1897*, pp. 6–7.

47. Butte (Mont.) *Bystander*, Nov. 6, 1897, p. 1. Montana Mine Inspector, *Report, 1898*, pp. 5–6. *Miners' Magazine*, August, 1900, pp. 4–8. Helena (Mont.) *Independent*, Jan. 9, 1900, p. 5. The ruling upholding the safety cage law is in *State v. Anaconda Copper-Mining Co.*, 59 Pacific 854 (Montana Supreme Court, 1900).

48. (1) General safety laws: Harry A. Lee, Colorado State Mining Bureau, Bulletin No. 1, *Recommendations for Safety Appliances in Mining* (1896), passim. *E/MJ*, Dec. 5, 1908, pp. 1088–1093. Idaho *Laws, 1909*, pp. 266–271. (2) Mine signals: California *Laws, 1893*, pp. 626–627. Montana Senate *Journal, 1895*, pp. 321, 325. *M/SP*, June 15, 1895, p. 383; March 28, 1903, p. 194; March 26, 1904, p. 208. Idaho Mine Inspector, *Report, 1904*, p. 17; *Report, 1908*, p. 22. Colorado *Laws, 1899*, p. 289; *Laws, 1903*, pp. 361–362. Arizona Territorial *Laws, 1907*, p. 118. (3) Use of Cages: Montana *Laws, 1903*, pp. 125–126; *Laws, 1897*, p. 246. Colorado *Laws, 1899*, p. 289; *Laws, 1903*, pp. 361–363. Idaho *Laws, 1909*, pp. 267–270. Montana Mine Inspector, *Report, 1900*, p. 15. Nevada *Laws, 1903*, chap. 13. *E/MJ*, June 16, 1906, p. 1148. Idaho Mine Inspector, *Report, 1908*, pp. 20–23. (4) Hoisting engineers: Montana *Laws, 1897*, pp. 67–68. Idaho *Laws, 1909*, p. 270. Colorado *Laws, 1903*, p. 361. Nevada *Laws, 1905*, pp. 212–213; *Laws, 1907*, pp. 407–408.

49. Colorado *Laws, 1893*, p. 129; *Laws, 1901*, pp. 161–162. John H. Murphy, WFM attorney, quoted in *Miners' Magazine*, August, 1901, p. 8. Thomas I. Parkinson, "Problems and Progress of Workmen's Compensation Legislation," *American Labor Legislation Review*, I:1 (January, 1911), pp. 57–58. Thos. McKaig, Pittsburgh, Pa., to Frederick Irwin, Dewey, Idaho, Feb. 23, 1909, Trade Dollar Co. papers (Idaho files). Utah *Laws, 1898*, Sec. 1343; *Laws, 1907*, Secs. 1342 and 1343. Arizona *Laws, 1901*, p. 734. *Vindicator Consol. Gold Min. Co. v. Firstbrook*, 86 Pacific 313 (Colorado Supreme Court, 1906). Montana *Laws, 1903*, pp. 156–157. U.S. *Statutes at Large* (59th Cong., 1st Sess., June 11, 1906), vol. 34, pt. 1, pp. 232–233; (60th Cong., 1st Sess., April 22, 1908), vol. 35, pt. 1, pp. 65–66. Nevada *Laws, 1907*, chap. 214. Idaho *Laws, 1909*, p. 34.

50. *Idaho Statesman*, Jan. 22, 1903, p. 3; Feb. 23, 1907, p. 3.

51. An excellent discussion of these changes is in Roy Lubove, "Workmen's Compensation and the Prerogatives of Voluntarism," *Labor History*, VIII:3 (Fall, 1967), p. 254 ff.

52. Harold U. Faulkner, *American Economic History* (New York, 1954), pp. 472–473. Lubove, "Workmen's Compensation," pp. 262–263. Early discussion of the English system appears in *MISP*, May 30, 1891, p. 344.

53. Montana Federation of Labor, 16th Convention *Proceedings* (1909), pp. 15–16. Montana *Laws, 1909*, pp. 81–86. See discussion in Crystal Eastman, *Work-Accidents and the Law* (New York, 1910), pp. 209, 296–299.

54. *Cunningham v. Northwestern Improvement Co.*, 119 Pacific 554 (Montana Supreme Court, 1911). Parkinson, "Workmen's Compensation Legislation," p. 59. Ernst Freund, "Employers' Liability, Workmen's Compensation and Insurance," *American Labor Legislation Review*, V:4 (December, 1915), pp. 724–727.

VIII: The Dilemma of Political Action

1. Western Federation of Miners, 10th Convention *Proceedings* (1902), pp. 100–101.

2. Much of the political activity by hard-rock miners in the 'nineties was conducted through the Populist and Labor parties. See Helena (Mont.) *Independent*, Oct. 5, 1900, p. 1; and Melvyn Dubofsky, "The Origins of Western Working Class Radicalism, 1890–1905," *Labor History*, VII:2 (Spring, 1966), pp. 140–141. Reports of miners' political activity may be noted in *Miners' Magazine*, December, 1900, p. 5; May, 1902, p. 47; March, 1903, p. 45; and May, 1903, p. 47.

3. Harry Seligson and George E. Bardwell, *Labor-Management Relations in Colorado* (Denver, 1961), p. 316. Thomas Tonge, "The Fourth Era of the Leadville Mining District," *Engineering and Mining Journal*, September, 1900, p. 824 [cited hereafter as *EIMJ*]. U.S. 12th Census (1900) *Reports*, vol. II, "Population," pt. II, p. cxxxvii. Colorado Mine Inspector, *Report, 1899–1900*, pp. 34–35.

4. Lynn Irwin Perrigo, "A Social History of Central City, Colorado, 1859–1900" (unpublished doctoral dissertation, University of Colorado, 1936), pp. 348–349. Butte (Mont.) *Miner*, Oct. 8, 1878, p. 4; Nov. 12, 1878, p. 4; Nov. 26, 1878, p. 4. Anti-Chinese activities are described in Chapter 2 above. *Miners' Magazine*, October, 1901, pp. 31–32. The speaker was John M. O'Neill, later the magazine's editor and an avid exponent of socialism. Records of Western legislatures during the period reveal progressively more specific laws on these subjects. Protections for workmen were strengthened in such areas as required patronage of the company store and boardinghouse, blacklisting, the mechanic's lien, and wage payment. A useful compilation is "Labor Laws of the United States with Decisions of Courts Relating Thereto," in U.S. Department of Commerce and Labor, *Twenty-Second Annual Report of the Commissioner of Labor—1907*. Also see Carl Ubbelohde, "The Labor Movement in Colorado—Patterns of the Era of Industrial Warfare," *The Denver Westerners Monthly Roundup*, XIX:10 (October, 1963), pp. 3–16. Such legislation came later in Alaska, due to the more slowly advancing industrialization of lode mining there. See William R. Hunt, *North of 53°—The Wild Days of the Alaska-Yukon Mining Frontier—1870–1914* (New York, 1974), p. 280.

5. *EIMJ*, Feb. 14, 1891, p. 216. Helena *Independent*, May 26, 1900, p. 7.

6. Eliot Lord, *Comstock Mining and Miners* (Washington, D.C., 1883; reprint 1959), p. 225. Dan DeQuille, *The Big Bonanza* (New York, 1876; 1947 reprint), p. 244. *Daily Alta California*, July 16, 1869, p. 2; July 23, 1869, p. 2; Aug. 7, 1869, p. 2. Richard E. Lingenfelter, *The Hardrock Miners: A History of the*

Mining Labor Movement in the American West, 1863–1893 (Berkeley, Calif., 1974), pp. 77–78. *Owyhee Avalanche*, Oct. 18, 1873, p. 3. *Idaho Tri-Weekly Statesman*, Feb. 26, 1876, p. 3; Sept. 4, 1877, p. 2. *Idaho World*, Nov. 27, 1877, p. 3. A. N. Rogers, Central City, Colo., to R. H. Rickard, New York, Nov. 16, 1880, Andrews N. Rogers letterpress book. George H. Holt, Leadville, to Little Chief Mine executive committee, n.p., n.d. (circa 1879), George H. Holt papers. Vernon H. Jensen, *Heritage of Conflict—Labor Relations in the Nonferrous Metals Industry up to 1930* (Ithaca, N.Y., 1950; 1968 reprint), p. 22. Carroll D. Wright, ed., *A Report on Labor Disturbances in the State of Colorado, from 1880 to 1904* . . . (58th Cong., 3d Sess., 1905, Senate Doc. No. 122), p. 69. *Mining and Scientific Press*, July 28, 1888, p. 61; Oct. 12, 1889, p. 283 [hereafter cited as *M/SP*]. Colorado Bureau of Labor Statistics, *Report, 1887–1888*, pp. 255–270.

7. For general background on the eight-hour day, see the following: Sidney Webb and Harold Cox, *The Eight Hours Day* (London, 1891), especially pp. 45–52, passim. John B. Andrews, "Nationalisation (1860–1877)," in John R. Commons et al., *History of Labour in the United States*, vol. II, pp. 86–109, 124–125, 151; Commons and Andrews, *Principles of Labor Legislation* (New York, 1936), pp. 120–127; Sidney Fine, "The Eight-Hour Day Movement in the United States, 1888–1891," *Mississippi Valley Historical Review*, XL:3 (December, 1953), pp. 441–444, 455–460; Marion Cotter Cahill, *Shorter Hours—A Study of the Movement since the Civil War* (New York, 1932), pp. 70 ff. Helena *Independent*, May 13, 1900, p. 4.

Western background is drawn from the following: *Montana Post*, Jan. 6, 1866, p. 2. Grass Valley (Calif.) *Daily National*, July 1, 1867, pp. 2, 4. *Alta California*, Feb. 16, 1869, p. 1; Feb. 25, 1869, p. 1; Aug. 5, 1869, p. 1. Nevada Assembly *Journal*, 4th Session (1869), pp. 91, 95, 100, 143, 192. Nevada Senate *Journal*, 4th Session (1869), p. 280. Jensen, *Heritage of Conflict*, pp. 96–97. Lingenfelter, *Hardrock Miners*, p. 63.

8. Cahill, *Shorter Hours*, pp. 49–51. Colorado Bureau of Labor Statistics, *Report, 1887–1888*, pp. 255–270; *Report, 1891–1892*, pp. 8, 13; *Report, 1895–1896*, p. 23. President's report in WFM 11th Convention *Proceedings* (1903), pp. 22–23. Testimony of Harry A. Lee, Denver, July 13, 1899, and Terhune: U.S. Industrial Commission, *Report* . . . *on the Relations and Conditions of Capital and Labor Employed in the Mining Industry* (57th Cong., 1st sess., 1901, House Doc. No. 181), vol. XII, pp. 235, 591–592. Wright, *Labor Disturbances in Colorado*, pp. 51, 137–138. *Miners' Magazine*, July, 1900, p. 8. Helena *Independent*, June 14, 1900, p. 4.

9. Montana Mine Inspector, *Report, 1889*, p. 89. Todd, "Cousin Jack in Idaho," p. 10. See comments by miners compiled in Colorado Bureau of Labor Statistics, *Report, 1887–1888*, pp. 255–270. *Deseret News*, Feb. 5, 1896, p. 2.

10. For example, both the 1890–1891 carpenters' eight-hour-day campaign in the East, and the 1891 Kansas law covering public employees were based heavily upon the philosophy of creating jobs. See Fine, "The Eight-Hour Day," p. 444; and Cahill, *Shorter Hours*, p. 104. For background on early hour laws for streetcar and railroad operators, see Commons and Andrews, *Principles of Labor Legislation*, pp. 122–127.

11. John A. Church, "Accidents in the Comstock Mines and Their Relation to Deep Mining," in William Ralston Balch, comp., *The Mines, Miners, and Mining Interests of the United States in 1882* (Philadelphia, 1882), p. 801. *Coeur d'Alene Miner*, June 24, 1893, p. 8. Montana *Laws, 1893*, p. 67.

12. Wyoming Constitution, 1889, Art. 19, Sec. 1.

13. Kearns later served as U.S. Senator from Utah from 1901 to 1904. Richard H. Peterson, "Conflict and Consensus: Labor Relations in Western Mining," *Journal of the West*, XII:1 (January, 1973), pp. 12, 15. Utah Constitution (1896), Art. XVI, Sec. 6.

14. Utah *Laws, 1896*, Title 36, Chap. 2, Sec. 1337. Utah House *Journal, 1st Session* (1896), pp. 186, 444. Utah Senate *Journal, 1st Session* (1896), pp. 450, 456.

15. Utah Senate *Journal, 1st Session* (1896), p. 457. Utah House *Journal, 1st Session* (1896), pp. 367–368, 484, 491–492. *Deseret News*, Jan. 28, 1896, p. 5; Feb. 26, 1896, p. 2; March 9, 1896, p. 5; March 16, 1896, p. 2; March 20, 1896, p. 4.

16. *E/MJ*, March 5, 1898, p. 276.

17. 46 Pacific 756–762 (Utah Supreme Court, 1896). See companion case on smelter worker: 46 Pacific 1105 (Utah Supreme Court, 1896). Discussed in Jensen, *Heritage of Conflict*, pp. 97–100. The plaintiff's brief is summarized in *Holden v. Hardy*, 169 U.S. 366–367, 373–379 (1898).

18. *Proceedings and Debates of the Constitutional Convention Held in the City of Helena, Montana . . . 1889* (Helena, 1921), pp. 213–214, 245. Jensen, *Heritage of Conflict*, p. 97. Lingenfelter, *Hardrock Miners*, p. 190. *E/MJ*, Nov. 29, 1890, p. 633; Dec. 6, 1890, p. 658; Feb. 14, 1891, p. 216.

19. Montana House *Journal, 2d Session* (1891), pp. 66–67. Butte (Mont.) *Mining Journal*, Feb. 22, 1891, p. 1; March 1, 1891, p. 1. Jensen, *Heritage of Conflict*, p. 100.

20. Helena *Independent*, June 14, 1900, p. 1. *Miners' Magazine*, September, 1900, pp. 11–12. The extent of the feud between mine owners was demonstrated in 1898 when Heinze closed the entire district briefly by claiming that the veins of three major mines joined in an apex on his tiny claim. His audacious act was soon overturned, but it entered Butte's legends as dramatic testimony to the extent of the mine owners' antagonism toward each other. See C. B. Glasscock, *The War of the Copper Kings—Builders of Butte and Wolves of Wall Street* (New York, 1935), pp. 227–229. Works Projects Administration, *Copper Camp—Stories of the World's Greatest Mining Town: Butte, Montana* (New York, 1943), pp. 32–39.

21. Glasscock, *War of the Copper Kings*, pp. 190–195. *E/MJ*, June 23, 1900, p. 749.

22. *E/MJ*, June 23, 1900, pp. 731, 749. Helena *Independent*, June 14, 1900, p. 1; June 22, 1900, p. 1; Aug. 23, 1900, p. 4; Sept. 7, 1900, p. 5; Sept. 25, 1900, p. 3; Oct. 7, 1900, p. 1; Oct. 17, 1900, p. 4; Nov. 7, 1900, p. 1; Nov. 8, 1900, p. 1. WPA, *Copper Camp*, p. 38. Glasscock, *War of the Copper Kings*, pp. 197–201, 229–230.

23. Identification with the bill was helpful to Montana politicians. John Quinn, who won a skirmish with another Butte legislator to submit the eight-hour-day bill, went on to win election as president of the Butte Miners' Union "immediately after" the successful legislative drive of early 1901. A year later, Quinn was elected sheriff of Silver Bow County. William Clark's election to the U.S. Senate was also based heavily upon his endorsement of the eight-hour day. Montana House *Journal, 7th Session* (1901), p. 72. Montana Senate *Journal, 7th Session* (1901), p. 61. Montana *Laws, 1901*, p. 62. Helena *Independent*, Jan. 9, 1901, p. 3; Jan. 11, 1901, p. 8; Jan. 14, 1901, p. 4; Jan. 24, 1901, p. 8; Jan. 26, 1901, p. 8; Feb. 2, 1901, p. 5. *Reveille*, Oct. 21, 1902, p. 1; Nov. 7, 1902, p. 1. *Miners' Magazine*, April, 1901, pp. 3–4.

24. The closed mine was the New Departure silver mine in Beaverhead

County. *M/SP*, May 25, 1901, p. 245. *Reveille*, Aug. 28, 1902, p. 5; Sept. 27, 1902, p. 3; Oct. 16, 1903, p. 1; Feb. 24, 1905, p. 4. *E/MJ*, April 27, 1901, p. 541; May 11, 1901, p. 601; May 18, 1901, p. 631; May 25, 1901, pp. 672–673. Montana Bureau of Agriculture, Labor, and Industry, *Report, 1902*, pp. 202–203, 205. *Miners' Magazine*, October, 1901, p. 6. WFM 11th Convention *Proceedings* (1903), pp. 147–148.

25. *Reveille*, Sept. 17, 1902, p. 1; Sept. 20, 1902, p. 5; Feb. 27, 1903, p. 1; March 28, 1904, p. 2. Helena *Independent*, Jan. 24, 1901, p. 1; Jan. 26, 1901, p. 8; March 3, 1903, p. 4; Jan. 12, 1905, p. 4. Montana Bureau of Agriculture, Labor, and Industry, *Report, 1906*, pp. 214 ff. Montana Constitution, Art. 18, Sec. 4. Montana *Laws, 1905*, pp. 105–106. The law was challenged in the courts on its coverage of public employees, not miners or smelter workers. See *State v. Livingston Concrete Bldg. & Mfg. Co.*, 87 Pacific 980 (Montana Supreme Court, 1906). *M/SP*, May 12, 1906, pp. 315–316. Jensen, *Heritage of Conflict*, pp. 100–101.

26. *Rocky Mountain News*, Jan. 11, 1887, p. 3; March 31, 1887, p. 2; April 4, 1887, p. 2; March 6, 1889, p. 6; March 10, 1889, p. 2. David Lawrence Lonsdale, "The Movement for an Eight-Hour Law in Colorado, 1893–1913" (master's thesis, University of Colorado, 1963), pp. 22–29, 32–34, 48–51. Colorado *Laws, 1893*, p. 305; *Laws, 1894*, pp. 85–86. Wright, *Labor Disturbances in Colorado*, pp. 51–52.

27. *In re Eight-Hour Bill*, 21 Colorado Reports 29 (Colorado Supreme Court, 1895). Discussed in Wright, *Labor Disturbances in Colorado*, pp. 51–52. Lonsdale, "Movement for Eight-Hour Law," pp. 57–59.

28. Campaign discussed in Lonsdale, "Movement for Eight-Hour Law," pp. 61–62, 66, 76, 83–85, 110–123. Colorado *Laws, 1899*, p. 232. Wright, *Labor Disturbances in Colorado*, p. 55. *In re Morgan*, 58 Pacific 1071, 1073–1074, 1078 (Colorado Supreme Court, 1899).

29. *American Law Register*, XXXIX:2 (February, 1900), p. 105.

30. *Miners' Magazine*, April, 1900, pp. 9–11.

31. Lonsdale, "Movement for Eight-Hour Law," pp. 139–141, 143–145. Wright, *Labor Disturbances in Colorado*, pp. 56–58. Colorado *Laws, 1901*, pp. 108–109.

32. George G. Suggs, Jr., *Colorado's War on Militant Unionism—James H. Peabody and the Western Federation of Miners* (Detroit, 1972), chap. 2. A mine engineer who arrived in Colorado during the strike had a highly negative view of the WFM. Under the leadership of the "inner ring," he wrote, were "terrorists, dynamiters, and gunmen, to whom murder was commonplace." The real reason for the strike was the "demand for a closed shop and domination by the union" (Gene M. Gressley, ed., *Bostonians and Bullion—The Journal of Robert Livermore, 1892–1915* [Lincoln, Nebr., 1968], pp. 92–93).

33. Wright, *Labor Disturbances in Colorado*, pp. 148–149. Peabody quoted in Suggs, *Colorado's War on Militant Unionism*, pp. 179–180.

34. Lonsdale, "Movement for Eight-Hour Law," pp. 165–166, 180. Bulletins No. 6, 7, and 11, issued early 1904, Denver, Colo.; copies in Edward P. Costigan papers.

35. Wright, *Labor Disturbances in Colorado*, pp. 62–63. Lonsdale, "Movement for Eight-Hour Law," p. 180.

36. Wright, *Labor Disturbances in Colorado*, pp. 61–67.

37. Melvyn Dubofsky, *We Shall Be All—A History of the Industrial Workers of the World* (Chicago, 1969), pp. 42–43: Chapter 3 covers the Colorado labor wars. Ubbelohde, "Labor Movement in Colorado," p. 9. Denver (Colo.) *Post*, Aug. 11, 1903, quoted in *Miners' Magazine*, Aug. 27, 1903, p. 7.

38. Information on the Cripple Creek strike is drawn heavily from the following: Suggs, *Colorado's War on Militant Unionism*, pp. 62–64, 75–80, 85, 90–108, 111–117, 119. Wright, *Labor Disturbances in Colorado*, pp. 137, 140, 151–159, 163, 170–175, 249–260. For Haywood's version of the Cripple Creek events, see his autobiography, *Bill Haywood's Book—The Autobiography of William D. Haywood* (New York, 1929; 1966 printing), chaps. 9 and 10.

39. Suggs, *Colorado's War on Militant Unionism*, pp. 21–22, 118–143. Wright, *Labor Disturbances in Colorado*, pp. 220–230. Jensen, *Heritage of Conflict*, pp. 144–146. Haywood, *Bill Haywood's Book*, pp. 140–141, 160–162.

40. Wright, *Labor Disturbances in Colorado*, pp. 228, 292. *Miners' Magazine*, Nov. 24, 1904, pp. 6, 11.

41. *Colorado Laws, 1905*, pp. 284–285. Lonsdale, "Movement for Eight-Hour Law," pp. 275–283. WFM 17th Convention *Proceedings* (1909), p. 33.

42. *Idaho Constitution* (1889), Art. XII, Sec. 2. A strike occurred in 1896 in Salmon City when miners claimed that the manager reneged on a nine hour-day agreement and required ten hours of work. *M/SP*, May 23, 1896, p. 423. Hours worked in various mines were reported by Idaho Mine Inspector, *Report, 1899*, pp. 20–34. U.S. Industrial Commission, *Report*, XII, 410–411. *M/SP*, March 24, 1900, p. 323.

43. *Idaho Laws, 1901*, pp. 311–312. *Idaho Statesman*, Jan. 31, 1903, p. 4.

44. Debates were reported in the following issues of *Idaho Statesman*: Jan. 6, 1903, p. 3; Jan. 7, 1903, pp. 1, 6; Jan. 11, 1903, p. 5; Jan. 28, 1903, p. 3; Jan. 31, 1903, p. 3; Feb. 4, 1903, p. 3; Feb. 5, 1903, p. 3; Feb. 12, 1903, pp. 3, 4, 6; Feb. 19, 1903, p. 4; Feb. 24, 1903, p. 5; Feb. 25, 1903, p. 3; March 1, 1903, p. 5; Dec. 31, 1904, p. 4; Jan. 27, 1905, p. 3. Also see Thos. B. McKaig, Pittsburgh, Pa., to Frederick Irwin, Dewey, Idaho, Feb. 3, 1903, Trade Dollar Co. papers (Idaho files). Idaho Mine Inspector, *Report, 1906*, p. 164; *Report, 1907*, pp. 141, 197. Idaho Senate *Journal, 9th Session* (1907), pp. 86, 99. *Idaho Laws, 1907*, p. 97. Representative Owen was censured by the Boise Federated Trades and Labor Council for his remarks, and later apologized.

45. The British Columbia eight-hour-day controversy is detailed in Merle W. Wells, "The WFM in British Columbia: The Eight Hour Statute, the Alien Labour Acts, and the Recognition Issue in the Kootenay Mines, 1899–1902" (paper presented May 14, 1976, 9th Annual Pacific Northwest Labor History Association Conference, Seattle, Washington), especially pp. 3–10. British Columbia *Laws, 1899*, p. 153. *M/SP*, April 22, 1899, p. 426; June 17, 1899, p. 634. *E/MJ*, Jan. 27, 1900, p. 121; Feb. 3, 1900, p. 151. *Miners' Magazine*, April, 1900, p. 15.

46. Gold Hill (Nev.) Miners Union, minute book, Sept. 23 and 30, 1889; Feb. 10 and 17, 1890. Nevada *Laws, 1903*, p. 33. *E/MJ*, March 7, 1903, p. 385; April 11, 1903, p. 575; July 11, 1903, p. 68. *M/SP*, July 18, 1903, p. 34. *In re Boyce*, 75 Pacific 1 (Nevada Supreme Court, 1904).

47. Arizona *Laws, 1903*, No. 8; *Laws, 1912*, pp. 59–61. James Ward Byrkit, "Life and Labor in Arizona, 1901–1921: With Particular Reference to the Deportations of 1917" (unpublished doctoral dissertation, Claremont Men's College, 1972), p. 90. *E/MJ*, April 14, 1903, p. 421. *Miners' Magazine*, Nov. 5, 1903, p. 7.

48. *E/MJ*, Dec. 29, 1906, p. 1225; June 15, 1907, p. 1157. *Report of Acting President Mahoney to the Fifteenth Annual Convention*, WFM (June, 1907), p. 6.

49. Jas. Opie, President, Tuolumne Miners Union No. 73, letter in *Miners' Magazine*, December, 1900, p. 32. WFM 16th Convention *Proceedings* (1908), p. 421; 17th Convention *Proceedings* (1909), p. 32. *E/MJ*, May 2, 1903, p. 682;

July 13, 1907, p. 79; March 27, 1909, p. 670; Feb. 19, 1910, p. 295. *California Laws, 1909*, p. 279. U.S. Immigration Commission, *Reports: Part 25, Japanese and Other Immigrant Races in the Pacific Coast and Rocky Mountain States* (61st Cong., 2d Sess., 1909–1910), pp. 140–141.

50. WFM 18th Convention *Proceedings* (1910), p. 15.

51. WFM 11th Convention *Proceedings* (1903), p. 22. *Report of Acting President Mahoney*, p. 6. *Miners' Magazine*, May, 1903, p. 37. Cahill, *Shorter Hours*, pp. 53–55. In 1915, it was noted that of the fourteen states and territories having an eight-hour-day law for miners, most were in the West, despite the fact that coal and metal mining were carried on in many areas of the country. The fourteen were Alaska, Arizona, California, Colorado, Idaho, Missouri, Montana, Nevada, Oklahoma, Oregon, Pennsylvania, Utah, Washington, and Wyoming. See Felix Frankfurter and Louis D. Brandeis, *The Case for the Shorter Work Day*, brief for the defendant, in *Franklin O. Bunting v. The State of Oregon*, 1915 (New York, n.d.), p. 1.

IX: Radicalism and the "Red-Hot Revolutionists"

1. Melvyn Dubofsky, "The Origins of Western Working Class Radicalism, 1890–1905," *Labor History*, VII:2 (Spring, 1966), p. 133.

2. Selig Perlman and Philip Taft, "Labor Movements," in John R. Commons et al., *History of Labour in the United States, 1896–1932*, vol. IV, pp. 169, 217. Dubofsky, "Origins of Western Working Class Radicalism," passim. John H. M. Laslett, *Labor and the Left—A Study of Socialist and Radical Influences in the American Labor Movement, 1881–1924*, pp. 241, 249, 278, 281, 299. William Preston, "Shall This Be All? U.S. Historians Versus William D. Haywood et al.," *Labor History*, XII:3 (Summer, 1971), pp. 437–439.

3. Preston, "Shall This Be All?", pp. 437–439.

4. Colorado remained an exception, for many major mines in the state were owned by such Coloradoans as Eben Smith and John Campion. U.S. Industrial Commission, *Final Report . . .* (57th Cong., 1st Sess., House Doc. No. 380, 1902), vol. XIX, pp. 228–229. Joseph Kinsey Howard, *Montana—High, Wide, and Handsome*, p. 83. *The Reveille*, June 26, 1903, p. 1. *Engineering and Mining Journal*, Nov. 21, 1903, p. 764 [hereafter cited as *E/MJ*]. Russell R. Elliott, *Nevada's Twentieth-Century Mining Boom—Tonopah, Goldfield, Ely* (Reno, 1966), pp. 18–19, 185. Nome (Alaska) *Gold Digger*, Nov. 29, 1907, quoted in William R. Hunt, *North of 53°—The Wild Days of the Alaska-Yukon Mining Frontier, 1870–1914* (New York, 1974), pp. 223–224.

5. *E/MJ*, May 2, 1885, p. 303; May 24, 1902, p. 718; Feb. 21, 1903, p. 285. Vernon Jensen, *Heritage of Conflict—Labor Relations in the Nonferrous Metals Industry Up to 1930* (Ithaca, N.Y., 1950; 1968 reprint), pp. 27–28. *Mining and Scientific Press*, May 2, 1885, p. 289; Sept. 7, 1895, p. 151; April 5, 1902, p. 186; July 18, 1903, p. 34; Dec. 26, 1903, p. 415; Jan. 16, 1904, p. 36 [hereafter cited as *M/SP*]. Robert W. Smith, "The Idaho Antecedents of the Western Federation of Miners—Labor Organization and Industrial Conflict in the Coeur d'Alene Mining District of Idaho, 1890 to 1893" (unpublished doctoral dissertation, University of California, Berkeley, 1937), pp. 55–56. Denver (Colo.) *Republican*, March 28, 1902. *Miners' Magazine*, February, 1903, p. 3. Carroll D. Wright, ed., *A Report on Labor Disturbances in the State of Colorado, from 1880 to 1904 . . .* (58th Cong., 3d Sess., Senate Doc. No. 122, 1905), pp. 46–50. George G. Suggs, Jr., *Colorado's War on Militant Unionism—James H. Peabody and the Western Federation of Miners* (Detroit, 1972), pp. 80, 150–152.

6. J. W. Finch, Goldfield, Nev., to A. L. Arnold, Cripple Creek, Colo., March 22, 1907; and Arnold to Finch, March 28, 1907, in James H. Hawley correspondence.

7. E. P. Weaver, Manufacturers Information Bureau Co., Denver, to Frederic Irwin, Manager, Trade Dollar Consolidated Mining Co., Dewey, Idaho, March 23, 1906; Weaver to Irwin, Nov. 10, 1906, in Trade Dollar Co. papers (Idaho files).

8. William D. Haywood, *Bill Haywood's Book—The Autobiography of William D. Haywood* (New York, 1929; 1966), pp. 80–81. *Miners' Magazine*, July, 1903, pp. 1, 25, 29.

9. *Miners' Magazine*, July, 1903, pp. 38–39.

10. Boyce was formerly in the Knights of Labor, whose national leader in 1882 urged members to buy rifles, bayonets, ammunition, and a Gatling gun for each local assembly. Within weeks after Boyce's 1897 recommendations, an Idaho National Guard shack in Mullan was raided and weapons seized, and the Engineering and Mining Journal concluded that WFM members "were simply taking their president's advice to arm themselves." Italian miners at Lake City, Colorado, stole rifles and ammunition from the state armory less than two years later. See Norman J. Ware, *The Labor Movement in the United States—1860–1895* (New York, 1929), p. 107. Melvyn Dubofsky, *We Shall Be All—A History of the Industrial Workers of the World* (Chicago, 1969), pp. 64–66. Wright, *Labor Disturbances in Colorado*, pp. 102–103. *Miners' Magazine*, Feb. 23, 1905, p. 4; June, 1903, pp. 52–54; March, 1900, pp. 37–40. *E/MJ*, May 29, 1897, p. 535. WFM 10th Convention *Proceedings* (1902), p. 9; 15th Convention *Proceedings* (1907), pp. 373–374. Suggs, *Colorado's War on Militant Unionism*, pp. 23–24.

11. Numerous letters on Haywood's plan appeared in *Miners' Magazine* in the Spring of 1902. *Miners' Magazine*, July, 1901, pp. 8–9; February, 1902, pp. 7–8; March, 1902, pp. 12–13; July, 1903, pp. 22, 24, 27–28. WFM 11th Convention *Proceedings* (1907), pp. 147, 307–352. *E/MJ*, May 29, 1897, p. 535. Jensen, *Heritage of Conflict*, pp. 70–71.

12. *Miners' Magazine*, November, 1901, pp. 8–9. Laslett, *Labor and the Left*, pp. 250–252. Dubofsky, *We Shall Be All*, pp. 60–61. Boyce-Gompers correspondence reprinted in "Labor Troubles in Idaho" (56th Cong., 1st Sess., Senate Doc. No. 42, 1899), pp. 6–13.

13. Dubofsky, *We Shall Be All*, p. 61. Haywood, *Bill Haywood's Book*, p. 95. *Miners' Magazine*, July, 1900, p. 16; November, 1901, p. 10; July, 1902, pp. 1, 31; November, 1902, pp. 6–8; December, 1902, p. 46; May, 1903, pp. 37–38; July, 1903, pp. 36–37. For examples of the continuing debate in the magazine's letters columns, see issues of July, 1900, pp. 41–45; September, 1900, p. 6; and October, 1900, pp. 38–40. WFM 10th Convention *Proceedings* (1902), pp. 100–101; 11th Convention *Proceedings* (1903), pp. 249, 252–254.

14. *Miners' Magazine*, May, 1900, p. 22; December, 1900, pp. 8–9. WFM 12th Convention *Proceedings* (1904), p. 170; 13th Convention *Proceedings* (1905), pp. 22–23.

15. *Miners' Magazine*, Nov. 17, 1904, pp. 3, 5–6, 11–12; Feb. 9, 1905, p. 4; Feb. 23, 1905, pp. 5, 11–12; March 30, 1905, pp. 5–6. WFM 12th Convention *Proceedings* (1904), pp. 201–202. Suggs, *Colorado's War on Militant Unionism*, pp. 186–187.

16. The birth and growth of the IWW have been extensively treated elsewhere. See especially Dubofsky, *We Shall Be All*, pp. 76–80, passim, and Paul F. Brissenden, *The IWW—A Study of American Syndicalism* (New

York, 1919; 1957 reprint). WFM 10th Convention *Proceedings* (1902), p. 14. *Miners' Magazine*, Jan. 26, 1905, p. 4.

17. Dubofsky, *We Shall Be All*, pp. 76–80. Haywood, *Bill Haywood's Book*, p. 186.

18. Brissenden, *IWW*, pp. 74–75, 104–105. Dubofsky, *We Shall Be All*, pp. 57, 73.

19. WFM 15th Convention *Proceedings* (1907), pp. 800–801, 808–810.

20. Brissenden, *IWW*, pp. 351–352.

21. Jensen, *Heritage of Conflict*, pp. 172 ff. Laslett, *Labor and the Left*, p. 264. Dubofsky, *We Shall Be All*, pp. 96–105, 115–116. Joseph R. Conlin, *Big Bill Haywood and the Radical Union Movement* (Syracuse, N.Y., 1969), pp. 79–80.

22. Laslett, *Labor and the Left*, p. 264. Brissenden, *IWW*, pp. 152–153. Jensen, *Heritage of Conflict*, pp. 176–181. Conlin, *Big Bill Haywood*, p. 81.

23. Jensen concludes that "Neither of the WFM groups of delegates were at home with their 'companions.'" Jensen, *Heritage of Conflict*, p. 176. WFM 15th Convention *Proceedings* (1907), pp. 178, 579–582, 587–588.

24. Ibid.

25. Brissenden, *IWW*, pp. 149–151, 216–217. Haywood, *Bill Haywood's Book*, pp. 227, 229–230. Dubofsky, *We Shall Be All*, pp. 116–119. Jensen, *Heritage of Conflict*, pp. 176–193. WFM 16th Convention *Proceedings* (1908), pp. 273–274.

26. Among other things, the IWW in Nome had taken over the miners' union newspaper and had disrupted a meeting of non-mining laborers. Information on the Alaska troubles is taken primarily from James C. Foster, "Syndicalism Northern Style—The Life and Death of WFM No. 193," *The Alaska Journal*, IV:3 (Summer, 1974), pp. 130–141. Hunt, *North of 53°*, pp. 274–280. WFM 17th Convention *Proceedings* (1909), pp. 257–262.

27. The best detailed account of the Goldfield strike is Elliott, *Nevada's Twentieth-Century Mining Boom*, chap. 5. This discussion suffers, however, from a lack of broad perspective regarding the IWW-WFM dispute. Also see Brissenden, *IWW*, pp. 191–203. WFM 15th Convention *Proceedings* (1907), pp. 33–35. *Idaho Statesman*, Jan. 21, 1907, p. 3.

28. Jensen, *Heritage of Conflict*, p. 235. WFM 16th Convention *Proceedings* (1908), pp. 13–14, 257–262, 268.

29. WFM 15th Convention *Proceedings* (1907), pp. 307–352. Jensen, *Heritage of Conflict*, chaps. 17 and 18, passim. K. Ross Toole, *Twentieth-Century Montana—A State of Extremes* (Norman, Oklahoma, 1972), pp. 126–138. *E/MJ*, Nov. 16, 1907, p. 943. *Reveille*, Nov. 1, 1907, p. 1. Dubofsky, *We Shall Be All*, pp. 301–307. Brissenden, *IWW*, pp. 320–325.

30. WFM 16th Convention *Proceedings* (1908), pp. 19, 339; 18th Convention *Proceedings* (1910), p. 352.

31. WFM 16th Convention *Proceedings* (1908), pp. 16, 18–19; 17th Convention *Proceedings* (1909), pp. 20–21.

32. WFM 15th Convention *Proceedings* (1907), pp. 304, 395–398, 916–917; 17th Convention *Proceedings* (1909), p. 22.

33. WFM 16th Convention *Proceedings* (1908), pp. 16–17.

34. WFM 16th Convention *Proceedings* (1908), pp. 273–274, 300–301.

35. *Miners' Magazine*, Oct. 8, 1903, p. 9.

36. Contributions to the WFM from around the country are listed in a special supplement to the *Miners' Magazine*, May 5, 1904; also see editorial of Feb. 25, 1904, p. 3. Jensen, *Heritage of Conflict*, pp. 238–239.

37. WFM 18th Convention *Proceedings* (1910), pp. 221, 316–317. Laslett,

Labor and the Left, pp. 269–270. Brissenden, *IWW*, pp. 215, 320. Jensen, *Heritage of Conflict*, p. 237.

38. Hunt, *North of 53°*, p. 278. Laslett, *Labor and the Left*, p. 281, note 17. Cf. Joseph G. Rayback, *History of American Labor* (New York, 1966), p. 234.

39. Haywood, *Bill Haywood's Book*, chap. 4, passim. Silver City (Idaho) Miners' Union No. 66, minute book, Sept. 13 and 20, 1897. The situation is paralleled today in newspaper and television coverage of labor. The mass media limit their coverage almost entirely to strikes and threats of strikes— with scarcely a word on the day-to-day life of unions protecting their members through grievance procedures and negotiations, or on employees confronting changes in their workplace.
Idaho mine employment totals are based on reports of the Idaho Mine Inspector rather than the census figures, which appear too low. The inspector was probably able to gauge sporadic and part-time mining more accurately. Cf. Idaho Mine Inspector, *Report, 1905*, p. 8; U.S. 12th Census (1900), *Abstract*, p. 429. *E/MJ*, Dec. 6, 1902, p. 762. *M/SP*, July 25, 1903, p. 57.

40. Frank Bulkley, Aspen, Colo., to President J. B. Wheeler, Aspen Mining and Smelting Co., Manitou, Colo., Oct. 4, 1893, in Bulkley copybook in D. R. C. Brown papers.

41. *Miners' Magazine*, December, 1900, p. 30; May, 1903, p. 38. Jay A. Carpenter, Russell R. Elliott, and Byrd Sawyer, *The History of Fifty Years of Mining at Tonopah, 1900–1950*, published as University of Nevada *Bulletin*, XLVII:1 (January, 1953), p. 31. WFM 15th Convention *Proceedings* (1907), pp. 32–35, 290–291.

42. Mine magnates cited in Richard H. Peterson, "Conflict and Consensus: Labor Relations in Western Mining," *Journal of the West*, XII:1 (January, 1973), pp. 1–17.

43. The wage increase for Butte miners amounted to 25 cents per day and was tied to a sliding scale based on the price of copper, then rising. *M/SP*, June 2, 1906, p. 371; Sept. 1, 1906, p. 253; Nov. 24, 1906, p. 612. *E/MJ*, Sept. 8, 1906, p. 453; Oct. 27, 1906, p. 788; Nov. 10, 1906, p. 897; Nov. 17, 1906, p. 930. Idaho Mine Inspector, *Report, 1907*, pp. 3, 141, 197. Laslett, *Labor and the Left*, pp. 302–303. Thos. B. McKaig, Pittsburgh, Pa., to Irwin, Dewey, Idaho, Nov. 16, 1906, Trade Dollar Co. papers (Idaho files).

44. Of course, this picture of the Homestake Mining Company is contradicted by what occurred in 1910, when a lockout was instituted after a sudden rise in union strength and reports of threats against non-union employees. Joseph Cash describes the company as basically benevolent until faced with what it regarded as flagrant union infringement upon management prerogatives. See Cash, *Working the Homestake* (Ames, Iowa, 1973), pp. 82–89 and passim. WFM 16th Convention *Proceedings* (1908), p. 298.

45. WFM 15th Convention *Proceedings* (1907), pp. 6–9. Peterson, "Conflict and Consensus," p. 17.

46. See discussion of this issue in Dubofsky, *We Shall Be All*, pp. 480–481; and Robert L. Tyler, "Comment," in John H. M. Laslett and Seymour Martin Lipset, eds., *Failure of a Dream?—Essays in the History of American Socialism* (Garden City, N.Y., 1974), p. 289. Brissenden, *IWW*, pp. 320–321. Laslett, *Labor and the Left*, p. 272. *Miners' Magazine*, July, 1903, p. 24.

47. Virginia City (Nev.) *Daily Territorial Enterprise*, May 4, 1867, p. 3. Eliot Lord, *Comstock Mining and Miners* (Washington, D.C., 1883; 1959 reprint), pp. 182, 379–380. Elliott, *Nevada's Twentieth-Century Mining Boom*,

p. 114. *Idaho Statesman*, Nov. 23, 1875, p. 2. *E/MJ*, May 11, 1901, p. 601; May 18, 1901, p. 631.

48. WFM 15th Convention *Proceedings* (1907), pp. 916–918.

49. *Miners' Magazine*, February, 1903, pp. 44–45; May, 1903, pp. 42–43. Brissenden, *IWW*, p. 127. WFM 15th Convention *Proceedings* (1907), p. 375; 16th Convention *Proceedings* (1908), p. 25; 17th Convention *Proceedings* (1909), pp. 32–33; 18th Convention *Proceedings* (1910), pp. 15, 279–280. Laslett, *Labor and the Left*, pp. 267–268.

50. *Miners' Magazine*, July, 1903, pp. 34–35. *E/MJ*, Nov. 14, 1903, p. 726. *M/SP*, Dec. 1, 1906, p. 644.

51. WFM 15th Convention *Proceedings* (1907), pp. 7, 39, 209, 294, 386, 390, 813–814. It should be noted that in 1903, when the spirit of radicalism was rising rapidly within the federation, a vote on political action which sought a "complete revolution of the present system of industrial slavery" still had 29 voting in opposition (out of 100 ballots), and a fourth of the convention delegates did not vote. WFM 11th Convention *Proceedings* (1903), pp. 249–254.

52. Testimony of Robert C. Chambers, Salt Lake City, Utah, Aug. 2, 1899, in U.S. Industrial Commission, *Report . . . on the Relations and Conditions of Capital and Labor Employed in the Mining Industry . . .* (57th Cong., 1st Sess., House Doc. No. 181, 1902), vol. XII, p. 585. *Miners' Magazine*, May, 1900, p. 24; March, 1901, pp. 12–14; May, 1902, p. 45. WFM 17th Convention *Proceedings* (1909), p. 288.

53. WFM 15th Convention *Proceedings* (1907), p. 149; 16th Convention *Proceedings* (1908), p. 269. Mobility as a brake on radicalism is discussed by Stephan Thernstrom, "Socialism and Social Mobility," in Laslett and Lipset, *Failure of a Dream?*, pp. 509–527.

54. WFM 16th Convention *Proceedings* (1908), pp. 269–275.

55. *Miners' Magazine*, June, 1900, p. 21; April, 1902, pp. 23–24; May, 1902, pp. 45–46. WFM 16th Convention *Proceedings* (1908), p. 214; 18th Convention *Proceedings* (1910), p. 197.

56. *Miners' Magazine*, May, 1900, p. 24; January, 1901, p. 43; Feb. 11, 1904, p. 6; Feb. 18, 1904, p. 7; April 21, 1904, pp. 14–15. WFM 15th Convention *Proceedings* (1907), pp. 164, 167; 16th Convention *Proceedings* (1908), pp. 272, 366–367.

X. Epilogue: End of the Pioneer Era

1. *Engineering and Mining Journal*, April 2, 1910, p. 694; April 16, 1910, p. 805.

2. WFM 18th Convention *Proceedings* (1910), p. 17.

3. In a revealing comment, a mine manager admitted following a mine accident in 1893: "I know nothing as to the identity of the person, never met him in life, hence cannot say from whence he came" (Gen. Mgr. C. L. Dahlen to Messrs. Story and Stevager, Ouray, Colorado, May 11, 1893, Iron Rod letterbook). *Miners' Magazine*, December, 1901, pp. 9–10.

4. Vernon H. Jensen, *Heritage of Conflict—Labor Relations in the Nonferrous Metals Industry up to 1930* (New York, 1950; 1968 reprint), chaps. 23 and 24.

BIBLIOGRAPHY

I. Manuscripts

A. Union Minutes and Correspondence

Clancy Miner's Union No. 30, WFM, Clancy, Montana. Minute Book, 1894–1896. Montana Historical Society.

Goldfield Miners' Union No. 220, WFM, Goldfield, Nevada. Records, 1904–1911. Western Historical Collections, University of Colorado Libraries.

Gold Hill Miners' Union, Gold Hill, Nevada. Constitution and By-Laws, Pledge and Minutes, 1866–1868, 1872–1875. Special Collections, University of Nevada Libraries. 2 vols.

———. Financial records and minutes, 1870–1900 (scattered). Beinecke Library, Yale University.

———. Minutes, 1889–1896. Nevada State Historical Society.

Silver City Miners' Union No. 66, WFM, Silver City, Idaho. Financial records and minutes, 1896–1898. Bancroft Library, University of California.

Telluride Miners' Union No. 63, WFM, Telluride, Colorado. Records, 1888–1918. Western Historical Collections, University of Colorado Libraries.

United Mine Workers of America, general correspondence [American Federation of Labor Files, series 7, Box 77]. Wisconsin State Historical Society.

Victor Miners' Union No. 32, WFM, Victor, Colorado. Ledger, 1894–1903. Wisconsin State Historical Society.

B. Records of Mining Companies and Management

Alta Concentrator Mill, Alta & Corbin Railroad. [Montana.] Payroll, 1894–1895. Montana Historical Society.

Bimetallic Mining Company. [Granite, Montana.] Correspondence files, 1887–1895. Montana Historical Society.

Brown, David Robinson Crocker. [Aspen, Colorado.] Mining company papers, latter nineteenth century. Western Historical Collections, University of Colorado.

Consolidated Virginia Mining Company. [Virginia City, Nevada.] Letterpress books, 1870–1878, 1892–1896. Special Collections, University of Nevada Libraries.

Curtis, Allen A. [Austin, Nevada.] Letterbook, 1870–1871. Beinecke Library, Yale University.

Foster, Ernest Le Neve. [Colorado.] Miscellaneous papers, 1886–1902. Western Historical Collections, Denver Public Library.

Gould & Curry Mining Co. [Virginia City, Nevada.] Letterpress book, 1867–1868. Special Collections, University of Nevada Libraries.

Graves, R. A. [Virginia City, Nevada.] Letterpress book, 1865–1866. Nevada State Historical Society.

Holman, Heber. [Virginia City, Nevada.] Diary, 1895. Special Collections, University of Nevada Libraries.

Holt, George H. [Leadville, Colorado.] Papers, 1878–1880. Western Historical Collections, University of Colorado.

Iron Rod Mining Company. [Madison County, Montana.] Letterpress book, 1879–1895. Bancroft Library, University of California.

Jones, J. E. [Gold Hill, Nevada.] Daily journal, 1878–1883. Special Collections, University of Nevada Libraries.

Kemp, John H. [Central City, Colorado.] Correspondence files, 1896–1897. Colorado State Historical Society.

La Crosse Gold Mining Co. [New York; Colorado.] Letterpress book, 1885–1905. Western History Collections, Denver Public Library.

Morgan, Cecil C. [Georgetown, Colorado.] Diary, 1878. Western History Collections, Denver Public Library.

Orford, Ernest P. [DeLamar, Idaho.] Letterbook, 1897–1898. Idaho Historical Society.

"Reply by mine owners of Leadville, Colo. area to Miners Union Thanksgiving Statement. Leadville, Dec. 15, 1896." Typescript. Wisconsin State Historical Society.

Rogers, Andrews N. [Central City, Colorado.] Letterpress book, 1879–1884. Colorado Historical Society.

Sizer, Frank L. [Montana.] Diaries, 1887–1900. Bancroft Library, University of California.

Smith, Eben. [Colorado.] Letterpress books, 1891–1896. Western History Collections, Denver Public Library.

Taylor, Thomas G. [Gold Hill, Nevada.] Letterpress book, 1882–1883. Special Collections, University of Nevada Libraries.

Trade Dollar Consolidated Mining and Milling Co. [Pennsylvania; Idaho.] Letters received, vouchers, 1891–1907. Bancroft Library, University of California.

————. Papers, 1891–1908. Idaho Historical Society.

Werner, Dr. Ed. [Colorado.] Letterpress book, 1895–1904. Colorado Historical Society.

C. Government Archives

San Miguel County, Colorado. Criminal Calendar, District Court, 1885–1898. San Miguel County Historical Society, Telluride, Colorado.

Teller County, Colorado. Coroner's Reports, 1902–1904. District Court, Cripple Creek, Colorado.

D. Other

Bowen, Arthur. [Leadville, Colorado.] Diary, 1882. Western History Collections, Denver Public Library.

Guyer, Henry. [Bannack City, Montana Territory.] Letters, 1866–1867. Beinecke Library, Yale University.

Hawley, James H. [Boise, Idaho.] Correspondence, 1890s and early 1900s. Idaho Historical Society.

Hofen, Leo. [Warrens, Idaho.] Dictation, 1879. Bancroft Library, University of California.

Hough, Frank. [Lake City, Colorado.] Diaries, 1900–1901. [In the Judge John Hough Collection.] Colorado Historical Society.

London Guarantee and Accident Company, Ltd., London, England. Casualty Policy issued to Old & Co., Lessees, Leadville, Colo., Oct. 26, 1896–Oct. 26, 1897. Western Historical Collections, University of Colorado.

Mine Engineer Reports, 1895–1908. Arthur Lakes Library, Colorado School of Mines.

Montana Dictations. Bancroft Library, University of California.

St. Peter's Hospital, Helena, Montana. Registers, 1884–1907. Used by permission of St. Peter's Hospital.

St. Vincent's Hospital, Leadville, Colorado. Registers, 1891–1918. Used by permission of St. Vincent's Hospital.

Sanford, Albert Byron. [Gunnison County, Colorado.] Diary, June 10, 1881–Sept. 4, 1881. Colorado Historical Society.

II. Federal and State Government Publications

A. Federal Publications

Boyce, Edward. "Coeur d'Alene Mining Troubles" [56th Cong., 1st Sess., Senate Document No. 25, Dec. 11, 1899].

Browne, J. Ross. *Mineral Resources of the States and Territories West of the Rocky Mountains* [40th Cong., 2d Sess., House Executive Document No. 202, 1868].

————. *A Report upon the Mineral Resources of the States and Territories West of the Rocky Mountains* [39th Cong., 2d Sess., House Executive Document No. 29, 1867].

Emmons, William H. *A Reconnaissance of Some Mining Camps in Elko, Lander, and Eureka Counties, Nevada* [U.S. Geological Survey, Bulletin No. 408, 1910].

Fessenden, Stephen D. "Present Status of Employers' Liability in the United States." *Bulletin of the Department of Labor*, No. 31 (November, 1900), 1157.

Hague, James D. *Mining Industry*, Vol. III of Clarence King, *Report of the Geological Exploration of the Fortieth Parallel* [Professional Papers of the Engineer Department, U.S. Army, No. 18, 1870].

Henderson, Charles W. *Mining in Colorado—A History of Discovery, Development, and Production* [Geological Survey, Professional Paper 138, 1926].

Kennedy, J. L. "Labor Troubles in Idaho" [56th Cong., 1st Sess., Senate Document No. 42, 1899].

"Labor Laws of the United States with Decisions of Courts Relating Thereto." *Twenty-Second Annual Report of the Commissioner of Labor, 1907.*

Laws Regulating Liability of Employers for Injuries to Employees [Report to U.S. Senate, published as 60th Cong., 1st Sess., Senate Document No. 207, 1908].

Merriam, Brig. Gen. H. C. "Coeur d'Alenes Mining Troubles" [56th Cong., 1st Sess., Senate Document No. 24, 1899].

Olmsted, Victor H., and Stephen D. Fessenden. "Employer and Employee Under the Common Law." *Bulletin of the Department of Labor*, Vol. I, No. 1 (November, 1895), 95.

Ransome, Frederick Leslie. *Preliminary Account of Goldfield, Bullfrog, and Other Mining Districts in Southern Nevada* [U.S. Geological Survey, Bulletin No. 303, 1907].

Raymond, Rossiter W. *Mineral Resources of the States and Territories West of the Rocky Mountains* [40th Cong., 3d Sess., House Executive Document No. 54, 1869].

————. *Mining Statistics West of the Rocky Mountains* [42d Cong., 1st Sess., House Executive Document No. 10, 1871].

————. *Statistics of Mines and Mining in the States and Territories West of the Rocky Mountains* [41st Cong., 2d Sess., House Executive Document No. 207, 1870].

————. *Statistics of Mines and Mining in the States and Territories West of the Rocky Mountains* [42d Cong., 2d Sess., House Executive Document No. 211, 1872].

U.S. Census Office [became Bureau in 1902]:

Ninth Census (1870), Vol. I, *The Statistics of the Population of the United States*. . . .

Ninth Census (1870), *A Compendium of the Ninth Census.*

Tenth Census (1880), part 13, *Statistics and Technology of the Precious Metals.*

Tenth Census (1880), *Compendium of the Tenth Census.*

Eleventh Census (1890), *Compendium of the Eleventh Census,* Vols. I–III.

Twelfth Census (1900), *Reports,* Vol. II, "Population." Pt. II.

Twelfth Census (1900), *Special Reports: Supplementary Analysis and Derivative Tables.*

Twelfth Census (1900), *Abstract of the Twelfth Census. . . .*

Thirteenth Census, Vol. II, *Population—1910—Alabama–Montana.*

Thirteenth Census, Vol. IV, *Population—1910: Occupation Statistics.*

Thirteenth Census, *Abstract of the Census.*

U.S. Congress, *Congressional Record.*

U.S. Geological Survey. *Mineral Resources of the United States,* annual and biennial reports, 1882–1893.

U.S. Immigration Commission. *Abstracts of Reports . . . ,* Vol. I [61st Cong., 3d Sess., Senate Document No. 747, 1911].

———. *Immigrants in Industries,* Part 17: *Copper Mining and Smelting;* Part 25: *Japanese and Other Immigrant Races in the Pacific Coast and Rocky Mountain States* [61st Cong., 2d Sess., Senate Document No. 633, 1911].

U.S. Industrial Commission. *Final Report . . . ,* Vol. XIX [57th Cong., 1st Sess., House Document No. 380, 1902].

———. *Report . . . on Labor Legislation,* Vol. V [56th Cong., 1st Sess., House Document No. 476, 1900].

———. *Report . . . on the Relations and Conditions of Capital and Labor Employed in the Mining Industry . . . ,* Vol. XII [57th Cong., 1st Sess., House Document No. 181, 1901].

U.S. Interior Department. *Idaho Territorial Papers, 1864–1890* (microfilm).

U.S. Senate, Committee on Military Affairs. "Home for Miners" [57th Cong., 1st Sess., Senate Report No. 877, 1902].

U.S. Statutes at Large.

"Workmen's Insurance and Benefit Funds in the United States." *Twenty-Third Annual Report of the Commissioner of Labor, 1908.*

Wright, Carroll D., ed. *A Report on Labor Disturbances in the State of Colorado, from 1880 to 1904, . . .* [58th Cong., 3d Sess., Senate Document No. 122, 1905].

B. State, Territory, and Province Publications

Arizona.

Acts, Resolutions and Memorials, 18th (1895), 21st (1901), 24th (1907), and 25th (1909) Territorial Legislative Assemblies; 1st (1912) State Legislature.

British Columbia.

Statutes, 1884, 1897, 1899, 1911.

California.

General Laws, 1909.

Colorado.

Bureau of Labor Statistics. *Biennial Report*, 1887–1888, 1889–1890, 1891–1892, 1893–1894, 1895–1896, 1899–1900.

Bureau of Mines. *Biennial Report*, 1897, 1899–1900, 1905–1906, 1907–1908, 1909–1910.

―――. *Bulletin No. 1*, 1896.

House Journal, 5th (1885) and 6th (1887) sessions.

Laws, 1877, 1879, 1881, 1883, 1885, 1887, 1889, 1891, 1893, 1894 (Extra Session), 1895, 1897, 1899, 1901, 1902 (Extra Session), 1903, 1905, 1907, 1909.

Metalliferous Mine Inspector. *Biennial Report*, 1889–1890, 1893–1894, 1898, 1899–1900, 1901–1902, 1903–1904.

Report of the Joint Special Legislative Committee of the Eleventh General Assembly on the Leadville Strike (1896).

Senate Journal, 6th (1887) and 7th (1889) sessions.

Idaho.

Council Journal, 1st (1863–1864), 7th (1872–1873), and 13th (1884–1885) territorial sessions.

House Journal, 1st (1890–1891), 2d (1893), 3d (1895), 4th (1897), 5th (1899), 6th (1901), 7th (1903), and 8th (1905) state legislative sessions.

Inspector of Mines. *Report*, 1899, 1900, 1901, 1902, 1903, 1904, 1905, 1906, 1907, 1908, 1909, 1910, 1911.

Laws, 1890–1891, 1893–1894, 1895, 1897, 1899, 1901, 1903, 1905, 1907, 1909, 1911, 1913, 1915, 1917.

Proceedings and Debates of the Constitutional Convention of Idaho—1889, Vols. I and II (1912).

Senate Journal, 1st (1890–1891), 2d (1893), 3d (1895), 4th (1897), 5th (1899), 6th (1901), 7th (1903), 8th (1905), and 9th (1907) state legislative sessions.

Illinois.

Bureau of Labor Statistics. *Statistics of Coal in Illinois—1893* (1894).

Montana.

Bureau of Agriculture, Labor, and Industry. *Annual Report*, 1893, 1902, 1906.

Council Journal, 2d (1866), 3d (1866), 4th (1867), 5th (1868–1869), 8th (1874), 10th (1877), 12th (1881), 13th (1883), and 16th (1889) territorial sessions.

House Journal, 2d (1866), 4th and extra (1867), 5th (1868), 6th (1869), 7th and extra (1873), 8th (1874), 10th (1877), 12th (1881), 13th (1883), and 16th (1889) territorial sessions; 2d (1891), 3d (1893),

4th (1895), 5th (1907), 7th (1901), 8th (1903), 9th (1905), 10th (1907), and 11th (1909) state legislative sessions.

Inspector of Mines. *Report*, 1889, 1891, 1892, 1898, 1899, 1900, 1902, 1905–1906, 1907–1908, 1909–1910.

Laws, 1864, 1871–1872, 1873, 1874, 1876, 1879, 1881, 1885, 1887, 1889, 1891, 1893, 1895, 1897, 1899, 1901, 1903, 1905, 1907, 1909.

Proceedings and Debates of the Constitutional Convention . . . 1889 (1921).

Senate Journal, 2d (1891), 3d (1893), 4th (1895), 5th (1897), 7th (1901), 8th (1903), 9th (1905), 10th (1907), and 11th (1909) sessions.

Nevada.

Assembly Journal, 4th (1869) territorial session.

Inspector of Mines. *Annual Report*, 1910, 1911.

Laws, 1885, 1893, 1895, 1897, 1899, 1901, 1903, 1905, 1907, 1908, 1909, 1911.

Miller, William C., and Eleanore Bushnell, eds. *Reports of the 1863 Constitutional Convention of the Territory of Nevada—As Written for The Territorial Enterprise by Andrew J. Marsh and Samuel L. Clemens and for The Virginia [City] Daily Union by Amos Bowman* (1972).

Senate Journal, 4th (1869) territorial session.

South Dakota.

Inspector of Mines. *Report*, 1897–1898.

Utah.

House Journal, 1st (1896) session.

Laws, 1896, 1897, 1899, 1901, 1903, 1905, 1907, 1909.

Senate Journal, 1st (1896) session.

III. Court Cases and Testimony

A. Federal Courts

Alaska Mining Company v. Whelan, 168 U.S. 86 (1897).

Alaska Treadwell Gold Min. Co. v. Whelan, 64 Fed. Reporter 462 (1894).

Browne v. King et al., 100 Fed. Reporter 561 (1900).

Bunker Hill & S. Mining & Concentrating Co. v. Schmelling, 79 Fed. Reporter 263 (1897).

Cantwell et al. v. State of Missouri, 26 S. Ct. 749 (1905).

Davis V. Trade Dollar Consol. Min. Co., 117 Fed. Reporter 122 (1902).

Hum Fay, Dear Yick, Hum Tong, and Huie Pock v. Frank Baldwin et al., 9th U.S. Circuit Court, District of Montana, record of testimony, Montana Historical Society (1898).

Frost v. Oregon Short Line Railroad, 69 Fed. Reporter 936 (1895).

Goldfield Consolidated Mines Co. v. Goldfield Miners Union No. 220, 9th U.S. Circuit Court, District of Nevada, record of testimony, Western History Collections, University of Colorado (1908).

Holden v. Hardy, 169 U.S. 366 (1898).

Homestake Min. Co. v. Fullerton, 69 Fed. Reporter 923 (1895).

Northern Pacific Railroad Company v. Hambly, 154 U.S. 349 (1894).

B. State Courts

Allen v. Bell, 32 Mont. 69, 79 Pacific 582 (1905).

In re Boyce, 27 Nev. 299, 75 Pacific 1 (1904).

Cunningham v. Northwestern Improvement Co., 44 Mont. 180, 119 Pacific 554 (1911).

Davidson v. Jennings et al., 27 Colo. 187, 60 Pacific 354 (1900).

Deep Mining & Drainage Co. v. Fitzgerald, 21 Colo. 533, 43 Pacific 210 (1895).

Dryburg v. Mercur Gold Min. & Mill. Co., 18 Utah 410, 55 Pacific 367 (1898).

Friel v. Kimberly-Montana Gold Mining Co., 34 Mont. 54, 85 Pacific 734 (1906).

Harvey v. Alturas Gold Min. Co., 3 Idaho [Hasb.] 510, 31 Pacific 819 (1893).

In re House Bill No. 147, 23 Colo. 504, 48 Pacific 512 (1897).

Kelley v. Cable Co., 7 Mont. 70, 14 Pacific 633 (1887).

Kelley v. Cable Co., 8 Mont. 440, 20 Pacific 669 (1889).

Kelley v. Fourth of July Min. Co., 16 Mont. 484, 41 Pacific 275 (1895).

Kelly [sic] *v. Fourth of July Min. Co. et al.*, 21 Mont. 291, 53 Pacific 959 (1898).

Last Chance Mining & Milling Co. v. Ames, 23 Colo. 167, 47 Pacific 382 (1896).

Mollie Gibson Consolidated Mining & Milling Co. v. Sharp, 5 Colo. A. 321, 38 Pacific 850 (1894).

In re Morgan, 26 Colo. 415, 58 Pacific 1071 (1899).

Schweizer v. Mansfield, 14 Colo. App. 236, 59 Pacific 843 (1900).

Shaw v. New Year Gold Mines Co., 31 Mont. 138, 77 Pacific 515 (1904).

Smith v. Sherman Min. Co., 12 Mont. 524, 31 Pacific 72 (1896).

State (of Montana) v. Anaconda Copper-Mining Co., 23 Mont. 498, 59 Pacific 854 (1900).

State (of Montana) v. Livingston Concrete Bldg. & Mfg. Co., 34 Mont. 570, 87 Pacific 980 (1906).

State of Utah v. Albert F. Holden, 14 Utah 71, 46 Pacific 756 (1896).

Stoll v. Daly Min. Co., 19 Utah 271, 57 Pacific 295 (1899).

Territory of Montana v. Lee, 2 Mont. 124 (1874).

Thompson v. Wise Boy Min. & Mill. Co., 9 Idaho 363, 74 Pacific 958 (1903).

Trewatha v. Buchanan Gold Mining & Milling Co., 96 Cal. 494, 28 Pacific 571 (1891).

Trihay v. Brooklyn Lead Min. Co., 4 Utah 468, 11 Pacific 612 (1886).

Union Gold Min. Co. v. Crawford, 29 Colo. 511, 69 Pacific 600 (1902).

Vindicator Consol. Gold Min. Co. v. Firstbrook, 36 Colo. 498, 86 Pacific 313 (1906).
Wells and others v. Coe, 9 Colo. 159, 11 Pacific 50 (1886).
Williams v. Sleepy Hollow Mining Co., 37 Colo. 62, 86 Pacific 337 (1906).

IV. Interviews

Clementi, Mrs. Albina. Telluride, Colorado, July 22, 1972.
Pangrazi, Mrs. Speranza. Telluride, Colorado. July 22, 1972.
Sterrett, Jim and Grace. Cripple Creek, Colorado. August 6, 1972.
Visintin, Mrs. Ermira. Telluride, Colorado. July 22, 1972.

V. Contemporary Periodicals

A. Newspapers

The Age. Boulder, Montana.
Boulder County News. Boulder, Colorado.
Butte Bystander. Butte, Montana.
Butte Miner. Butte, Montana.
Butte Mining Journal. Butte, Montana.
Carson Daily Appeal. Carson City, Nevada.
Carthage Press. Carthage, Missouri.
Coeur d'Alene Miner. Wallace, Idaho.
Colorado Miner. Georgetown, Colorado.
Daily Alta California. San Francisco, California.
Daily Mining Journal. Black Hawk, Colorado.
Daily National. Grass Valley, California.
Daily Pioche Review. Pioche, Nevada.
Daily Territorial Enterprise. Virginia City, Nevada.
Denver Republican. Denver, Colorado.
Denver Times. Denver, Colorado.
Deseret Evening News. Salt Lake City, Utah.
Gilpin County Observer. Central City, Colorado.
Gogebic Advocate. Ironwood, Michigan.
Gold Hill Daily News [also called *Evening News*]. Gold Hill, Nevada.
Helena Daily Herald. Helena, Montana.
Helena Independent. Helena, Montana.
Idaho Tri-Weekly Statesman. Boise, Idaho.
Idaho World. Idaho City, Idaho.
Jefferson County Sentinel. Boulder, Montana.
Joplin Daily Globe. Joplin, Missouri.
Leadville Weekly Herald. Leadville, Colorado.
Lump City Miner [later renamed *Clancy Miner*]. Lump City and Clancy, Montana.
Menominee Range [later renamed *The Iron Range* and then *The Range-Tribune*]. Iron Mountain, Michigan.

Montana Post. Virginia City [later Helena], Montana.
Owyhee Avalanche. Ruby City [later Silver City], Idaho.
Owyhee Semi-Weekly Tidal Wave. Silver City, Idaho.
The Reveille. Butte, Montana.
Rocky Mountain News. Denver, Colorado.
The Sun. Grantsville, Nevada.
Tri-Weekly Miner's Register [later renamed *Daily Miner's Register, Daily Central City Register, Daily Register-Call*]. Central City, Colorado.
Wallace Miner. Wallace, Idaho.
Wallace Press. Wallace, Idaho.
The Weekly News. Denver, Colorado.
The Weekly Tribune. Butte, Montana.

B. Journals

American Labor Legislation Review. New York, N.Y.
Engineering and Mining Journal. New York, N.Y.
Journal of United Labor. Marblehead, Mass. [also Pittsburgh and Philadelphia, Pa.].
Miners' Magazine. Butte, Montana [also Denver, Colorado].
Mining. Spokane, Washington.
Mining and Scientific Press. San Francisco, California.
Nevada Miner. Golconda, Nevada.
Nevada Monthly. Virginia City, Nevada.

C. Scrapbooks of Newspaper Clippings

Ellis, J. C. (Carson City, Nevada). Scrapbook of Nevada newspapers, 1860s and 1870s. Washoe County Library, Reno, Nevada.

Mine accidents in Georgetown, Colorado, area, 1863–1902. Scrapbook of clippings in Western History Collections, Denver Public Library.

Telluride, Colorado, area. Scrapbook of clippings in San Miguel County Historical Museum, Telluride, Colorado.

U.S. Bureau of Mines, Denver, Colorado. Scrapbooks of clippings on Colorado mines, Colorado State Historical Society.

VI. Published Proceedings and Other Records of Labor Unions

Constitution, By-Laws, Order of Business, and Rules of Order of the Miner's Union, of Gold Hill, Nev. Virginia City, Nev., 1871.

Constitution, By-Laws, Order of Business and Rules of Order of the Miners' Union, of Virginia [City], Nevada. Virginia City, Nev., 1876.

Constitution and By-Laws of San Juan District Union and Silverton Miners Union No. 26, Sky City Miners Union No. 27, Ouray Miners' Union No. 15, 16 to 1 Miners Union No. 63, Bryan Miners Union No. 64, Rico Miners Union No. 36, Henson Miners Union No. 69. N.p., 1898.

Forty-fifth Anniversary Program—Virginia [City] Miners Union. Virginia City, Nev., 1912.

General Laws and By-Laws of the Miners' and Mechanics' Mutual Aid Association of Colorado. Georgetown, Colo., circa 1874.

Montana Federation of Labor. *Proceedings of the . . . Annual Convention* [14th, 1907; 15th, 1908; and 16th, 1909] (Helena).

Montana State Trades and Labor Council and Butte Industrial Conference. *Proceedings of the . . . Convention . . .* [2d, 1895; 8th, 1901] (Butte).

Western Federation of Miners. *Constitution* (1893).

———. *Official Proceedings of the . . . Annual Convention* [10th, 1902; 11th, 1903; 12th, 1904; 13th, 1905; 14th, 1906; 15th, 1907; 16th, 1908; 17th, 1909; 18th, 1910; 19th, 1911] (Denver).

———. *Report of Acting President Mahoney to the Fifteenth Annual Convention.* N.p., 1907.

VII. Pamphlets

Bulletin No. 6, Bulletin No. 7, Bulletin No. 11. N.p., apparently 1903. [Anonymous pamphlets in Colorado eight-hour-day controversy; copies in Edward P. Costigan papers, Western Historical Collections, University of Colorado Libraries.]

Church, John A. *The Heat of the Comstock Mines.* N.p., 1878.

Frankfurter, Felix, and Louis D. Brandeis, assisted by Josephine Goldmark. *The Case for the Shorter Work Day.* New York, circa 1915. [Brief for defendant in error, *Franklin O. Bunting v. The State of Oregon*, U.S. Supreme Court, 1915.]

Idaho Historical Society. *Mining in Idaho* (Reference Series No. 9). N.p., n.d.

Letter No. 1 of Joseph Aron to the President of the Sutro Tunnel Co. Paris, France (?), 1889.

Mine Inspectors' Institute of the United States of America. *Proceedings.* St. Louis, Mo., 1915.

Report by A. MacDonald to the Members of the Miners' National Union on the Conditions and Prospects of Labour in the United States. N.p., circa 1877.

Statement by John C. Osgood Before the House Committee on Mines and Mining—February 16, 1903, at Denver Colorado. N.p., n.d. [Copy in Costigan papers.]

Slosson, H. L., Jr. *Deep Mining on the Comstock.* San Francisco, n.d.

Sutro, Adolph. "Lecture on Mines and Mining, Delivered by Adolph Sutro, at Piper's Opera House, Virginia City, and in all the principal towns and Mining Camps in the State of Nevada," supplement to *The Daily Independent*, Virginia City, Nevada, Oct. 31, 1874.

Tonge, Thomas. "The Fourth Era of the Leadville Mining District."

Reprinted from *The Engineering Magazine* (New York and London), September, 1900.

Young, George J. *The Ventilating System at the Comstock Mines, Nevada*. University of Nevada *Bulletin*, Vol. III, No. 4 (Oct. 1, 1909).

VIII. Autobiographies, Journal

Crampton, Frank A. *Deep Enough—A Working Stiff in the Western Mine Camps*. Denver: Sage, 1956.

Gressley, Gene M., ed. *Bostonians and Bullion—The Journal of Robert Livermore, 1892–1915*. Lincoln: University of Nebraska Press, 1968.

Hamilton, Alice. *Exploring the Dangerous Trades—The Autobiography of Alice Hamilton, M.D.* Boston: Little, Brown, 1943.

Haywood, William D. *Bill Haywood's Book—The Autobiography of William D. Haywood*. New York: International Publishers, 1929, 1966.

IX. Books

A. Special Interest

Athearn, Robert G. *Westward the Briton*. New York: Scribner's, 1953.

Balch, William Ralston, comp. *The Mines, Miners and Mining Interests of the United States in 1882*. Philadelphia: The Mining Industrial Publishing Bureau, 1882.

Bancroft, Hubert Howe. *History of Washington, Idaho, and Montana—1845–1899*. San Francisco: The History Co., 1890. Vol. XXXI in Bancroft's *Works*.

Brissenden, Paul F. *The IWW—A Study of American Syndicalism*. New York: Russell & Russell, 1919, 1957 reprint.

Carpenter, Jay A., Russell Richard Elliott, and Byrd Fanita Wall Sawyer. *The History of Fifty Years of Mining at Tonopah, 1900–1950*. Published as University of Nevada *Bulletin*, Vol. XLVII, No. 1 (January, 1953).

Cash, Joseph H. *Working the Homestake*. Ames: Iowa State University Press, 1973.

Chiu, Ping. *Chinese Labor in California, 1850–1880—An Economic Study*. Madison: State Historical Society of Wisconsin, 1963.

Church, John A. *The Comstock Lode—Its Formation and History*. New York: John Wiley, 1879.

Conlin, Joseph R. *Big Bill Haywood and the Radical Union Movement*. Syracuse, N.Y.: Syracuse University Press, 1969.

Crane, Walter R. *Gold and Silver*. New York: John Wiley, 1908.

———. *Ore Mining Methods*. New York: John Wiley, 1910.

Davies, D. C. *A Treatise on Metalliferous Minerals and Mining*. London: Crosby Lockwood and Son, 1888.

DeQuille, Dan [William Wright]. *The Big Bonanza*. Hartford, Conn.: American Publishing Co., 1876; reissued by Knopf, 1947.

———. *A History of the Comstock Silver Lode and Mines*. Virginia City, Nevada: F. Boegle, 1889.

Dorset, Phyllis Flanders. *The New Eldorado—The Story of Colorado's Gold and Silver Rushes*. New York: Macmillan, 1970.

Dubofsky, Melvyn. *We Shall Be All—A History of the Industrial Workers of the World*. Chicago: Quadrangle Books, 1969.

Elliott, Russell R. *Nevada's Twentieth-Century Mining Boom—Tonopah, Goldfield, Ely*. Reno: University of Nevada Press, 1966.

Glasscock, C. B. *The War of the Copper Kings—Builders of Butte and Wolves of Wall Street*. New York: Grosset and Dunlap, 1935.

Greever, William S. *The Bonanza West—The Story of the Western Mining Rushes, 1848–1900*. Norman: University of Oklahoma Press, 1963.

Griswold, Don L., and Jean Harvey Griswold. *The Carbonate Camp Called Leadville*. Denver: University of Denver Press, 1951.

Harris, Beth Kay. *The Towns of Tintic*. Denver: Sage Books, 1961.

Howard, Joseph Kinsey. *Montana—High, Wide, and Handsome*. New Haven: Yale University Press, 1943.

Hunt, William R. *North of 53°—The Wild Days of the Alaska-Yukon Mining Frontier—1870–1914*. New York: Macmillan, 1974.

Jackson, W..Turrentine. *Treasure Hill—Portrait of a Silver Mining Camp*. Tucson: University of Arizona Press, 1963.

Jenkin, A. K. Hamilton. *The Cornish Miner—An Account of His Life Above and Underground from Early Times*. London: Allen and Unwin, 1927, 1948.

Jensen, Vernon H. *Heritage of Conflict—Labor Relations in the Nonferrous Metals Industry Up to 1930*. Ithaca: Cornell University Press, 1950, 1968.

Langdon, Emma F. *The Cripple Creek Strike—A History of Industrial Wars in Colorado 1903–4–5*. Denver: Great Western, 1904–1905; reprinted 1969 by Arno.

Laslett, John H. M. *Labor and the Left—A Study of Socialist and Radical Influences in the American Labor Movement, 1881–1924*. New York: Basic Books, 1970.

———, and Seymour Martin Lipset, eds. *Failure of a Dream? Essays in the History of American Socialism*. Garden City, N.Y.: Anchor Books, 1974.

Lingenfelter, Richard E. *The Hardrock Miners: A History of the Mining Labor Movement in the American West, 1863–1893*. Berkeley: University of California Press, 1974.

Livingston-Little, D. E. *An Economic History of North Idaho, 1800–1900*. Los Angeles: L. L. and C. S. Morrison, 1965.

Lock, C. G. Warnford. *Miners' Pocket-Book—A Reference Book for En-*

gineers and Others Engaged in Metalliferous Mining. New York: Spon and Chamberlain, 1901.

Lord, Eliot. *Comstock Mining and Miners. A Reprint of the 1883 Edition.* Washington, D.C.: U.S. Geological Survey, 1883; reprinted 1959 by Howell-North.

MacKnight, James Arthur. *The Mines of Montana—Their History and Development to Date*. Helena: C. K. Wells Co., 1892.

Magnuson, Richard G. *Coeur d'Alene Diary—The First Ten Years of Hardrock Mining in North Idaho*. Portland, Oregon: Metropolitan Press, 1968.

Malone, Michael P., and Richard B. Roeder, eds. *The Montana Past—An Anthology*. Missoula: University of Montana Press, 1969.

Owyhee Avalanche Publishing Company. *A Historical, Descriptive, and Commercial Directory of Owyhee County, Idaho*. Silver City, Idaho: Owyhee Avalanche Press, 1898.

Paul, Rodman W. *California Gold—The Beginning of Mining in the Far West*. Cambridge: Harvard University Press, 1947.

———. *Mining Frontiers of the Far West, 1848–1880*. New York: Holt, Rinehart and Winston, 1963.

Raymond, Rossiter W. *Mines and Mining of the Rocky Mountains, the Inland Basin, and the Pacific Slope*. New York: J. B. Ford, 1871.

Rickard, T. A. *Across the San Juan Mountains*. New York: Engineering and Mining Journal, 1903.

———. *A History of American Mining*. New York: McGraw-Hill, 1932; reprinted 1966 by Johnson Reprint Corp.

———. *Interviews with Mining Engineers*. San Francisco: Mining and Scientific Press, 1922.

Risdon Iron and Locomotive Works. *Gold Mines and Mining in California—A New Gold Era Dawning on the State*. San Francisco: Spaulding, 1885.

Rothwell, Richard P., ed. *The Mineral Industry, Its Statistics, Technology and Trade, in the United States and Other Countries—From the Earliest Times to the End of 1893*. Vol. II (Statistical Supplement of the Engineering and Mining Journal). New York: Scientific Publishing Co., 1894.

Rowe, John. *The Hard-Rock Men—Cornish Immigrants and the North American Mining Frontier*. New York: Barnes & Noble, 1974.

Saxton, Alexander. *The Indispensable Enemy—Labor and the Anti-Chinese Movement in California*. Berkeley: University of California Press, 1971.

Shepperson, Wilbur S. *Restless Strangers—Nevada's Immigrants and Their Interpreters*. Reno: University of Nevada Press, 1970.

Smith, Duane A. *Horace Tabor—His Life and the Legend*. Boulder: Colorado Associated Universities Press, 1973.

————. *Rocky Mountain Mining Camps—The Urban Frontier*. Blooming-ton: Indiana University Press, 1967.

————. *Silver Saga—The Story of Caribou, Colorado*. Boulder: Pruett Publishing Co., 1974.

Smith, Grant H. *The History of the Comstock Lode, 1850–1920*. Issued as University of Nevada *Bulletin*, Vol. XXXVII, No. 3 (July 1, 1943).

Spence, Clark C. *British Investments and the American Mining Frontier, 1860–1901*. Ithaca: Cornell University Press, 1958.

Sprague, Marshall, *Money Mountain—The Story of Cripple Creek Gold*. Boston: Little, Brown, 1953.

Suggs, George G., Jr. *Colorado's War on Militant Unionism—James H. Peabody and the Western Federation of Miners*. Detroit: Wayne State University Press, 1972.

Thomas, Herbert. *Cornish Mining Interviews*. Camborne, England: Camborne Printing and Stationery Co., 1896.

Todd, Arthur Cecil. *The Cornish Miner in America*. Glendale, Calif.: Arthur H. Clark Co., 1967.

Toole, K. Ross. *Montana—An Uncommon Land*. Norman: University of Oklahoma Press, 1959.

————. *Twentieth-Century Montana—A State of Extremes*. Norman: University of Oklahoma Press, 1972.

Trimble, William J. *The Mining Advance into the Inland Empire*. Pub-lished as University of Wisconsin *Bulletin*, No. 638 (History Series, Vol. III, No. 2), 1914.

Works Projects Administration. *Copper Camp—Stories of the World's Greatest Mining Town: Butte, Montana*. New York: Hastings House, 1943.

Wyman, Walker D., ed. *California Emigrant Letters—The Forty Niners Write Home*. New York: Bookman, 1952.

Young, Otis E., Jr. *Black Powder and Hand Steel—Miners and Machines on the Old Western Frontier*. Norman: University of Oklahoma Press, 1975.

————. *How They Dug the Gold—An Informal History of Frontier Pros-pecting, Placering, Lode-Mining, and Milling in Arizona and the South-west*. Tucson: Arizona Pioneers' Historical Society, 1967.

————. *Western Mining—An Informal Account of Precious-Metals Pros-pecting, Placering, Lode Mining, and Milling on the American Frontier from Spanish Times to 1893*. Norman: University of Oklahoma Press, 1970.

B. General Interest

Allen, James B. *The Company Town in the American West*. Norman: University of Oklahoma Press, 1966.

Ashton, T. S. *The Industrial Revolution, 1760–1830*. New York: Oxford University Press, 1972.

Bardwell, George E., and Harry Seligson. *Organized Labor and Political Action in Colorado: 1900–1960*. Denver: College of Business Administration, University of Denver, 1959.

Barth, Gunther. *Bitter Strength—A History of the Chinese in the United States, 1850–1870*. Cambridge: Harvard University Press, 1964.

Berthoff, Rowland Tappan. *British Immigrants in Industrial America, 1790–1950*. Cambridge: Harvard University Press, 1953.

Billington, Ray Allen. *America's Frontier Heritage*. New York: Holt, Rinehart and Winston, 1966.

Brody, David. *Steelworkers in America—The Non-union Era*. Cambridge: Harvard University Press, 1960.

Brown, E. H. Phelps, with Margaret H. Browne. *A Century of Pay— The Course of Pay and Production in France, Germany, Sweden, the United Kingdom, and the United States of America, 1860– 1960*. New York: St. Martin's, 1968.

Bureau of Economic Research. *Trends in the American Economy in the Nineteenth Century*. Princeton, N.J.: Princeton University Press, 1960.

Cahill, Marion Cotter. *Shorter Hours—A Study of the Movement Since the Civil War*. New York: Columbia University Press, 1932.

Commons, John R., ed. *Trade Unionism and Labor Problems*. New York: Ginn, 1905.

Commons, John R., and John B. Andrews. *Principles of Labor Legislation*. New York: Harper and Brothers, 1916, 1936.

Commons, John R., et al. *History of Labour in the United States*. Vols. II and IV. New York: Macmillan, 1918, 1935; 1966 reprint by Augustus M. Kelley.

Douglas, Paul H. *Real Wages in the United States, 1890–1926*. Boston: Houghton Mifflin, 1930.

Eastman, Crystal. *Work-Accidents and the Law*. New York: Russell Sage, 1910.

Faulkner, Harold U. *American Economic History*. New York: Harper and Brothers, 1954.

Gibson, Arrell M. *Wilderness Bonanza—The Tri-State District of Missouri, Kansas, and Oklahoma*. Norman: University of Oklahoma Press, 1972.

Glück, Elsie. *John Mitchell—Miner—Labor's Bargain with the Gilded Age*. New York: John Day, 1929; 1969 reprint by Greenwood.

Greene, Victor R. *The Slavic Community on Strike—Immigrant Labor in Pennsylvania Anthracite*. South Bend, Indiana: University of Notre Dame Press, 1968.

Guice, John D. W. *The Rocky Mountain Bench—The Territorial Supreme*

Courts of Colorado, Montana, and Wyoming, 1861–1890. New Haven: Yale University Press, 1972.

Gutman, Herbert G. *Work, Culture, and Society in Industrializing America—Essays in American Working-Class and Social History*. New York: Knopf, 1976.

Hicks, John D. *The Populist Revolt—A History of the Farmers' Alliance and the People's Party*. Minneapolis: University of Minnesota Press, 1931; 1961 reprint by University of Nebraska Press.

Kirkland, Edward C. *Industry Comes of Age—Business, Labor, and Public Policy—1860–1897*. Chicago: Quadrangle, 1961, 1967.

Long, Clarence D. *Wages and Earnings in the United States, 1860–1890*. Princeton, N.J.: Princeton University Press, 1960.

McMurry, Donald L. *Coxey's Army—A Study of the Industrial Army Movement of 1894*. Seattle: University of Washington Press, 1929; 1968 reprint by University of Washington Press.

Neufeld, Maurice F. *Italy: School for Awakening Countries—The Italian Labor Movement in Its Political, Social, and Economic Setting from 1800 to 1960*. Ithaca: New York State School of Industrial and Labor Relations, Cornell University, 1961.

Perlman, Selig. *A History of Trade Unionism in the United States*. New York: Macmillan, 1923.

———. *A Theory of the Labor Movement*. New York: Macmillan, 1928; 1949 reprint by Augustus Kelley.

Rolle, Andrew F. *The Immigrant Upraised—Italian Adventurers and Colonists in an Expanding America*. Norman: University of Oklahoma Press, 1968.

Rosen, George. *The History of Miners' Diseases—A Medical and Social Interpretation*. New York: Schuman's, 1943.

Rosenblum, Gerald. *Immigrant Workers—Their Impact on American Labor Radicalism*. New York: Basic Books, 1973.

Seligson, Harry, and George E. Bardwell. *Labor-Management Relations in Colorado*. Denver: Sage, 1961.

Strahorn, Robert E. *To the Rockies and Beyond, or a Summer on the Union Pacific Railroad and Branches*. Omaha, Nebr.: New West, 1879.

Ware, Norman J. *The Labor Movement in the United States, 1860–1895—A Study in Democracy*. New York: D. Appleton, 1929; undated reprint by Vintage.

Webb, Sidney, and Harold Cox. *The Eight Hours Day*. London: Walter Scott, 1891.

Webb, Sidney, and Beatrice Webb. *Industrial Democracy*. London: Longmans, Green and Co., 1902.

Webb, Walter Prescott. *The Great Plains*. New York: Ginn, 1931, 1972.

Wolff, Leon. *Lockout—The Story of the Homestead Strike of 1892: A Study of Violence, Unionism, and the Carnegie Steel Empire*. New York: Harper & Row, 1965.

Yellowitz, Irwin. *Industrialization and the American Labor Movement, 1850–1900*. Port Washington, N.Y.: National University Publications, 1977.

X. Articles

Brissenden, Paul F. "The Butte Miners and the Rustling Card." *The American Economic Review*, Vol. X, No. 4 (December, 1920), 755.

Cushman, Dan. "Cordova Lode Comstock." *Montana—The Magazine of Western History*, Vol. IX, No. 4 (October, 1959), 12.

————. "Garnet—Montana's Last Booming Gold Camp." *Montana—The Magazine of Western History*, Vol. XIV, No. 3 (July, 1964), 38.

Davies, J. Kenneth. "Utah Labor Before Statehood." *Utah Historical Quarterly*, Vol. XXXIV, No. 3 (Summer, 1966), 202.

Derig, Betty. "Celestials in the Diggings." *Idaho Yesterdays*, Vol. XVI, No. 3 (Fall, 1972), 2.

————. "The Chinese of Silver City." *Idaho Yesterdays*, Vol. II, No. 4 (Winter, 1958–1959), 2.

Dubofsky, Melvyn. "The Origins of Western Working Class Radicalism, 1890–1905." *Labor History*, Vol. VII, No. 2 (Spring, 1966), 131.

Fine, Sidney. "The Eight-Hour Day Movement in the United States, 1888–1891." *Mississippi Valley Historical Review*, Vol. XL, No. 3 (December, 1953), 441.

Foster, James C. "Syndicalism Northern Style—The Life and Death of WFM No. 193." *The Alaska Journal*, Vol. IV, No. 3 (Summer, 1974), 130.

Gazzam, Joseph P. "The Leadville Strike of 1896." *Bulletin of the Missouri Historical Society*, Vol. VII, No. 1 (October, 1950), 89.

Gutman, Herbert G. "Work, Culture, and Society in Industrializing America, 1815–1919." *American Historical Review*, LXXVIII, No. 3 (June, 1973), 531.

Hough, Merrill. "Leadville and the Western Federation of Miners." *Colorado Magazine*, Vol. XLIX, No. 1 (Winter, 1972), 19.

Hutchinson, William H. "The Cowboy and the Class Struggle (Or, Never Put Marx in the Saddle)." *Arizona and the West*, Vol. XIV, No. 4 (Winter, 1972), 321.

Jackson, W. Turrentine. "The Irish Fox and the British Lion—The Story of Tommy Cruse, the Drum Lummon, and The Montana Company, Limited (British)." *Montana—The Magazine of Western History*, Vol. IX, No. 2 (April, 1959), 28.

Lubove, Roy. "Workmen's Compensation and the Prerogatives of Voluntarism." *Labor History*, Vol. VIII, No. 3 (Fall, 1967), 254.

McMillan, Rev. A. C. "A Young Clergyman Looks at Granite's Glittering Glory." *Montana—The Magazine of Western History*, Vol. XIV, No. 3 (July, 1964), 62.

Noxon, Victor I. [as told to Forest Crossen]. "Hard Rock Drilling Contests in Colorado." *Colorado Magazine*, Vol. XI, No. 3 (May, 1934), 81.

Papanikolas, Helen Zeese. "Life and Labor Among the Immigrants of Bingham Canyon." *Utah Historical Quarterly*, Vol. XXXIII, No. 4 (Fall, 1965), 289.

Paul, Rodman Wilson. "Colorado as a Pioneer of Science in the Mining West." *Mississippi Valley Historical Review*, Vol. XLVII, No. 1 (June, 1960), 34.

Peterson, Richard H. "Conflict and Consensus: Labor Relations in Western Mining." *Journal of the West*, Vol. XII, No. 1 (January, 1973), 1.

————. "The Frontier Thesis and Social Mobility on the Mining Frontier." *Pacific Historical Review*, Vol. XLIV, No. 1 (February, 1975), 52.

Preston, William. "Shall This Be All? U.S. Historians Versus William D. Haywood et al." *Labor History*, Vol. XII, No. 3 (Summer, 1971), 435.

"Progress of the Law—Constitutional Law." *American Law Register*, Vol. XXXIX, n.s., No. 2 (February, 1900), 105.

Smith, Duane A. "Colorado's Urban-Mining Safety Valve." *Colorado Magazine*, Vol. XLVIII, No. 4 (Fall, 1971), 299.

Todd, A. C. "Cousin Jack in Idaho." *Idaho Yesterdays*, Vol. VIII, No. 4 (Winter, 1964–1965), 8.

Tondel, Frank P. "As I Remember Goldfield." *Nevada Historical Society Quarterly*, Vol. III, No. 3 (Summer, 1960), 13.

Ubbelohde, Carl. "The Labor Movement in Colorado—Patterns of the Era of Industrial Warfare." *The Denver Westerners Monthly Roundup*, Vol. XIX, No. 10 (October, 1963), 3.

XI. Unpublished Studies

Balibrera, Dana Evans. "Virginia City and the Immigrant." Master's thesis, University of Nevada, 1965.

BeDunnah, Gary P. "A History of the Chinese in Nevada: 1855–1904." Master's thesis, University of Nevada, 1966.

Brown, Ronald Conklin. "Hard-Rock Miners of the Great Basin and Rocky Mountain West, 1860–1920." Doctoral dissertation, University of Illinois, 1975.

Byrkit, James Ward. "Life and Labor in Arizona, 1901–1921: With Particular Reference to the Deportations of 1917." Doctoral dissertation, Claremont Graduate School, 1972.

Cash, Joseph Harper. "Labor in the West: The Homestake Mining

Company and Its Workers, 1877–1942." Doctoral dissertation, University of Iowa, 1966.

Elliott, Russell R. "The History of White Pine County." Unpublished paper in possession of the Nevada State Historical Society, n.d.

Grazeola, Franklin. "The Charcoal Burners War of 1879: A Study of the Italian Immigrant in Nevada." Master's thesis, University of Nevada, 1969.

Hiester, Arthur J., E. S. Geary, and E. H. Murchison. "Air Drills and Modern High Explosives." Graduation thesis, Colorado School of Mines, 1912.

Hough, Charles Merrill. "Leadville, Colorado, 1878 to 1898: A Study in Unionism." Master's thesis, University of Colorado, 1958.

Hulse, James W. "A History of Lincoln County, Nevada—1864–1909." Master's thesis, University of Nevada, 1958.

King, Joseph Edward. "'It Takes a Mine to Run a Mine': Financing Colorado's Precious-Metals Mining Industry, 1859–1902." Doctoral dissertation, University of Illinois, 1971.

Lonsdale, David Lawrence. "The Movement for an Eight-Hour Law in Colorado, 1893–1913." Doctoral dissertation, University of Colorado, 1963.

McCormick, D. Ford. "Mine Ventilation, with Special Reference to the Vulcan Mine." E. M. thesis, Colorado School of Mines, 1910.

Mann, Ralph Emerson, II. "The Social and Political Structure of Two California Mining Towns, 1850–1870." Doctoral dissertation, Stanford University, 1970.

Merrifield, Robert B. "Nevada, 1859–1881: The Impact of an Advanced Technological Society upon a Frontier Area." Doctoral dissertation, University of Chicago, 1957.

Ozawa, Fumio. "Japanese in Colorado, 1900–1910." Master's thesis, University of Denver, 1954.

Pawar, Sheelwant Bapurao. "An Environmental Study of the Development of the Utah Labor Movement: 1860–1935." Doctoral dissertation, University of Utah, 1968.

Perrigo, Lynn Irwin. "A Social History of Central City, Colorado, 1859–1900." Doctoral dissertation, University of Colorado, 1936.

Romig, Robert Lawrence. "The South Boise Quartz Mines, 1863–1892: A Study in Western Mining Industry and Finance." Master's thesis, University of California, Berkeley, 1950.

Rudolph, Gerald E. "The Chinese in Colorado, 1869–1911." Master's thesis, Denver University, 1964.

Sawyer, Byrd. "Labor Conditions in Tonopah and Goldfield." Master's thesis, University of California, Berkeley, 1931.

Smith, Robert Wayne. "The Idaho Antecedents of the Western Federation of Miners—Labor Organization and Industrial Conflict in the

Coeur d'Alenes Mining District of Idaho, 1890 to 1893." Doctoral dissertation, University of California, Berkeley, 1937.

Vacek, Vincent F. "A Study of Electrical Installations in Colorado Mines." Graduation thesis, Colorado School of Mines, 1910.

Watts, Alfred C., and Herbert E. Badger, "Hoisting and Haulage in the Cripple Creek District." Graduation thesis, Colorado School of Mines, 1902.

Wells, Merle W. "The WFM in British Columbia: The Eight Hour Statute, the Alien Labour Acts, and the Recognition Issue in the Kootenay Mines, 1899–1902." Paper presented May 14, 1976, before the Ninth Annual Pacific Northwest Labor History Association Conference, Seattle, Washington.

White, Forest Lowell. "The Panic of 1893 in Colorado." Master's thesis, University of Colorado, 1932.

INDEX

323

Designer:	Dave Comstock
Compositor:	G & S Typesetters, Inc.
Text:	VIP Palatino 11 pt.
Display:	Typositor Clarendon Bold
Printer:	Maple-Vail Book Mfg. Group
Binder:	Maple-Vail Book Mfg. Group